How to build your ow

Supercar

2

Also from Veloce Publishing

Speedpro Series
4-cylinder Engine – How To Blueprint & Build A Short Block For High Performance (Hammill)
Alfa Romeo DOHC High-performance Manual (Kartalamakis)
Alfa Romeo V6 Engine High-performance Manual (Kartalamakis)
BMC 998cc A-series Engine – How To Power Tune (Hammill)
1275cc A-series High-performance Manual (Hammill)
Camshafts – How To Choose & Time Them For Maximum Power (Hammill)
Competition Car Datalogging Manual, The (Templeman)
Cylinder Heads – How To Build, Modify & Power Tune Updated & Revised Edition (Burgess & Gollan)
Distributor-type Ignition Systems – How To Build & Power Tune (Hammill)
Fast Road Car – How To Plan And Build Revised & Updated Colour New Edition (Stapleton)
Ford SOHC 'Pinto' & Sierra Cosworth DOHC Engines – How To Power Tune Updated & Enlarged Edition (Hammill)
Ford V8 – How To Power Tune Small Block Engines (Hammill)
Harley-Davidson Evolution Engines – How To Build & Power Tune (Hammill)
Holley Carburetors – How To Build & Power Tune Revised & Updated Edition (Hammill)
Jaguar XK Engines – How To Power Tune Revised & Updated Colour Edition (Hammill)
MG Midget & Austin-Healey Sprite – How To Power Tune Updated & Revised Edition (Stapleton)
MGB 4-cylinder Engine – How To Power Tune (Burgess)
MGB V8 Power – How To Give Your, Third Colour Edition (Williams)
MGB, MGC & MGB V8 – How To Improve (Williams)
Mini Engines – How To Power Tune On A Small Budget Colour Edition (Hammill)
Motorcycle-engined Racing Car – How To Build (Pashley)
Motorsport – Getting Started in (Collins)
Nitrous Oxide High-performance Manual, The (Langfield)
Rover V8 Engines – How To Power Tune (Hammill)
Sportscar/kitcar Suspension & Brakes – How To Build & Modify Enlarged & Updated 2nd Edition (Hammill)
SU Carburettor High-performance Manual (Hammill)
Supercar, How To Build (Thompson)
Suzuki 4x4 – How To Modify For Serious Off-road Action (Richardson)
Tiger Avon Sportscar – How To Build Your Own Updated & Revised 2nd Edition (Dudley)
TR2, 3 & TR4 – How To Improve (Williams)
TR5, 250 & TR6 – How To Improve (Williams)
TR7 & TR8 – How To Improve (Williams)
V8 Engine – How To Build A Short Block For High Performance (Hammill)
Volkswagen Beetle Suspension, Brakes & Chassis – How To Modify For High Performance (Hale)
Volkswagen Bus Suspension, Brakes & Chassis – How To Modify For High Performance (Hale)
Weber DCOE, & Dellorto DHLA Carburetors – How To Build & Power Tune 3rd Edition (Hammill)

Those Were The Days ... Series
Alpine Trials & Rallies 1910-1973 (Pfundner)
Austerity Motoring (Bobbitt)
Brighton National Speed Trials (Gardiner)
British Police Cars (Walker)
British Woodies (Peck)
Dune Buggy Phenomenon (Hale)
Dune Buggy Phenomenon Volume 2 (Hale)
Hot Rod & Stock Car Racing in Britain In The 1980s (Neil)
MG's Abingdon Factory (Moylan)
Motor Racing At Brands Hatch In The Seventies (Parker)
Motor Racing At Crystal Palace (Collins)
Motor Racing At Goodwood In The Sixties (Gardiner)
Motor Racing At Nassau In The 1950s & 1960s (O'Neil)
Motor Racing At Oulton Park In The 1960s (Mcfadyen)
Motor Racing At Oulton Park In The 1970s (Mcfadyen)
Three Wheelers (Bobbitt)

Enthusiast's Restoration Manual Series
Citroën 2CV, How To Restore (Porter)
Classic Car Bodywork, How To Restore (Thaddeus)
Classic Car Electrics (Thaddeus)
Classic Cars, How To Paint (Thaddeus)
Reliant Regal, How To Restore (Payne)
Triumph TR2/3/3A, How To Restore (Williams)
Triumph TR4/4A, How To Restore (Williams)
Triumph TR5/250 & 6, How To Restore (Williams)
Triumph TR7/8, How To Restore (Williams)
Volkswagen Beetle, How To Restore (Tyler)
VW Bay Window Bus (Paxton)
Yamaha FS1-E, How To Restore (Watts)

Essential Buyer's Guide Series
Alfa GT (Booker)
Alfa Romeo Spider Giulia (Booker & Talbott)
BMW GS (Henshaw)
BSA Bantam (Henshaw)
BSA Twins (Henshaw)
Citroën 2CV (Paxton)
Citroën ID & DS (Heilig)
Fiat 500 & 600 (Bobbitt)
Jaguar E-type 3.8 & 4.2-litre (Crespin)
Jaguar E-type V12 5.3-litre (Crespin)
Jaguar/Daimler XJ6, XJ12 & Sovereign (Crespin)
Jaguar XJ-S (Crespin)
MGB & MGB GT (Williams)
Mercedes-Benz 280SL-560DSL Roadsters (Bass)
Mercedes-Benz 'Pagoda' 230SL, 250SL & 280SL Roadsters & Coupés (Bass)
Morris Minor & 1000 (Newell)
Porsche 928 (Hemmings)
Rolls-Royce Silver Shadow & Bentley T-Series (Bobbitt)
Subaru Impreza (Hobbs)
Triumph Bonneville (Henshaw)
Triumph TR6 (Williams)
VW Beetle (Cservenka & Copping)
VW Bus (Cservenka & Copping)

Auto-Graphics Series
Fiat-based Abarths (Sparrow)
Jaguar MKI & II Saloons (Sparrow)
Lambretta Li Series Scooters (Sparrow)

Rally Giants Series
Audi Quattro (Robson)
Austin Healey 100-6 & 3000 (Robson)
Fiat 131 Abarth (Robson)
Ford Escort MkI (Robson)
Ford Escort RS Cosworth & World Rally Car (Robson)
Ford Escort RS1800 (Robson)
Lancia Stratos (Robson)
Peugeot 205 T16 (Robson)
Subaru Impreza (Robson)

General
1½-litre GP Racing 1961-1965 (Whitelock)
AC Two-litre Saloons & Buckland Sportscars (Archibald)
Alfa Romeo Giulia Coupé GT & GTA (Tipler)
Alfa Romeo Montreal – The Essential Companion (Taylor)
Alfa Tipo 33 (McDonough & Collins)
Alpine & Renault – The Development Of The Revolutionary Turbo F1 Car 1968 to 1979 (Smith)
Anatomy Of The Works Minis (Moylan)
Armstrong-Siddeley (Smith)
Autodrome (Collins & Ireland)
Automotive A-Z, Lane's Dictionary Of Automotive Terms (Lane)
Automotive Mascots (Kay & Springate)
Bahamas Speed Weeks, The (O'Neil)
Bentley Continental, Corniche And Azure (Bennett)
Bentley MkVI, Rolls-Royce Silver Wraith, Dawn & Cloud/Bentley R & S-Series (Nutland)
BMC Competitions Department Secrets (Turner, Chambers Browning)
BMW 5-Series (Cranswick)
BMW Z-Cars (Taylor)
Britains Farm Model Balers & Combines 1967 to 2007 (Pullen)
British 250cc Racing Motorcycles (Pereira)
British Cars, The Complete Catalogue Of, 1895-1975 (Culshaw & Horrobin)
BRM – A Mechanic's Tale (Salmon)
BRM V16 (Ludvigsen)
BSA Bantam Bible, The (Henshaw)
Bugatti Type 40 (Price)
Bugatti 46/50 Updated Edition (Price & Arbey)
Bugatti T44 & T49 (Price & Arbey)
Bugatti 57 2nd Edition (Price)
Caravans, The Illustrated History 1919-1959 (Jenkinson)
Caravans, The Illustrated History From 1960 (Jenkinson)
Carrera Panamericana, La (Tipler)
Chrysler 300 – America's Most Powerful Car 2nd Edition (Ackerson)
Chrysler PT Cruiser (Ackerson)
Citroën DS (Bobbitt)
Cliff Allison – From The Fells To Ferrari (Gauld)
Cobra – The Real Thing! (Legate)
Cortina – Ford's Bestseller (Robson)
Coventry Climax Racing Engines (Hammill)
Daimler SP250 New Edition (Long)
Datsun Fairlady Roadster To 280ZX – The Z-Car Story (Long)
Dino – The V6 Ferrari (Long)
Dodge Charger – Enduring Thunder (Ackerson)
Dodge Dynamite! (Grist)
Donington (Boddy)
Draw & Paint Cars – How To (Gardiner)
Drive On The Wild Side, A – 20 Extreme Driving Adventures From Around The World (Weaver)
Ducati 750 Bible, The (Falloon)
Ducati 860, 900 And Mille Bible, The (Falloon)
Dune Buggy, Building A – The Essential Manual (Shakespeare)
Dune Buggy Files (Hale)
Dune Buggy Handbook (Hale)
Edward Turner: The Man Behind The Motorcycles (Clew)
Fiat & Abarth 124 Spider & Coupé (Tipler)
Fiat & Abarth 500 & 600 2nd Edition (Bobbitt)
Fiats, Great Small (Ward)
Fine Art Of The Motorcycle Engine, The (Peirce)
Ford F100/F150 Pick-up 1948-1996 (Ackerson)
Ford F150 Pick-up 1997-2005 (Ackerson)
Ford GT – Then, And Now (Streather)
Ford GT40 (Legate)
Ford In Miniature (Olson)
Ford Model Y (Roberts)
Ford Thunderbird From 1954, The Book Of The (Long)
Forza Minardi! (Vigar)
Funky Mopeds (Skelton)
Gentleman Jack (Gauld)
GM In Miniature (Olson)
GT – The World's Best GT Cars 1953-73 (Dawson)
Hillclimbing & Sprinting – The Essential Manual (Short & Wilkinson)
Honda NSX (Long)
Jaguar, The Rise Of (Price)
Jaguar XJ-S (Long)
Jeep CJ (Ackerson)
Jeep Wrangler (Ackerson)
Karmann-Ghia Coupé & Convertible (Bobbitt)
Lamborghini Miura Bible, The (Sackey)
Lambretta Bible, The (Davies)
Lancia 037 (Collins)
Lancia Delta HF Integrale (Blaettel & Wagner)
Land Rover, The Half-ton Military (Cook)
Laverda Twins & Triples Bible 1968-1986 (Falloon)
Lea-Francis Story, The (Price)
Lexus Story, The (Long)
little book of smart, the (Jackson)
Lola – The Illustrated History (1957-1977) (Starkey)
Lola – All The Sports Racing & Single-seater Racing Cars 1978-1997 (Starkey)
Lola T70 – The Racing History & Individual Chassis Record 4th Edition (Starkey)
Lotus 49 (Oliver)
Marketingmobiles, The Wonderful Wacky World Of (Hale)
Mazda MX-5/Miata 1.6 Enthusiast's Workshop Manual (Grainger & Shoemark)
Mazda MX-5/Miata 1.8 Enthusiast's Workshop Manual (Grainger & Shoemark)
Mazda MX-5 Miata: The Book Of The World's Favourite Sportscar (Long)
Mazda MX-5 Miata Roadster (Long)
MGA (Price Williams)
MGB & MGB GT– Expert Guide (Auto-doc Series) (Williams)
MGB Electrical Systems (Astley)
Micro Caravans (Jenkinson)
Micro Trucks (Mort)
Microcars At Large! (Quellin)
Mini Cooper – The Real Thing! (Tipler)
Mitsubishi Lancer Evo, The Road Car & WRC Story (Long)
Montlhéry, The Story Of The Paris Autodrome (Boddy)
Morgan Maverick (Lawrence)
Morris Minor, 60 Years On The Road (Newell)
Moto Guzzi Sport & Le Mans Bible (Falloon)
Motor Movies – The Posters! (Veysey)
Motor Racing – Reflections Of A Lost Era (Carter)
Motorcycle Apprentice (Cakebread)
Motorcycle Road & Racing Chassis Designs (Noakes)
Motorhomes, The Illustrated History (Jenkinson)
Motorsport In colour, 1950s (Wainwright)
Nissan 300ZX & 350Z – The Z-Car Story (Long)
Off-Road Giants! – Heroes of 1960s Motorcycle Sport (Westlake)
Pass The Theory And Practical Driving Tests (Gibson & Hoole)
Peking To Paris 2007 (Young)
Plastic Toy Cars Of The 1950s & 1960s (Ralston)
Pontiac Firebird (Cranswick)
Porsche Boxster (Long)
Porsche 964, 993 & 996 Data Plate Code Breaker (Streather)
Porsche 356 (2nd Edition) (Long)
Porsche 911 Carrera – The Last Of The Evolution (Corlett)
Porsche 911R, RS & RSR, 4th Edition (Starkey)
Porsche 911 – The Definitive History 1963-1971 (Long)
Porsche 911 – The Definitive History 1971-1977 (Long)
Porsche 911 – The Definitive History 1977-1987 (Long)
Porsche 911 – The Definitive History 1987-1997 (Long)
Porsche 911 – The Definitive History 1997-2004 (Long)
Porsche 911SC 'Super Carrera' – The Essential Companion (Streather)
Porsche 914 & 914-6: The Definitive History Of The Road & Competition Cars (Long)
Porsche 924 (Long)
Porsche 944 (Long)
Porsche 993 'King Of Porsche' – The Essential Companion (Streather)
Porsche 996 'Supreme Porsche' – The Essential Companion (Streather)
Porsche Racing Cars – 1953 To 1975 (Long)
Porsche Racing Cars – 1976 On (Long)
Porsche – The Rally Story (Meredith)
Porsche: Three Generations Of Genius (Meredith)
RAC Rally Action! (Gardiner)
Rallye Sport Fords: The Inside Story (Moreton)
Redman, Jim – 6 Times World Motorcycle Champion: The Autobiography (Redman)
Rolls-Royce Silver Shadow/Bentley T Series Corniche & Camargue Revised & Enlarged Edition (Bobbitt)
Rolls-Royce Silver Spirit, Silver Spur & Bentley Mulsanne 2nd Edition (Bobbitt)
RX-7 – Mazda's Rotary Engine Sportscar (Updated & Revised New Edition) (Long)
Scooters & Microcars, The A-Z Of Popular (Dan)
Scooter Lifestyle (Grainger)
Singer Story: Cars, Commercial Vehicles, Bicycles & Motorcycles (Atkinson)
SM – Citroën's Maserati-engined Supercar (Long & Claverol)
Subaru Impreza: The Road Car And WRC Story (Long)
Taxi! The Story Of The 'London' Taxicab (Bobbitt)
Tinplate Toy Cars Of The 1950s & 1960s (Ralston)
Toyota Celica & Supra, The Book Of Toyota's Sports Coupés (Long)
Toyota MR2 Coupés & Spyders (Long)
Triumph Motorcycles & The Meriden Factory (Hancox)
Triumph Speed Twin & Thunderbird Bible (Woolridge)
Triumph Tiger Cub Bible (Estall)
Triumph Trophy Bible (Woolridge)
Triumph TR6 (Kimberley)
Unraced (Collins)
Velocette Motorcycles – MSS To Thruxton Updated & Revised (Burris)
Virgil Exner – Visioneer: The Official Biography Of Virgil M Exner Designer Extraordinaire (Grist)
Volkswagen Bus Book, The (Bobbitt)
Volkswagen Bus Or Van To Camper, How To Convert (Porter)
Volkswagens Of The World (Glen)
VW Beetle Cabriolet (Bobbitt)
VW Beetle – The Car Of The 20th Century (Copping)
VW Bus – 40 Years Of Splitties, Bays & Wedges (Copping)
VW Bus Book, The (Bobbitt)
VW Golf: Five Generations Of Fun (Copping & Cservenka)
VW – The Air-cooled Era (Copping)
VW T5 Camper Conversion Manual (Porter)
VW Campers (Copping)
Works Minis, The Last (Purves & Brenchley)
Works Rally Mechanic (Moylan)

www.veloce.co.uk

First published in July 2008 by Veloce Publishing Limited, 33 Trinity Street, Dorchester DT1 1TT, England. Fax 01305 268864/e-mail info@veloce.co.uk/web www.veloce.co.uk or www.velocebooks.com.
ISBN: 978-1-84584-166-9/UPC: 6-36847-04166-3

Readers with ideas for automotive books, or books on other transport or related hobby subjects, are invited to write to the editorial director of Veloce Publishing at the above address.
British Library Cataloguing in Publication Data - A catalogue record for this book is available from the British Library. Typesetting, design and page make-up all by Veloce Publishing Ltd on Apple Mac.
Printed in India by Replika Press.

THE ESSENTIAL MANUAL™

How to build **your own** Supercar

Amazing self-build techniques for builders of supercars, kit-cars, racing cars, hot-rods and custom cars. Includes glassfibre moulding techniques, vacuum-forming polycarbonates, creating interior trim, adapting standard mass-production components and much, much more.

Brian Thompson

Contents

Introduction & thanks

INTRODUCTION

A while ago I spent nine years of my life crafting a unique supercar from a mock-up body shell, which was originally created to star in a television advertising campaign for an insurance company. The project was very demanding physically and mentally, and I sometimes wonder why I put myself through such an ordeal. I suppose I like a challenge, especially if it results in such a fantastic-looking vehicle. There were countless problems to be solved along the way, and this book details some of the various techniques and solutions used to make the car a reality. But, first, a brief history of how and why this concept car came about.

In the late 1980s, the Norwich Union company sought to highlight the investment side of its business, and recruited advertising agency Burkitt, Weinreich, Bryant, Clients & Co, which came up with the idea of a fictional new sports car from the Soviet Union that a forward-looking company like Norwich Union would spot as a good investment opportunity before its rivals. The job of constructing two cars fell to specialist props designer, Jon Bunker, who, along with his team, built two mock-ups in only a few weeks, which were given the suitably Russian-sounding name of Mirov II.

The author with the Mirov in its original condition.

Both cars started life as M6 GTR kit cars made by the Unique Vehicle and Accessory Company (UVA) in England. The M6 GTR was a development of the Manta Montage, an American kit car that closely resembled Bruce McLaren's 1969 M6 road car. All the exterior GTR panels were cut off and thrown away, which left only the centre cockpit section. A full size clay body buck was constructed from which fibreglass moulds were taken to produce the new panels. The specially-moulded Mirov body panels were then attached, filled and painted, and, in a short time, two

The Mirov after nine years of hard work.

Much time and effort was spent creating all the opening panels.

cars had been created that were good enough to fool the cameras.

After seeing the adverts on television and becoming curious, I first saw one of the cars in the flesh at the Royal Norfolk Showground, and fell in love with the shape. Knowing of its kit car origins, I had a good look and realised it had potential to be a great build project. The cars featured in TV adverts and various shows around the country for nearly five years before they were deemed surplus to requirements, and one was put up for auction. I eventually managed to buy the other one, which was languishing in a Norwich Union private car park, with a view to putting it on the road after a three year build. This proved a bit optimistic ...

Once installed in my workshop, the most important part of any new car project was carried out; the ritual sit in the driver's seat (accompanying engine noises optional). After a record lap of Silverstone it was time to take stock of what I had bought.

The only opening panels on the car were two flimsy, ill-fitting gull wing 'doors' with fixed plastic windows. Each was single skinned only and attached to the roof by one domestic door butt hinge held by a couple of wood screws. The doors were removed before they fell off on their own.

Inside, the complete centre tunnel had been cut out to fit some mock-up, medium density, fibreboard (MDF) seats, and there were no front or rear bulkheads to speak of. The original inner M6 GTR sill was not directly attached to the outer Mirov sill panel, the garage floor being clearly visible through the large gap between them; looking around the door apertures it was clear that the front and rear wings were similarly not attached.

It was obvious that the body could not be removed from the chassis at this stage without collapsing. In order to build a roadgoing car the entire structure required major consolidation.

The creation of a structurally sound working body with doors and opening panels, etc, was undoubtedly the major part of this build as this took up seven of the eventual nine years of the project. Halfway through the build the British government introduced the Single Vehicle Approval (SVA) test, which examines all aspects of amateur vehicle construction – from structural integrity to seat belt positioning and exhaust emissions – before registration for the road can be obtained. The Mirov had to be built with these exacting standards in mind, so an SVA test manual was obtained as soon as possible to ensure compliance.

The aim of the project was to end up with a unique, fast car to be enjoyed on high days and holidays. A mid-mounted, 2.7 litre Renault V6 was fitted to ensure lively performance, and many practical touches – such as a small boot, electric windows, and effective weather sealing on the gull wing doors – combined to make the end product easy to live with and a joy to drive.

The finished car looks very similar to the original as bought, which belies the immense amount of work that went into the project. Some of the more interesting techniques and solutions developed during build are detailed in this book. Firstly, a few basic fibreglass techniques are covered, along with a selection of tools that proved very useful. Chapters 2, 3 and 4 detail all the major alterations carried out to make the body shell road legal, with chapter 5 dedicated entirely to the manufacture of the gull wing doors. Chapter 6 deals with systems, such as the exhaust and twin fuel tanks, and finishes with a small

The author driving his first red car. (Courtesy Harold Thompson)

The author's second red car is significantly sleeker than the first!

section revealing a few novel solutions employed to solve various problems. Lastly, chapter 7 relates how an expensive-looking interior was achieved on a budget.

Even though everything covered is specific to the creation of the Mirov, there's no reason why the ideas cannot be adapted and used in any car build. This book is intended to encourage you to have a go, and shows just what can be done if you're prepared to put in the hours. I hope you find it interesting, useful, and – ultimately – inspiring.

THANKS

The first two people I would like to thank are my parents, Reneé and Harold, for sharing with me their creativity and practical approach to life. They provided my introduction to motoring by giving me my first red car, albeit pedal-powered. Also as a young boy I had the good fortune to receive one of the best toys ever invented: Meccano. This provided hours of fun and invention, introducing basic engineering and nurturing the manual dexterity that has seen me through thirty years as an aircraft technician, plus, of course, the nine years spent building the Mirov II.

More thanks must go to all my friends and work colleagues who lent their support – moral and practical – to the project. Special mention goes to Fred, Jim, and Dave who provided valuable machining services, and Ray, who carried out specialist welding on the fuel tanks and original driveshafts. Thanks also to Steve, who lent his many talents, including machining and painting, and my friend and neighbour, Simon, for transportation of the unfinished car on many occasions.

The most thanks, however, must go to my partner, Marian. Trying to maintain some semblance of normal living throughout the project was quite a juggling act, but the fact that we're still together after my 6000 hours of car building says more about her patience and understanding than my juggling ability. I dedicate this book to Marian in appreciation of her unfailing love and support.

Brian Thompson

Mirov II specification

GENERAL DIMENSIONS & WEIGHTS

Weight 1280kg
Distribution
Front 500kg
Rear 780kg
Length (including rear wing)4000mm (13ft 1 1/2in)
Width 2030mm (6ft 8in)
Height 1140mm (3ft 9in) (1200mm (3ft 11 1/2in) including wing)
Front track 1750mm (5ft 9in)
Rear track 1900mm (6ft 3in)

ENGINE & TRANSMISSION

Engine Mid-mounted Renault V6 Aluminium alloy with cast iron wet cylinder liners
Capacity 2664cc (162.6 cu in)
Gearbox 4 speed manual
Driveshafts Modified Ford Sierra

FUEL SYSTEM

Tanks Custom-made twin aluminium tanks, interlinked
Total capacity 64 litres (14 imperial gallons)
Pump Mechanical, driven by LH cylinder bank camshaft
Carburettor Twin choke Weber

EXHAUST SYSTEM

Custom-made mild steel consisting of a central collector/balance box and twin straight through silencers terminating in multiple tail pipes

COOLING SYSTEM

Radiator Mid-mounted modified Renault 30 with under car air scoop and ducting from RH air intake.
Pump Electric, thermostatically controlled. Engine-driven pump impeller removed
Fan Electric 405mm (16in) thermostatically controlled
No engine thermostat fitted
Cooling fins fitted to oil filter case

SUSPENSION & STEERING

Front suspension UVA double wishbone with VW Beetle stub axles
Rear suspension VW Beetle independent
Front shock absorbers AVO adjustable
Rear shock absorbers AVO adjustable
Front springs 450lb coils with adjustable spring seats
Rear springs Heavy duty torsion bars with adjustable spring plates
Steering rack Austin Metro fitted with Ford Cortina track rods and Ford Sierra track rod ends
Steering column Vauxhall Cavalier Mk3, adjustable

BRAKES

Master cylinder and servo Ford Cortina MkIV
Front VW Beetle 280mm (11in) disc. Tarox 6 pot callipers.
Rear VW Beetle 280mm (11in) disc. Renault single pot callipers with handbrake facility

WHEELS & TYRES

Front wheels Compomotive FH 3 piece split rim. 8x15in
Rear wheels Compomotive FH 3 piece split rim 10x16in
Front tyres 225/50ZR15
Rear tyres 255/50ZR16

Chapter 1

Materials, tools & techniques

1. SAFETY

When working with fibreglass and its associated materials, prevent skin and eye contact by wearing the appropriate protective clothing, and work in a well ventilated area. Store all the materials in a cool, dry place, away from direct sunlight.

When handling any of the raw fabrics, the fine glass fibres can irritate skin, so wear protective gloves – disposable latex gloves are cheap and ideal. Always wear protective overalls. Disposable paper or thick cotton ones were found to be best, as thin nylon types tend to let spilt resin straight through onto clothes or skin.

When cutting or sanding fibreglass or polyurethane foam, wear a good pair of goggles or safety glasses to protect the eyes, and wear an effective dust mask. If using power tools, it's advisable to wear some form of ear protection; headphone-type ear defenders are most efficient.

When working with resin, catalyst and acetone, because the vapours produced are flammable, refrain from smoking, and do not use a naked flame.

Always keep the work area tidy, and use an old vacuum cleaner to clean up at the end of the day; the less dust the better.

If in doubt about any of the materials you intend using, contact the supplier or manufacturer.

2. MATERIALS

The following is a list of the fibreglass and related materials used in the Mirov project. It's not intended to be a definitive record of all the products available, and the descriptions and uses of the products are for guidance only. In all cases, the manufacturer's instructions should be followed.

2.1. Polyester resins

(a) Polyester resin 'A' (lay-up resin)

This is a general-purpose, clear resin that is mixed with a liquid catalyst in a ratio of approximately 100/1. If used in a low ambient temperature, this mix ratio can be increased slightly to, say, 100/2 or even 100/3 to shorten cure time. The chemical reaction is exothermic, so don't add too much catalyst because there's a risk of the resin smoking or catching fire due to the generated heat not being able to dissipate quickly enough. I speak from experience here because, on a cold day, a little too much catalyst was impatiently added to a batch of resin and applied too thickly. When my back was turned it began to smoke, though, luckily, did not catch fire and the Mirov was saved. I learnt my lesson ...

Reblended resin was used when it was available, as it was cheaper than the top quality product, and slightly thicker, which was an advantage in awkward vertical or upside down lay-up situations. In the manufacture of resin, if the cure time does not fall within specified limits, then that batch is sent for reblending with similar batches to end up with a product that has a more predictable cure rate. A commercial production environment demands a predictable cure rate, but it wasn't a problem with the Mirov project.

(b) Polyester Resin 'B' unwaxed (gel coat resin)

Resin 'B' or gel coat is a thick resin used to produce the smooth outside surface of a moulding, and is mixed in a 100/2-100/3 ratio with a catalyst. Unwaxed Resin 'B' is usually used as the first gel coat layer in a mould as an absence of air cures the resin completely. Waxed Resin 'B' is used as a flow coat painted on top of a moulding, the wax helping the resin to cure in the presence of air. However, for this project unwaxed Resin 'B' was used as a flow coat to take advantage of the resulting surface tackiness, because, due to the prototype nature of all the panels, it was never certain whether further lay-ups would have to be added, so to have a tacky surface to bond to was ideal. When a panel was deemed finished the thin tacky layer could be lightly sanded, or, if the job was a long one, the resin was left and would be fully cured after a few weeks anyway. Colour-impregnated Resin 'B' was used in either white or light grey as opposed to clear because surface irregularities could be more easily spotted when finish-sanding, especially when using the grey.

2.2. Catalyst (organic peroxide)

As mentioned earlier, this is mixed with the various resins at a ratio of 1-3 per cent to promote the cure. Care must be taken when handling the catalyst as it is highly flammable and can spontaneously combust in contact with some substances when stored above 50 degrees C. Store it in a cool, dry place and all will be fine.

2.3. Glassfibres

Three types were used.

(a) Chopped strand mat (CSM)

This is made up of a collection of short glass fibres pressed into a mat and held together with a bonding agent that dissolves in contact with the resin mix. It is available in a variety of thickness (weights), the most common being 300g, 450g and 600g per square metre (1oz, 1.5oz, 2oz per square foot). The first weight was used for the Mirov as it is more easily worked into awkward corners and shapes. Category 2 CSM was purchased if it was available as it was slightly cheaper; the quality was not as good as Category 1 inasmuch as thickness was not uniform throughout the roll, but as this was not a production situation it was not a problem.

(b) Rovings

Rovings are a loose rope of continuous glass strands, used as reinforcement in a lay-up, providing great strength in one direction. Rovings were used in the 'A' and 'B' posts during door manufacture.

(c) Woven rovings (cloth)

These are continuous glass strands of rovings that have been woven into a cloth. When incorporated into a moulding they impart good strength, but, because they are of regular construction, the thicker weights are harder to form into complex shapes.

2.4. Fillers

(a) Filler powder

Glass blooms are microscopic glass spheres that, together, form a very light powder that thickens resin 'A' to give a very useful filler paste. It is used for bonding together panels as well as being a filler.

(b) Polyester filler

Probably better known as body filler, this is a fast setting, two pack filler used for filling shallow surface irregularities.

2.5. Core materials

(a) Rigid expanded polyurethane (REP) foam

This is available in sheets of different thickness; on the Mirov 25mm (1in) and 50mm (2in) thick sheets were used. It is very light and easily cut with a saw or sharp knife, and can be sanded to shape with minimal effort. It was used between fibreglass panels to add stiffness without a weight penalty.

(b) Polyurethane foam aerosol

Also known as builder's foam, this is available in most DIY stores. It was found that, once a can was started, the nozzle blocked easily, so it was best to use the whole lot in one go. The advantage with this over the rigid foam was that it could be injected into an already formed box section to expand and solidify, thereby bracing the whole structure: the lower part of the Mirov sills are so filled.

(c) Plywood

When plywood was used as a core material, the resulting structure was very strong, but also heavy. It was used in the front bulkhead area where strength was the main criteria.

2.6. Release agent

Release agent is applied to a mould to prevent the laminate from sticking to the mould surface. The wax-type release agent was used for this project, two to three applications being applied to mould surfaces and polished between each coat. Never rush this part of the job because if any of the mould surface is missed it could ruin the mould and the part being made.

2.7. Acetone

Acetone effectively removes resin from brushes and is highly flammable, so care should be taken with its storage and use. This was always used to thoroughly clean panels of dirt and dust before laminating to ensure a good permanent bond.

2.8. Mixing pots

Graduated mixing pots are available from fibreglass stockists, but there are cheaper alternatives. Cut-down milk containers were used because household life yielded a free one every week, and they are made from the right type of plastic that does not adhere to resin. Comparison with the graduated pots revealed how much resin they held to allow the correct mix ratio to be achieved. As with the commercial pots, any excess resin was left to cure and then removed by giving the pot a squeeze; all the flakes of cured resin then fell out, leaving it clean for the next mix. Several pots were used so a clean one was always ready whilst others awaited cleaning.

3. TOOLS

3.1. Power tools

(a) Variable speed electric drill

A truly invaluable piece of kit in both mains-powered and rechargeable battery forms. Its most obvious use is drilling holes, which is where the variable speed facility comes into its own, as it is far more controllable when starting a hole, preventing the drill bit from skipping off across the panel. The physical size of a power drill should be considered as access can sometimes be limited, so a small bodied drill with a reasonable chuck capacity of 13mm (½in) is ideal.

When access was still a problem, a couple of attachments made life a lot easier. The first is a flexible drive, essentially an outer cable with a small chuck mounted on the end of an inner cable about 600mm (2ft) in length, and driven by the chuck of the power drill. This was very good in tight situations, but it is a two-handed operation, and limited to small drill bit sizes as the inner cable drive tends to wind up under load. If a larger capacity is required then a right angle drive chuck attachment is the answer. The chuck is driven at right angles by bevel gears in a housing mounted in the power drill, and, like the flexible drive, requires both hands to operate. Being more positively driven, however, it handles larger loads and is easier to control.

A set of hole saws proved very useful to have, and, used with a power drill at slow speed, gave a very neat cut. I own twenty three different sizes from 14mm (9/16in) to 95mm (3¾in) but the hole diameter required always seemed to fall between the sizes, which leads neatly onto the next items.

To remove material from a panel edge or increase the size of a hole, various rotary tools were used in a power drill. For small work, rotary files – sometimes called rotary burrs – were used to make complex shaping simplicity itself; for larger areas there are flap wheels and drum sanders.

A versatile tool for drilling small holes of varying diameter is the cone cutter, which is basically a stubby conical drill that can produce holes of any diameter between a minimum and maximum range. The one used on the Mirov has a capacity of from 6mm (¼in) up to 20mm (¾in).

Last on the list of tools used in a power drill is an unusual one; a 5mm (3/16in) tapered reamer. It was used to cut holes of any shape in panels by inserting it in a pilot hole and then dragging it along the marked cut line like a freehand router. A surprisingly neat and accurate cut was achieved, and this method was used with great success on sheets of fibreglass, wood, aluminium and mild steel. The only thing to watch is not to put too much sideways pressure on the reamer, otherwise it will snap.

(b) Angle grinder

This is an absolutely brilliant piece of kit that wasn't even new when purchased, but a reconditioned unit that takes 110mm (4½in) discs. Over the nine year car build it received a lot of abuse and had to be fitted with a new set of motor brushes and a new switch.

Equipped with a sanding disc it was ideal for rapid material removal, while, for cutting fibreglass panels, I found a stone cutting disc to be excellent. The only drawback with using the angle grinder was the mess it created; clouds of dust billowed everywhere and full protective clothing was a must, including heavy leather gauntlets for the hands, eye protection,

A selection of rotary files.

A cone cutter.

The indispensable Powerfile.

and ear defenders as it was easily the loudest tool used.

(c) Powerfile

Made by Black and Decker, this is a sort of narrow belt sander where the 12mm (½in) wide belt runs around a protruding finger with a roller on the end. It was probably the most used power tool of the entire project, in a working environment so hostile that two went bang, failure being due to the small bearing at the end of the motor shaft succumbing to the ingestion of cooling air laden with abrasive glass dust. For detail shaping work in small areas it is unbeatable. Apart from the regular bearing failures this tool was excellent as it could reach into all sorts of places to remove material quicker than anything else, and it is thoroughly recommended.

(d) Belt sander

This was of the hand-held variety, used for fast removal of material to shape a panel, or to smooth gel coat prior to filling or finish sanding. It had to be kept on the move to prevent a build-up of friction heat between the belt and the panel, as this could make the surface soft and tacky. Panels were trimmed straight with ease by running it along the edge, and it gave a more accurate finish than a sanding disc in the angle grinder, although it was almost as noisy.

(e) Variable speed jigsaw

Where access was good the jigsaw was used to cut fibreglass panels, and it worked best using fine metal cutting blades at a slow speed because the glass content of the panels would blunt the blades quite quickly if used on a fast setting.

(f) Orbital sanders

Sanding and finishing all the manufactured panels took hundreds of hours, and all of the sanding tools saw really heavy use, with two of them having to be replaced. Three types were used: ⅓rd sheet, palm, and detail sanders.

The detail sander had a small triangular head with a Velcro hook and loop-type fastening system for the abrasive pads. A very good tool, even though the small head could have done with being even smaller at times. The palm sander was about half the size of the ⅓rd sheet type, and gave a good rate of removal. It was very smooth in operation; being relatively small to a certain extent it could be used on concave surfaces. The ⅓rd sheet orbital sander was used when access was good and speed not important; very good for edge work.

(g) Miniature hobby tool

This little variable speed multi tool accepts small drill bits, rotary files, cutting discs, drum sanders, and wire brushes. When access was restricted – such as when working in the doors or the fuel tank pods – it was excellent. Despite its diminutive size it was a very capable performer, just right for intricate work such as cleaning hardened resin from bonded-in screw threads and sanding excess fibreglass from around fixing holes.

3.2. Hand tools

(a) Hacksaws

A hacksaw fitted with a 24TPI blade proved very capable in the accurate cutting of fibreglass panels, along with its smaller stablemate, the junior hacksaw. Occasionally, when access was limited, the blade had to be held in a special pad saw-type holder, though care had to be taken as, with little support, it was very easy to buckle the blade.

(b) Metal shears (tin snips)

As well as being used for normal metal cutting duties, hand-held shears or snips were a quick and easy way to cut the thin, pre-formed fibreglass sheet to shape before being bonded in and fibreglassed over. Good quality shears/snips are recommended because glass fibres can be tough customers, and cutting a laminate up to a maximum of 600g (2oz) (ie two layers of 300g (1oz) or one layer of 600g (2oz)) only is advised because, any thicker, and the shears struggle with the glassfibre, which tends to shatter along the cut and leave furry edges.

(c) Files

The various profiles of ordinary hand-held, second cut files were useful for fine shaping and finishing, a special rasp with a rough surface very similar to coarse aluminium oxide paper being ideally suited for fast material removal, leaving a smooth surface. When filing across the edge of a panel, it's best to work in one direction, from the outside inward, otherwise there is a risk of chipping the gel coat layer.

(d) Sanding & shaping

After rough working with power tools, it was necessary to hand-finish the majority of panels, especially complex areas such as the rain channelling and doors. Abrasive aluminium oxide paper – from rough 80 grit, right up through the grades to 1200 grit wet or dry paper – was employed with a variety of shaped sanding blocks of all sizes. General sanding was carried out with the usual flat rubber block, whereas detailed sanding required wooden blocks to be tailormade to the exact profile of the areas to be worked, the abrasive paper stapled around the blocks to ensure slip-free operation. If the paper became clogged it was easily revived with light use of a clean wire brush and vacuum cleaner.

One of the most useful sanding blocks made for the project was a flat wooden version, measuring 460mm (18in) x 100mm (4in), with a handle screwed to the back for extra grip. When used in a long, sweeping action, a really good surface finish was obtained on larger panels.

4. PRACTICAL FIBREGLASS TECHNIQUES

Designing a complex structure for maximum strength and minimum weight is a science in itself, but, for the home builder, the maxim "If it looks right, it is right," plays a big part. Panel thickness and shape contribute to the strength of the finished structure: get the shape right and a weight-saving can be made by using a thinner lay-up. Avoid large, flat, unsupported expanses, and always try to envisage the actual loading on a part when in use – will it be in compression, tension, or torsion? – then build accordingly. Inevitably, this may result in some parts being over-engineered, but this is no bad thing for a road car, and preferable to being too weak.

To understand the construction methods used on the Mirov, it is best to start with the simple techniques used, which, together, form the basis for the complex structures that were tackled in the build.

4.1. Simple moulds

(a) Flat panels

When constructing the body shell and creating new panels in situ, it was sometimes easier to pre-fabricate thin, flat fibreglass sheets. These were cut to shape and bonded in place on the car before being fibreglassed over to form the finished structure.

Most flat, non-porous surfaces can be used to create a fibreglass panel, but, from a safety point of view, it is best to avoid using a sheet of glass as it is too smooth and the resin will tend to stick. To produce a panel of worthwhile size, a 1800mm (6ft) x 610mm (2ft) sheet of white melamine-covered chipboard was given two coats of release wax, and polished between each coat. Two layers of 300g (1oz) CSM that had been cut to size were added, one at a time with the lay-up Resin 'A' being worked into each in turn with a brush or a roller, after which it was left to cure. The finished panel was peeled off the board and put to one side ready for use. A good example of fibreglass sheet construction is the rear bulkhead, which is covered in chapter 3.

If a panel was required to form a component with a ready-finished surface, such as the door skins, then the initial coating on the melamine board was gel coat Resin 'B,' after which the required number of CSM layers were added.

(b) Angles & curves

Having just covered the manufacture of a flat panel, it is easy to see that, if two pieces of melamine-covered chipboard are screwed together at right angles, a right angled fibreglass panel can be made. Add a third piece and a corner mould is the result; add

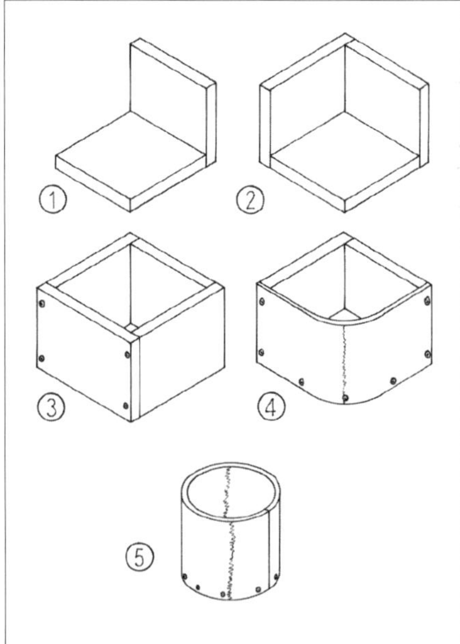

1) Two pieces of board screwed together form a simple angled mould. 2) Add a third board and the result is a corner mould. 3) A fourth and fifth side give a box mould. 4) Remove the last two additions, round off the corner and add a flexible material to give a more complex result. 5) With a completely circular base, a tubular mould evolves.

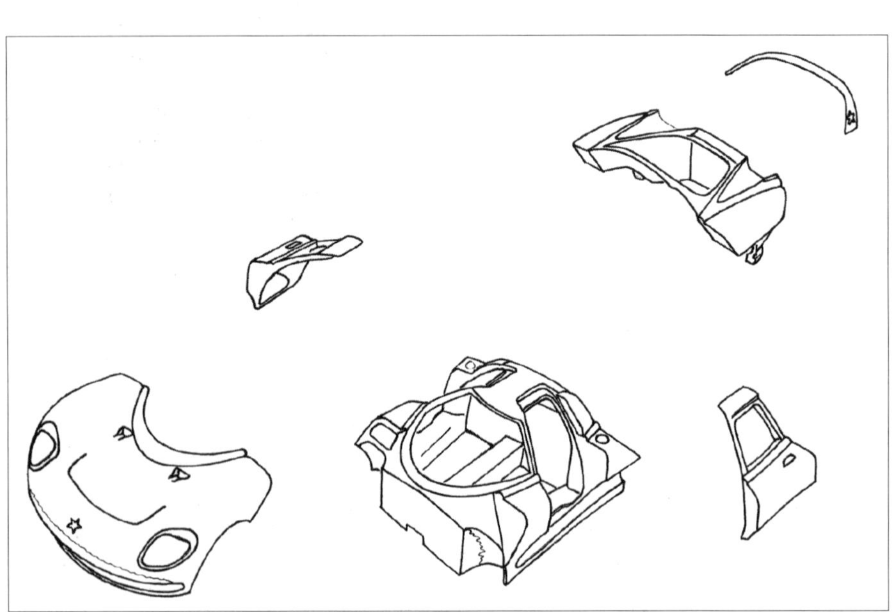

A combination of the techniques covered in this chapter was used to construct all of the Mirov body components.

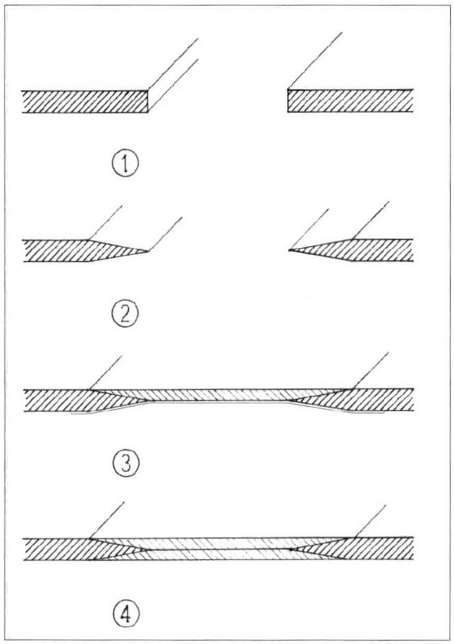

The evolution of a strong feathered joint that, with attention to finishing, can be made invisible. 1) The hole or panels to be joined. 2) The edges are feathered on both sides. 3) The first lay-up is added over a temporary support. 4) The second lamination backs up the first.

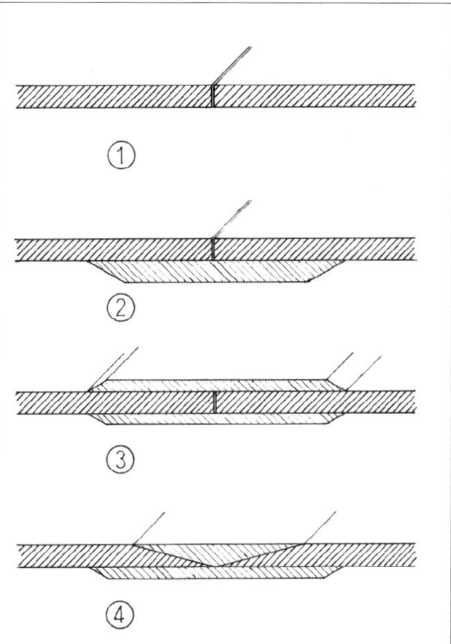

Variations on the butt joint. 1) The two panels are cleaned, sanded for a close fit, and pushed together. 2) A single lay-up on the reverse side may be all that is needed if the join is not to be seen. 3) A second layer can be added on top for extra strength. 4) Alternatively, the top could be ground out to form a feathered join for a flush

fourth and fifth pieces and you have an open-topped box mould. The beauty of this technique is that, with everything screwed together from the outside, once the box has been created in the mould the entire assembly can be dismantled around it.

For curved panels a flexible mould material is required, and this can be almost anything: hardboard, metal, rubber, plastic, cardboard, the list goes on, but the common link between each mould used in the Mirov project is that they were cheap or free. So recycle those breakfast cereal packets, milk containers and hardboard, etc, as it's all useful 'junk.'

If two adjacent sides are removed from the box mould and the exposed corner of the base is cut into a curve, the two sides can be replaced by a single piece of flexible material, and a box with a rounded corner made. Take this to its logical conclusion and replace all of the sides with flexible material fixed to a circular base, and a round box mould is the result.

This basic method makes an appearance in the Mirov build, combined with fibreglass techniques to produce more complex structures such as the boot box (chapter 2), rear spoiler (chapter 4), and doors (chapter 5).

4.2. Joining panels

One of the basic techniques used throughout the build was joining together fibreglass panels, old and new. The Mirov chassis consists of a front and rear subframe connected by four 38mm (1½in) square 18SWG steel box sections at floor level. In itself it is not very rigid, so it was clear that the body would have to be a structural element in the design, which meant that any join would have to be of excellent quality; due to the nature of the project, there would be plenty of them ...

The first consideration was cleanliness; all mating surfaces had to be free of grease and dust to ensure a good bond, and this was achieved using acetone on a tack-free cloth, which cleaned and slightly softened the cured resin surface. A few moments had to be allowed for any surplus acetone to evaporate before work began, otherwise joint strength could be compromised.

Although the joint methods covered here were used to construct the body shell of the Mirov, they could equally be used to repair an existing fibreglass body.

(a) Feathered joint

If done correctly this method is very strong, and, with careful rubbing down, can be made invisible. As the name suggests, the key is feathering the panel edges to be joined; this means they are tapered in thickness to increase the bonded area, and thereby increase join strength.

The tools found to produce quick and neat feathered edges were an angle grinder fitted with a sanding disc, and a Powerfile belt sander, although, in areas with highly restricted access, hand tools were also used.

With both panel edges feathered inside and out, the two panels are supported in position and the gap bridged by a piece of waxed board or metal, as the join will be tackled one side at a time. Narrow strips of CSM and resin are applied to the middle of the resulting shallow 'V' section, with subsequently applied strips being slightly wider than the last until marginally under the level of the panel surface. This lay-up is left to cure, after which the backing board can be removed and, if possible, the whole assembly turned upside down for ease of work. After a thorough clean, the lay-up procedure can be repeated for the underside, but this time the CSM can overlap the edges of the 'V' for added strength as this side will be out of sight when finished. When cured, the entire assembly is righted and initial lay-up finished off with a layer of flow coat. With great attention paid to the finish sanding of the outer surface, a perfectly smooth, undetectable join can be achieved.

(b) Butt joint

A butt joint is usually meant to go unseen; it is very functional in appearance and tends to be used on inside surfaces. It is quick and easy to carry out, and is a convenient and strong method of combining panels.

If one side of the panels to be joined is finished in smooth gel coat, then that should be scuffed up with coarse abrasive paper first. The two panels are butted up against each other

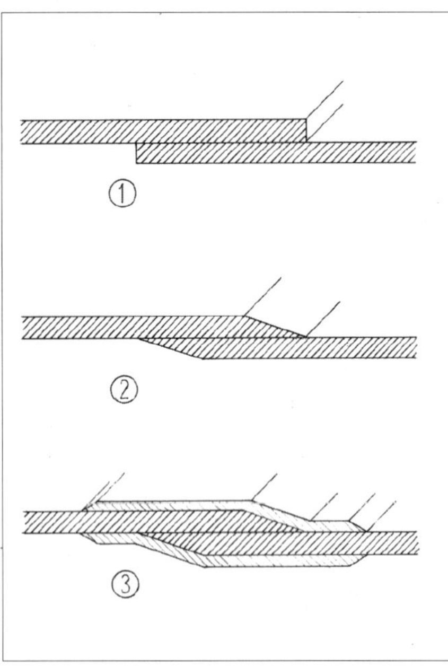

1) Two panels are positioned for a lap joint. 2) The edges are feathered. 3) Lay-up is added each side for a strong join.

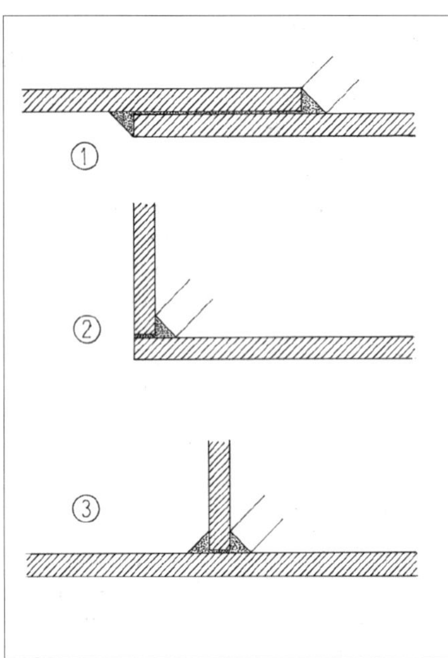

Three types of simple bonded joint. 1) A bonded lap joint. 2) A right angle. 3) A 'T' joint.

and layers of CSM and resin applied to bridge the join on one or both sides. The technique can be amended to join panels at different angles, or even in a T-shape, and the number and extent of laminations can be increased for more strength.

(c) Lap joint

The lap joint is very similar to the butt joint, but slightly stronger as the subject surfaces are overlapped a certain amount with a resin interface before being laminated on both sides. It is also easier to position and clamp together the pieces before work begins.

(d) Bonded joint

If access is restricted, the bonded joint may be the answer, although, because the bonded surface area is invariably smaller than with the previous two methods, the resultant joint tends not to be as strong. With the Mirov this type of joint was used for non-load bearing items only (such as the air box for the windscreen demister vents) and for initial fixing before permanent lamination.

The bonded joint consists of two surfaces that are held together with resin. If the surfaces are not perfectly flat, a way of ensuring good resin contact must be found. This was done in two ways: the use of a single layer of CSM in the joint to act as a carrier for the resin; the use of glass blooms to thicken the resin into a paste. Recommended are clamps or weights on the joint to apply moderate pressure until the resin has cured; spread the pressure with lengths of wood protected by a sheet of polythene to prevent them from sticking to the job.

4.3. Dealing with gel coat cracks

Finding spidery star cracks on a fibreglass car is a common problem, and is a result of local stresses in the panels, which can be caused by a knock in the form of accident damage, impact from a flying stone, or the twisting of bodywork on a less than rigid chassis, the latter cause nearly always giving cracks in the corners of door apertures. In most cases the cracking is only cosmetic, and necessitates local repairs to the gel coat; if the damage extends into the fibreglass, however, a more extensive repair is required.

(a) Cosmetic cracks

The way to deal with this minor type of damage is to grind it out along the path of the crack down to the fibreglass laminations, ensuring that the crack does not continue into the underlying structure. The best tools to use for this

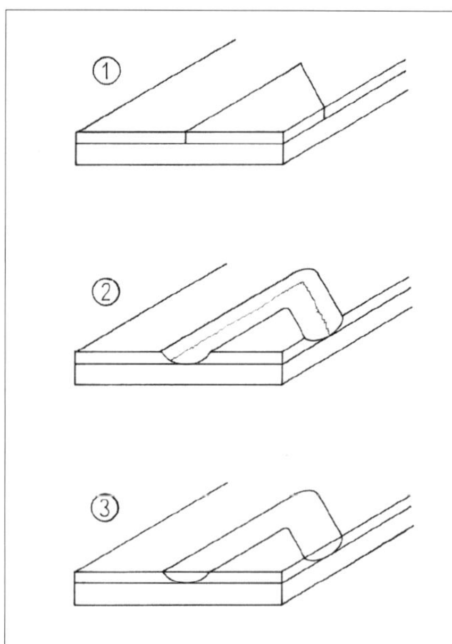

1) A typical gel coat crack. 2) Grind out along the crack. 3) Fill with gel coat or polyester filler.

are a ball rotary burr powered by an electric drill, or the tip of a Powerfile, both of which will cut a smooth channel with a semicircular cross-section. Avoid using a file or burr with a pointed end as the resulting V-shaped channel will tend to concentrate stresses, and soon allow the repair to crack again and undo all your hard work.

When all of the cracks have been ground out, they should be thoroughly cleaned with acetone. If the reworked areas are large and shallow, or small and deep, good quality polyester filler can be used, but it is best to fill them with fresh gel coat using a small brush. The latter method is more time-consuming, but filling with the same material ensures a good quality repair. When thoroughly cured, both types of repair can be rubbed down, and any low spots filled and sanded to give a smooth finish ready for paint.

(b) Deeper damage

If, after grinding out the cracks, it is found that the damage extends down into the fibreglass structure, the channel will have to be widened using a sanding disc in an angle grinder, taking out all of the damage. The resulting hole with feathered edges can then be repaired using the methods described in section 4.2. joining panels.

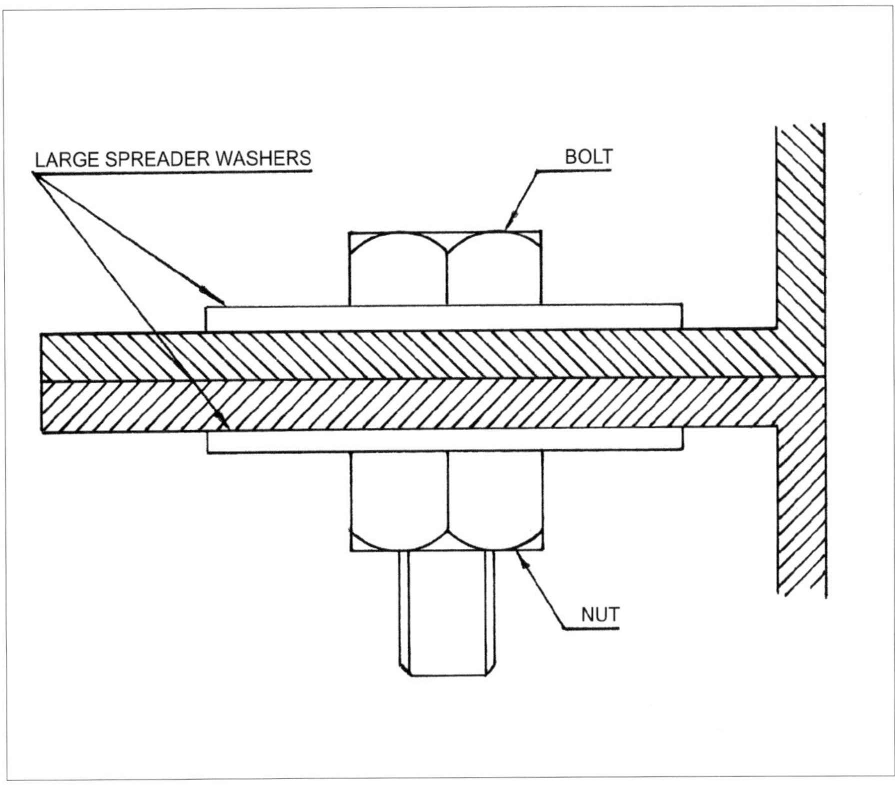

Always try to spread the load at a fibreglass panel join. Large washers are ideal for this.

Here are four of the six nut plates that were bonded to the rear bulkhead to accept body mounting bolts.

4.4. Fixings

When fitting items to fibreglass panels it is sensible to spread the load to prevent localised cracking of gel coat and the possibility of laminate failure. The Mirov front bodywork hinges are mounted with just two bolts, but each one is fitted with a 50mm (2in) steel washer each side of the fibreglass, and a local box section forming the number plate mount helps distribute the stresses into the surrounding structure. Another example of load spreading is the bonded-in nut plates that secure the body to the chassis in some locations.

(a) Spreader washers

As outlined above, when bolting through fibreglass the key is to spread the load of the fixing with large washers each side of the panels concerned. If this is not done localised cracking of the gel coat and ultimate failure of the panel will ultimately result. As well as using spreader washers under nuts and bolts, it's a good idea to use them when installing pop rivets, as well. Always use them under the tail of a rivet to prevent it pulling through the panel when being formed, but, ideally, use them under the head, too.

(b) Nut plates

Perforated steel plates with welded-on nuts were bonded to the inside of the central body unit to permit the mounting bolts to be tightened from one side only, which eased assembly, and the large plate spread the load of the mounting point over a wide area to enhance structural integrity.

Steel plates measuring about 30mm (1¼in) x 150mm (6in) x 3mm (⅛in) had M10 nuts welded over a central 10mm (⅜in) hole, and were drilled with many smaller holes to allow the plates to be securely bonded in position with resin paste. A couple of self-tapping screws held each plate while the body mounting bolts were inserted and tightened to seat the plates securely before they were laminated over with CSM and resin.

A variation on this theme is the use of bolt plates. Bolts are inserted through holes drilled in a small plate and the heads are welded to the plate. The bolts are then pushed through corresponding holes in a panel, and the component is mounted with nuts trapping the fibreglass panel between the two. This method was used to secure the rear clamshell catch brackets.

(c) Studs

These took the form of bonded-in mounting studs, and were used for light duty fixings such as inside the doors

The rear clamshell catch brackets were fitted using bolt plates.

to fit the handle assemblies and lock mechanism bellcranks, as well as being used to mount the additional rear light units.

The head of an M5 bolt of the required length was welded to a 50mm (2in) square piece of 1.2mm (18swg) perforated steel sheet to make the stud assembly. The thread was taped over to protect it from resin, and then the plate was pressed onto a bed of resin paste and laminated over, leaving the bolt thread accessible. The square plate guards against future failure because it tends to resist torque better than a round plate, and so will not begin to spin when trying to undo the nut at a later date.

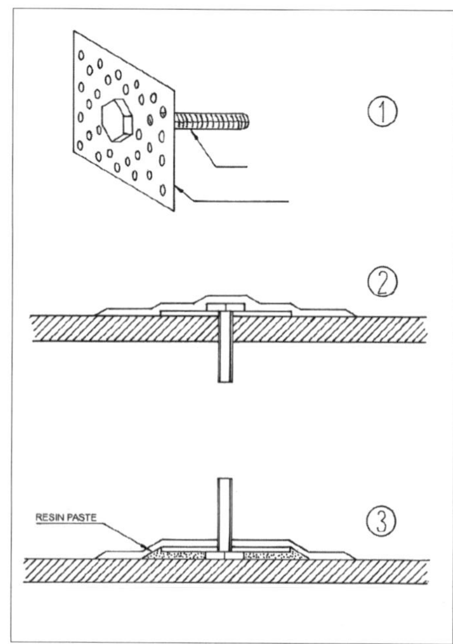

A captive fixing will make future maintenance easier. Here are two ways of securing a stud. 1) Made from a bolt welded to a square of perforated steel. 2) Here, the stud is secured to the back of a panel with a layer of chopped strand mat. 3) The stud can also be fixed to the same side of the panel as the item to be secured. In the Mirov this method was used to hold the mounting studs for the rear lights and door handles.

Chapter 2

Front bodywork

This chapter covers the creation of the front part of the car from the original one piece body shell, and details the different techniques used for each stage. The basic panel needed much work to ensure it was practically and legally fit for road use. Practical measures were ensuring it was strong enough by adding box section stiffening around the hinges, which doubled as a number plate mount, further stiffening being provided by inner wheelarches moulded in situ. More practical alterations included moulding intake ducts to supply the heater unit, and widening of the whole assembly to allow the suspension to work unhindered when on full steering lock. The legal side of things concerned altering the wing profile to house purpose-made headlight units at the required height, along with clear polycarbonate fairings, which were made by vacuum-forming.

The beauty of working with fibreglass is that tasks can be tackled with confidence in the knowledge that any mistakes are possible to correct. The techniques described put into practice some of the basic joint methods outlined in Chapter 1, and can be adapted to suit most problems encountered when working with a fibreglass body.

The front clamshell panel had to be cut and created from the original body. The hinge is as far forward as possible to allow maximum access.

1. FLIP FRONT

The Mirov was never intended for road use, and this threw up many problems, the first of which was the lack of access panels. The easiest solution to this was to cut and hinge the complete front and rear of the body to create two clamshells, which would break the car down into three manageable sections and provide excellent access.

The car was very wide, and the finished panel was going to be quite

Inner wheelarches and headlight boxes were added, which helped stiffen the whole structure.

The front bodywork cut and hinged open for the first time. Note the original dummy headlight covers.

The new clamshell panel viewed from the rear showing the lack of internal stiffening structure.

The wooden jig in position to assist with marking out the cut lines.

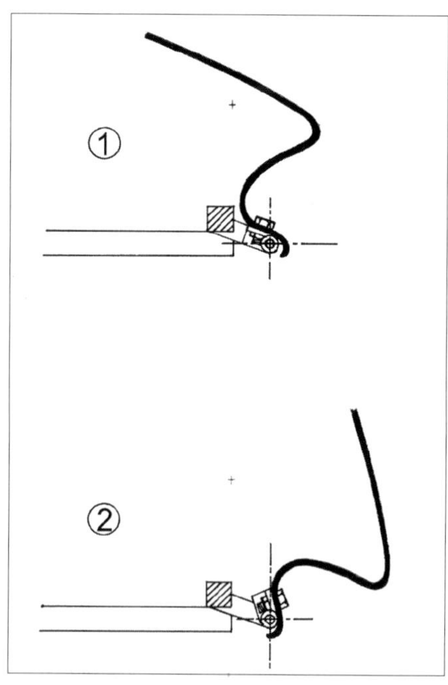

A cross-sectional view across the nose of the car, showing the hinge bolted to the lip of the air dam to get the pivot point as far forward as possible.

large and awkward to handle, so the hinge points were fabricated and fitted underneath before any cuts were made in the bodywork. This ensured perfect alignment and eliminated the need to build in any adjustment for the hinges.

The chassis finished 460mm (18in) behind the front of the car, the nose section of the body being self-supporting. To allow the body to open wide, the hinge was to be mounted as far forward as possible, so a supporting framework was welded onto the chassis. This would eliminate the E-type

Jaguar problem of the bonnet almost hitting the ground and restricting access because the hinges are quite a way back. Each hinge was bolted to the lip of the air dam at the bottom of the nose, using large washers each side to spread the load on the fibreglass.

With the hinges secured the next step was to decide where to cut the wings each side of the windscreen, a choice complicated by the car not being symmetrical. To aid matters, a wooden jig was made in the form of a pair of uprights, separated by a crossbar long enough to straddle the width of the car. This was placed square across the car by measuring from the suspension points. From this a plumb line was used to plot cut lines on each wing with a chinagraph pencil. Due to the car's asymmetry, the lines had to be finalised with a touch of freehand adjustment to get both sides looking similar.

A combination of jigsaw and pad saw cut the fibreglass along the lines, and, using an old steel rule with one end sharpened to a knife edge, the bonds at the base of the windscreen and the original wooden support midway along the bonnet were separated to allow the whole front end to be hinged open.

2. WIDENING THE FRONT WINGS

When proper double wishbone suspension was fitted to replace the transverse rigid steel tubes originally installed to hold on the wheels, it was clear that the tyres and wheelarches would come into contact during full suspension movement: the wings would have to be widened. A line was marked about 75mm (3in) from the lip of each wheelarch, and a cut made with a jigsaw, leaving a small portion still attached at the front and rear of each cut. Wooden wedges were driven into the cuts, which moved the top of each wheelarch outward about 25mm (1in). The exposed edges were prepared for a feathered joint (page 15, Joining panels) by sanding back 25mm (1in) from the cut.

The raw edges were cleaned with acetone, and a strip of cardboard covered with brown parcel tape was waxed and fixed with masking tape

With a wheel and tyre in position, a cut line is drawn around the wheelarch.

The first cut is wedged open and fibreglassed. Polythene sheet protects the tyre and workshop floor from resin drips.

The modified wheelarch has been sanded to shape and is ready for an application of flow coat resin.

to the underside of each cut, which supported the outer laminations of fibreglass applied to bridge the gaps. When this had cured, the wedges were removed and the remaining gap fibreglassed over. The cardboard was removed and the reverse of each cut was feathered back to allow more layers of mat and resin to be applied. The outer face was sanded back and finished with a flow coat of resin 'B,' which was sanded smooth when fully cured.

A little while after widening the wings, the versatility of fibreglass construction was demonstrated when it became apparent that the wings had not been widened enough, and the whole process was repeated to double the width increase.

3. ADDING STRENGTH

3.1. Box sections

When the front body was cut and hinged to create one large opening panel, it proved quite flexible. One of the measures to counter this was the manufacture of a box section across the inside of the nose to reinforce the hinge mounting area on the front spoiler lip.

At this early stage in the project I was still experimenting with different techniques, and this box section was formed by laminating onto several thin plywood sheets that had been bonded in place across the inside of the nose with polyester filler. This reduced panel wobble by half, and most of the remaining flex was eliminated by constructing a second box section in front of the hinge attachments with fibreglass sheet, which doubled as a number plate mounting point.

Three pieces of prefabricated fibreglass sheet were cut to form the box and bonded in position with resin paste. The air dam was sanded back through the gel coat and into the fibreglass around the box; this allowed subsequent laminations over the sheet sections to be blended flush into the surrounding bodywork. Flow coat was brushed on the whole area and left to cure before being sanded to give a neat finish.

3.2. Stiffening ribs

Another way of adding strength to a panel is to incorporate ribs. The large, hinged front panel had already been braced by the addition of two box sections, and, to further stiffen it, a pair of longitudinal ribs – which doubled as inner wheelarches – and a transverse drip rail were moulded onto the underside.

The drip rail was formed by moulding small pieces of chopped strand mat (CSM) onto a long, thin cardboard former braced by wooden blocks, and held in place with masking tape. Its purpose is to intercept rainwater running down the underside of the panel before it gets to the boot seal.

To make the inner wheelarches, two waxed pieces of melamine-faced board were cut to match the forward sloping profile of the body, and clamped vertically to each side of the chassis; the front panel was then closed on them, making sure they were a snug fit. Working inside each wheelarch in turn, the new inner arches were laid up

The right-hand wheelarch being widened for the second time.

Creating the first box section stiffening across the nose by laminating over thin plywood diaphragms.

The finished box section number plate mount made by laminating over sheet fibreglass sections.

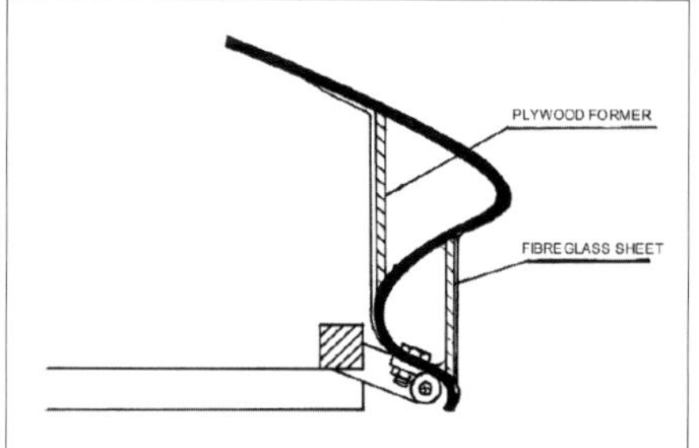

A cross section of the clamshell nose showing how both box sections combine to reinforce the hinge mounting points.

The drip rail being moulded across the underside of the front panel.

Both the inner arches and drip rail stiffen the front clamshell panel. The two boxes built to house the headlight units add additional strength.

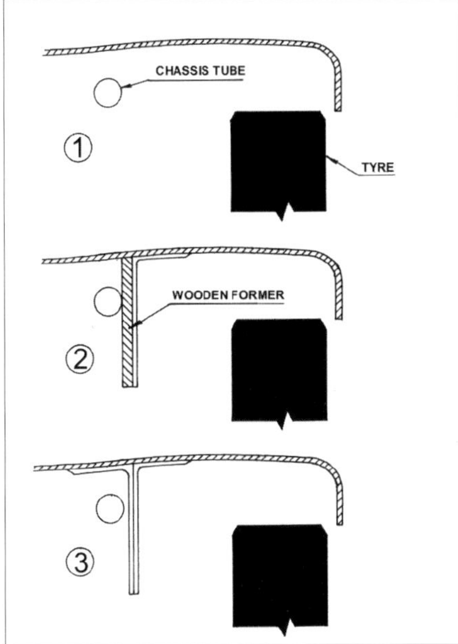

A cross-sectional view through the right-hand front wing looking forward (1), showing creation of the inner wheelarches. A wooden former is clamped to the chassis rail (2), and the inner wheelarch is laminated onto it. The board is then removed to allow fibreglass to be applied to the reverse of the new panel (3).

in situ onto the boards and up onto the underside of the body and nose box section.

When cured, the clamps were released and the front panel opened up, complete with boards, which were then removed to allow the reverse side of each new moulding to be roughed up and cleaned with acetone. A second lay-up was applied to the reverse of each new inner wheelarch panel, across onto the bodywork to provide further stiffening, and effectively double the bonded attachment area of the inner arches.

Curved rear sections were added to each new inner wheelarch in the same manner with the front panel shut, but this time laminating onto some waxed cardboard taped in place. With everything cured, the cardboard was removed and the arches trimmed to shape.

3.3. Return flange

As well as adding strength a return flange can also improve the look of a panel, such as the cut edges of the front panel where it was separated from the central body section. A quick way to form these flanges is to use fibreglass sheet.

Using cardboard templates the fibreglass flanges were cut from sheet and bonded in place with resin paste, and masking tape to hold them until cured. A gloved finger was wiped around the inside to smooth the paste before it set to allow easier application of mat and resin on the inside, which reinforced the join. Flow coat was brushed on and rubbed down to eliminate the outer join line.

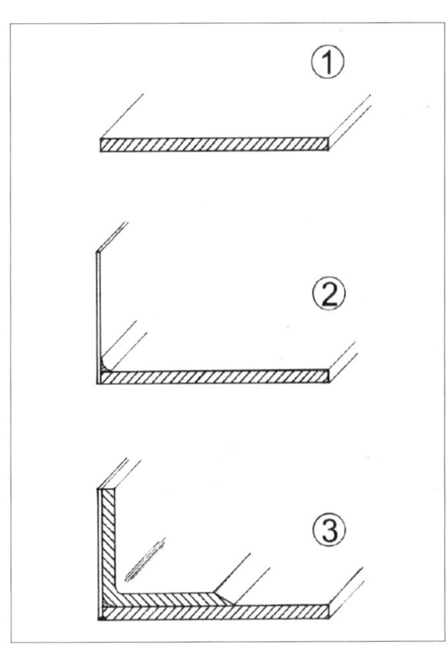

Diagrams showing return lip creation starting with the cut panel edge (1). The sheet fibreglass is bonded on with resin paste (2), and then laminations of fibreglass matting back up and reinforce the new return lip (3).

4. BOOT BOX

For the sake of practicality the front of the car was going to house a small boot area, so some form of box had to be made to fit between the chassis rails. Fibreglass allowed the box to be closely tailored to the chassis tubes to maximise boot capacity.

A transverse chassis tube divided

Here, the back of the right-hand front wing section of the clamshell has a piece of fibreglass sheet attached with resin paste to create a return flange.

the available space and dictated that the boot box would have two compartments, front and back. The mould was fashioned using pieces of plywood and cardboard clamped, taped and wedged in place over the chassis rails, taking care with the overall shape to make sure the finished moulding could be lifted off the chassis without having to cut it about. When satisfied with the shape and size, the entire mould was covered with brown parcel tape. The smooth surface of the plastic tape allowed the easy application of wax release agent, which was followed by several layers of CSM and resin.

The piecemeal mould construction allowed partial disassembly to aid removal of the new moulding, which lifted off vertically as planned. After removing the rest of the mould sections, the boot box was placed back on the chassis to allow four mounting holes to be drilled. The top edge was progressively trimmed back until it was a close fit under the front panel, with enough clearance to permit the fitting of a rubber seal. With the box once again removed, the surface irregularities caused by small wrinkles in the parcel tape were corrected with polyester filler before the outside was painted black.

This is the same return lip fully finished.

The various mould parts are held in position by clamps and masking tape. Even the scrunched up newspaper on the left is playing a supporting role.

The boot mould takes shape on the chassis.

After initial laminations a revised rear section is added using sheet fibreglass.

The inverted boot moulding awaits final trimming.

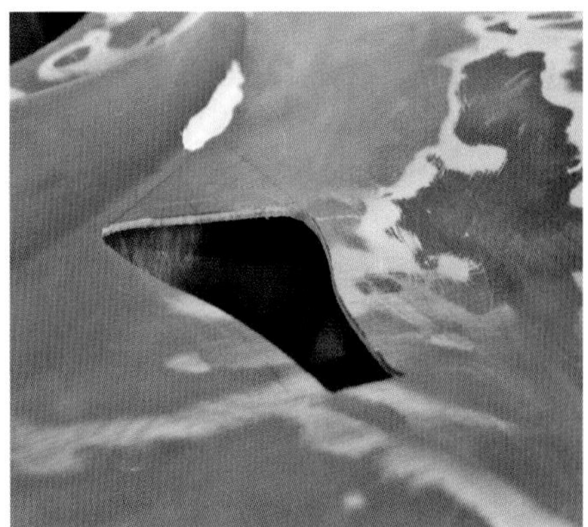

An air intake is cut in the front panel.

Card mould elements taped in place and stapled to rectangular wooden formers.

The finished boot box trimmed with red-edged black carpet and topped by a weather seal. Note the twin windscreen washer reservoirs.

5. AIR INTAKES

The heater blower motor was going to be fitted to the left-hand side of the front bulkhead, so some kind of air intake had to be added. This took the form of a NACA-style duct moulded in situ underneath the front panel just in front of the windscreen, using a simple, three-piece waxed cardboard mould held together with masking tape. Small moulds such as this are easy to form from thin cardboard, whereas anything bigger would require too much bracing, in which case metal or hardboard would be more suitable. To balance the look of the car, a matching, non-functional intake was added to the right-hand side of the panel.

Firstly, the holes in the front panel were marked out and cut with a jigsaw, then the sides were formed from a cereal packet and taped in place behind each hole, after which the lower part of the mould was added and fixed with tape. The three parts of the mould were stapled to a rectangular chipboard support, which ensured that everything remained square, and then the shiny outer face of the cereal packet mould surface was polished gently with wax release agent.

Gel coat resin 'B' was applied and left to go off for a few hours before laminating with four layers of CSM and resin overlapping onto the surrounding bodywork. After curing, the cardboard was removed and the gel coat cleaned with acetone to allow final finishing with flow coat of some low spots. The complete assemblies were rubbed

With the card mould removed, the freshly formed intake awaits final finishing.

The foam cubes are sanded to shape, ensuring both sides are as symmetrical as possible.

After rubbing down, filling and painting, the new intakes blend in well.

down to blend into the surrounding bodywork, and, as a finishing touch, after the car was painted, fine metal mesh was bonded to the back of each duct with resin paste.

6. FITTING HEADLIGHTS

The SVA test rules stipulate the legal positioning criteria for the various light units. The minimum height requirement for headlights is 500mm (19¾in) measured to the dipped beam cut-off point on the lens. The Mirov as purchased had no headlights, and, as the front wings were a very close fit around each tyre, there was no room to accommodate any either. Bearing in mind that the ultra compact light units of today were not available at the time of this project ,all attempts to fit headlights – even pop-up units – met with failure. There was simply no way that the minimum height requirement could be met.

From day one the intention was to preserve as much of the original body design as possible, but the shape of the front end had to change to make things legal. To create the necessary space, drastic surgery was called for, but care had to be taken to ensure the work did not ruin the look of the car.

6.1. Altering the wings

(a) REP foam formers

The wing lines swept sharply downward just forward of each wheelarch, which looked great but, unfortunately, had to change. Careful

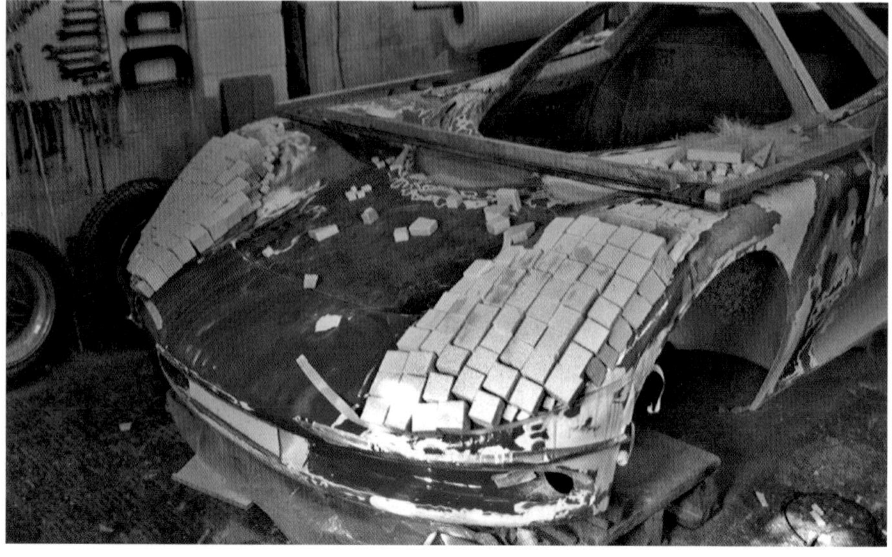

REP foam cubes are fixed in place on each wing.

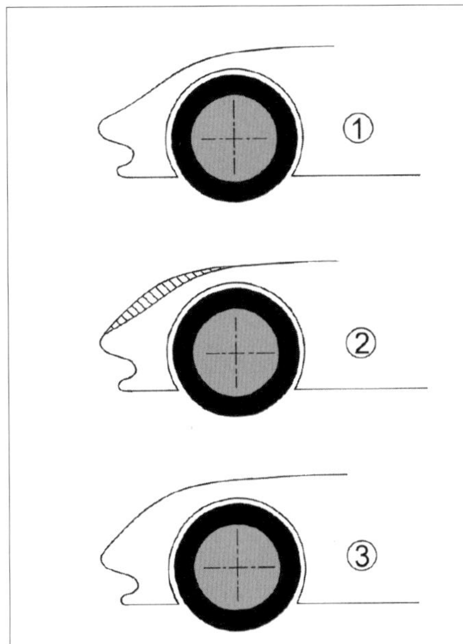

Three diagrams illustrating the change of wing profile, starting with the existing wing line (1). The foam cubes are added and sanded to shape (2). The original wing is cut away from underneath and the foam removed to allow the back of the new wing skin to be laminated (3).

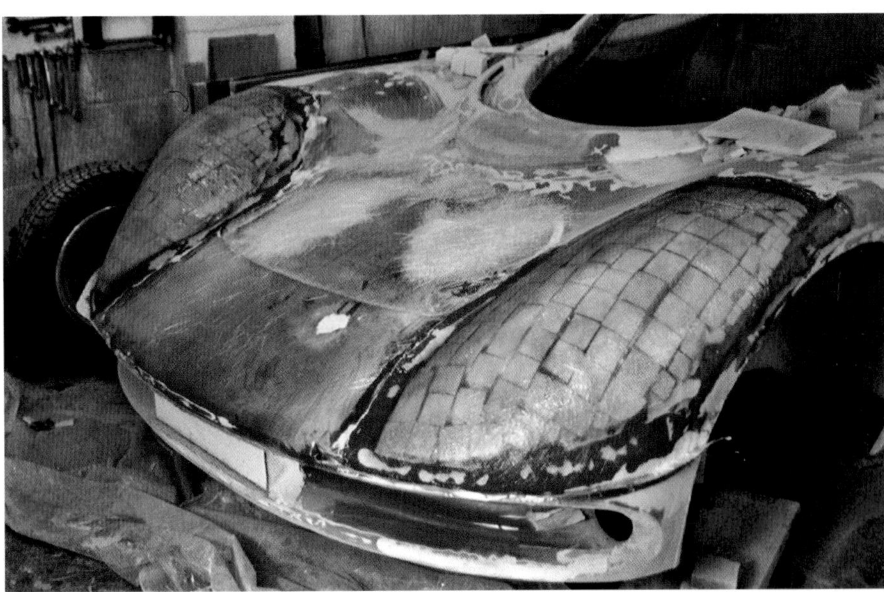

The new wing is created by laminating onto the foam core. Note that the surrounding gel coat has been ground back to ensure a flush join.

The re-profiled wings have new holes cut to house the proposed headlight units.

measurement confirmed that the wing need not be raised because a fixed headlight assembly could be accommodated at a legal height if the line of the wing was moved forward slightly. It would just meet the minimum height requirements of the SVA test, and could be accomplished with the minimum disturbance to the svelte shape.

Firstly, the front of each wing was covered with 50mm (2in) cubes of REP foam stuck on with resin 'A.' With these securely held in place, work commenced on one wing with carefully sanding down the foam to give a new profile that blended into the surrounding bodywork to look as if the car had been designed that way. Care had to be taken when sanding the foam because, although rigid, it is very soft when attacked with abrasive paper, and it is very easy to take off too much, so it was a case of "gently does it." When satisfied with the new shape, vertical cardboard templates were taken of the new profile at two locations to assist in creating a mirror image with the foam on the other wing.

(b) Making the new outer skin

With both areas of foam sanded to the new profile, the surrounding gel coat was sanded back to ensure that the layers of mat and resin which followed sat flush to the existing bodywork for an invisible join.

When cured, the new lay-up was painted with three applications of white resin 'B' flow coat, then left for a few days to harden, after which it was sanded to blend in with the original bodywork, filling any low spots with more resin 'B' until everything was totally smooth.

At this point, as a precaution, a mould was taken of each wing to preserve the new profile so that major foul-ups could be corrected easily and brought back into shape with the

A rebate lip being laminated in one of the wing moulds.

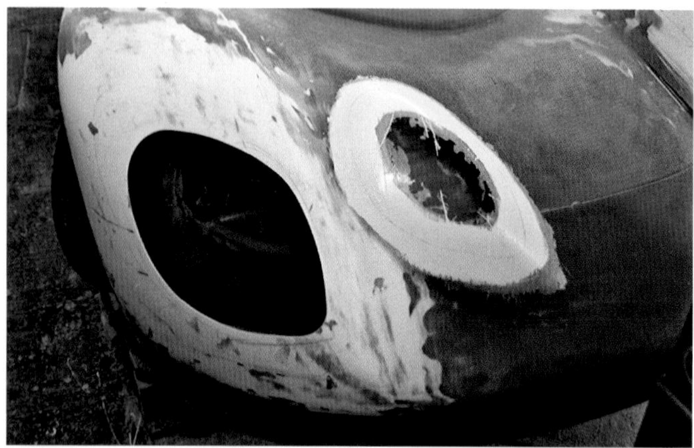

The right-hand rebate lip fresh from the mould, showing it has exactly the same profile as the new wing.

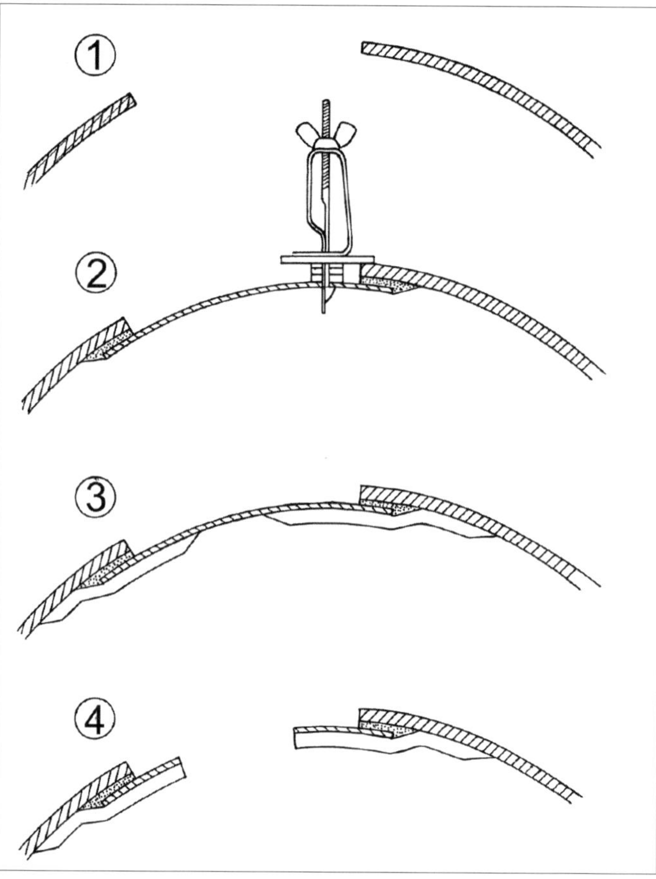

These diagrams demonstrate how an even depth rebate is achieved around a curved aperture (1). The rebate panel is held in place with grip pins and spacing washers to ensure even depth (2). The initial resin paste fix is supported by a lay-up of CSM (3). The finished lip is trimmed to size (4).

The left-hand rebate is held in place with grip pins and spacing washers during initial fixing with resin paste.

The finished rebate trimmed to width.

Headlight units began with the manufacture of stepped base mouldings from basic wooden moulds.

The base mouldings have been trimmed to shape and had scalloped sections added to accommodate the headlights.

minimum of fuss. As the headlight installation was incomplete and fresh additions would be required, it was decided not to contaminate the surface with release wax, and so the new area of each wing was covered with brown parcel tape and waxed before being subjected to a layer of gel coat resin 'B,' plus three applications of CSM and resin 'A.' When cured, the mouldings were pulled off and the tape removed, any stubborn areas of sticky residue being shifted with the help of white spirit, which does not harm the gel coat.

To complete joining of the new wing profile to the existing skin, the front body was hinged upward and secured in the open position; this allowed the old wing skin to be cut and sanded away from underneath to reveal the underside of the foam cubes. These were removed to expose the reverse side of the new fibreglass skin. The edges of the original skin were feathered to meet the new skin, and, after cleaning with acetone, four or five laminations were applied inside the wings and the alteration was complete.

Even after drastically altering the front wing profile, space was still a problem, so headlight positioning was critical. Several paper templates were tried on the new wings until the shape of the headlight apertures was finalised. After drawing around the template, each hole was cut out with a jigsaw.

(c) Fitting rebates

To allow the planned fairings to sit flush, it was decided to add some form of rebate flange around each hole. The moulds taken of the new wing profiles were used to create the two rebate flanges, which then had to be bonded to the underside of each wing. The outer edges of the rings were trimmed until they were 20mm (¾in) larger than the apertures, and then trial fitted and centralised; the outline of the hole was marked on them in pencil. Positions of the transparent cover fixing holes were determined, and eight drilled in each rebate ring, 5mm (3/16in) in diameter.

The edge of each rebate, and the area around the underside of each aperture, was keyed with abrasive paper and cleaned with acetone, then bonded in place on a bed of resin paste and held with grip pins, ensuring that the depth of the rebate was equal all around the hole by using spacing washers on each pin. Grip pins – sometimes referred to as skin pins – are used in the aircraft industry to hold panels together prior to riveting. They are easy to get hold of because they are always popping up on e-Bay. It is definitely worthwhile acquiring some as they will prove invaluable. When the resin paste had cured the grip pins were removed and the outer edge of each rebate panel inside the wings was feathered, which allowed the application of CSM to augment the bonded join from behind.

The oversize rebate flange was

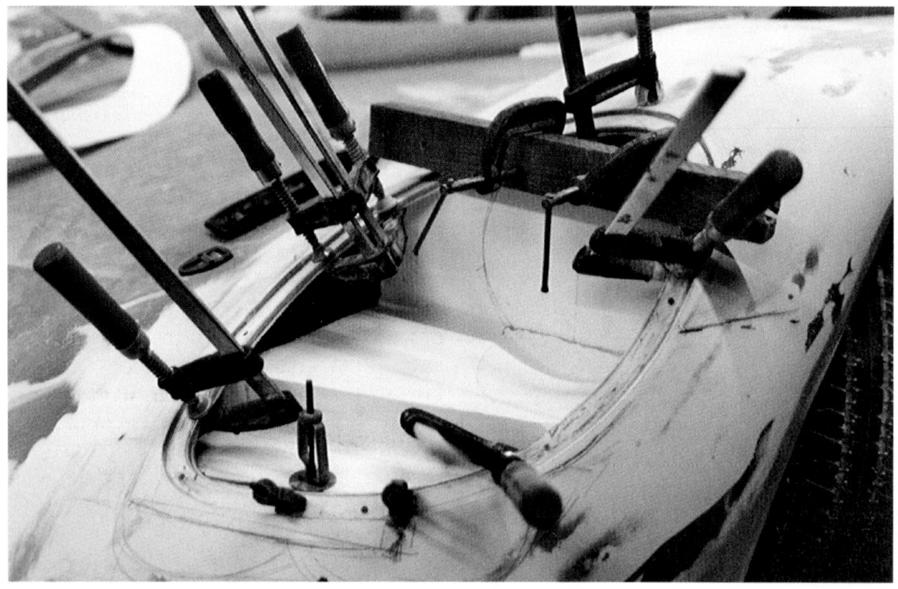

The left-hand base unit being bonded to its mounting ring in situ.

trimmed to a neat 20mm (3/4in) in width after inserting a pencil into a washer of the correct radius, and rolling it around the circumference of the aperture to mark the cut line equidistant from the edge of the hole.

6.2. Creating headlight units

Lack of available rearward depth dictated the use of 145mm (5¾in) sealed beam headlights on each side, which were nice and shallow, and left room for a projector beam spotlight just inboard and an indicator/sidelight unit to the front. Some sort of pod on which to mount these various units had to be made.

Very basic left- and right-handed moulds for the base of each headlight unit were made from four pieces of melamine-covered chipboard screwed together to form a stepped mould, the front step angled to match the nose of the car. After waxing the moulds, a layer of gel coat resin preceded three applications of CSM and resin to form the basic structure for each pod.

When trial fitted the headlamps protruded too much above the wing line, so, to drop them slightly – and still keep within the minimum height requirement – a scallop was added to the base of each unit. A circular cardboard template that represented the headlight was held in position on the vertical back section of each moulding to determine how deep the scallop needed to be to house the headlight by recessing it into the horizontal portion of the moulding. A cut-out was made in each panel and cardboard taped in place over the holes and waxed to allow each scallop to be moulded in fibreglass.

Using a plumb line and the goalpost jig originally created to cut the front bodywork, reference points were marked on each side of the headlight apertures to align the two base mouldings with each other, and make sure that the headlight mounting faces were vertical and at right angles to the centreline of the car. The mouldings

Both base units fixed to their respective mounting rings.

The right-hand assembly in place with holes cut for the headlight and indicator/sidelight units.

The lights are trial fitted to the left-hand housing.

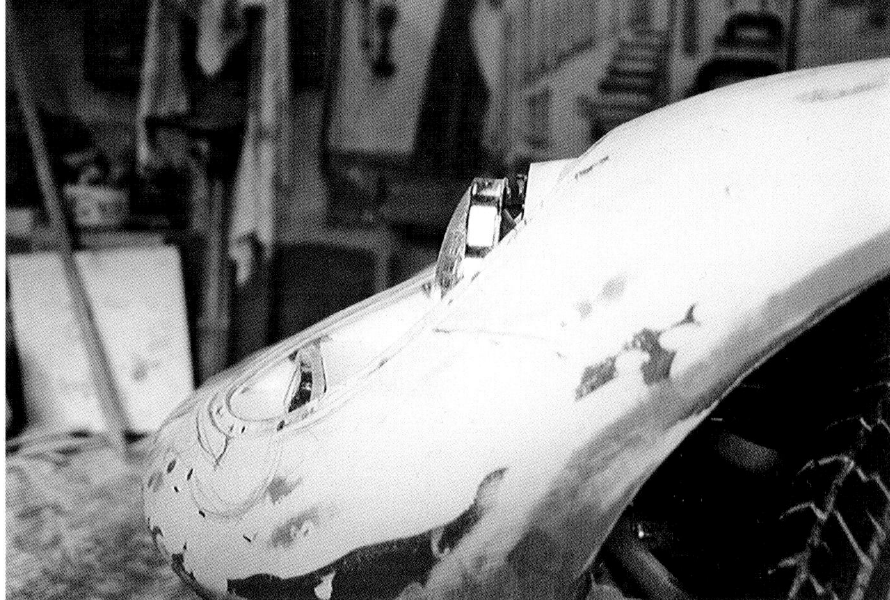

Even with the re-profiled wings space was still at a premium, and the headlights protruded slightly above the wing line.

were then trial fitted in each wing to allow excess material to be trimmed off a little at a time to obtain a good fit.

To allow the light housings to be fitted snugly behind the rebate flanges around the holes, two more mouldings were taken from the wing moulds to produce a pair of mounting rings the same shape as the rebates. These were trimmed to ensure that the centre hole was exactly the same size as the hole in the rebate flange to assist positioning.

Each mounting ring was clamped to the back of its corresponding rebate, after which the base mouldings of each pod were bonded with resin paste inside their respective rings, and held in place with a grip pin at the front and wood clamped across the rear aligned with the pencil reference lines. Using a small spirit level they were checked for level.

When these assemblies had cured they were removed and all the odd-shaped gaps between the bases and the mounting rings bridged with cardboard and moulded over with fibreglass; the cardboard was then removed to reveal two basic headlight pods. Holes were cut in the base of each pod for the lights to be tried in place to give an idea of the finished product. At this stage, provision was made to fit small 12V computer cooling fans to each pod to be wired in to come on with the lights and provide a demisting facility for the fairings; all that remained was to manufacture the fairings themselves.

6.3. Vacuum forming headlight fairings

The style of fairing had already been partially decided by the fact that the sealed beam headlights protruded slightly above the line of the wing contour, which meant they needed a blister to accommodate them. The shape was going to be quite complex and called for some fancy thinking.

Back at school in the 1970s, my woodwork teacher demonstrated the art of vacuum forming, using nothing more than a plaster mould, a thin sheet of acetate, a two-bar electric fire, and a vacuum cleaner to make a body for a slot racing car. That impressed me at the time and has lingered in my mind, just awaiting an opportunity to be used. That time had come; vacuum forming was the answer to this particular problem.

(a) Making patterns

The first task was to make fibreglass patterns of the required shape for the fairing to allow it to be moulded in plaster of Paris. The two sections of wing previously cut out were temporarily refitted and taped in place on the rebates. For aesthetic reasons there were to be two blisters on each fairing, so two ovals of 25mm (1in) thick REP foam were stuck onto each replaced panel with double-sided tape and sanded to form four blisters, each about 20mm (¾in) high. Brown parcel tape was then applied to the foam blisters and the area around them to allow moulds to be taken. From the resulting female moulds two more

Foam blisters are added before being covered with parcel tape to allow moulds to be taken.

Gel coat is applied over the parcel tape, followed by several layers of CSM and resin.

moulds were taken to reproduce the blisters in fibreglass. These mouldings were treated to final filling and sanding to refine the shape, after which they were trimmed down until about 20mm (¾in) larger than the holes in the wings. These were the patterns needed to make the vacuum moulds.

(b) Constructing the vacuum moulds

With one of the fibreglass patterns face up on the bench, a 180mm (7in) high aluminium collar was formed snugly around it, overlapping the ends and sealed with silicone sealant and secured with self-tapping screws. The next stage was to pour in plaster of Paris to form a mould of the fibreglass pattern within the aluminium collar. To provide a key to anchor the plaster, self-tapping screws were inserted through the sides of the collar just above the pattern. Once the plaster of Paris was mixed, it was necessary to move fast as it sets quite quickly, and it was poured into the aluminium collar onto the pattern to give a central depth of 50mm (2in), which, due to the curvature of the pattern, increased towards the sides to about 130mm (5in) deep. Any trapped air bubbles were released by vibrating the mould with an orbital sander with the paper removed, after which it was left for several days to dry out.

When completely dry, the assembly was inverted and the fibreglass pattern removed, allowing the aluminium collar to be trimmed flush to the plaster. Two hundred 2mm (3⁄32in) diameter air holes were drilled right through the plaster mould face at a spacing of 13mm (½in).

The bottom of the collar was blanked off with a 13mm (½in) thick piece of MDF sheet cut to fit, screwed in place and sealed with high temperature silicone sealant. This left a 38mm (1½in) deep air chamber between the bottom of the plaster and the board. A 20mm (¾in) hole for the vacuum supply was cut through the side of the collar into the air chamber, and a thick bead of silicone sealant was applied around it and left to cure to form a seal for the vacuum nozzle.

(c) Forming the fairings

2mm (3⁄32in) thick polycarbonate sheet was chosen for the fairings because, with two hundred and fifty times the impact resistance of glass, and

The blister mouldings are each wrapped in a collar of aluminium to allow plaster of Paris to be poured in.

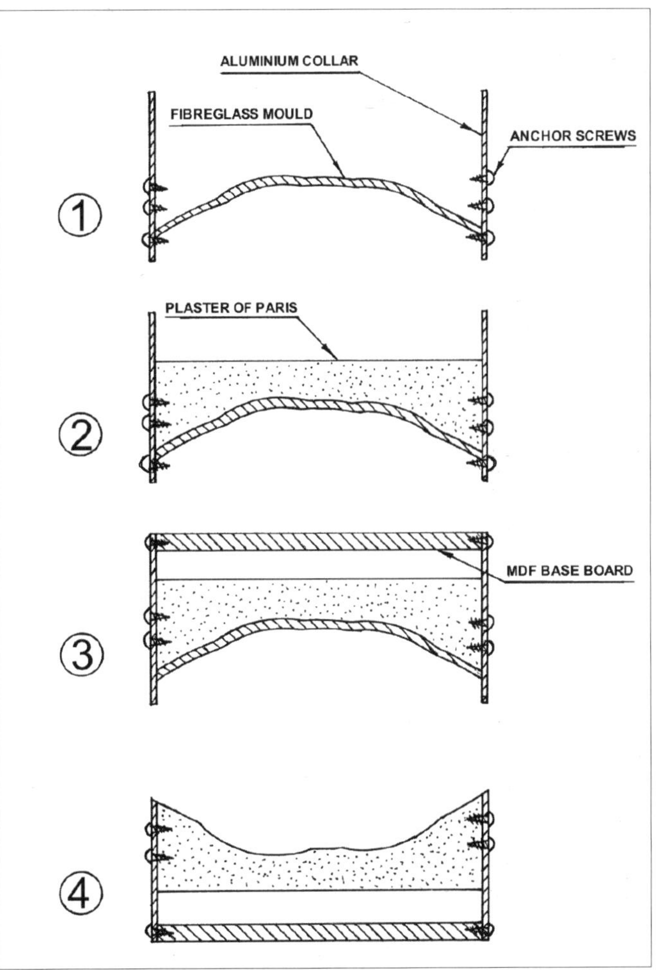

The four stages of vacuum mould manufacture. First, the blister moulding is placed in an aluminium collar (1) and screws inserted to provide a key for the plaster. The collar is filled with plaster of Paris (2). An MDF base board is added (3), leaving an air gap above the plaster. The entire assembly is then inverted (4), and the blister moulding removed to allow the aluminium collar to be trimmed flush to the plaster. It then only remains to drill the plaster with 200 air holes and cut the vacuum hole in the side of the air chamber.

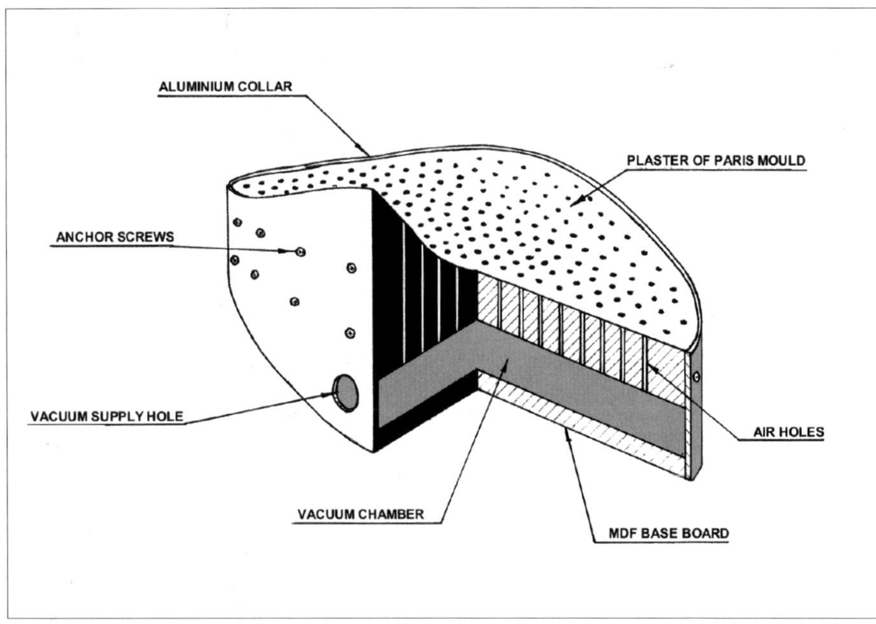

A three quarter cross-section of the finished vacuum mould showing the small air holes in the plaster and the vacuum supply hole in the side through to the vacuum chamber.

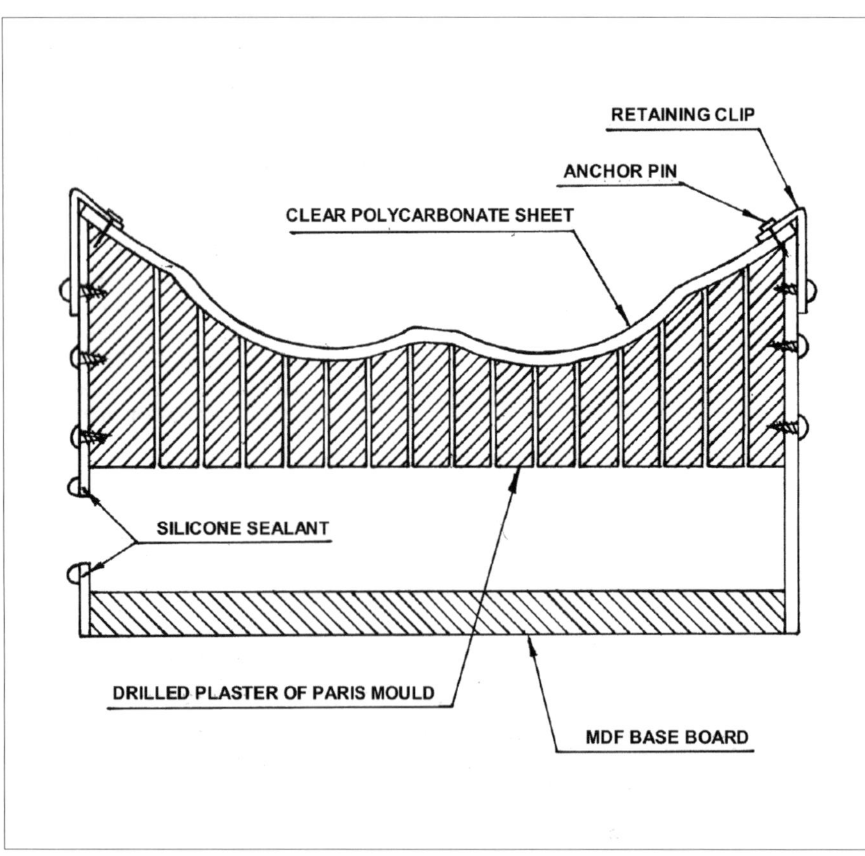

A cross-section of the vacuum mould showing the formed polycarbonate sheet and how it is anchored along the edge to prevent slippage.

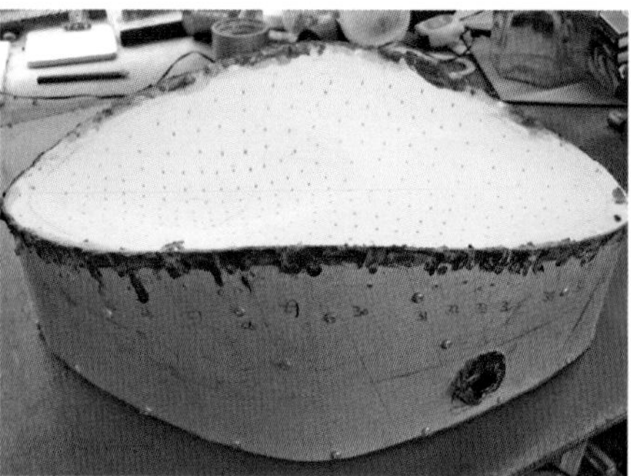

One of the finished vacuum moulds, which only just fitted in the oven, showing the seal around the vacuum supply hole.

good UV stability, it would be virtually unbreakable and not become opaque after a few weeks' use. Also, being thin, it was ideal for the fairly primitive vacuum forming operation that was to follow.

To hold the polycarbonate in position, 40 holes were drilled through the aluminium collar around the top of the plaster mould to accept small steel, right angled brackets held on with self-tapping screws. A cardboard template was taken of the plaster mould and the polycarbonate cut to shape. It was pushed down into the curve of the mould with a bead of high temperature silicone sealant around the edge to ensure an airtight fit, and fixed in place with the brackets. Small holes were drilled in the top of each securing bracket, through the fairing material and into the mould to allow small panel pins to be pushed in to anchor the edges of the polycarbonate and prevent slippage during the forming process. The complete assembly was left overnight for the sealant to fully cure.

To maintain domestic harmony, permission to use the kitchen oven was sought and given. Measurements revealed that the mould assembly would fit in the oven – just – much to my relief, because I had not checked this before making the mould! The theory was to place the mould in the oven to heat up, and then quickly open the oven door with a vacuum cleaner running and place the nozzle on the air box outlet to suck the polycarbonate into the mould. The vacuum cleaner was prepared by taking out the dust bag and filters to reduce the risk of fire and increase suction.

The left-hand headlight cover displaying its twin blisters fresh from the mould, trimmed to size and trial fitted.

The finished headlight fairings with their bonded black rubber gaskets.

The length of time in the oven and the required temperature were arrived at by trial and error. The first attempt wrinkled at the edge of the polycarbonate through not being hot enough, and the second was too hot and distorted the plastic: eventually, a delicate balance was reached.

Because the cure time for the sealant around the edge of the moulding was so long, all attempts had to be twenty four hours apart, which was very frustrating. With hindsight, a more direct heat in the form of a radiant electric fire, or even the cooker grill, would probably have been more successful and less risky to the vacuum cleaner, as it would have been sucking cool air which would have made it more efficient, as well.

The next attempt was a complete success, with two neat blisters being formed and the polycarbonate retaining the curve of the mould. The process was repeated using the other mould with equal success. The two oversize fairings were laid in place on each wing, and the excess material marked and trimmed off with a pair of metal shears. They were put back on the wings to mark the fixing holes, which were then drilled. To hide the face of the mounting rebate, and to bring the fairings flush to the wing skin, gaskets were cut from 3mm (1/8in) thick black rubber sheet and bonded onto the back of each fairing with black silicone sealant.

If attempting this sort of thing yourself, it would be best to carry out your own experiments with degree of heat and amount of time because your heat source and mould size will be different to the ones used here. Always be extra careful with this sort of thing, and be aware of the risk of fire by having an extinguisher to hand. The best piece of advice is that, if in any doubt about what you are planning, DON'T DO IT!

6.4. Finishing detail

(a) Headlight trim

The black border around the fairings effectively hid from view the top of the headlight adjusting mechanism. However, the area between the headlight and spot lamp looked a little untidy, so an embossed aluminium trim panel was made to hide the light fixings.

Firstly, a cardboard template was made to determine the shape of the panel and a pair of MDF formers cut. Some thin embossed aluminium – slightly larger than the formers – was placed between them and bolted in place. The narrow edge of the metal was then tapped over to form a flange. The two panels were screwed in place

The MDF formers used to create the headlight trim.

After failure of the rubber bond, the headlight fairings were treated to a new finish using satin black acrylic paint, which was found to adhere to the polycarbonate extremely well without using primer.

The LH trim in place between the headlight and spot lamp. Spacers are used to hold the trim flush to the headlight rim.

between the lights with spacers to hold them flush to the headlight rims.

(b) Black borders

The appearance of the headlight fairing black surrounds relied on the rubber gasket fitted to the underside being viewed through the clear polycarbonate, but, unfortunately, the black silicone sealant was not up to the job and the rubber began to come away, which ruined the external appearance. Various experiments with painted finishes revealed that acrylic satin black spray paint adheres extremely well to polycarbonate sheet with minimal preparation and without using primer. After wiping with a soft, dry cloth, each headlight cover was masked and received a satin black border, which, to date, has withstood a few thousand miles with no chips or scratches.

Chapter 3

Central body unit

The main strength of the original UVA M6 GTR car, on which the Mirov is based, was achieved by uniting a structural fibreglass body unit with a fairly simple chassis that combined to form a very strong assembly. Unfortunately, when the Mirov was created, the centre body was chopped about so much, the main structural element of the design was lost. The sills were removed along with the centre tunnel and most of the rear bulkhead to leave one rather floppy car. To replace the missing bits and unite all of the original UVA parts with the Mirov panels, many different techniques have been used to help form a major new structural part of the final design.

The UVA chassis at the heart of the Mirov has only four 37mm (1½in) square chassis rails, running at floor level and linking front and rear halves, so a stiff body section is vital. With work of this nature, all of the joins in the fibreglass have to be scrupulously clean to ensure good strong bonds, and this was achieved by thorough cleaning with acetone on tack-free rags prior to any work being carried out.

To make the central body tub every panel had to be modified in some way, much of it being made from scratch.

After reinstating the sills, bulkheads and tunnel to ensure the body/chassis unit was as stiff as possible, new mounting points were added along both floor pans to increase the original 13 points to 33. Large steel plates with welded-on nuts were welded to the four longitudinal chassis rails to allow holes to be drilled through the floor to take M12 bolts.

Apart from the structural side, there were many details to attend

The workshop floor is clearly visible through the left-hand sill. One of the many wooden infill panels that had to be removed can be seen in the top left of the picture on the 'A' post. Note how the original kit car structure has been cut off, leaving wide, horizontal flanges.

Here, the base of the left-hand sill has been partially constructed in fibreglass. The board used to support the lay-up has been removed for clarity.

to as well in order to end up with a professional-looking and functional body shell. The manufacture of return lips where the front and rear body had been cut off, and rain channel and seal flanges around the door apertures, took a lot of time to get right, though the end result was well worth the effort. The construction of the doors themselves was a major task and is covered in chapter 5.

When tackling this scale of work, don't become intimidated by looking at the project as a whole, always try to break things down into manageable tasks. If solutions to problems are not readily apparent, go and do something else or sleep on it; it's amazing how the subconscious brain will continue working on that problem. With this project I was fortunate to have plenty of time, and found that simple solutions to problems would come to mind days, weeks, or even months later.

1. SILLS

The Mirov as bought was nothing more than a hastily assembled collection of fibreglass panels with little unitary strength. To survive the rigours of road use, all the panels had to be bonded together correctly, and extra reinforcing sections added where necessary. Longitudinal strength in most cars is derived from the centre tunnel and sills running between the front and rear wheels on each side. The Mirov had no centre tunnel, and only fresh air joining the remains of the original M6 GTR inner sills with the new outer skin, so additional structure was needed to connect the two. The sills were constructed in several stages, which resulted in a strong, though rather complex, assembly.

During the original construction of the Mirov mock-up the sills had been cut off, leaving a fairly wide, horizontal flange at floor level. To create a good key for the new fibreglass laminations, this was initially feathered on the top side only, then the inner face of the outer skin panel was lightly sanded to key the surface. To ensure a strong permanent bond, both surfaces were thoroughly cleaned with acetone.

With the car at a comfortable working height on axle stands, a piece of waxed melamine-covered chipboard was held in place under each sill in turn, two old scissor jacks making sure that it sat level, and a large polythene sheet protecting the workshop floor from resin drips.

Working inside the sill, the first stage of the new lower skin was laid up on the board, overlapping onto the existing structure by at least 100mm (4in). After cure, the board was removed and the process repeated for the other sill. The underside of each join was completed at a later date when the

The plywood centre diaphragm is trial fitted.

Initial sill construction is complete and laminating over sheet fibreglass sections has consolidated the 'A' post.

Here, a top layer of 25mm (1in) REP foam has been added to the sill, and the first incarnation of door seal flange constructed.

Using a cardboard mould the top of the sill is modified to accept a door catch.

body was strong enough to be removed from the chassis and inverted.

The next stage involved fibreglassing over a plywood diaphragm, bonded in place at the top of the sill with resin paste to form a box. Small gaps at each end allowed polyurethane foam to be injected from an aerosol, which expanded and solidified to add rigidity.

On this top skin a door seal flange was moulded onto a wooden former, before a layer of 25mm (1in) thick REP foam was added, which had its inner edge rounded to ease access to the seats, when fitted. The foam was encapsulated by CSM and resin, layered down onto the inner sill and

An inner view of the taller seal flange moulding. Note how the edge of the REP foam has been rounded off to blend with the inner sill.

The top of the sill has been built up with a second layer of REP foam, flush with the revised seal flange.

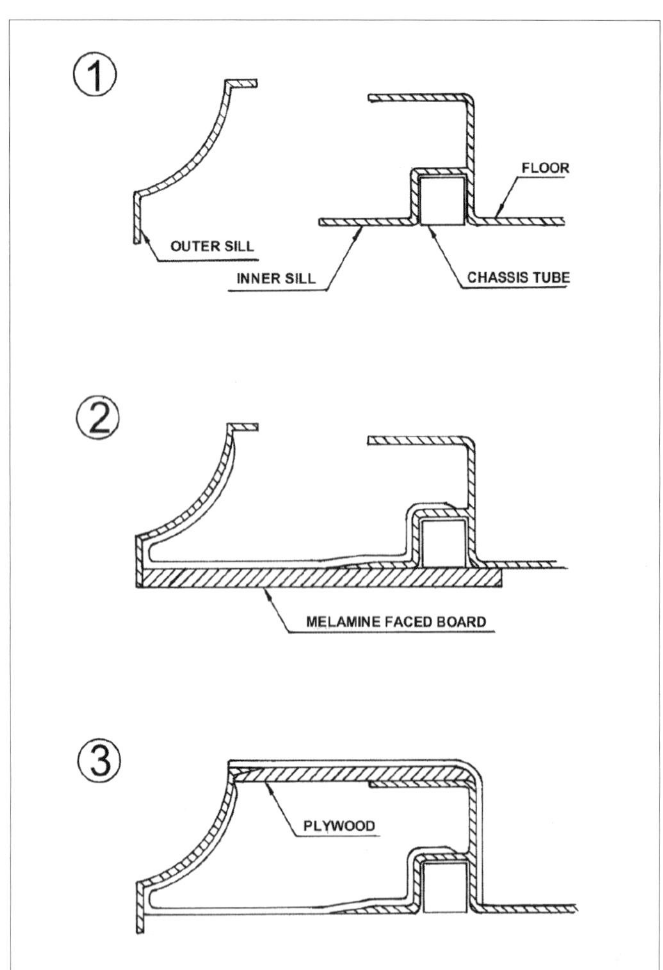

A series of sectional diagrams showing construction of the sills. 1) A cross-section through the original sill. 2) The bottom of the sill is laminated onto a waxed board. 3) The upper plywood section is added.

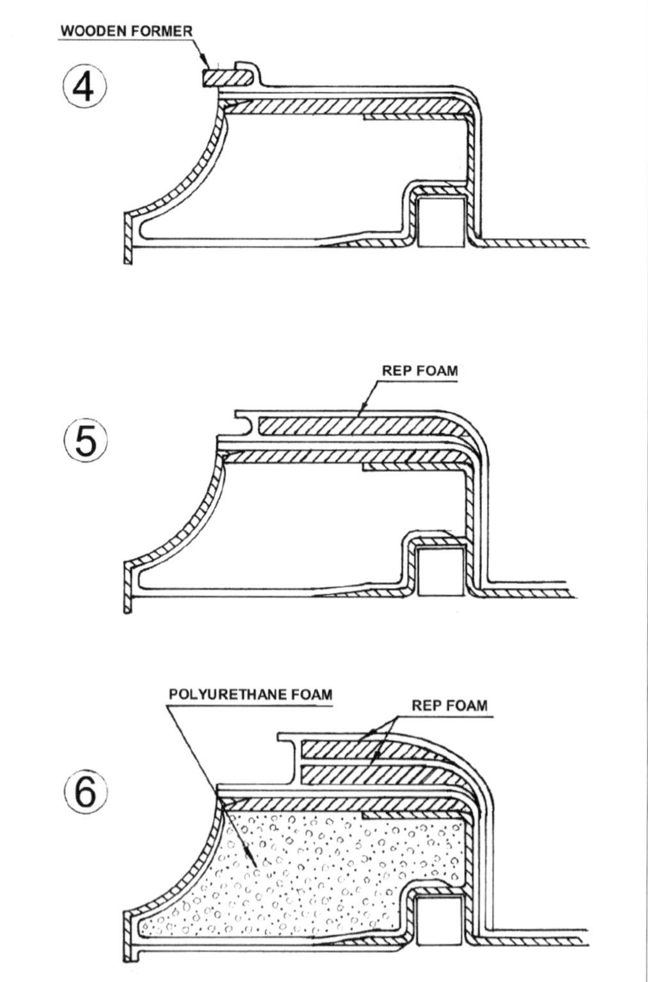

4) The initial seal flange is created over a wooden former. 5) REP foam is added to make the top surface flush. 6) The final construction detail showing the extra layer of REP foam, deeper rain channel, and aerosol foam filling.

The finished left-hand sill.

The two rear side sections of centre tunnel are laminated in.

The sheet fibreglass tunnel sides are bonded in whilst being supported by wood and cardboard spacers.

floor for strength to form a second box section. When it was realised that no provision had been made for the mounting of a door catch, the lower seal flange was removed and rebuilt taller with an inward kink. The increase in height was taken up by adding a second layer of 25mm (1in) REP foam, and laminating over it to form a third box section.

The resulting triple box section sill joined the original fibreglass floor to the Mirov outer panels, and added the necessary strength for road use.

2. CENTRE TUNNEL

Following the construction of the new sills, the next task was to reinstate the centre tunnel, which had been cut out to make room to fit a pair of fabulous-looking MDF seats.

After the very pretty – but very heavy and uncomfortable – MDF seats were removed, the outline of the original centre tunnel could be seen on the remains of the front and rear bulkheads, which indicated it had been quite a deep structure. The replacement was to be shallower, with a solid bottom and bolt-on removable top panels to improve access to things like the handbrake cable, gear linkage, heater pipes, and throttle cable.

2.1. Replacing the structure

The starting point was the remaining 38mm (1½in) lip that traced the outline of the original tunnel on the floor of the car. The lip was feathered on the only side that was accessible, and the excess on the rear bulkhead above the new tunnel height was removed with a sanding disc, the gap filled in with prefabricated fibreglass sheet. Four sections of sheet were cut to fit the length of the cockpit to form the tunnel sides, the two shorter sections forming the rear portion that flared out, following the chassis rails, to meet the bulkhead, the longer pieces running parallel from these to the front bulkhead. Both sides were held onto the chassis rails with masking tape, and held apart by taped-on wood and folded cardboard spacers, whilst resin paste cured to hold them in position.

With all the component parts held securely, several layers of mat and resin were laid up from the floor of the car, and up onto the new tunnel sides, then left to cure.

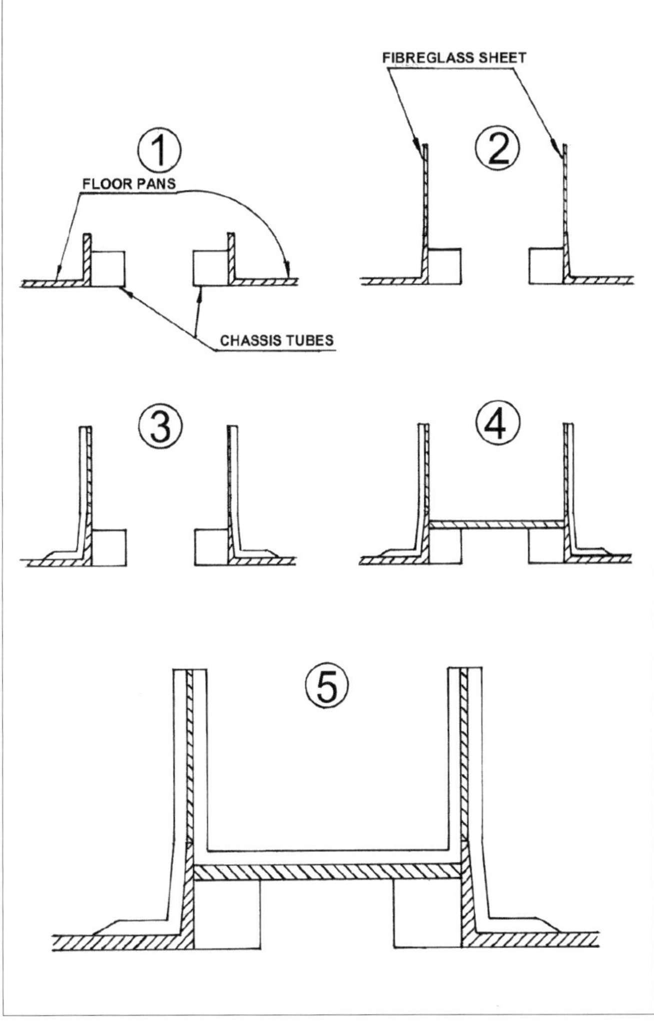

A series of sectional diagrams showing construction of the centre tunnel. 1) A cross-section looking forward through where the original tunnel has been cut out, leaving separate floor pans each side. 2) Sheet fibreglass sides are added. 3) The sides are laminated in. 4) A sheet bottom is positioned. 5) A final lay-up bonds the bottom and reinforces the sides.

With the new sides fixed in position, the wood and cardboard supports were removed from between them and the masking tape peeled off. To form the bottom of the tunnel, a long strip of fibreglass sheet was laid, gel coat side down, onto the chassis rails between the new tunnel sides, and held from underneath with masking tape. Several applications of mat and resin inside the tunnel simultaneously reinforced the new sides and bonded in the new bottom.

The underside of the feathered join along the length of the tunnel was tackled at the same time as the bottom of the sills when the body was inverted at a later stage in the project. Any irregularities in the floor to tunnel join were ground out and made good with mat and resin or resin filler, ensuring a smooth finish was obtained for a close fit around the chassis rails.

The top closing panels were made from folded aluminium, with the exception of the handbrake panel which was moulded in fibreglass, and is covered in the next section.

Three stages of handbrake panel construction. 1) The wooden mould. 2) The basic panel moulding produced. 3) The finished panel upside down showing the slot for the handbrake, and reinforcing steel nut plates.

2.2. Handbrake panel

An example of using a simple wooden mould to manufacture the handbrake panel, which is fitted to the top of the centre tunnel. The required plan form of the panel was transferred onto a small section of melamine-faced chipboard laid on top of the centre tunnel, by marking with a pencil from underneath.

The board was then righted and laid on the bench, and, by using the marked lines as a guide, blocks of wood were screwed in place from underneath to form the 50mm (2in) high sides of the mould: the front and back were left open.

After polishing the mould with release wax, several layers of CSM

The panel in place on the centre tunnel yet to be bolted in.

The finished handbrake installation.

and resin were applied to give a thick laminate able to take the load of the handbrake. When fully cured, the blocks forming the mould sides were unscrewed and the panel removed and trimmed to size. For extra security nuts were welded to the bent down ends of two 1.6mm (16swg) thick steel reinforcement straps, which were fitted under the panel to provide a rigid mounting for the handbrake and help spread the load in operation.

3. BULKHEADS

3.1. Front bulkhead

The top of the front bulkhead was missing, with the forward part of the windscreen supported by a centrally-mounted steel tube tack welded to the chassis and surrounded by fresh air. The tube could not be removed without providing some form of support for the windscreen, but, luckily, it was in such a position that it could be worked around whilst adding the necessary structure and removed later.

As well as providing support for the windscreen and other components, completion of the front bulkhead was vital for body stiffness, so it had to be a substantial assembly joined securely to the existing bodywork.

(a) Forming the core

A core of 10mm (⅜in) plywood was used to construct the missing bulkhead. Firstly, a cardboard template was made and the forward section of bulkhead cut from plywood. This was bonded in place with resin filler paste just behind the steel tube windscreen support on top of the existing bulkhead. A pair of plywood sides were cut and secured with resin filler paste to butt up against the ends of the forward section of plywood, leaving two triangular areas on top to be filled by another pair of plywood panels. The steel tube support was then removed.

The corners of the wooden core assembly were rounded off to give a smoother path for the fibreglass matting, and the triangular panels sanded with an angle grinder to give a slight compound curve, which carried on the curve of the windscreen for a good smooth profile, and ensured that the front body panel could be shut with adequate clearance.

(b) Laminating

Before any fibreglass was applied all of the internal corners between the plywood sections received a finger wipe of resin filler paste to increase the radius of the corner, ease routing of the

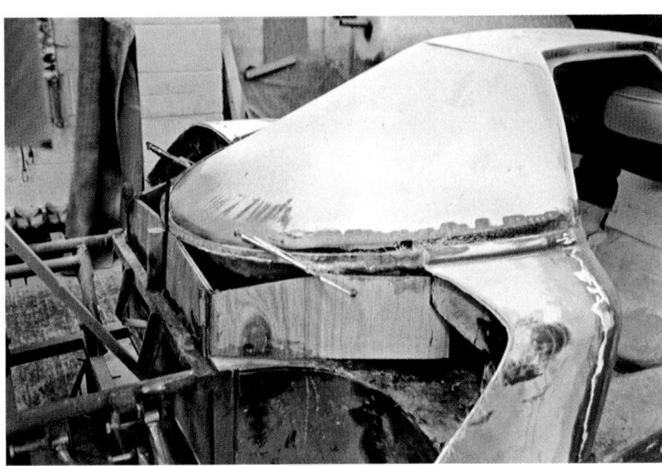

The front bulkhead plywood core being initially bonded in place.

The first layers of CSM are added.

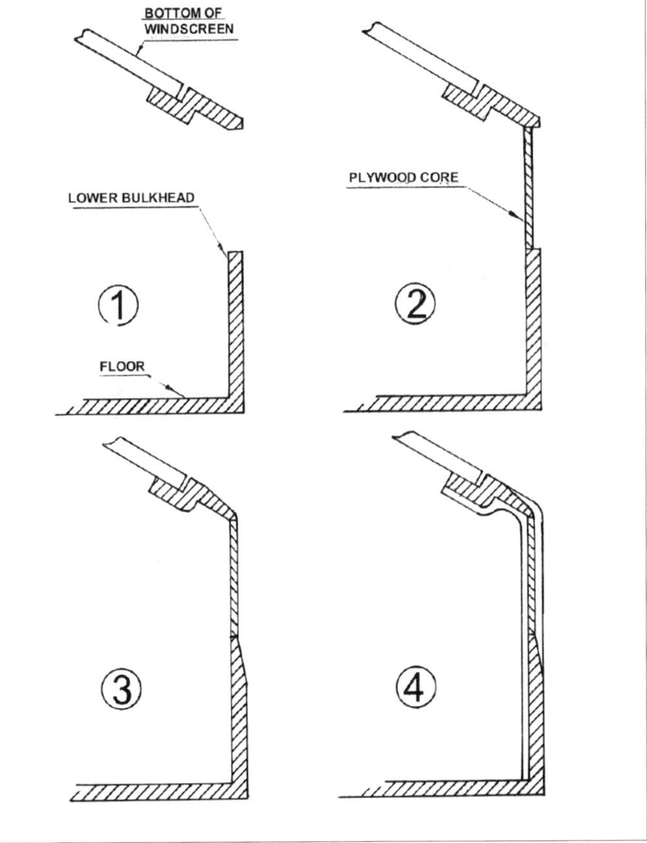

A series of sectional diagrams showing construction of the front bulkhead. 1) The gap between the top of the bulkhead and the base of the windscreen. 2) The plywood core is positioned. 3) The existing fibreglass is tapered down to the plywood for a better join. 4) The core is sandwiched between inner and outer laminations of CSM.

The finished front bulkhead sporting a home-made data plate on the nearside.

Pre-fabricated fibreglass sheet is clamped and wedged in position to form the basis of the rear bulkhead.

More sheet sections are used to construct the fuel tank enclosures within the wings.

glassfibre matting, and minimise the possibility of air gaps. When satisfied with the plywood core, the entire assembly was covered inside and out with several layers of mat and resin to form a substantial, double-skinned structure. Inside the cockpit the lay-up overlapped onto the existing bulkhead for a good strong join, the outer part of which was hidden behind a transverse chassis tube and feathered and joined properly at a later date when the body was removed from the chassis. When cured, the outer surfaces were painted with flow coat and sanded smooth for a neat finish.

3.2. Rear bulkhead & window

The situation at the rear was similar to that at the front, with most of the bulkhead missing. Apart from the roof the only thing holding together left and right halves of the car at this point was a thin sliver of fibreglass, just above where the centre tunnel had been removed. Not only had the bulkhead to be replaced, but some form of window surround had to be made as well. It had already been decided to use a double glazed window to try and reduce engine noise in the cabin, so the surround was made deep enough to take this.

A large piece of fibreglass sheet, the full width of the interior, was clamped to the chassis tubes immediately behind the cabin, up to the proposed window line. It was thin enough to be bent slightly to form a curve which added a little strength and followed the line of the chassis tubes. Masking tape held the lower edge in position, whilst resin paste provided an initial fix for the whole panel before lamination on the inside face, with a

The rear of the centre tub lacked much in the way of structure.

The wooden rear window former is taped and wedged in position.

Hidden in front of the Renault V6, the completed rear bulkhead displays the double-glazed window fitted for extra sound-proofing.

An interior view of the rear bulkhead showing the step of the window aperture.

Here, the former has been removed to reveal the deep window recess.

generous overlap onto the existing lower part of the bulkhead and sides of the body for a permanent join.

Making a recess deep enough to house a double glazed window unit filled the gap between the top of the new bulkhead and the roof. A 25mm (1in) thick wooden pattern, taped and wedged in position against the roof and chassis rails, allowed the window surround to be moulded in situ from the inside. When cured, the former was removed to permit the window aperture to be cut out, leaving a 13mm (½in) flange all round.

A sheet of 25mm (1in) thick REP foam was butted up to the bottom of the resulting window recess, and bonded to the inside of the new bulkhead with resin 'A' carried in a layer of CSM. The foam was laminated over to form a second skin on the new bulkhead section, tapering down to the original, single-skinned lower part. The resulting rear bulkhead, combined with the new front bulkhead and sills, made the centre body section a major structural element of the car once again.

4. DETAILING

4.1. Fitting a flush filler cap

The following procedure to make rebates for flush-fitting fuel caps is very similar to the formation of rebates for the headlight fairings covered in the previous chapter, except that, being on a flat surface ,the fuel caps are easier to accommodate.

When the position of the fuel tanks was finalised, recesses were formed on top of each wing section behind the doors to permit flush fitting of the filler caps. The diameter of the filler cap was measured and a hole a fraction bigger cut in the top of each wing section. The thickness of the caps determined that the rebates would have to be 6.4mm (¼in) deep, but the lay-up thickness of the wings around the holes varied, so some form of jigging procedure was required to ensure even spacing of the rebate flange during the bonding process.

An interior view of the fully trimmed rear bulkhead.

A disc of fibreglass sheet, 25mm (1in) greater in diameter than the hole in the wing, was drilled with four holes

A disc of fibreglass sheet is bonded in position inside the rear wing to form one of the fuel filler cap recesses. The plywood spacer ensures equal depth all round.

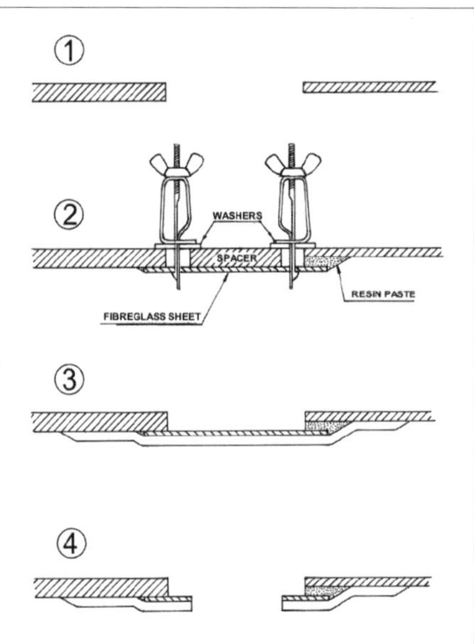

A series of sectional drawings showing the production of a fuel filler cap mounting recess. 1) Firstly, a hole is cut in the wing. 2) Fibreglass sheet is held in place with grip pins whilst being bonded with resin paste. The spacer ensures an equal depth is achieved all round. 3) A lay-up of CSM is added underneath to ensure a strong flange. 4) Finally, a hole is cut to accommodate the fuel cap, leaving a narrow lip all round.

A fuel cap recess before being cut out to leave a narrow lip all round.

The flush-mounted fuel cap installed with a neat bead of polyurethane sealant.

at a pitch circle diameter (PCD) slightly less than the cap diameter. After a generous coating of resin paste, applied all around the edge, the disc was lightly pressed in place across the underside of the hole in the wing, and held with four grip pins, although nuts and bolts could equally be used. An even depth of rebate was achieved by using a 6.4mm (¼in) thick plywood disc as a spacer, any variation in the thickness of the original wing lay-up taken up by the resin paste.

Inside the wings the excess resin paste squeezed out from the edge of the fibreglass discs was smoothed over with a gloved finger before it cured, which enabled a later reinforcing lay-up to be smoothly applied across the disc. When everything had fully hardened, the centre of the disc was cut out with a hole saw to form the finished rebate flange, which was drilled with eight mounting holes to take the flush-fitting fuel filler cap.

4.2. Rain channel & seal flange

The one-off nature of the build meant it was inevitable that some tasks – such as moulding the door rain channel and seal lip – necessitated several attempts to achieve the correct result. The fibreglass construction allowed many alterations during the course of the project; for example, when it transpired that more clearance was needed for the rear gas struts on the doors, and when an extra one was needed at the front to provide enough support for the increasing weight of each door. Both occasions necessitated partial removal and rebuild of the rain channel, with the forward one being modified very late in the project.

The door apertures on the Mirov had no seal flange to speak of, and no rain channel whatsoever. With gull wing doors, a lot of attention had to be paid to weather sealing, and deep rain channels were planned that incorporated small uprights to accept rubber door seals.

The channel was moulded around wooden formers screwed in place around the door aperture, and, because the area to be worked was a complex shape, it was divided into six with a wooden former tailormade to fit each section. The six separate operations were split thus: an upper and lower former for the front doorpost; the same for the back, and one each for the top and bottom.

Firstly, the small lip that already existed around the door opening was feathered to a point and thoroughly cleaned with acetone. Each former was provisionally positioned using double-sided tape to allow two fixing holes to be drilled right through into the car body to accept a pair of self-tapping screws, and then removed.

The new channel was attached to the existing lip using a feathered join. The edge of the first two layers of matting were applied to the outside of the existing lip with resin, and the former screwed back on, trapping the edge of the matting underneath it and leaving the rest hanging down. With the former secure, the matting was wrapped around it and wetted with resin, after which three more laminations were applied to the former to wrap around onto the back of the original lip, thereby encapsulating it and forming the new channel and flange,

Moulding part of the passenger door rain channel/seal flange over wooden formers clamped and screwed in place.

The basic rain channel sections with formers removed. The top half of the door frame has yet to be tackled.

The initial rain channel is complete. Note the altered lower section and the narrow top, which has yet to be modified to accept the door hinge.

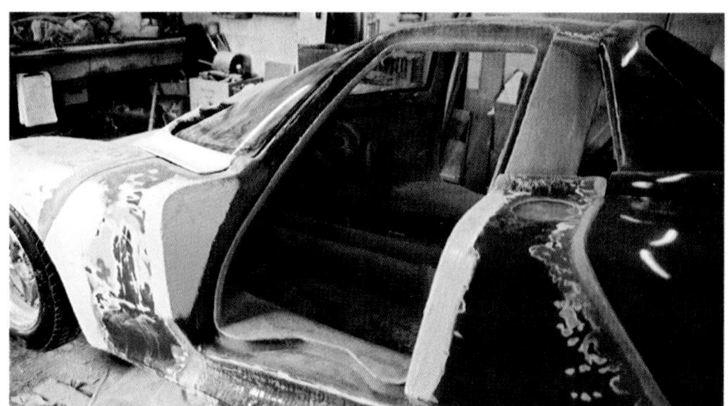

completing the feathered join all in one process.

This was repeated all around the door aperture using different shaped formers, the corners tackled last. These were formed with masking tape bridging the gaps, before being laminated over; when cured, the tape was removed and another lay-up applied to the other side to complete the structure. The rain channel was

The finished rain channel on the nearside 'A' post.

The nearside 'B' post rain channel.

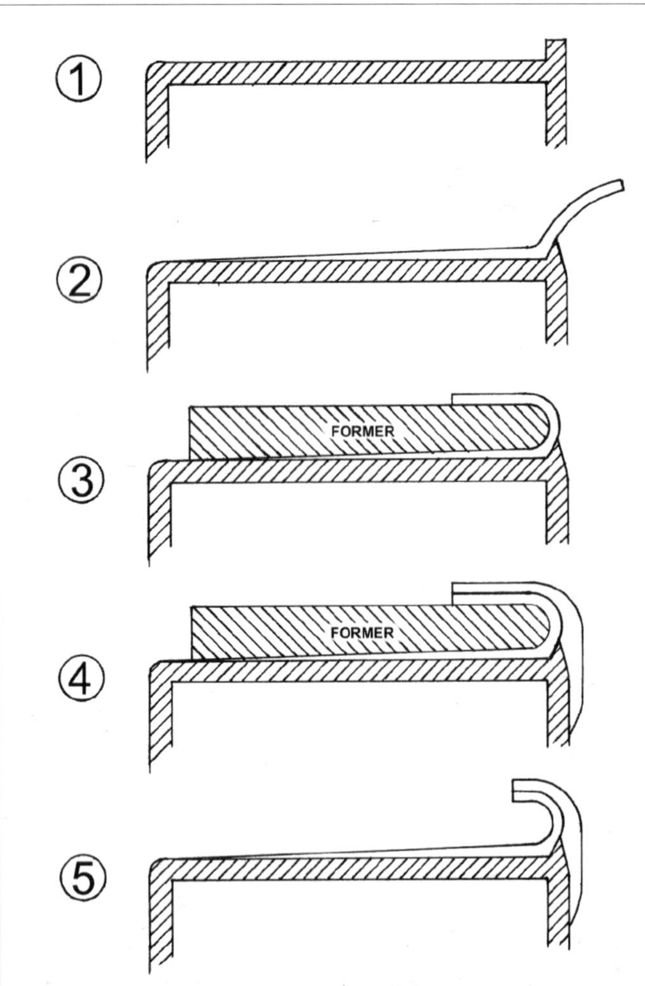

A series of sectional views showing the manufacture of a rain channel. 1) A cross-section looking down through a doorpost. 2) The existing lip has been feathered and CSM applied to the doorpost, leaving one edge free. 3) The wooden former is positioned and the free end of CSM wrapped over it. 4) The first lay-up is augmented by a second that runs behind the original lip section. 5) The former is removed to reveal the rain channel, which has been trimmed to length.

The top of the 'B' post rain channel that had to be wide enough to accommodate the rear gas strut.

then trimmed to size and flow-coated. This was followed by hours of rubbing down using specially-shaped sanding blocks to give a smooth, uniform finish.

4.3. Return flanges

Where the fibreglass had been cut return flanges were added to the front and rear of the central body unit in a similar manner to the front body section using fibreglass sheet. It pays to spend time making sure the cardboard templates are accurate to ensure the fibreglass sections will be a good fit.

4.4. Door striker plate cover

This feature was born out of necessity to conform to SVA test rules regarding sharp projections. The door striker plates sit on specially-made angled brackets on top of each sill, held in place with two M8 bolts apiece. The bolt heads fall foul of the minimum radius requirement and are classed as sharp projections. There were two solutions; use different rounded bolt heads, or cover them up. The latter course was chosen because it also hides the unsightly bracket.

A wooden pattern was made of the desired shape and bolted to a melamine-covered baseboard. The whole assembly was polished with release wax and a fibreglass mould taken. With this removed from the board the wooden pattern was unscrewed and reduced in height, width and length by about 2mm all over, and refitted to the board and waxed again. The fibreglass mould was also waxed before receiving a thin covering of gel coat, followed by two applications of matting. The fibreglass female mould was then pressed down onto the wooden male mould and held in place with a heavy weight. This had the effect of squeezing out any trapped air to form a very thin, strong moulding that was smooth on both sides. After trimming to size, it was held in place by trapping it between the angled bracket and striker plate. When finally painted to match the car, it looked very smart.

4.5. Repeater indicators

When trying to fit a standard part to a fibreglass car, the thickness of the body sometimes poses problems. One example is the side repeater indicators used on the Mirov that have clips

A rectangular ring of fibreglass sheet is taped in place whilst being bonded with resin paste and CSM on the inside.

The finished RH fuel tank enclosure and return lip.

The door latch bracket in place. Note the exposed bolt heads.

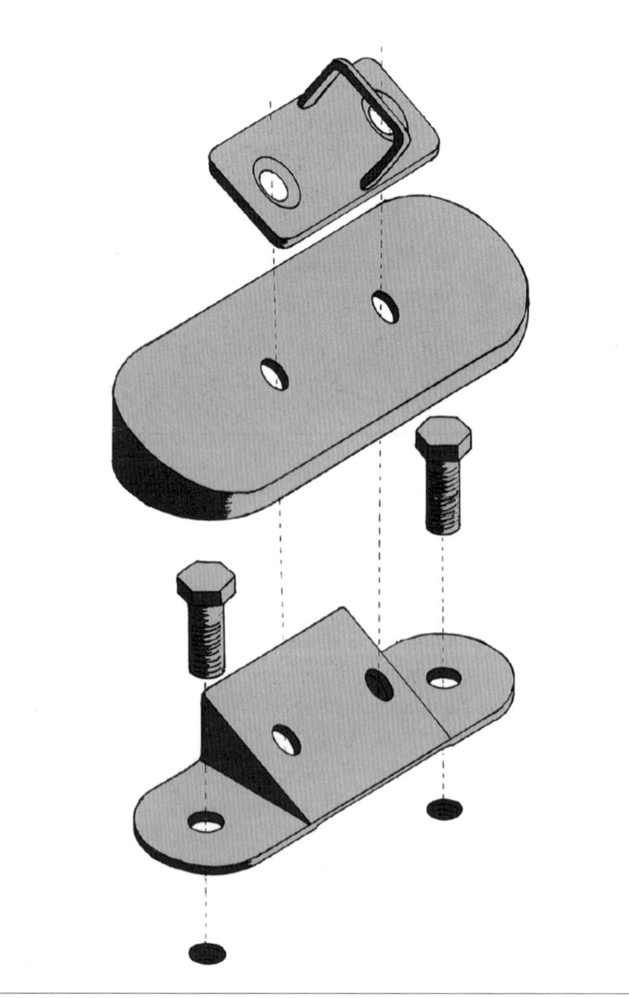

An exploded drawing showing how the cover is held in place by being trapped between the latch and bracket.

designed to fit into a thin steel wing, which do not provide enough grip when presented with thick fibreglass. The following solution was employed to fit and enhance the overall look of the indicator units.

The front wing skin at the repeater indicator location was about 6mm (¼in) thick, and the clips were struggling to keep a positive grip as they were not long enough to locate on the back of the panel. Also, the edges of the plastic lens were reverse tapered to fit in a pressed recess on a steel wing and looked a little odd just perched on the surface of the wing.

The edge of the lens was tackled first by cutting an oval ring from a piece of aluminium sheet the same thickness as the lens edge. The inside of the ring was filed to match the sloping edge of the lens until it was a snug fit, after which the outer edge of the ring was chamfered to continue the profile of the lens.

A hole to mount the repeater unit was cut into an oval aluminium sheet base plate the same size as the oval ring. The base was fixed to the wing with two stainless steel, countersunk M5 set screws after two holes had been drilled and tapped to accept them. The repeater unit was then clipped in place on the base plate, trapping the oval surround under the reverse chamfer of the lens edge. The assembly was dismantled and the surround painted satin black before reassembly. The finished result ensures a secure light unit, and adds a professional touch to what would otherwise have looked like a slapped on afterthought.

The finished bracket and cover in place on the left-hand sill.

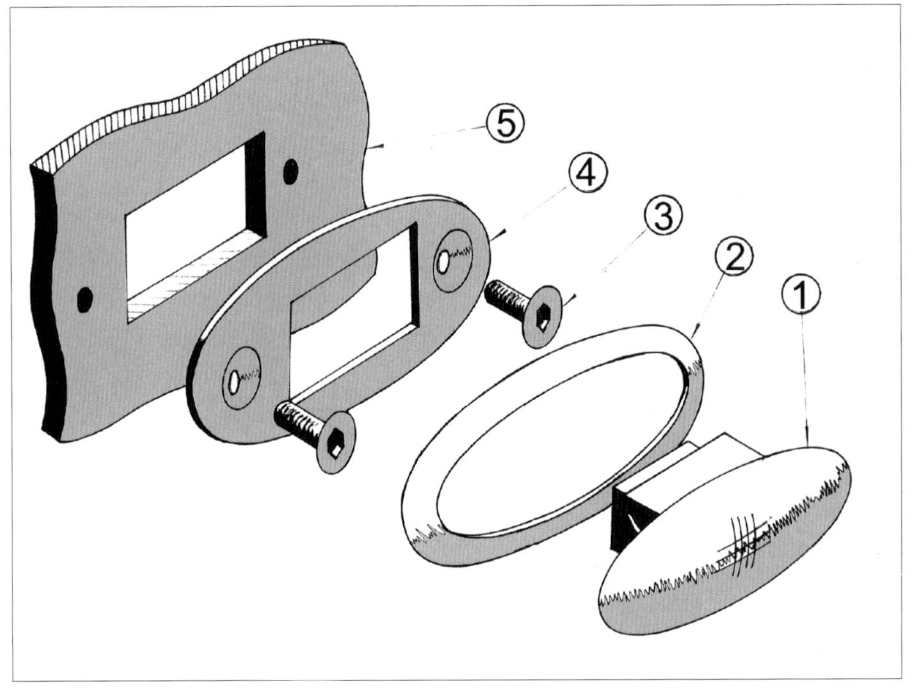

The completed indicator assembly.

An exploded diagram showing the repeater indicator fitment. 1) The indicator unit. 2) Trim ring. 3) Countersunk screws. 4) Base plate. 5) The fibreglass wing surface.

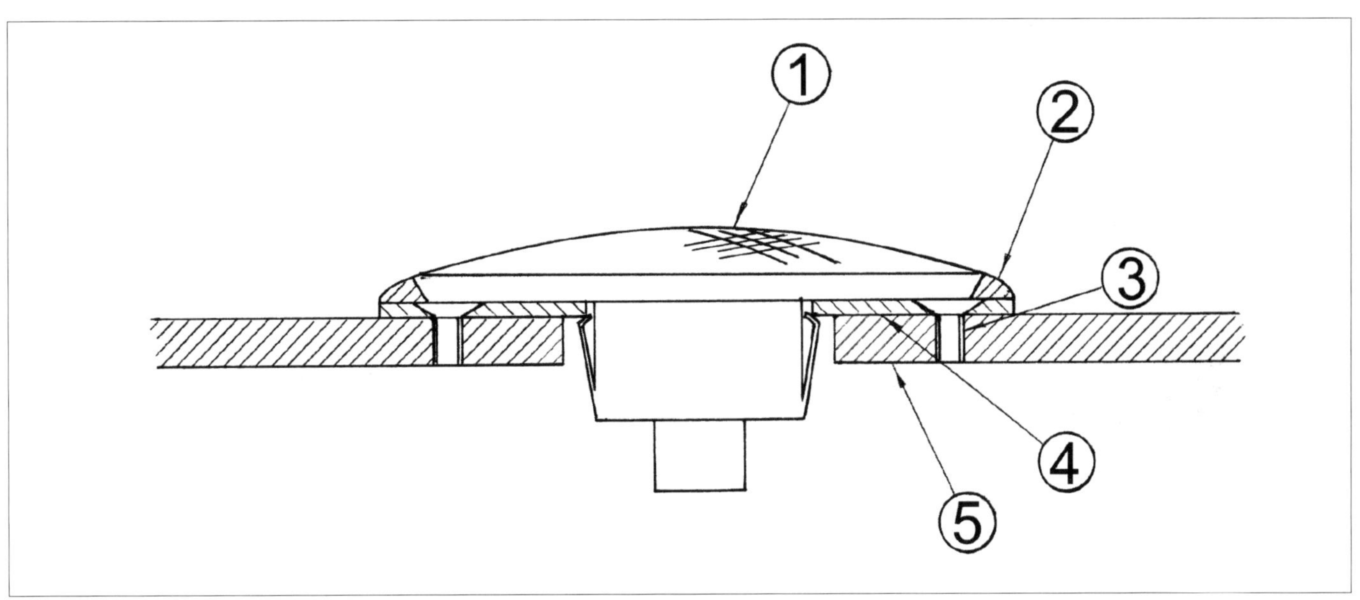

A cross-section through the indicator showing how the trim ring (2) is retained by the edge of the lens (1), and how the retaining clips positively locate through the base plate (4), which, in turn, is held onto the wing (5) by the countersunk screws (3).

Chapter 4

Rear bodywork

The separation of the rear body as an opening panel was achieved in a similar fashion to that of the front, with the hinge being fitted before any cuts were made. First, though, everything had to be consolidated as there was nothing to bolt a hinge to. The lower part of the rear body is made up of two separate bolt-on panels, which had to be rigidly attached to the main section. Strong, wide mounting flanges were added to the panels before everything was bolted together to allow a large pair of fabricated pivot points to be fitted to the back of the chassis. The goal post jig used to mark the cut lines for the front body section was again employed to mark the lines for the rear wings, which were then cut, the panel finally being separated by sawing along the rear roof section. The complete panel was then hinged upward. The same lack of rigidity that was found at the front had to be tackled in a similar manner at the rear.

The entire rear of the car was made to tilt open for maximum accessibility.

This chapter deals with the main tasks that were required to achieve a fully functional, hinged rear body section. Just like the front end, when proper suspension was fitted at the back, the lack of symmetry meant there were clearance issues to resolve as the right-hand tyre was fouling the wing. Then there was the mock-up nature of the stylish spoiler, which led to the manufacture of a replacement with a built-in brake light constructed in a temporary wooden mould. Again, legal requirements dictated the position of the lights, with extra units having to be added; the proximity of the number plate to the exhaust system necessitated the design and manufacture of a slimline number plate light.

The fibreglass techniques used for this work are similar to those employed for the front and centre body sections, and further show how they can be adapted to suit different situations.

1. RETURN FLANGES

The construction of return lips using fibreglass sheet is covered in other chapters, but this section illustrates another method that forms and bonds a return flange to a panel in one operation. As well as stiffening panels the addition of return flanges or lips along an edge provides an excellent means of attachment, and this was the case with the rear valance panels of the Mirov. As mentioned, the rear panels had to be firmly fixed to the car to provide a sound means of attachment for the proposed hinges.

The original mouldings had the smallest of flanges, which contributed nothing to their sturdiness or security. To increase the size of the return lips the small existing lips were feathered, and each panel was stood and supported at the correct angle on a waxed melamine-covered board placed on the floor of the workshop. The top edge of the upper panel was stepped down in the middle, so blocks of wood had to be stacked to support a piece of waxed board at the required height; this way, the two outer flanges and centre stepped one were created simultaneously to produce three horizontal returns at two different levels. About six layers of CSM and resin were then laid on the board and up the back of each panel, which bonded and created the new return flanges in one operation.

When cured, each panel was turned over and the process repeated for the other edges. To accept the valance panels, horizontal mating flanges were moulded onto the lower edge of each rear wing in a similar manner, using waxed boards clamped to the car and supported with blocks of wood. With the return flanges complete, these were trimmed to the required shape and width before the panels were clamped together on the car to allow drilling of fixing holes. Numerous nuts, bolts and large penny washers – to spread the fixing load – were then used to assemble the reworked rear end.

The sheer size of the rear clamshell demanded substantial internal bracing in the form of partitions and box sections.

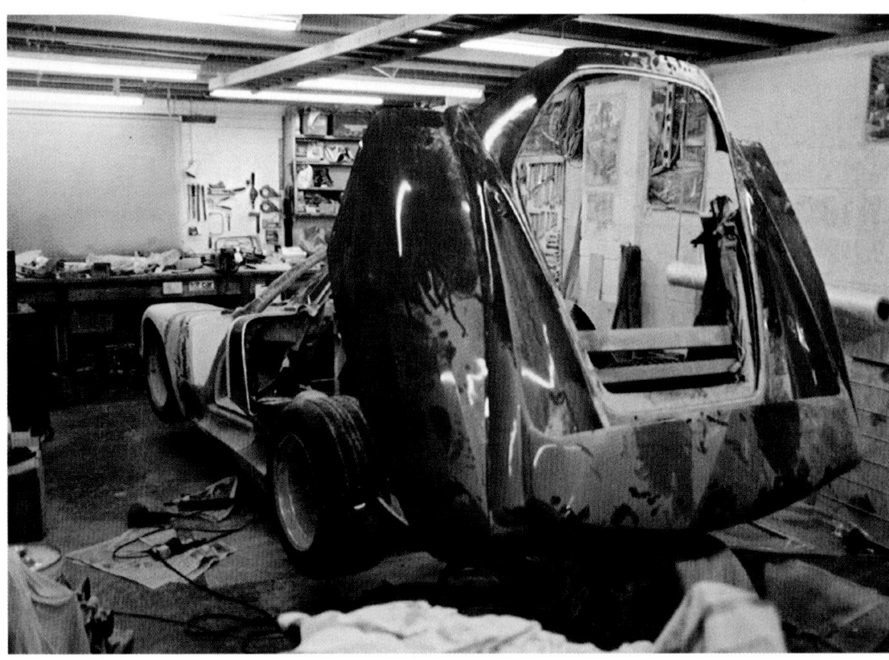

The rear panel cut and hinged open for the first time. Note the wooden bracing across the window aperture, a legacy of the car's mock-up nature.

2. FLARING THE REAR WINGS

As mentioned previously, the Mirov had originally been built in a rush as a mock-up, so little attention had been paid to symmetry. When the rear suspension was fitted it was found that the right-hand tyre pressed hard up against the wraparound rear wing. Upon investigation, it was found that the top of the wing looked similar to

Moulding the lower return lip on the rear valance panel. The upper lip has already been formed.

The foreground shows the lower rear valance upside down, sporting a newly-created return flange.

The hand-made rear hinges are bolted onto the body with their pivot points as far back as possible within the lower valance.

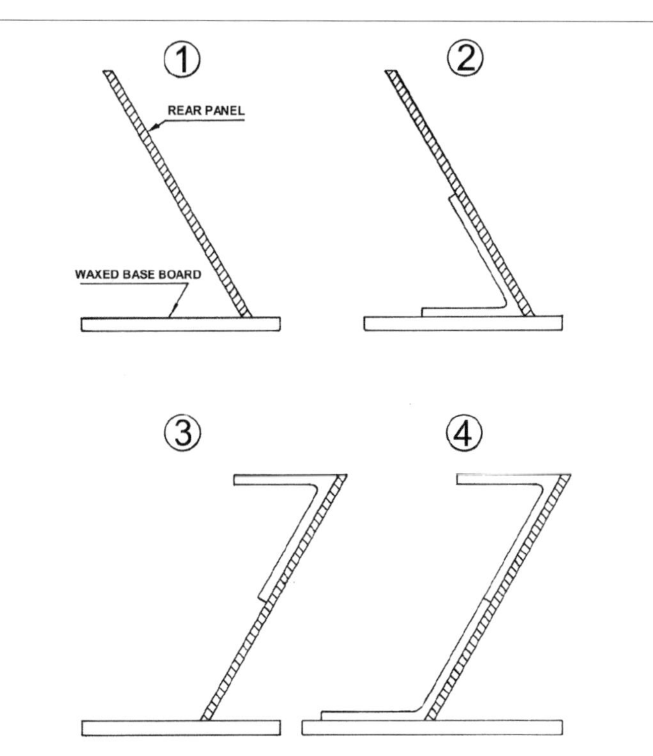

Four cross-sectional diagrams showing the manufacture of return lips on the rear panel. 1) Firstly, the panel is supported at the correct angle on a waxed board. 2) The lip is laminated. 3) The panel is inverted and supported. 4) The second lip is added.

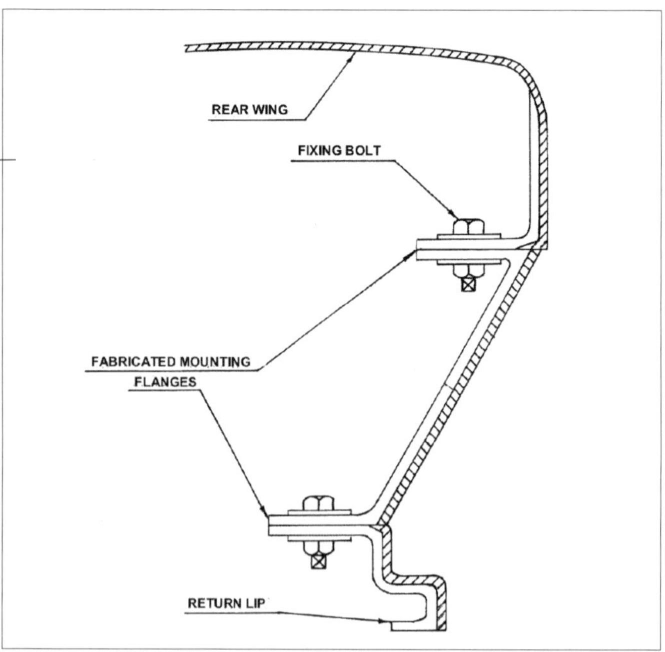

A cross-section looking across the back of the car, showing how the three sections are bolted together through their flanges.

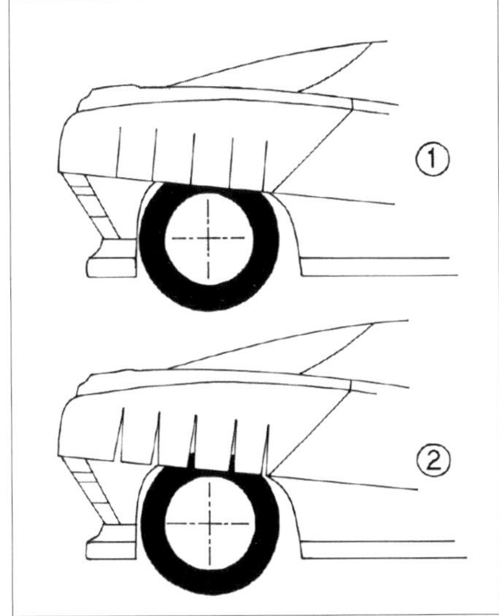

Two views of the right-hand rear wing showing the vertical cuts (1), and how they were splayed out (2) to create clearance around the tyre before being fibreglassed together.

The rear body off the car, showing how the LH wing has been fibreglassed to its new profile.

Flow coat has been applied to the wing prior to being rubbed down smooth.

the left-hand side, but, whereas the left wing flared out around the tyre, in contrast, the right one was fairly flat.

The remedy was to cut the wing into vertical 'petals' with a jigsaw and push these out the required distance by bracing wooden blocks against the tyre. The edges of the petals were feathered back to allow the outside of each cut to be laminated using the feathered join technique, after which the rear panel was opened and the inner face repaired. The outer surface was sanded after the flow coat had been applied and the surgery was completely hidden.

The finished wing with plenty of clearance around the tyre.

This shot shows how the same technique was used to alter the body profile to match the rear window glass.

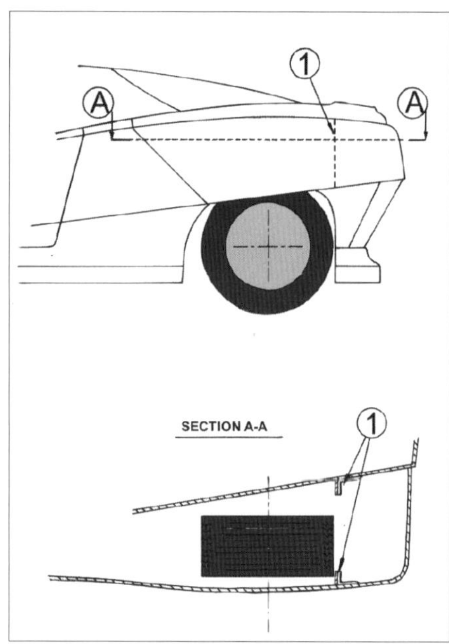

Cross-section A-A looking down through the left-hand rear wing showing the position of the panel mounting flange.

Once repaired and painted, the alteration is invisible.

This technique is quite versatile and was also used to bring the body into profile with the rear windscreen. 'Petals' were cut and the body skin pulled up to the level of the glass and held in place with grip pins to allow the 'petals' to be feathered and laminated into their new position.

3. COMBINED STIFFENING RIB & MOUNTING FLANGE

This is a variation of the sheet fibreglass return lip described in chapter 2, which has two functions: an internal stiffening rib that doubles as a mounting flange for an aluminium closing panel, which seals off the area behind the wheels where the tail light assemblies are housed.

Due to the asymmetric body, two slightly different cardboard templates had to be cut to fit vertically across the inside of each wing. After trimming to ensure a good fit, these shapes were transferred to a sheet of pre-formed fibreglass sheet and cut out with a pair of metal shears. The resulting panels were bonded in place vertically with resin paste just behind the rear wheel location. When set the paste was augmented with laminations of mat and resin, joining the reverse side of each panel to the inner and outer wings to give a stronger join.

With the new panels in place the centre section of each was cut out to leave an upside down, 'U'-shaped lip that braced the outer wings and was a perfect mounting for the aluminium closing panels.

4. MOULDING REPLACEMENT COMPONENTS

The nature of this project meant that several fibreglass parts had to be remade, either for a better fit or because they had not been correctly made in the first place. The following two examples fall into the latter category and illustrate methods of wooden mould construction; one simple and one fairly complex.

The finished flange with panel removed, revealing that birds have made a nest in the rear light wiring!

The original MDF quarter panel. Note the big blobs of filler that originally held it in place.

The panel is installed to close off the rear part of the wheel arch and keep all the road muck out.

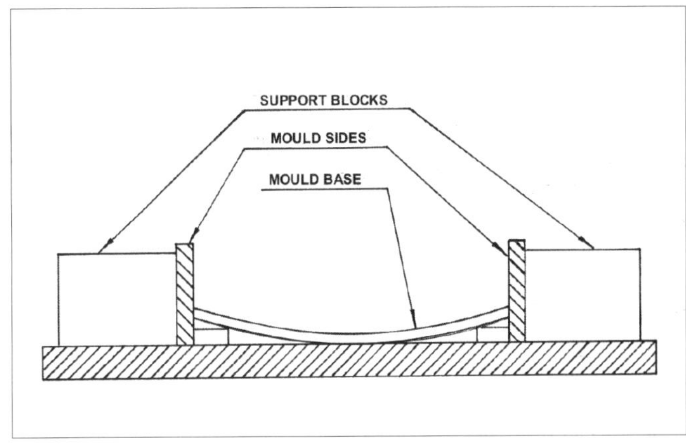

A cross-section through the quarter panel mould showing how the base is propped up at the edges to form a curve.

4.1. Quarter panels

The original triangular quarter panels behind the rear wheels looked fine until closer scrutiny revealed they were made from painted MDF, which would not have been weatherproof in use. They mated with the lower edge of the wings and forward edge of the rear light clusters, both of which were curved although the MDF panels were flat. New fibreglass panels with a slight double curvature were necessary to blend in more successfully.

The overall shape of each panel when viewed from the side was fine, so the shape was replicated in thin hardboard. This was nailed onto a

The two moulds painted with gel coat resin awaiting CSM lay-up.

The new LH quarter panel fresh out of the mould.

The same panel completed and in position.

melamine-faced board in the centre only, the corners supported by aluminium shims, which formed the required slight double curvature along the edges of the mould.

The edge of the mould was made with an upright fence of thin, fabric-reinforced conveyor belt rubber wrapped around the hardboard base, and supported by wooden blocks and masking tape to form a wide return lip. After gel coat and a few layers of matting were applied and left to cure, the rubber sides were dismantled to free the new mouldings. The panels produced required only the minimum of final finishing, and the generous return lips allowed secure nuts and bolts fixing to the rear wings and lower valance.

4.2. Rear spoiler

The original low rear spoiler was, like the quarter panels, only a mock-up. It was made from a central core of MDF encased in body filler, which, though shaped to look fantastic, was not structurally sound and weighed far too much. A new one had to be made, so ways of improving on the original were considered.

It was noted that the cross-section and angle of the original wing would have produced positive lift – not a desirable tendency – and the low mounting interfered with rearward vision, which could have constituted an SVA test failure, so the decision was taken to produce a higher wing of the correct aerofoil cross-section.

(a) Mould construction

Much consideration was given to how the new wing should blend in with the shape of the car. It was decided that, in side view, it should slope back and finish slightly behind the rear of the bodywork, the overall shape looking from the rear mimicking the curve of the roof and sides of the cockpit section. The plan view took into account the gentle curve of the central box section that protruded from the rear panel, and so completed the third dimension and provided enough information to sketch out a mould.

The body mounting points for the wing complicated matters because they were neither horizontal nor parallel, but angled up and in at the front. To form the supports for the mould, three different width chipboard formers were cut, all different heights to replicate the angled mounting points on the car and achieve the correct angle of attack for the new aerofoil section. Each support mirrored the curve of the roofline, and was screwed to a chipboard base with the tallest and widest of the three at the back and the shortest and narrowest one at the front. The difference in height and width of the formers ensured that the ends of the wing would be moulded at the correct angle to exactly mate with the body mounting points.

A sheet of hardboard was laid into the curve of the formers and held in place with small panel pins. The excess length was trimmed off until the

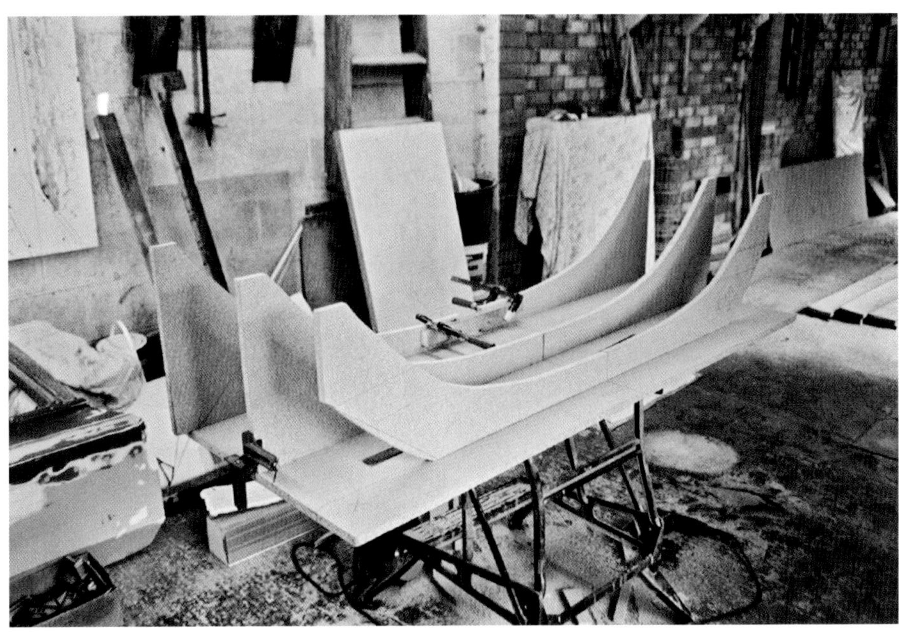

The three different formers being attached to the base board.

Hardboard is fixed in the formers to create the main mould shape, after which the outline of the wing spoiler is formed with shallow fences of hardboard supported by small wooden blocks.

hardboard was flush with the tops of the formers at each end.

The plan view of the new wing was then drawn onto the hardboard mould surface, with reference to a cardboard pattern of the desired curve taken from the back of the car. To define the leading and trailing edges, hardboard fences were produced using card templates and nailed to small wooden blocks. These were positioned on the mould and held in place with double-sided tape. The join between the main mould and the hardboard fences was sealed with a finger wipe of polyester body filler. To make more of an aerofoil shape a piece of card was taped into the bottom of the mould over a slim packer to form a concave shape in the upper surface of finished wing. The mould was now ready to use.

(b) Moulding the spoiler

Two coats of release wax were applied to the new mould and polished before white gel coat was brushed on – three coats thickly applied into the front and rear corners of the mould edges to allow for greater shaping when finish sanding in these areas. Five laminations of mat and resin were laid in place, onto which a core of REP foam sanded into an aerofoil section was placed and weighted in position until the resin had cured. Small cuts were made in the foam to help it conform to the shape of the mould.

When making the rear fence of the mould the centre part of the trailing edge was made taller than the rest to allow the incorporation of a brake light housing. The 12V supply wires for this were embedded into the REP foam with four wires running from the centre, two to each side in case one failed.

A jig was made to ensure accurate positioning of the mounting studs that were to be built into each end of the wing moulding. A wooden board was placed across the car and the mounting holes transferred to the board by drilling up from underneath. End plates for the new wing were made by shaping two pieces of fibreglass sheet to the same footprint as the mounting points on the car, and drilling them to allow the studs to poke through. For each side of the wing a pair of M8 bolts were welded to a perforated stainless steel sheet, then folded close to the bolt heads to form mounting stud assemblies that could be bonded to each end of the wing. The fibreglass end plates were placed over the mounting studs and the studs then fixed to each end of the wooden jig, trapping the end plates in position. A hole was drilled through each end plate and jig between the bolt heads. When the entire assembly was lowered into place on the moulding, the supply wires were fed through the holes in the jig. With hindsight it would have been easier to take advantage of the fibreglass body construction and wire the supply directly to the mounting studs within the wing moulding, with one side positive and the other side earth.

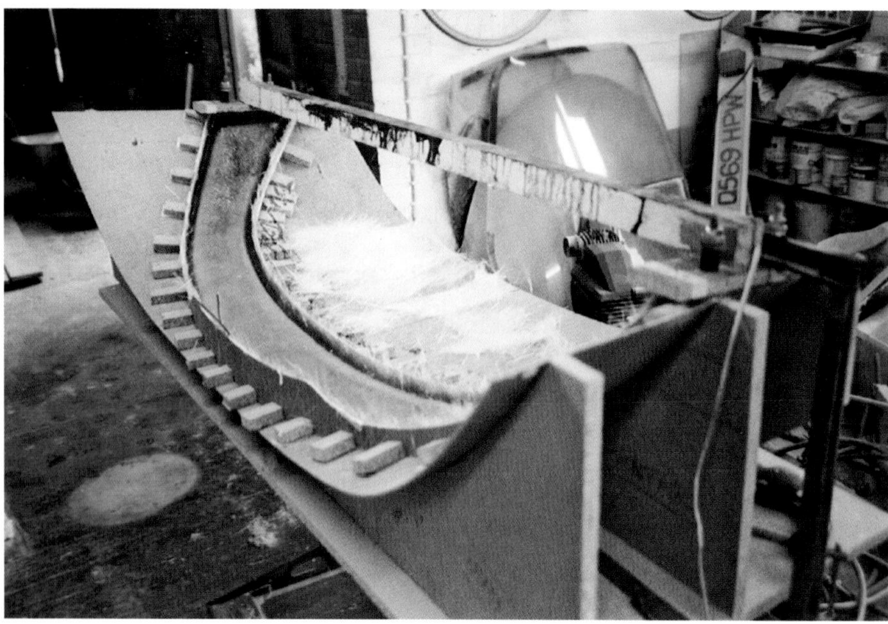

The wooden jig straddles the mould to hold the mounting studs in position whilst they are laminated in place.

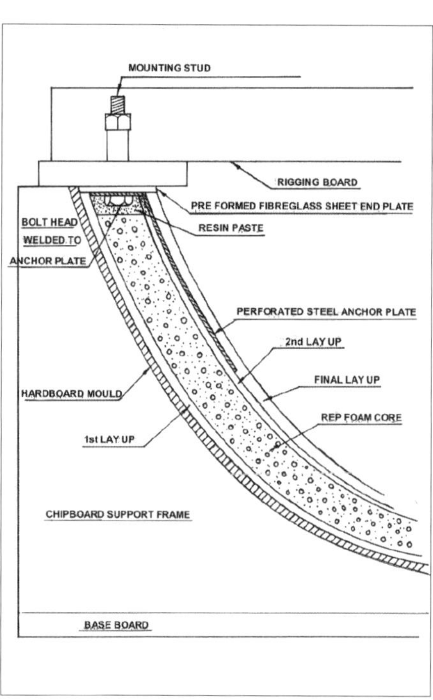

A cross-section through one end of the mould showing the layered construction of the wing and how the mounting studs are anchored using a perforated steel plate.

The untrimmed rear wing is trial fitted: note the deeper middle section to accommodate the brake light installation. One of the supply wires can be seen hanging down on the right.

The perforated stainless steel sheets were trapped between lay-ups of matting and initially anchored with a pair of self-tapping screws before being laminated in completely. More layers of mat and resin followed over the whole of the upper surface of the moulding to form the lower skin of the wing, the lay-up at each end of the mould increased to ensure it matched the footprint of the end plates. When the last lay-up had cured a final three applications of flow coat were applied to allow a good amount of finish sanding. A couple of days later the nuts were unscrewed and the jig lifted

After many hours of rubbing down, the finished wing belies the simple mould that produced it.

The centre section houses a high level brake light.

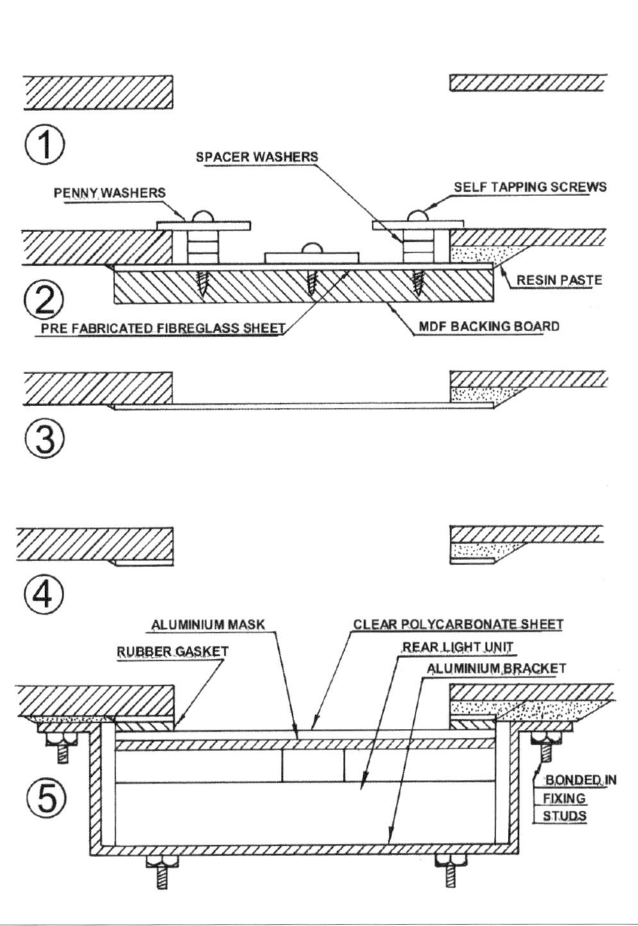

A series of cross-sectional views showing the rear light installation. 1) Firstly, the hole is cut in the wing: note the uneven lay-up thickness of the panel. 2) Fibreglass sheet is bonded to the back of the panel with resin paste, ensuring equal depth all round using spacer washers. 3) The MDF backing board is then removed. 4) The hole is cut in the fibreglass sheet, which leaves an even panel thickness all round. 5) After studs are bonded in the light unit is bolted in place using a large aluminium bracket.

off before the new wing was removed from the mould and trial fitted to the car, the studs exactly lining up with the mounting holes.

After trimming off the excess with an angle grinder, the rest of the shaping was done by hand with the help of a sanding block. A light guide coat of black spray paint was applied to highlight any low spots; these were filled with more flow coat which took a day or more to harden enough to sand, so the whole process was very protracted. After sanding off almost as much flow coat as was put on, the new wing spoiler looked great, a vast improvement on the original.

5. LIGHTS

5.1. Additional rear lights

The Mirov was originally built with rear light clusters, not wired in, of course, which came from a Renault 5 Mk2 and were fitted upside down and swapped left to right. They looked great and would have remained but, because they had swapped sides, the cluster with the fog light was now on the wrong side to be legal. This was overcome by buying another light unit intended for a left-hand drive car but all was still not well, however, as the height of the indicator and tail light lenses was right on the SVA minimum height limit, plus, when the rear body was open, the lights could not be seen from certain angles; another fail point.

A different set of lights had to be fitted higher on the car in order to comply with these regulations, and a pair of plain rectangular light units – intended for use on a trailer or caravan – were mounted inside the rear wings. After many fancy-shaped templates had been tried, a plain hole with rounded ends was cut in the back of each wing. To counter the varying thickness of fibreglass, and to ensure that the light units were mounted parallel to the wing surface, a sheet of fibreglass was bonded inside each wing with resin paste and held parallel to the outer surface with spacer washers whilst curing in a similar manner to that of the fuel cap rebate. The resulting fibreglass sheet across the hole was cut out to leave a 10mm (⅜in) thick panel edge all around the hole and a totally flat mounting face inside the wing.

The lights were to be held in

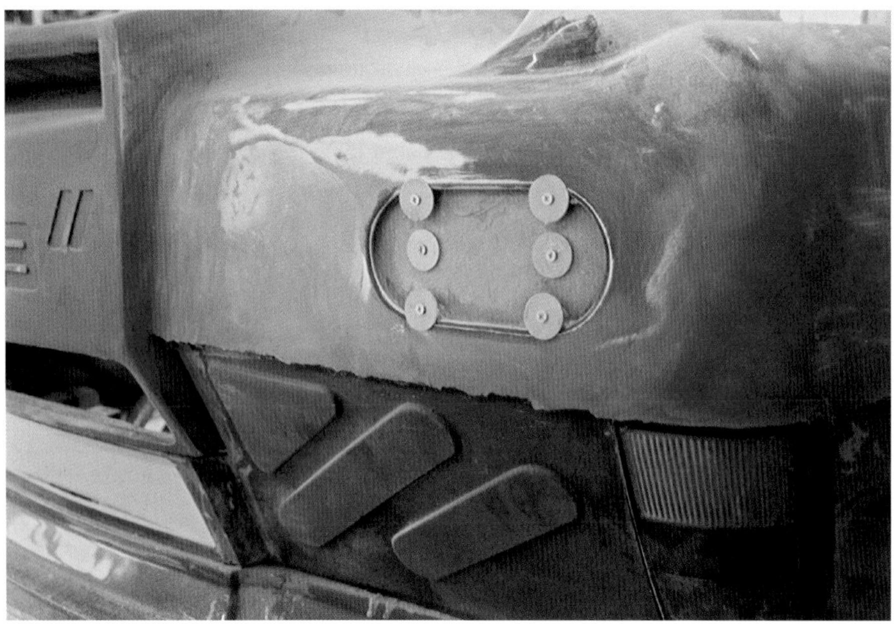

The fibreglass sheet being bonded to the inside of the right-hand rear wing with resin paste. Spacers on each screw ensure a regular depth.

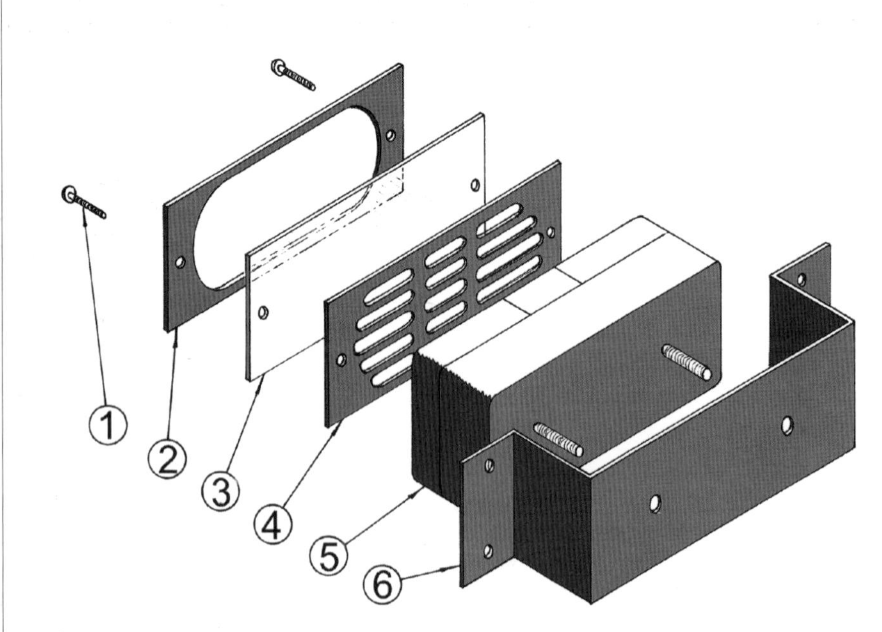

An exploded view of the rear light installation showing the lens screws (1) that secure the rubber gasket (2), clear polycarbonate sheet (3), and aluminium mask (4) to the light unit (5). The complete assembly is held in place by the large aluminium top hat bracket.

place with a top hat aluminium bracket bridging the whole unit and fixing to both sides of each hole. To accept this a pair of mounting studs were bonded inside each wing, each side of the fibreglass sheet around the holes.

To enhance the appearance of the plain lenses, a sheet of aluminium alloy was milled with a number of slots, and painted satin black to create a mask. Each light cluster was assembled with its bracket and mask; to keep the mask clear of road dirt, a transparent polycarbonate sheet was placed over each one, a rubber gasket going on last before both assemblies were secured to the studs inside each wing.

The result is pleasing to the eye and belies the light units' humble origins.

5.2. Slim number plate light

The rear number plate recess was formed in the only space available on the rear panel below the exhaust tail pipes, which was fine except for one thing: there was no room to fit any commercially available number plate lamp units, which meant that a very slim unit had to be designed and made from scratch.

A long, narrow, aluminium box was folded so that it was big enough to house two festoon bulbs and electrical contacts liberated from two old courtesy light units. A slot to accommodate this box was cut in the rear panel flange above the number plate and below the exhaust. On this was placed a rubber gasket, cut to fit, followed by a clear lens cut from polycarbonate sheet, which was covered by a polished aluminium surround to make a number plate lamp of about 20mm (¾in) total depth, half of which was recessed within the panel flange.

The extra right-hand light unit being trial fitted, showing the unpainted mask.

The finished light installation.

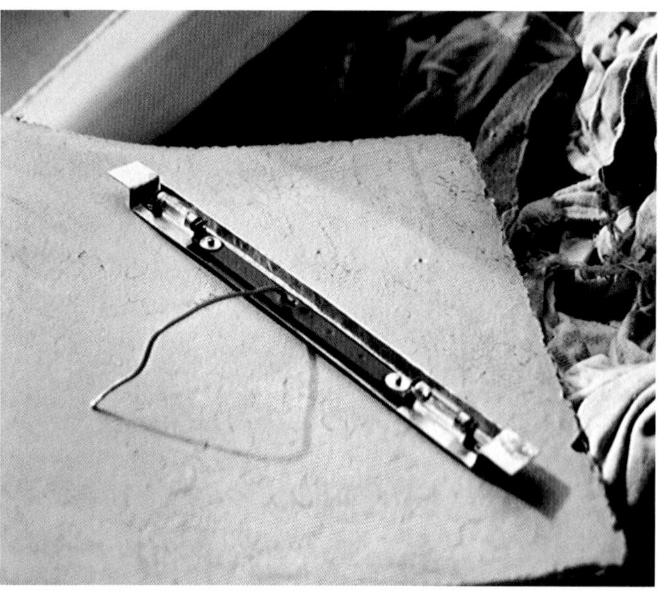

The folded aluminium lamp housing. The inner bulb contacts are insulated from the housing by strips of insulating tape and nylon inserts around the pop rivets that hold in place the central positive supply wire.

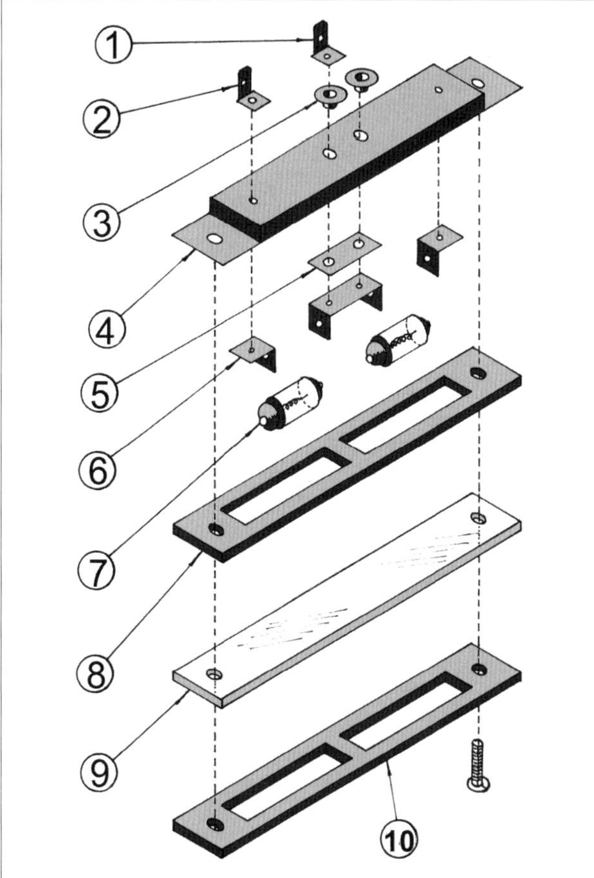

An exploded picture showing the number plate lamp construction. The spade terminals (1) & (2) are pop riveted to the housing (4). The positive terminal (1) is insulated from the housing by nylon washers (3) and insulating tape (5). Earthing for the festoon bulbs (7) is via the end clips (6). The fixing screws clamp the polished aluminium surround (10) to the clear polycarbonate sheet (9) and rubber gasket (8).

The finished number plate light unit fitted just below the tail pipes. The rear edge is curved to match the body.

Chapter 5

Door construction

Planning and making the doors – using the wooden mould techniques already covered – was undoubtedly the most challenging part of this project. Their construction illustrates how complex the process can become and so deserved a chapter of its own.

When purchased, the Mirov had no doors to speak of, and the prospect of having to make a pair from scratch was very daunting. To complicate matters, the shape of the car favoured a gull wing style, and – as if this wasn't bad enough – I wanted to fit electric windows as well: all in all, a real test.

Once the rain channelling and seal flange were finalised the idea was to use the door apertures themselves to support the various mould components in the required shapes and make the doors on the car. The inner door shells were formed first, along with the 'A' and 'B' pillars of the door window, the window frames and outer skins being added later.

The construction process has been broken down into five sections to explain exactly how the doors took shape.

One of the most demanding aspects of the build was designing and making the gull wing doors.

1. THE MOULD

1.1. Preparation

The two original, floppy door skins were attached by just one 50mm (2in) domestic door hinge, which was not good for the super car image, so something altogether more robust and corrosion-resistant was needed. A touch of serendipity produced an old aircraft cargo door hinge in excellent condition. It was nearly 1m (39in) long and made of thick aluminium alloy with a 6mm (¼in) stainless steel hinge pin. After some redundant flanges were cut off, two 270mm (10½in) lengths

Even shut lines add to the overall quality feel of the car.

The gull wing doors allow unhindered access to the interior.

were cut to form the two door hinges. The thickness of metal allowed one half of each hinge to be drilled with six fixing holes and tapped, before being bolted in position at the top of the door apertures on the broad horizontal part of the rain channel moulding.

The idea was to build the door mould around the hinge and bond the upper half of the hinge into the door during the moulding process. To provide good anchorage, the top half of the hinge had several large holes drilled through it to allow the resin to penetrate and hold it firmly, and a perforated stainless steel sheet was screwed to it to increase the bonded area.

Taking advantage of the fibreglass construction, electrical supply to the doors was to be through the hinge assembly, earth being via the catch on the sill; that way there would be no ugly wiring loom bridging the hinge area. A pair of wires was attached to the upper hinge section, with loop terminals ready

The original 'doors' removed from the car.

Positioning the door catch bracket.

Sections of hardboard cut and positioned to form the front and rear of each door mould.

to be bonded into the door down the 'A' and 'B' pillars during moulding.

The door lock mechanism was planned to be flush-mounted in the bottom of the new doors at the same angle as the catch on the sill. This area of the mould would be fairly complex to construct, so the catch bracket was bolted in position on the sill to ensure that the correct angle was achieved.

1.2. Constructing the mould

The front and rear of the mould was tackled first, each part an oversize facsimile of the front and rear of the door aperture cut from white-painted hardboard, held in position with countersunk self-tapping screws.

The next stage was to add the back, which was to form the inner skin. One graceful curve of plain hardboard was held in place with clamps on the 'A' and 'B' pillars, the lower half held in shape by two vertical wooden formers fitted to the back of the panel.

Before mould construction continued, precautions were taken to ensure sufficient clearance between the door and the weather seal flange. Two layers of thick, sound-proofing felt material were taped over all the seal flanges to simulate the thickness of compressed rubber door seal and provide the correct clearance around the door. A lot of masking tape was applied across it to join the sides of the mould to the back.

Next, the lower part was made from three sections of white hardboard, the centre one resting at an angle on the catch bracket bolted to the sill. Clearance for the weather seal at the bottom of the mould was provided by two panels of thick hardboard bent to follow the contour of the seal flange, and secured with countersunk screws to a section of melamine-covered chipboard that formed the base of the inner part of the mould.

The lower half of the hinge was covered with hardboard, leaving the upper half temporarily sticking up in mid air; at the top of the window area a

The inner face of the right-hand door mould is clamped in place. Note the vertical formers holding the lower half in shape.

The right-hand mould taking shape. The top section is built around the hinge, while the bottom follows the angle of the catch bracket.

After covering the intricate areas with parcel tape, the mould is ready for the application of release wax. Note the gas strut clearance blister formed in the middle of the 'B' post.

Gel coat resin is applied, leaving the window area clear.

cardboard addition ensured adequate headroom in the finished moulding. A small clearance blister, shaped from wood, was added to the centre of the 'B' post to accept the lower end of the intended door gas strut when in the stowed position. The entire perimeter area was covered with masking tape to tie everything together, followed by brown parcel tape for a smooth surface. The mould was now ready for wax.

2. MAKING THE DOORS

2.1. Inner shell

After carefully waxing and polishing all of the various nooks and crannies, paying particular attention to the plain hardboard inner section, the mould was painted with grey gel coat resin 'B,' leaving the centre of the window area clear. When tacky, the gel coat was followed by several applications of CSM and resin 'A.' The area over the lower half of the hinge was built up until the upper half of the hinge could be swung down to sit level. It was then embedded in resin paste and the electrical wires from it routed down the 'A' and 'B' pillars and fibreglassed in position. The top of the window section

The first layers of CSM and resin have been applied and the power supply wires positioned down the 'A' and 'B' pillars. Note the block of REP foam fitted to raise the door top to roof level.

The foam has been fibreglassed over and the lower window edge is being formed in line with the bottom of the windscreen.

The window rain channel is moulded separately. Note the temporary brace across the bottom of the moulding.

Here, the door has been removed from the mould, trimmed to size, and refitted. The window surround is being trial fitted.

received a block of REP foam to build it up to the roof line, and this was laminated in along with the top half of the hinge.

The lower edge of the window was the next to be formed by laminating over a section of prefabricated fibreglass sheet taped in position, making sure that it lined up with the bottom of the windscreen.

The back of the mould was removed first, after which the hinge was unbolted to allow the new door moulding to be freed. The mould materials were removed and the door bolted back in place. Then, using the surrounding bodywork as a guide, a pencil mark denoted where to trim off the excess fibreglass.

The electric windows were to be flush-glazed with the glass pane swinging outward before retracting into the door; this meant it would sit on a rubber seal and have a rain channel just like the doors themselves. This channel was moulded separately using three lengths of wood sanded to shape and fixed to a board following the same outline as the front, top and back of each side window. After lamination, a length of wood was temporarily added between the lower ends of the rain channel to prevent them twisting out of line during bonding to the door.

Before bonding on the window channelling, the 'A' and 'B' posts of the door moulding were treated to a lay-up of glass rovings to increase their strength, as they would support the entire weight of the open door when finished. The weather channel moulding was pressed into place on a bed of resin paste and left to cure.

From inside the car the basic shell looked very boxy, so, in order to improve appearance and increase interior space, a large, scallop shape was marked out which echoed the scallop on the side of the car. This was cut out and a mould was formed over the hole by taping on a section of conveyor belt rubber. After moulding the scallop from inside the door the rubber was removed.

To try and create an interior door trim panel in plywood, or similar, would have been impossible because of the complex shape of the inner door, so fibreglass examples were created. The door shell was covered with brown parcel tape and waxed to allow a fibreglass trim panel to be laid-up on top, which, when cured, was removed and put aside for future use.

2.2. The outer skin

The original skin did not fit at all well, and was not of good enough quality to be used in its entirety. The required shape was very complex, and would have been hard to mould in one piece, so was formed in four parts, with the top two taken from the original skin and the lower two brand new without the need for moulds.

Apart from having to provide access to fit and maintain all of the electric

The window surround is bonded in position with resin paste.

The inside of the door moulding was found to be a bit boxy and intrusive.

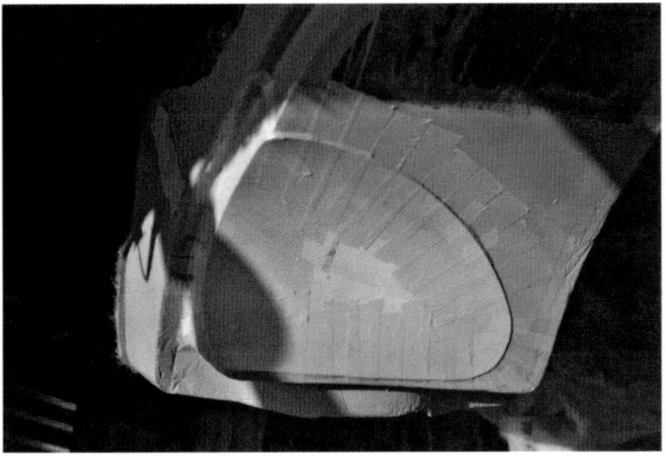

The offending section of door has been cut out and a piece of thin conveyor belt rubber taped across the hole to form a mould.

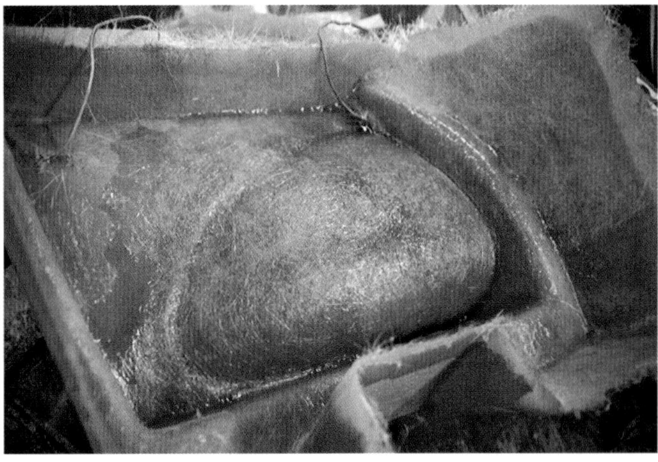

The rubber is laminated on the inside of the door.

Here, the new inner door shape is covered in parcel tape to allow a mould to be taken for future use as a door trim panel.

window and door lock components, the immediate concern was how to make and install a new skin? Taking into account all of the door furniture and window mechanism mounting points, a large hole was cut in the inner skin moulding to ensure adequate access to use a resin-filled brush.

To allow the new skin to sit flush to the surrounding bodywork, the exposed edges of the inner moulding were taken back a touch further than they had already been trimmed. A line about 5mm ($^{3}/_{16}$in) was drawn all around the edge and the excess cut off with a jigsaw and sanding disc. Care was taken around the door latch area with the angle of the lower moulding. There was a subtle twist in the side of the car so the angle of the lower moulding had to match up to the different angles, front and rear.

Any hopes of using the original skins were dashed when a trial fit proved that they were totally the wrong shape. Initial dismay gave way to gradual realisation that the top section in isolation could be used, which was great because it incorporated a section of moulded feature that ran from the front of the windscreen, along the base of the side windows, all the way to the back of the car, and would have been difficult to replicate.

The skin was cut in half horizontally and the lower part put aside. The top part was trial fitted on its own, but the radius between the vertical and horizontal sections did not match the radius on the surrounding car body. The two halves were cut along the radius, which confirmed that both parts could be persuaded to fit, the difference in radius being corrected later. Once satisfied with the fit of the top skin section, it was bonded in position with resin paste, giving the interior part of the join a small radius by wiping the excess paste smooth with a gloved finger. Next, the vertical part of useable skin was bonded on and held in place, short aluminium strips bridging the gap to the existing bodywork, and secured with self-tapping screws.

The shape of the lower half of the door skin would have been tricky to produce as a whole, so it was tackled in two parts – upper and lower – with the split made at the fold that formed the top edge of the large scallop feature in the side of the body shell.

Using cardboard templates the two missing skins were cut from prefabricated, flat fibreglass sheet. Two pieces of hardboard were cut and screwed to the front and rear wings across the door, and the position of the lower edge of the skin already fitted was marked on the inside of the hardboard, along with two lines marking the front and rear of the doors. The hardboard was then removed.

Using the marks as a guide, the sheet fibreglass sections were fixed to the inside of the hardboard panels with screws inserted from the outside. Both hardboard panels were then positioned back on the side of the car and secured using the previously made screw holes, which ensured the new panels were accurately located on the doors. A finger wipe of resin paste around the inside where the new panels abutted the existing structure provided an initial fix, and plugged any holes to retain the resin used in the next stage.

The initial fix of the new skins was consolidated by laminating with mat and resin inside the doors. With the new skins joined permanently to the rest of the door, the hardboard was unscrewed from the outside and the

The two useable sections of original door skin are held in place with aluminium strips whilst being bonded on.

Forming the lower half of door skin, with two fibreglass sheets held in position using hardboard across the door to line up everything with the front and rear wings.

The hardboard has been removed to reveal the new door skin, which follows the complex shape of the side of the car.

The completed door skin.

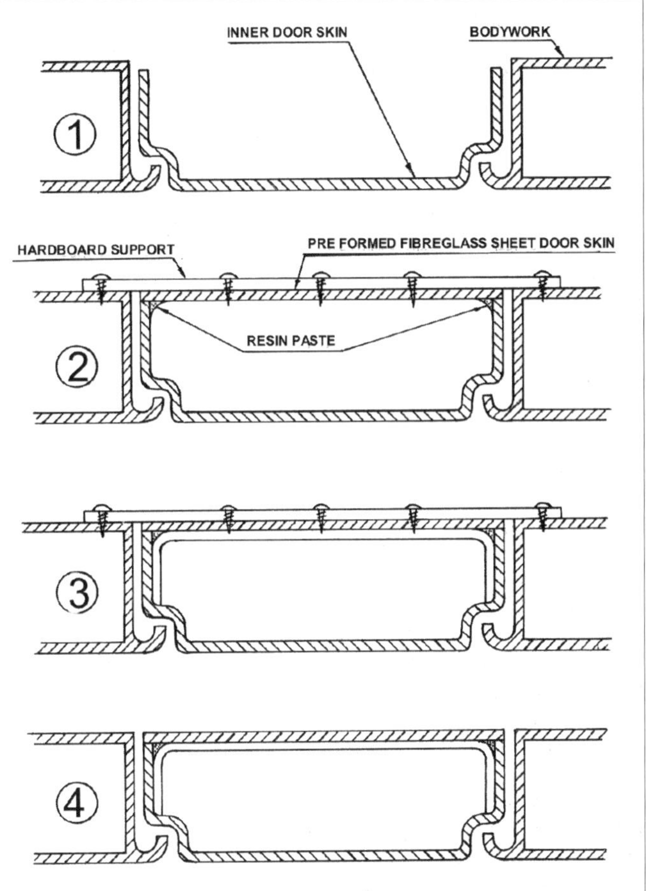

A series of sectional diagrams through a door moulding, showing the process of forming a new door skin. 1) The inner door skin is trimmed to slightly below the level of the surrounding bodywork. 2) Pre-formed fibreglass sheet is held in place with hardboard across the door and bonded with resin paste. 3) The initial bond is augmented with layers of CSM and resin inside the door. 4) The hardboard is removed and the screw holes filled to reveal the new door skin.

result admired. The lowest section had acquired a subtle twist that ensured it blended in with the scallop feature of the surrounding bodywork.

The only thing left to do was tidy up the joins between all the various sections of fibreglass. The top join with the incorrect radius profile was sanded back hard and the two panel edges feathered before a bridging piece of cardboard was taped inside. The outer surface was formed with mat and resin before the inside was tackled after removing the card support. The outer face was finished with gel coat resin to allow it to be sanded smooth to the correct profile.

The only attention required at the centre and lower joins was grinding out some small areas and filling with gel coat to lose the join after sanding.

3. DETAILING

The main carcass of each door was complete but there was much work to do before they could be described as finished. As the initial moulds had been only temporary affairs, there was a lot of remedial surface work to be done, especially the areas that had been moulded onto brown parcel tape. When the tape was applied every effort was made to keep the surface as smooth as possible, but wrinkles were inevitable and the resulting small irregularities required hours of rectification.

To assist progress several shaped wooden sanding blocks were made to suit different locations, and these sometimes had the abrasive paper stapled to them because it was tricky to hold it in place with the fingers. This much work could probably be considered quite a drawback to the temporary mould technique, but for one-off panels it is ideal. When the finished shape and detail are impossible to predict, this step-by-step method is eminently suitable. Any additions and alterations needed are easily accommodated and there are no large fibreglass mould assemblies to manufacture and store.

Without permanent moulds future

The flush door handle assembly is made from layers of riveted aluminium sheet.

The internal Renault handle is accessed through a spring loaded flap.

repair could be a problem, but I am of the opinion that the panels have been formed once so there is no reason to doubt that they can be formed again; hard work but not impossible.

An addition to the inside of the door, which, to make it easier, should have been carried out without the outer skin in place, was the installation of internal channelling to divert rainwater from the window channel straight to the drain holes at the bottom of the door. The internal channel angles were made in a simple folded aluminium mould and bonded in place with resin paste.

On the subject of rain, during the first year of use after the car was finished, another waterproofing addition was needed when it was noted that rainwater entered the car by dripping off the bottom of the window glass and running down the inside of the fibreglass trim panel – and through the electric window switch! Installing a polythene membrane over the inside of the door before fitting the trim panel, just like some production cars, resolved this.

The bottom of the handle assembly showing the plastic Renault handle and the angle bracket that supports the spring loaded hinge.

3.1. Flush door handles

The door handles came about out of a desire to keep the external appearance of the Mirov looking much as it did in the original TV adverts, in which the door handles were shown as incorporating a fingerprint recognition entry system: entirely fictional, of course, but the top of the door skin – which was about the only part of the original door to be reused – had a dummy fingerprint scanner fitted, which, when removed, left a hole that matched the plan view of the door skin. It was decided to fabricate a flush door handle in polished aluminium to fit this hole.

By chance, the door handles on the Renault 30 donor car were of the type that were hidden within the door and accessed through a hole. These handles were pressed into service, fitted behind custom-made, spring loaded aluminium flaps. The flap assemblies and surrounds were fabricated from a three layer sandwich of 3.2mm (⅛in) aluminium sheets riveted together with a spring loaded hinge and the Renault handles. The construction details can be seen in the accompanying diagrams (opposite).

The lower layer is the rectangular mounting plate that is fixed to the underside of the door skin with four bonded-in studs, as described in Chapter 1. On one side of this is riveted a right angled bracket that has the hinge bolted to it, and opposite this is fixed the Renault handle. The middle

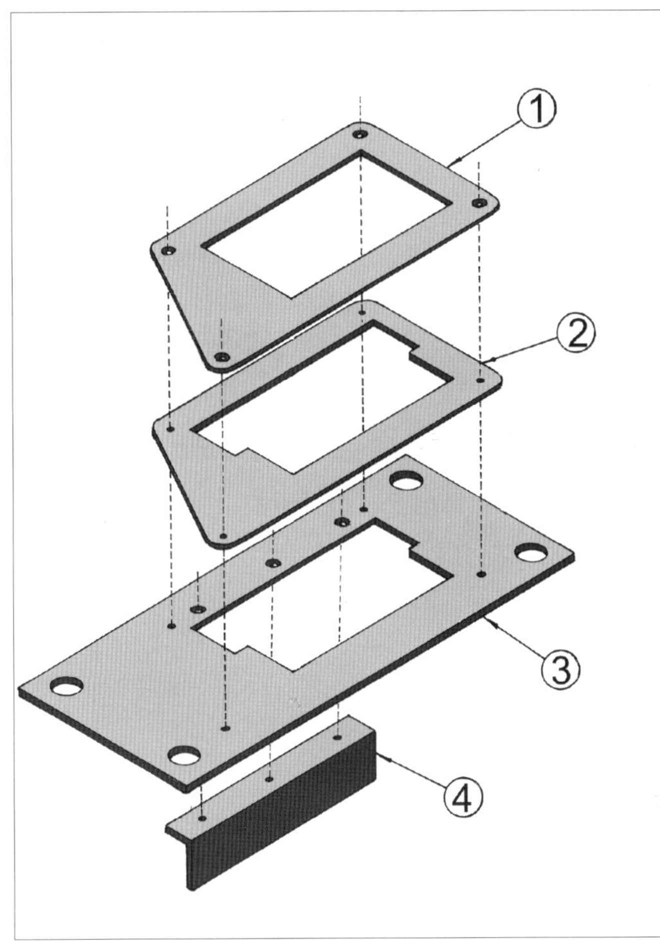

An exploded diagram showing the aluminium component parts of the handle assembly. The polished outer surround (1) is riveted to the spacer (2) and base plate (3), and the angle (4) is attached underneath to accept the hinge.

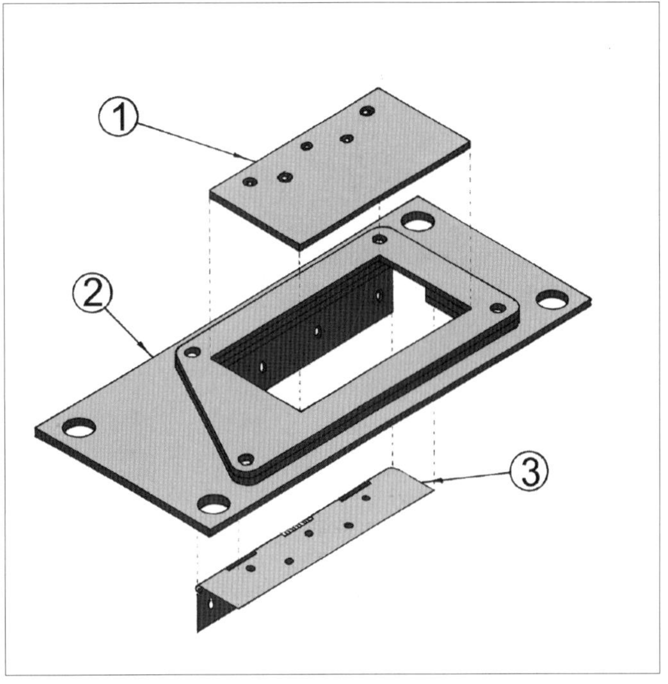

The riveted handle assembly (2) receives the spring loaded hinge (3) and cover plate (1).

piece of aluminium is there as a spacer to ensure that the polished top layer sits flush with the door skin. This top piece also acts as a stop for the spring loaded hinge to ensure the flap remains flush in the close fitting hole.

3.2. Door locks

The door locks came from the Renault 30 donor on which they were fixed with a spring clip inside the steel door skin. To use the same fixing on the thicker Mirov fibreglass door, a large hole was cut that allowed the lock to sit flush to the skin. A perforated steel plate was then bonded over the hole inside the door, and a hole cut in it to accept the lock, which was then secured with the spring clip.

3.3. Connecting door lock rods

When all the lock components were

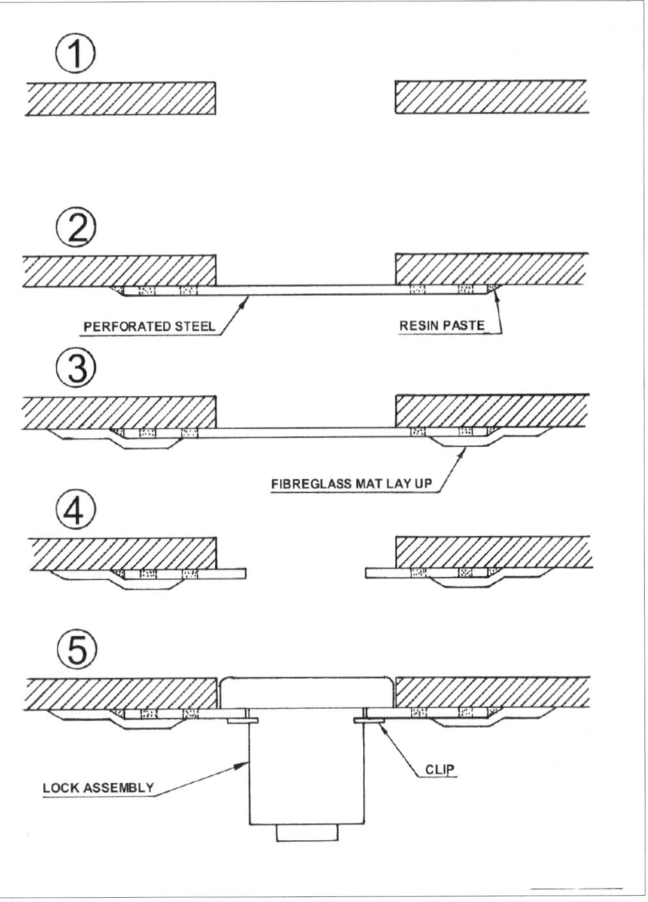

A series of sectional diagrams showing how the standard door lock was fitted to the fibreglass door. Firstly, a hole was made to accommodate the lock assembly (1). Perforated steel sheet was bonded across the back of the hole with resin paste (2). This was augmented with a layer of CSM (3). A hole was cut in the steel (4) to allow the lock to be flush fitted using its original spring clip (5).

The finished lock and handle assembly fitted flush to the door skin.

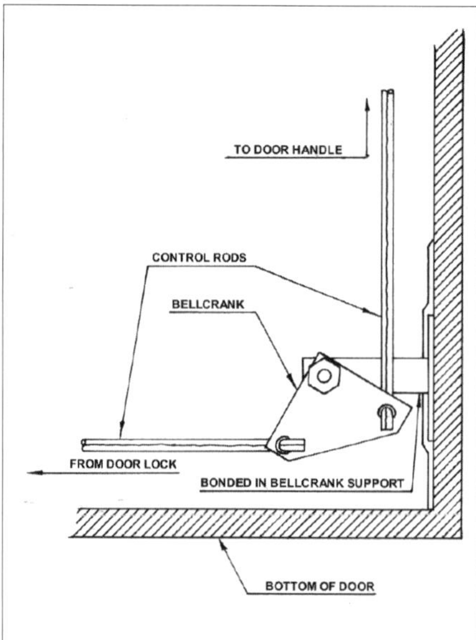

This illustrates the type of bellcrank installation fitted to the bottom rear corner of each door that is used to link the handles to the lock mechanisms.

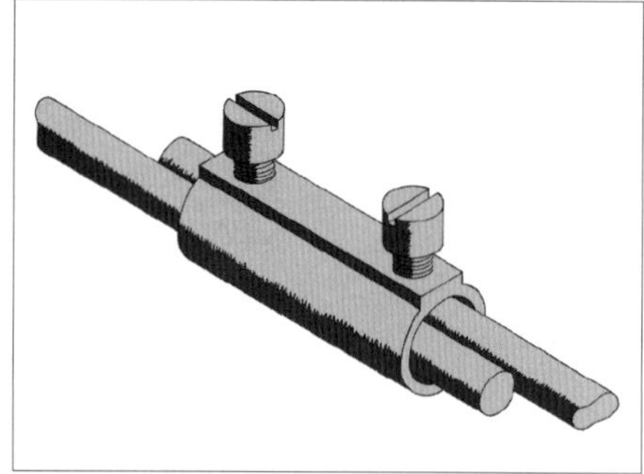

To ease installation and adjustment, each control rod was made in two parts and joined using the metal clamps taken from large electrical terminal blocks.

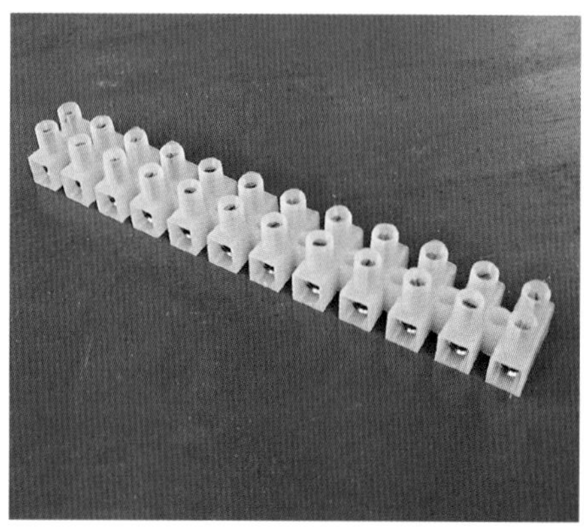

Large-type electrical 'chocolate block' connector.

installed in the doors it was time to think about linking them to operate together. The stout wire used for the operating rods was actually a mixture of rods from the Renault donor and sections of wire coat hanger.

On a normal door the lock and exterior handle are situated very close to the latch mechanism; on the Mirov gull wing doors, however, all of the components were scattered about, with direct links unable to be made due to the path of the retracting window glass, the four different mounting planes of the interior handle on the inner skin, the latch mechanism on the door bottom, the external handle on the top outer skin, and the lock on the side of the outer skin.

Small steel bellcranks had to be manufactured and fitted to brackets fibreglassed inside the door to change the control rod directions. There was one each for the exterior handle rod, the lock barrel, the interior handle, and the interior lock plunger, which had been located horizontally at the bottom of the door next to the handle.

With four bellcranks there were far more connecting rods than with a conventional door, and trying to cut and bend each rod to the correct length would have been a nightmare. The answer was to make every rod in two pieces, joined by a clamp, which would allow easy installation and infinite adjustment. The clamps were made from the metal screw clamp sections of large electrical terminal blocks, sometimes referred to as 'chocolate block' connectors. The block had to be big enough to allow two rods to be inserted side-by-side in one of its wire terminal clamps. Each terminal was removed from its plastic block by first taking out the screws and then pushing out the main body of the clamp. One terminal was fitted to each rod assembly, and, after installation, each rod could be easily adjusted to ensure correct lock operation.

3.4. Window mechanism

The tilting window mechanism created for the Mirov gull wing doors is a development of an idea I first used on a Cox GTM kit car restoration, which originally came about through my dislike of the GTM sliding window arrangement. Because the doors were so thin, the only way to get the proposed flat glass to wind down was to have it swing out first before disappearing into the door. Specially-made flat glass was to be used on the Mirov as well, and, initially, because the door was so wide, it was thought that the glass could be made to operate without any fancy gymnastics. Unfortunately, the pronounced tumblehome – the angle at which the window is from vertical – meant that the glass would hit the inside of the door before it was fully open, so the tilting mechanism would have to make a repeat appearance.

Basically, the glass is attached to the lifting mechanism with a horizontal hinge. A short pair of arms on the glass carrier engage with the lower window frame when the pane travels up to tilt it inward onto the seal. When opening, the arms come away from the window frame, which then allows rollers on the frame to push out the glass as the carrier travels down. To make life as easy as possible the window mechanism was developed midway through the construction of the door shells before the outer skins were fitted. As with the GTM there were to be no runners to carry the glass; it would rely completely on the lifting mechanism for location, which was of the cable type of Ford origin and bolted to the inner skin of the driver's door.

Another piece of aircraft hinge was bolted horizontally to the slider of the lifting mechanism, and the glass was fitted to the hinge via a pair of brackets with built-in adjustable stops. The adjuster screws on the arms were also used to ensure the glass sat square in

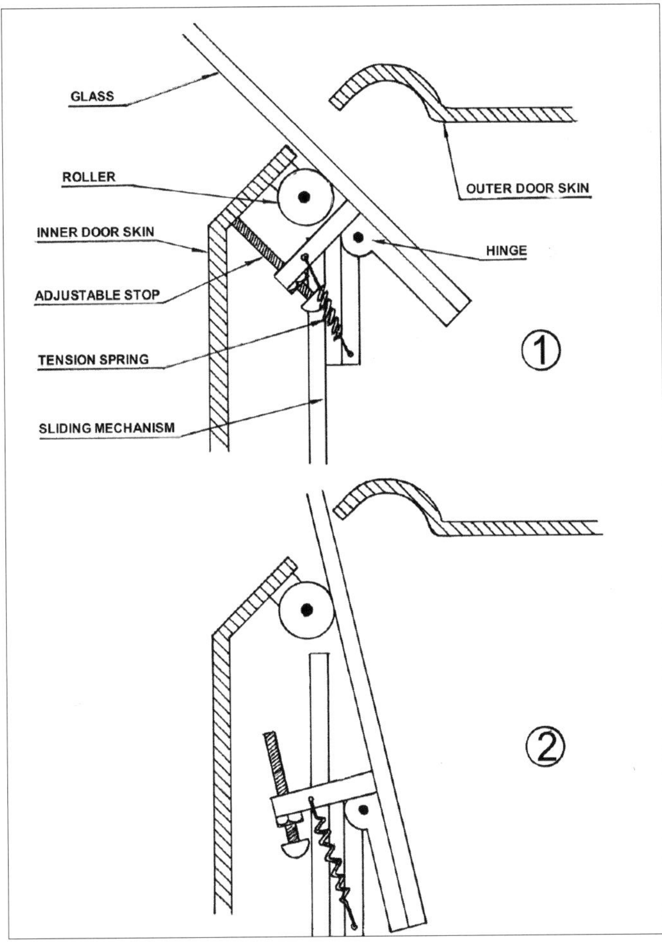

Two cross-sectional views showing the action of the tilting window mechanism. Diagram (1) shows the window in the up position tilted on its hinge by the action of the adjustable stop hitting the door. Diagram (2) shows the window lowered and forced into an upright position by the fixed roller and downward motion of the slider.

the frame when closed, and eliminated the misalignment any wear in the slider mechanism or hinge would cause. A small tension spring was connected between the end of each bracket and the slider assembly, which would tend to steady the glass as it travelled by subjecting it to gentle pressure that constantly attempted to tilt it inward.

The Renault donor car supplied the motors, which were nice compact units, although from the lever type of window mechanism, so an adapter was made that allowed them to directly drive the spigot on the cable lifting mechanism.

The system worked but there was a lot of friction between the glass and the lower part of the window seal when in operation. The offending seal rubber was cut away and a pair of small rubber rollers with integral bearings, sourced from an old tape recorder, were fitted to a pair of brackets. These were bolted in place just under the lower window frame to take the spring pressure as the glass moved up and down.

The window shut and sitting totally flush to the door.

As the glass moves down, the fixed rollers force it to assume a more upright attitude.

Halfway down.

The window in the fully open position.

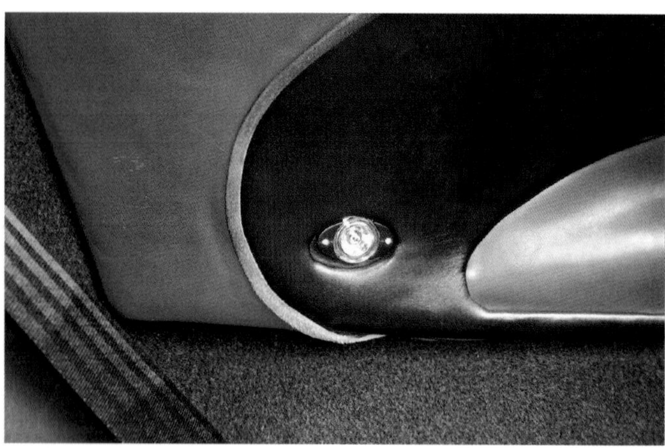

The rechargeable torch fits in an oval aperture in the door panels.

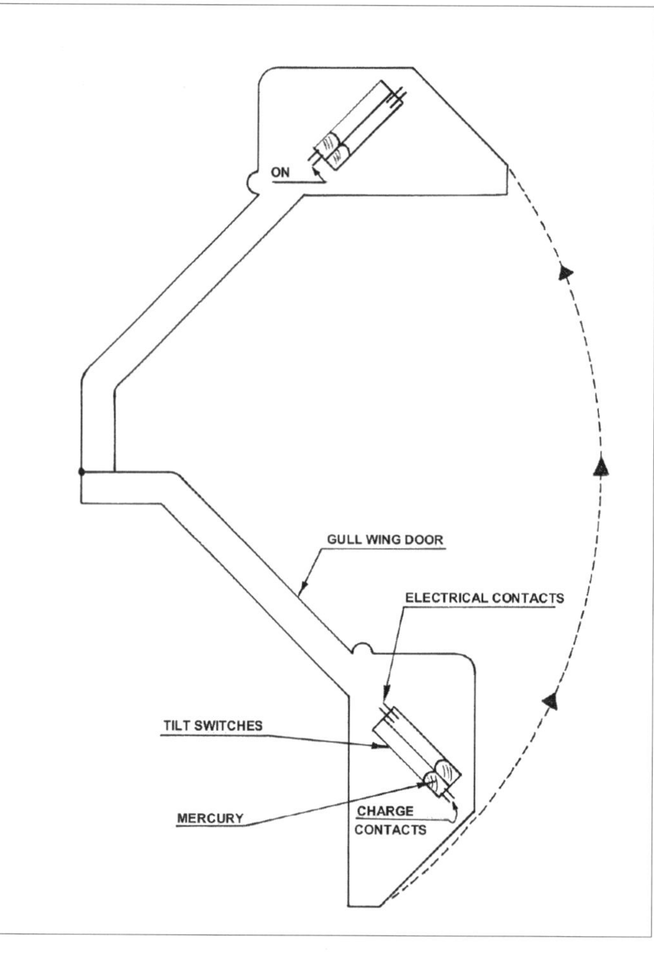

These diagrams show the arrangement and operation of the mercury tilt switches within the doors. In the closed position the torch is in 'charge' mode. The motion of the opening door alters the angle of the tilt switches to turn the torch from 'charge' to 'on.'

The entire system was tested using an MDF blank to ensure it all worked before having a pair of 5mm ($^3/_{16}$in) toughened glass windows made. The glass was made this thick because the unique window lifting mechanism, when fully up, puts a sideways load on the glass to press it against the seal; any thinner and it would flex too much.

3.5. Wireless courtesy lights

To take advantage of the fibreglass body construction, the power supply to the gull wing doors was routed through the hinge and earthed through the catch on the sill. This had the effect of keeping the hinge area clear of any wiring, but meant that power was only supplied to the door when it was shut. It was felt that it would be a good idea to have a courtesy light in the door trim panel which would shine down on the sill when the door was open, but there was no power to the door when in the open position. Switching would also be a problem.

After a great deal of thought a solution was found involving small rechargeable torches of the type that plug into a cigar lighter socket. These were equipped with a three position switch – ON, OFF, CHARGE – and to replace this it was decided to take advantage of the gull wing door action and use mercury tilt switches arranged to automatically change from CHARGE to ON as the door was opened. These tilt switches consist of a sealed plastic capsule with a pair of internal electrical contacts that are made by a blob of mercury, depending on the attitude of the capsule. Two of these tilt switches, at 180° to each other, were fitted at 45° inside each door and wired into the torches to permit them to charge when the doors were shut and come on when open.

The system works, and would be even better if the car was used on a daily basis. The limited mileage tends to leave the batteries undercharged, although, after a long run, everything works very well.

Chapter 6

Systems & solutions

1. SINGLE WINDSCREEN WIPER

The shape of the Mirov windscreen indictated the use of a single wiper for optimum coverage, which meant that the angle of sweep was a lot smaller than with a conventional system. The solution to this involved modification of an ordinary twin wiper system; in this case, the one from the donor Renault 30, which was of the crank and lever variety.

A position at the centre of the front bulkhead was chosen to be the pivot point for the wiper arm and a suitable bracket made and fitted. Measurements were taken from here to the rear edge of the windscreen to determine the length of wiper arm required (610mm (24in) with a 610mm (24in) blade). One of the original Renault arms was cut and extended by riveting on a specially-made aluminium alloy extension piece. By placing this new arm assembly on the windscreen in the park position and maximum sweep position, the angle between the two was measured at 80°.

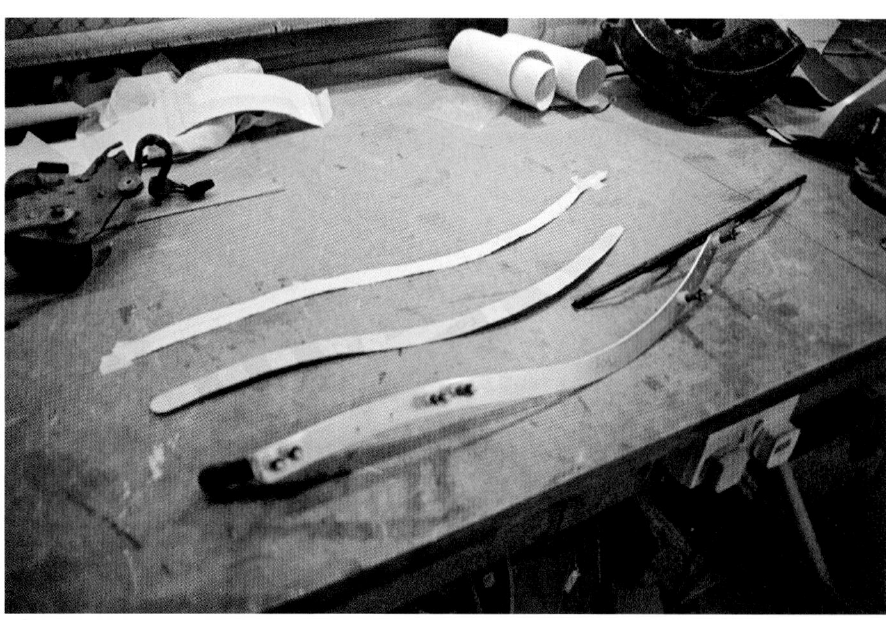

The wiper arm showing the original paper and card templates used to make the aluminium alloy extension piece.

The motor was fixed to another bracket a short distance from the wiper spindle. The motor crank length was 40mm (1⁹⁄₁₆in), which, in one complete revolution, gave a linear motion of twice this figure (80mm (3⅛in)). Using this crank to move the arm through the required 80° meant that the length of lever at the wiper spindle would have to be altered. The system was drawn out on paper to work out exactly what this length needed to be. A centre line was drawn, followed by one line each side at 40° to it to represent park and maximum sweep. By setting a pair of compasses at 40mm (1⁹⁄₁₆in), arcs were drawn each side of the centre line and linked to give two lines parallel to the centreline and 80mm (3⅛in) apart. The point where these two lines crossed the angled ones marked the length of lever

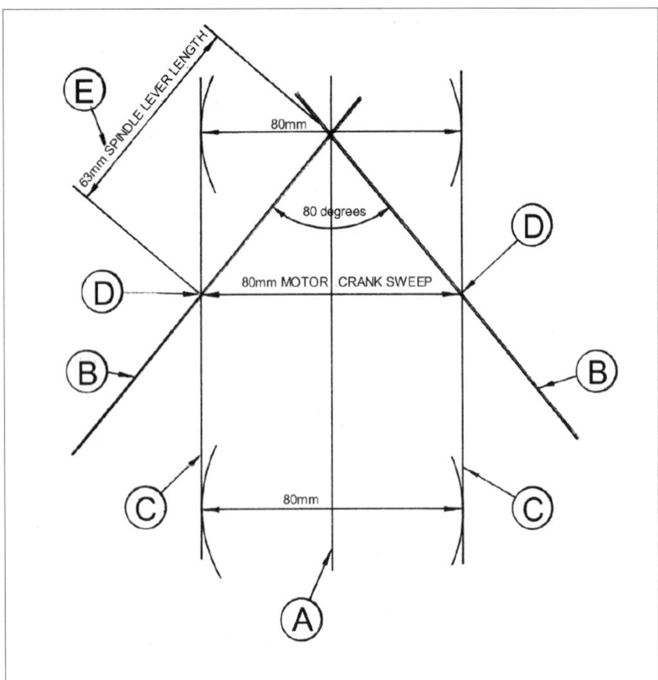

This geometric diagram shows how the 80° angle of sweep and 80mm (3⅛in) crank movement were used to deduce the required length of wiper spindle lever. Firstly, the centreline (A) was drawn, followed by two lines (B) 80° apart, which represented the angle of sweep required, arranged equidistant each side of the centreline. Onto this the 80mm (3⅛in) crank movement was superimposed by drawing two parallel lines (C) 80mm apart, arranged equally about the centreline. The point (D) where line (C) crossed line (B) gave the required length of spindle lever measured to pivot point (E).

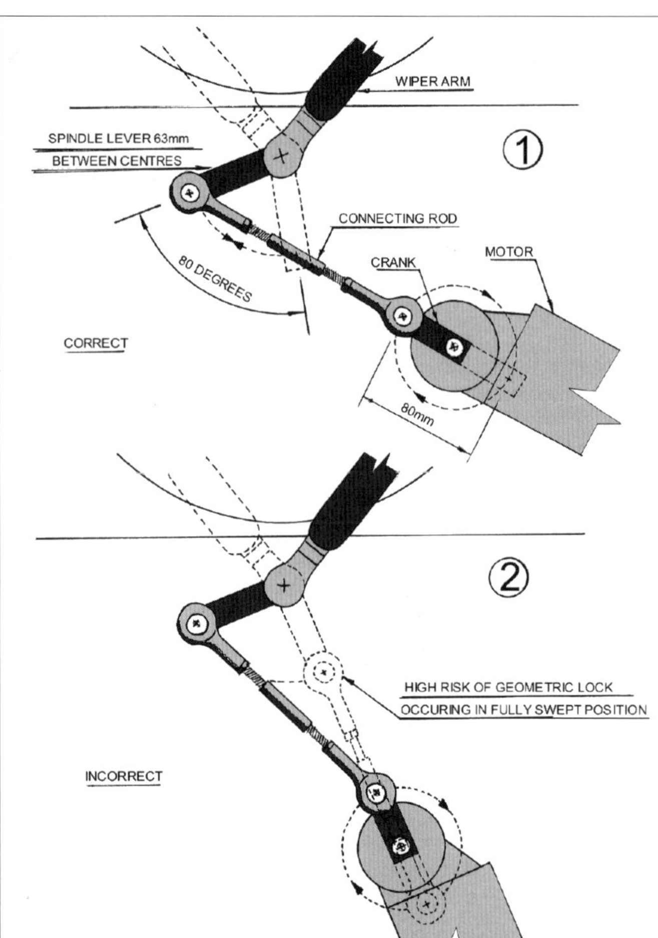

Diagram (1) shows the correct arrangement of mechanism to achieve smooth wiper operation. Diagram (2) shows how an incorrect arrangement could lead to the mechanism locking up.

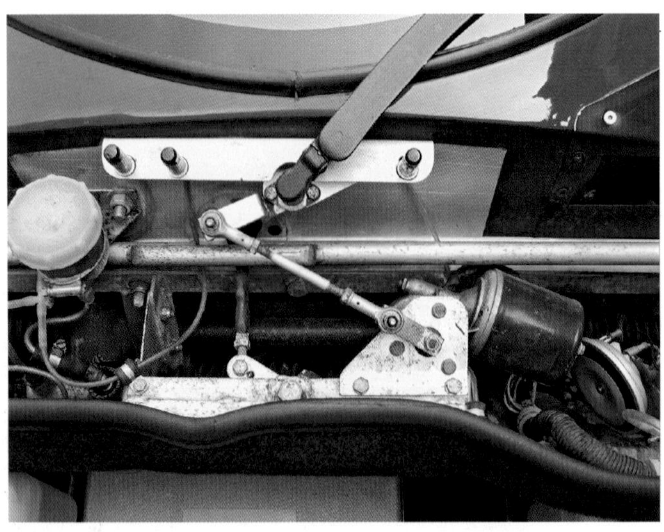

The finished wiper mechanism installed.

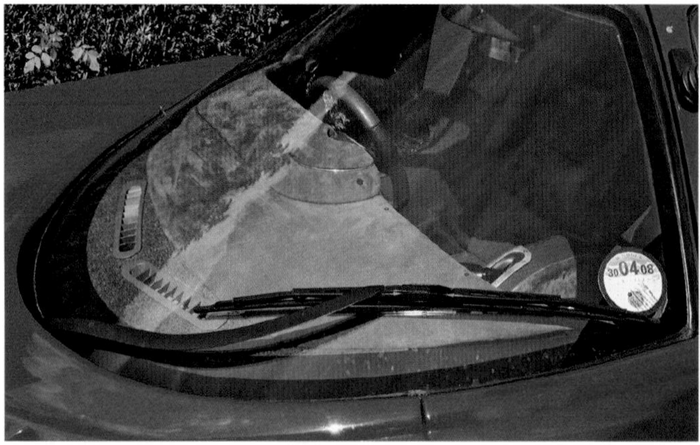

The new wiper arm painted satin black and fitted with a 600mm (2ft) blade.

required at the wiper spindle, which, in this case, was 63mm (2½in).

With the spindle lever modified and in position, an adjustable rod was made to connect it to the motor crank. By making the rod adjustable, the park position on the windscreen could be fine tuned if necessary.

When connecting up it's best to have everything in the park position, lining up the connecting rod with the crank and with the end of the spindle lever when in its parked and projected fully swept position. Failing to do this will mean that wiper speed will not be constant throughout the range of sweep, plus there is a risk of the mechanism locking up because of incorrect geometry.

2. GEAR LINKAGE

Owning and driving a mid-engined car is great, but it's not until you actually build one from scratch that you appreciate the amount of development involved in such things as the gear change mechanism. At first glance the problem seems very complex, but apply a spot of logic and the solution actually proves very straightforward.

When the transmission was in the Renault driving the front wheels, the engine was in front of the axle with the gearbox behind it, which meant that the gear lever was in close proximity to the gearbox, making connection fairly simple for the manufacturer. With the complete drive train located in the back half of the Mirov, the gearbox was now as far away from the gear lever as it could get – over 2m (6ft 6in) away, in fact.

I was fortunate in that the Cox GTM rebuild completed a few years earlier had provided experience of this problem. The main thing was to minimise the amount of joints in the system, which would ensure positive gear selection with minimal lost motion. Running the gear change rod backward from the lever, instead of forward, does not, as some might think, reverse the gate pattern. The original Renault 30 mechanism had a short selector rod running from the lever, approaching the gearbox from behind. When first gear was selected, viewed from behind, the gear lever in the cockpit was pushed to the left and forward, which resulted in the lower end of the lever swinging to the right and back. This motion was transmitted to the gearbox via the selector rod, which swung the gearbox lever over to the right and pulled it back, thereby selecting first gear.

If we look at the selection of first gear again, but this time imagine the lever in front of the gearbox as with the Mirov, the movement left and forward of the gear lever produces the same swing to the right and backward movement of the lower end as before. The motion is transmitted rearward via a long selector rod, which swings the gearbox lever to the right and pushes it backward, selecting first gear as before.

2.1. Construction

To simplify matters as much as possible the gear lever and housing from the Renault 30 donor car were used. The lower end of the lever was mounted in a nylon ball, which, in turn, was fitted in a nylon housing with a spring. To select reverse the lever had to be pushed down against the spring to allow the lower end to ride under a detent moulded into the nylon housing. The actual selector rod was connected to the lower end of the lever with a single pivot, so it was easy enough to swing it back through 180° to face the rear.

A mounting plate for the lever was formed in steel, with a right angled fold along each edge to stiffen it and a large hole to accept the lever. The nylon housing was bolted to the underside of the plate with the lever poking through the hole. Two rubber mounts fixed the complete assembly to a steel bracket bolted across the centre tunnel of the car, taking care to keep it high enough to allow passage of the various services that had to run in the tunnel.

Before the selector linkage was designed and fitted, it was important to fabricate a tie bar with which to solidly connect the engine to the lever assembly mounting plate. This would ensure that they moved as one unit when the engine rocked about on its mountings, eliminating false inputs and preventing it jumping out of gear.

A suitable location on the left-hand side of the engine block was found, which had three unused threaded holes. A bracket was made and bolted to the block, and measurements taken from this to the lever mounting plate to allow a tubular steel tie bar to be made and fitted.

On the gearbox, gear selection is performed by a single lever on the back of the gearbox, mounted on a sliding pivot, which allows the lever to swing backward and forward and slide from side-to-side. The selector rod attaches to the gearbox in the horizontal plane by a floating link, which allows it to rotate via a ball and socket joint. A short arm drops from the selector rod and attaches to the gearbox lever by a second ball and socket, which locates it vertically.

To enable connection of a selector rod that approached from the front instead of behind, as on the donor car, both the gearbox lever and the floating link had to be moved to the left by about 75mm (3in). The complete floating link was relocated by moving its mounting bracket across on an adaptor plate

The top rod ties the rubber mounted gear lever housing rigidly to the engine. The lower rod transmits the gear lever action to the mechanism at the back of the gearbox.

bolted to the back of the gearbox, and the gearbox lever had an extension welded to it to move the ball joint across by the same amount. This enabled the floating link and selector lever to be directly accessed from the front down the left-hand side of the gearbox.

With both ends of the mechanism sorted, all that remained was to find a route for a one-piece selector rod to connect them, which avoided the water pipes in the tunnel, the fuel cross feed pipes, the handbrake mechanism, the engine, chassis rails, and gearbox mounts: simple!

The engine had ended up slightly higher in the chassis than intended because of the wide sump not fitting between the chassis rails, which was a good thing, actually, because it meant that a more direct route for the gear change rod was available by running directly under the engine.

The new extended rod was made up from bits of tubular steel conduit and curved sections of tube cut from an old chair. Initially, each section was clamped together until I was satisfied with the shape and routing. The rod ran straight under the engine, angled to the left until it was roughly underneath the left-hand driveshaft. A slight kink was incorporated so that it ran parallel to the chassis rail until it met the gearbox mount, where two, right angled curves were added to run it up and over to the modified mechanism at the back of the gearbox.

The drop link arm from the end of the original Renault rod was cut in two, the top half turned around to face forward, and welded back on, then welded onto the end of the new rod so that the ball could be inserted directly into the end of the floating link, which located the rod in the lateral plane. The lower part, which retained its upward-facing socket attached to a short piece of the original rod, was pressed onto the gearbox lever ball joint, which supported the rod in the vertical plane.

With everything tack welded it was checked for correct operation and clearance along the route. Once proved to be fine, it was taken off and finally welded together.

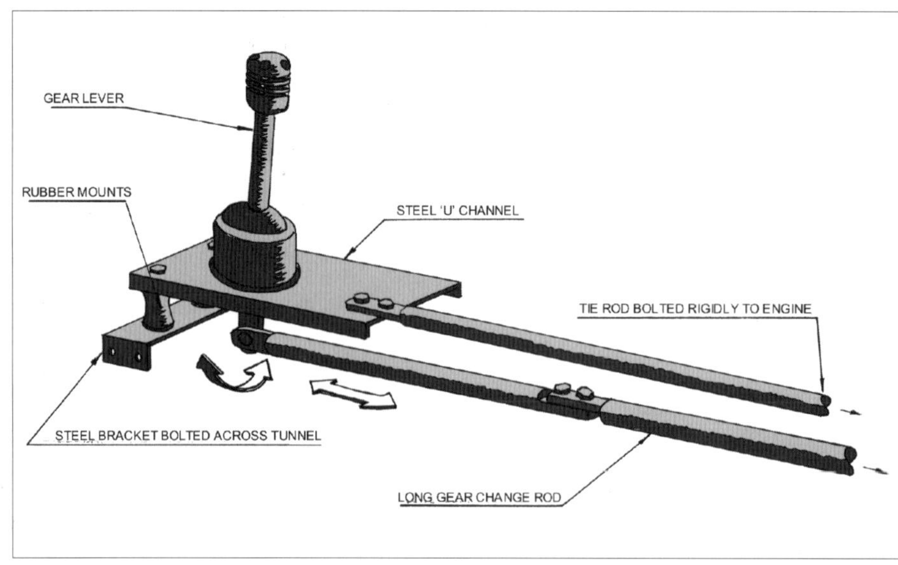

This sketch shows how the gear lever is fitted to a steel channel, which is bolted across the centre tunnel and supported by two rubber bobbins at the front. The rear is supported by the tie rod attached to the front of the engine.

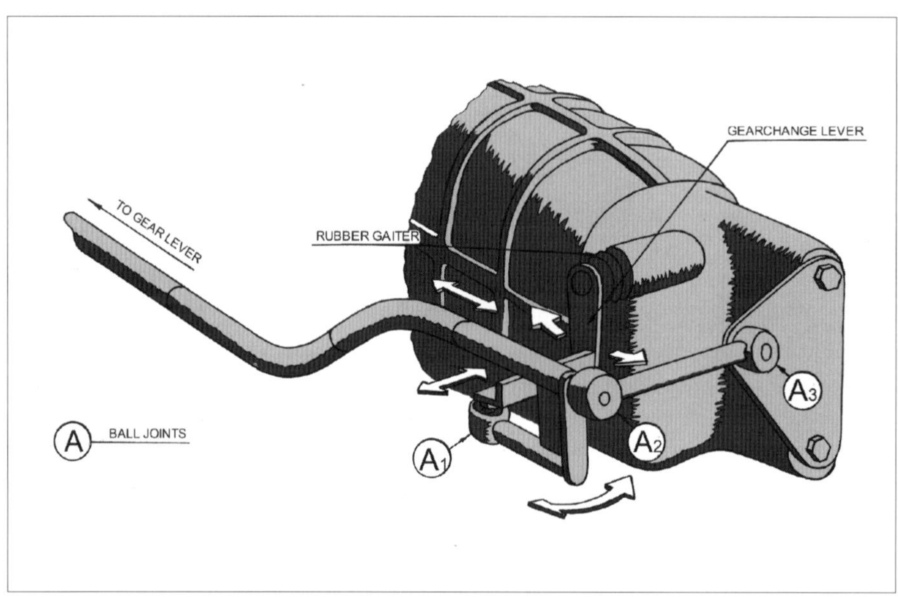

This sketch illustrates the fixing of the gear change rod to the gearbox. The rod is supported at the gearbox by the small ball joint (A^1) and located sideways by joint (A^2). The gear change lever can swing forward and backward and slide from side-to-side. To allow the gear change rod to connect from the front, ball joints (A^1) and (A^3) have been moved across to the left by a welded angle on the gear change lever and a triangular adaptor plate respectively.

3. TWIN FUEL TANKS

Using a badly designed twin fuel tank system can be very inconvenient, especially if the tanks are not interlinked and have to be filled separately. Some systems are interlinked so that both tanks can be filled from either side of the car, and have a connecting pipe which is too small. This results in the fuel backing up in the tank being filled until such time as it can run through the pipe and equalise. Other considerations – such as adequate venting – also have to be taken into account. Here, I show you the layout of the Mirov fuel tanks, designed to be easy to live with and very effective since the car has been on the road.

To maximise capacity, twin interlinked fuel tanks were fitted. The left-hand tank supplies the engine.

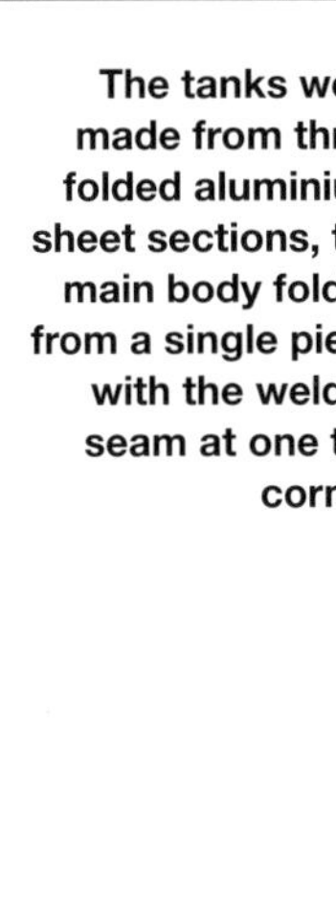

The tanks were made from three folded aluminium sheet sections, the main body folded from a single piece with the welded seam at one top corner.

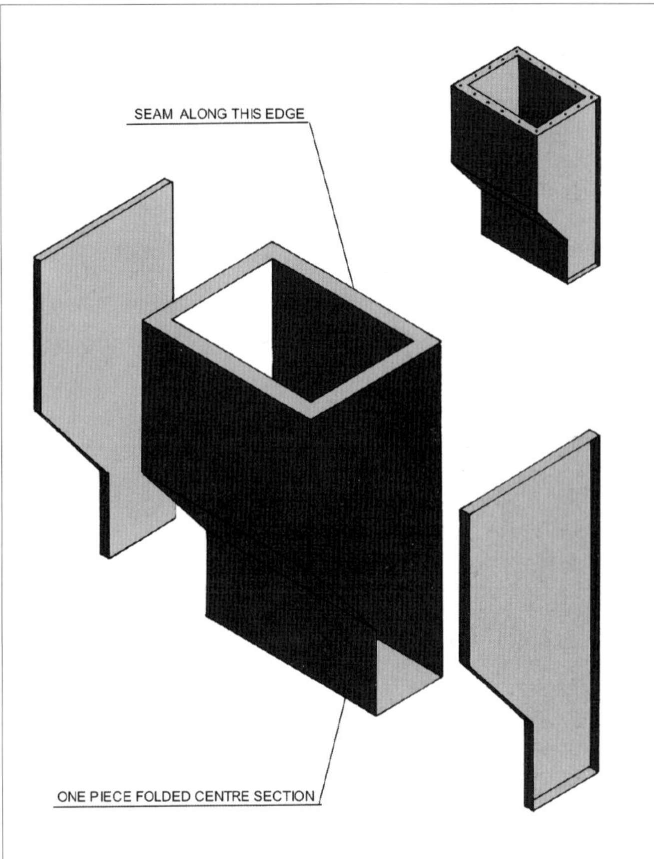

The right-hand tank houses the sender unit. Note the air balance pipe connected to the top panel and running across to the LH tank.

To simplify the installation the cross feed pipes were the only connections fitted to the main body of the tanks, all other connections sprouting from the removable top panels that would also allow unrestricted internal access if required. A target capacity of 45 litres (10 gallons) was established to ensure an adequate range of at least 320km (200 miles). A finished capacity of 64 litres (14 gallons) was squeezed out of the space available, which includes the fuel contained in the double cross feed pipes. On a good, steady run, fuel consumption was better than expected at 9.5 litres/100km (30mpg), which gave a useful range of up to 474km (296 miles); not bad for a 2.7 litre V6.

3.1. The tanks

For lightness and ease of manufacture, aluminium was the chosen material for the tanks. Because the intended tank locations were such an awkward shape, a dummy wooden tank which would fit both sides was made as a pattern. The bottom of the tank ended up very narrow, which was an advantage as it alleviated the need to fit any baffles to prevent fuel surge. The dummy tank was trial fitted in both sides, and, when satisfied with the size and shape, the component parts were cut and formed in 16swg aluminium sheet. Each tank consisted of a front and rear panel with short, 6mm (¼in) right angled flanges folded along all the edges for added strength. The top, sides and bottom of each tank were folded from one piece of aluminium, and the middle of the top was cut out to leave a 25mm (1in) lip all round.

After all the parts had been clamped together, to ensure a good fit they were professionally welded and leak tested by filling with water and standing on absorbent paper for a few hours. Each tank had a small leak in one lower corner, revealed by a damp patch on the paper. They were welded and tested again, when both tanks proved leak-free.

An aluminium panel was cut to fit the top of each tank, and secured with 18 bolts fitted into an anchor nut ring riveted under each tank flange. All of the services, bar the fuel cross feed pipes, would connect to these panels.

3.2. Fitting

To secure the tanks a heavy duty version of a diagonal battery clamp was devised and fixed in the side pods of the car, making sure that adequate clearance was maintained to allow

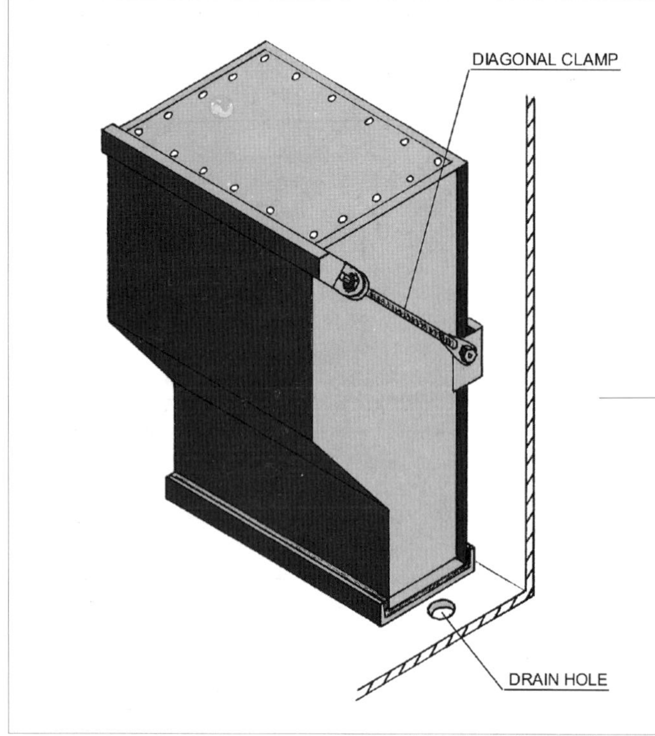

Each tank sits in a rubber-lined fibreglass channel and is held secure by substantial diagonal clamps. Note the water drain hole that also prevents the build-up of petrol vapour.

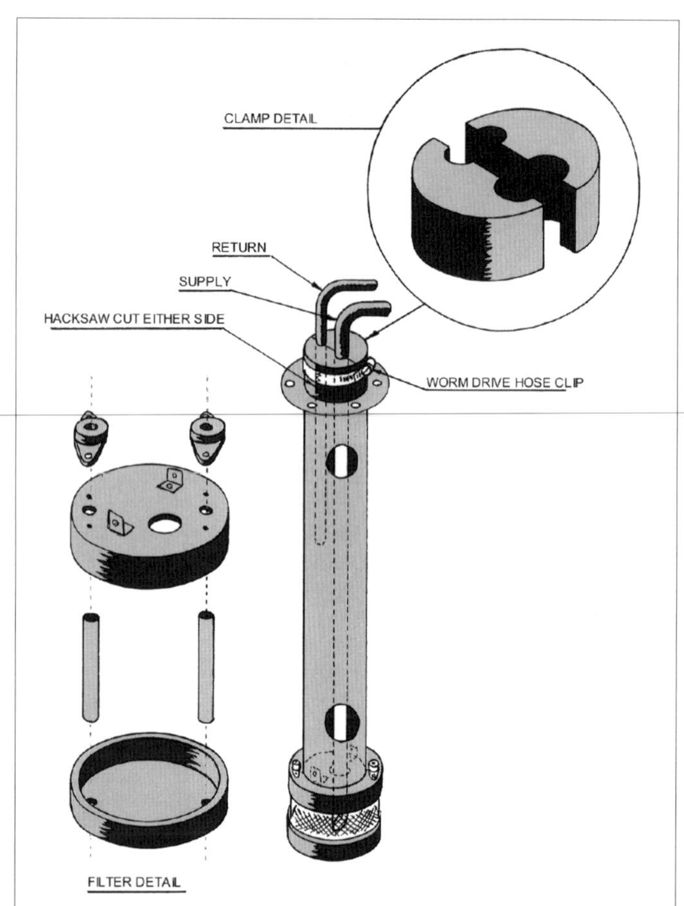

Detail of the tubular steel housing that holds the fuel supply, return pipes and filter assembly in the LH tank.

the top panels to be removed with the clamps in place. A fibreglass channel for the base of each tank to sit in was fashioned from a simple aluminium mould, lined with rubber and bonded to the floor of the side pods with the tanks in place to ensure accurate positioning.

Because the fuel tank housings had closed bottoms, there was a risk of petrol vapour – which is heavier than air – becoming trapped around the tanks, so two 13mm (½in) diameter holes were cut in the base of each pod to allow vapour or rain water to disperse or drain out.

Apart from the fuel transfer pipes linking the tanks, all other connections were fitted to the bolt-on top panels for ease of maintenance. The filler necks were made from steel tube, with a welded flange that allowed them to be bolted to the panels.

3.3. Fuel feed

The V6 fuel pump was located on the left-hand side of the engine, which dictated that the supply and return pipes be fitted to the LH fuel tank. Both pipes were clamped in the top

The top of the left-hand tank showing the filler neck, fuel pipe assembly, and air balance vent connection.

of a tubular housing made from a new length of 44mm (1¾in) exhaust pipe, which ran the full depth of the tank and had a mesh filter fitted to the end. The top had a mounting flange welded just below the pipe clamp, and the entire assembly fitted through a 50mm (2in) hole in the top panel to be secured with six bolts.

3.4. Sender unit

When installing the electrics, the donor Renault 30 wiring loom was used in modified form, complete with all ancillaries, which, to ensure accurate readings, included the fuel gauge and sender unit. However, at 510mm (20in) high, the new tanks were more than twice as deep as the original Renault tank, which would cause problems regarding the accurate measurement of low fuel levels. With the fuel pick-up already fitted in the left-hand tank, the sender unit was mounted in the right-hand one.

To minimise the risk of running out of petrol, the sender unit had to be adapted to give good low fuel readings in the deeper tank, whereas an accurate full reading was not strictly necessary. This was achieved by mounting the unit halfway down the tank on a long bracket dropped from the top panel; the electrical connections were extended as necessary, with the positive terminal passing through the top panel within an insulating nylon top hat washer assembly. The length of the float arm was increased to cover a greater depth range for the same angular movement. The original float was cut off and the remaining arm extended with another float from a different sender unit, attached using a terminal block wire clamp in a similar manner to that of the door lock rods mentioned in Chapter 5. The complete assembly was mounted diagonally across the tank to accommodate as long a float arm as possible.

For ease of maintenance the sender unit was mounted to its own separate panel, bolted into the rear right-hand corner of the main top panel via five of the existing top panel bolts and three new ones, which screwed into an 'L'-shaped nut plate.

3.5. Linking the tanks

To enable both tanks to be filled from either side of the car, their bases had to be interconnected via a fuel cross feed pipe. This was fine in theory, but, in practice, several things were in the way, such as the engine, gear change mechanism, radiator supports, and chassis rails, so a straight route was not possible. The pipes would have to run inboard a short distance before turning at 45° to run forward to the bulkhead, performing another 45° turn to run parallel to the bulkhead and meet in the middle.

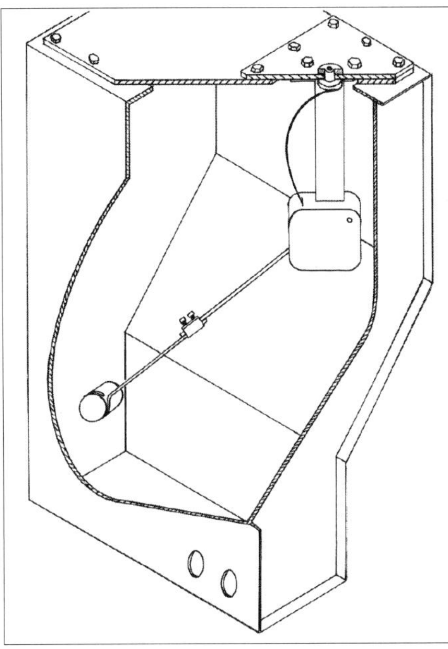

A cutaway view of the right-hand tank showing the sender unit on its extended bracket mounted diagonally across the tank. Note the float arm extension fitted using a terminal block clamp, and the separate corner panel that allows access to the sender without disturbing the tank main top panel.

The plan was to use 22mm (⅞in) diameter copper tubing, as this could be easily formed with a plumber's bending spring, although there was concern that this would not provide enough flow to allow both tanks to fill uniformly. The answer was to use two pipes running parallel, which doubled capacity although also doubled manufacturing problems, plus, there would be twice the chance of leaks at the tank connections.

The intended route was carefully surveyed, and detailed measurements enabled the required pipe shapes to be mapped out full size on a board to act as an assembly jig. After a couple of aborted attempts at fabricating the pipes in a single piece, they were eventually made in four sections, each section containing one bend. They were then laid on the jig and cut to length before being joined together with in-line soldered fittings. The tank connections were made with standard brass water tank compression fittings augmented by fuel-proof sealant.

These pipes were fitted to allow

The top of the right-hand tank showing the air balance vent pipe, filler neck, and sender unit panel.

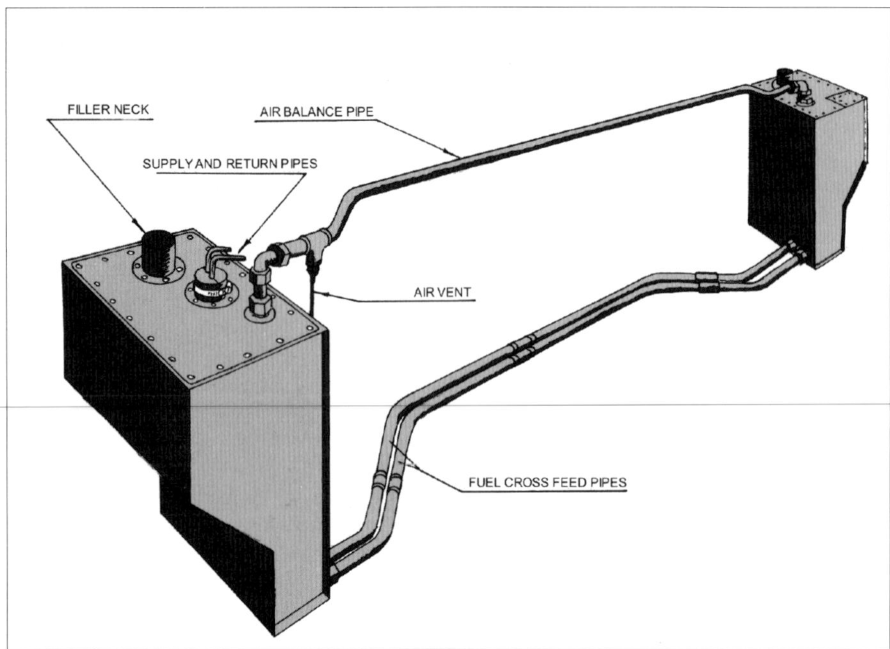

Here is the general arrangement of the twin fuel tank installation that illustrates the features required to ensure such a set-up works as it should. Always have cross feed pipes of adequate capacity, and remember to fit an air balance pipe and static air vent.

both tanks to be filled from one side of the car, but the air displaced by incoming fuel in the far tank had to have an escape route. To supply this an air balance pipe was fitted between each tank top panel using the same diameter tubing, which would allow the air to vent from whichever filler neck was in use.

To statically vent the tanks a 'T'-piece adapter was fitted toward the left-hand side of the air balance pipe, which accepted a small bore rubber hose that terminated with a small hole in a blanking cap level with the bottom of the tanks.

3.6. Sealing

To ensure fuel-tight connections on all bolted flanges, thick gasket card was used in each join, and to make the top panels totally leak-free the gaskets were fitted using fuel-proof sealant. To ease future access the panels received a thin smear of grease as a release agent before being bolted on. This allowed future removal without disturbing the perfect seal formed on the tank flange.

4. EXHAUST SYSTEM

The decision had been made to carry a full-size spare wheel. This had a knock-on effect because, with a rear wheel and tyre assembly in position on its support frame over the gearbox, there was very little room underneath to install an exhaust system. Total length from the exhaust manifold outlets to the back of the car was about 600mm (24in), and that space had to accommodate the silencers, plus the entire connecting pipework. This meant that the size of the silencer boxes and positioning of all inlet and outlet connections was critical if everything was to fit. The obvious solution was to design and manufacture the complete exhaust system from scratch.

Manufacturing something that physically fitted the space was relatively easy, and the real test was if it actually worked and allowed the engine to operate effectively without restriction. The other consideration was the SVA test noise limit of 101dbA measured 500mm (19⅝in) from the exhaust outlet.

One solution that would allow the engine to breathe efficiently and cut noise at the same time was a balance pipe that linked the two separate exhaust systems running from each cylinder bank. This would harmonise the pressure of the exhaust pulses, reducing noise and promoting better scavenging of the waste gases from each cylinder.

Common sense engineering achieved a design that ensured a free flow of gas and an SVA noise limit pass for a total materials cost of not more than £20, with the added bonus of a deep, throaty exhaust note and good performance.

4.1. Planning

The original cast iron exhaust manifolds were retained for simplicity because their outlets were conveniently positioned quite high and almost flush with the rear of the cylinder block. Not the most efficient set-up, granted, but very compact. There was a gap under the front of the spare wheel carrier on top of the differential and bell housing, just about level with the outlets, which provided the ideal site to transversely fit a combined expansion and balance box.

Two silencer boxes could just be accommodated each side of the gearbox under the rear half of the spare wheel. The back panel of the Mirov was very low and did not provide an obvious place for the exhaust to exit. Finally, the decision was decided by a portion of bodywork, just above the position earmarked for the number plate, which was ideally styled and placed to provide a neat exit slot. The entire panel was cut out to give a large rectangular exit hole about the same size as the number plate housing below it.

4.2. Manufacture

Careful measurement determined the maximum size of exhaust box that could be accommodated, and it transpired that all of the boxes could be made with the same cross section,

With space at a premium, the logical thing to do was tailor-make an exhaust system to fit. This is where the expansion/balance box fits under the front of the spare wheel.

Sheet steel for the end plates is clamped between two MDF formers ...

... and then gently tapped over with a hammer ...

... to form an end plate with a 6mm (¼in) flange all round.

Right angled folds were formed along the edge of each silencer skin.

which simplified the tooling. A sheet of 0.9mm (20swg) mild steel was used to form all the box component parts, except for the integral tail pipes, which were made of square tube.

The 180mm (7in) x 100mm (4in) end plates of the boxes were tackled first. The simple, round-ended shape was first cut from ⅜in (10mm) MDF to make a pair of formers, which could be joined together with two bolts. A piece of steel sheet was then cut to the same shape but 6mm (¼in) larger all round and bolted between the MDF formers and held in a vice. This allowed the exposed edge of steel to be gently tapped over, being careful not to hit the metal too hard as this could have stretched it and caused wrinkles. The resulting right angled flange all around the perimeter of the plate stiffened it and provided a good clamping point for the skins during manufacture. The procedure was repeated to create the remaining five end plates and four baffle plates.

All the boxes were to be 320mm (12½in) in length. The circumference of the end plates was measured and, as the skins were to be made in halves, the measurement was divided by two to give the size of the top and bottom skins. A small amount was added to form a flange, which would allow the two halves of skin to be welded together along their length. Each steel sheet for the skins was bent around the main upright of a pillar drill, which gave just the right amount of curvature to fit the end plates, after which the full-length flanges were formed by clamping each skin in a vice between two steel angles and tapping over.

Inlet and outlet holes were cut in two end plates, which were welded to the lower skin of the expansion/balance box, and a 'T'-shaped baffle introduced, incorporating two large holes to allow the exhaust gases to mix. The skeletal box was propped in position across the top of the differential housing to install inlet piping from the exhaust manifolds. This was made from curved sections of the donor car exhaust cut and welded to fit.

The rearmost silencer end plates each received three square tail pipes, and the front ones a single round inlet pipe. These plates were added to two lower skin halves to form the

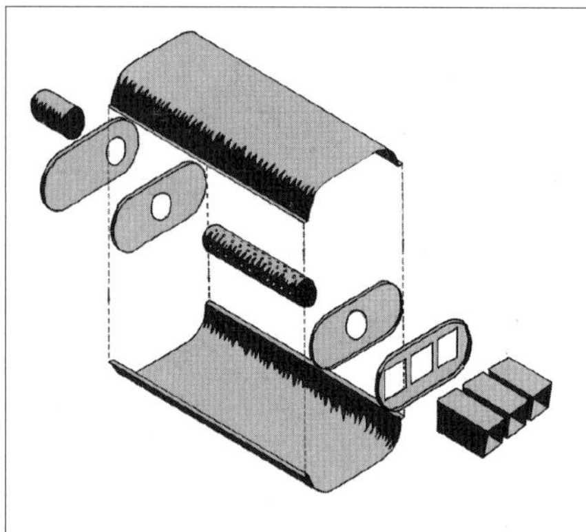

An exploded drawing of a silencer showing its component parts.

The left-hand silencer box being made. The perforated pipe has yet to receive a wrapping of fibreglass cloth, after which the top skin will be welded on.

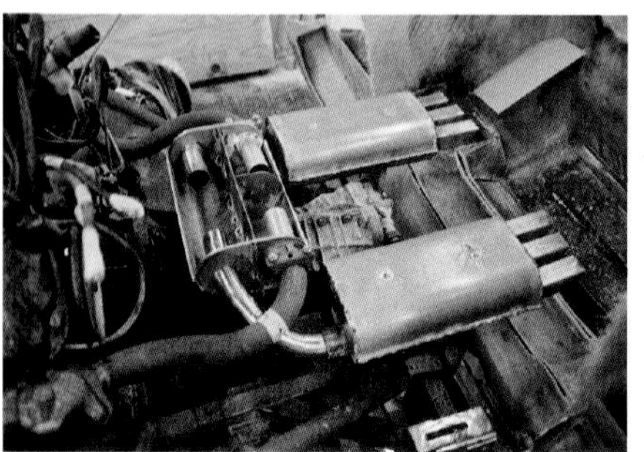

Trial fitting the exhaust. The top of the centre box has yet to be fitted.

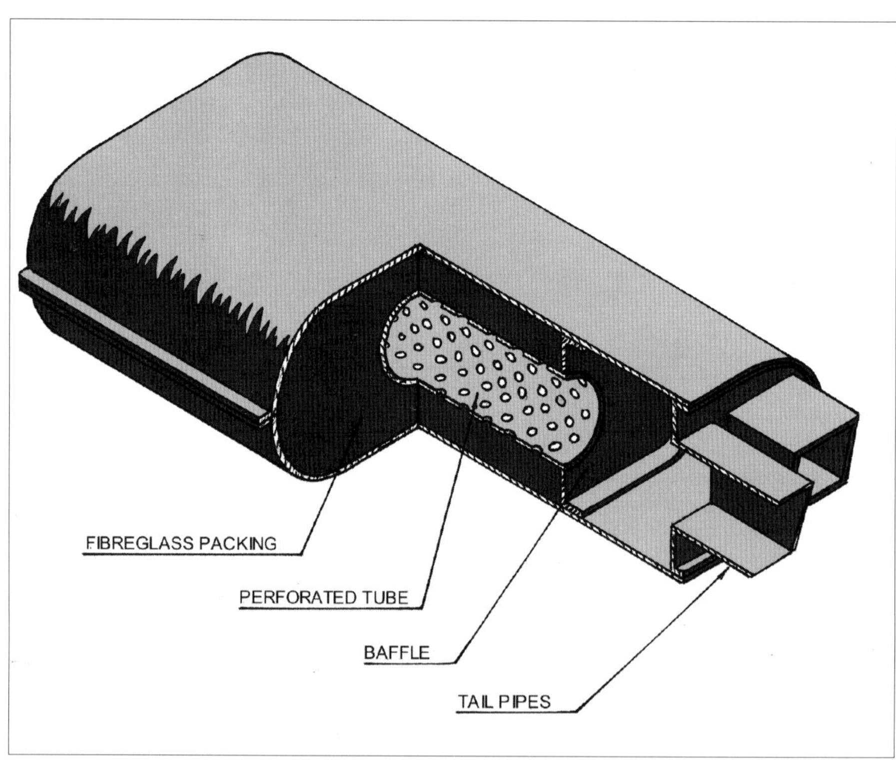

A cutaway of the exhaust silencer showing the perforated pipe surrounded by fibreglass packing.

basis for the silencers. The four baffle plates formed to fit inside the silencers supported perforated tubes between them that had been liberated from the donor exhaust system. Before the top skin was welded on, fibreglass cloth was wound around the perforated tubes and held in place with stainless steel locking wire. Around this CSM fibreglass was packed to fill the remaining gaps and the top skin welded on, the baffles plug welded to hold them steady.

The silencers were propped in position each side of the gearbox to allow the fabrication of connecting pipes to the expansion/balance box; again, made from sections of the Renault donor car exhaust.

4.3. Tail pipes

The final tail pipe layout just sort of evolved; there was no initial intention of being so outrageous. To support the exhaust system, the rear of each silencer was linked by a steel angle, which bolted to a bonded rubber mount fixed to an upright on the back of the chassis.

With the new exhaust installed, the six square tail pipes looked lost in the large slot cut in the rear panel, so four dummy tail pipes were welded between the six real pipes on the steel angle support to form a row of ten. This still looked a little inadequate so the decision was taken to go completely

Six tail pipes look a bit lost in that large exit slot.

Four dummy pipes are added, but it still doesn't look right.

That's better. The entire top row is fake.

over the top and a further row of ten dummy tail pipes was created and fitted above the original ten, which filled the aperture to perfection. It has since amused many children at car shows who, after counting, have excitedly shouted things like "Wow! Dad it's got twenty exhaust pipes!"

To finish off all of the pipes were ground back flush to the bodywork to follow its curved profile and get rid of any projections that might cause a problem at the SVA test.

The exhaust system was stripped and grit blasted before receiving a coat of silver high temperature exhaust paint. Because the exhaust occupied the same environment as the engine, there was a risk of trapped heat causing problems, not least to the spare wheel directly above. To try and counter this, each exhaust box was wrapped in an insulating blanket of aluminium foil faced fibreglass cloth.

The finished tail pipe setup, with all the tubes ground back to follow the profile of the rear body.

5. SOLUTIONS

Every car build is different and throws up many problems, which can be resolved in various ways. It always pays to think outside the box when confronted with tricky situations, and this section details some ideas used on the Mirov project. Hopefully, they will be of use, directly or indirectly through inspiration, to help you arrive at a tailor-made answer to your own particular predicament.

5.1. Pipe clamps

It is common sense – and a requirement of the SVA test – that all brake and fuel pipes are securely fixed at regular

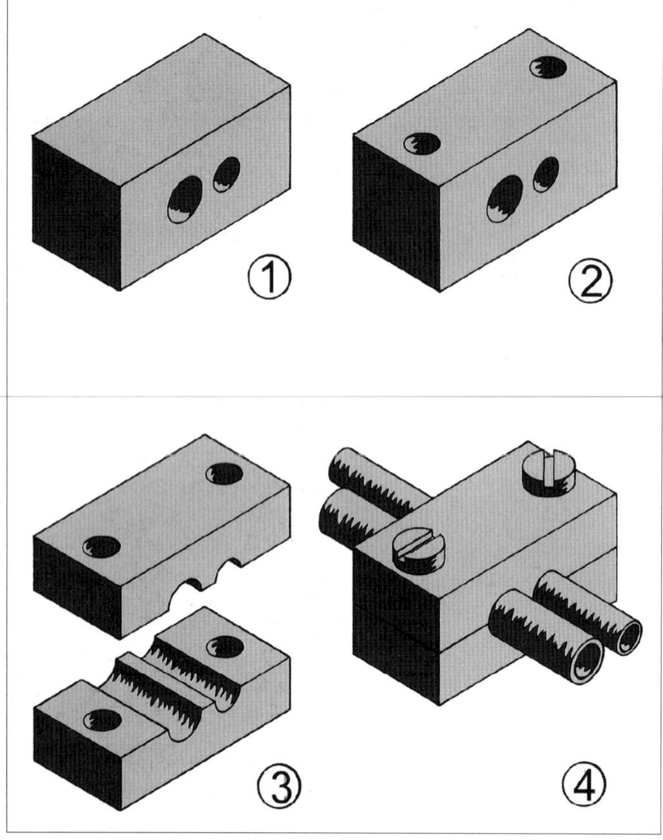

How to make a split clamp. Firstly, drill holes in your block of metal, nylon, or similar (1). Then drill holes for fixing screws at right angles (2). Cut the block in half (3), and, finally, clamp your pipes (4).

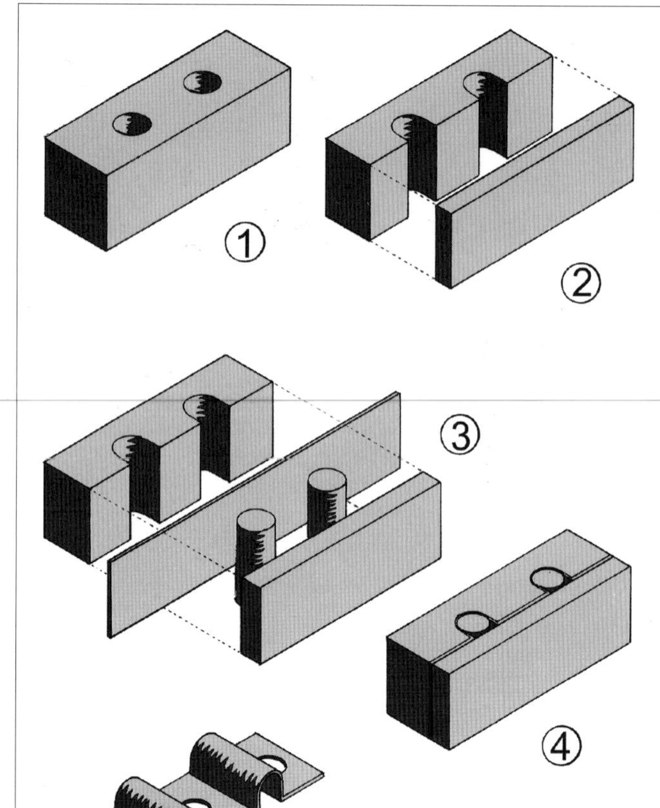

How to make a pressed metal clamp. First, drill a block of wood, MDF, nylon, or similar (1). Cut off the side and file out the holes to the edge (2). Insert a strip of steel or aluminium, and short sections of metal rod or bolt shanks (3). Then grip the assembly in a vice (4) and squash the metal into the slots to form a clamp (5).

intervals. If they are all neatly routed, this adds to the quality appearance of the finished enterprise. 'P' clips or tie wraps can be used, but, if more than one pipe needs retaining, tailor-made clamps are a neater answer.

(a) Split clamp

This type of clamp is very easy to make. A 20mm (¾in) square block of suitable material such as aluminium, nylon or Tufnol is first cut to the required length and drilled with holes for the pipes along its centre line. Turn the block 90° and drill holes for fixing bolts, then cut along the centre line to end up with identical halves, which will hold the pipes firmly in place when clamped together. If required, the holes for the pipes can be drilled a little oversize to allow for rubber or plastic lining.

(b) Pressed clamp

This is a bit more involved to manufacture because tooling must be made for each size of pipe to be clamped. Drill a 20mm (¾in) square block of metal or Tufnol with holes slightly larger than the pipes, then cut the block, not through the centre of the holes as for the split clamp, but so the cut just touches the edge of them. File the holes to the edge to form 'U'-shaped notches. Cut a 20mm (¾in) strip of aluminium or steel and position it across the notches, then use a vice to push the metal into the notches with suitably sized bolts or bits of metal rod to form the clamp. Again, the clamp can be lined with rubber or insulation tape if required.

5.2. Wheel centre caps

Amateur car builders, as a breed, tend to be very innovative, and good at lateral thinking to come up with solutions to the various problems encountered. I once used a pair of cut down plastic cutlery trays as air intakes on a Cox GTM, and a pair of Scotchbrite pads sprayed satin black

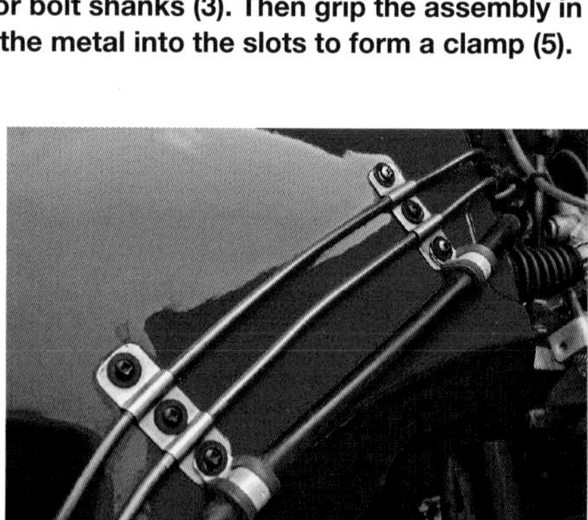

Pressed stainless steel clamps securing the brake pipes. They are lined with insulating tape.

Some solutions are not always obvious ...

... such as this pudding basin used as a wheel centre cap.

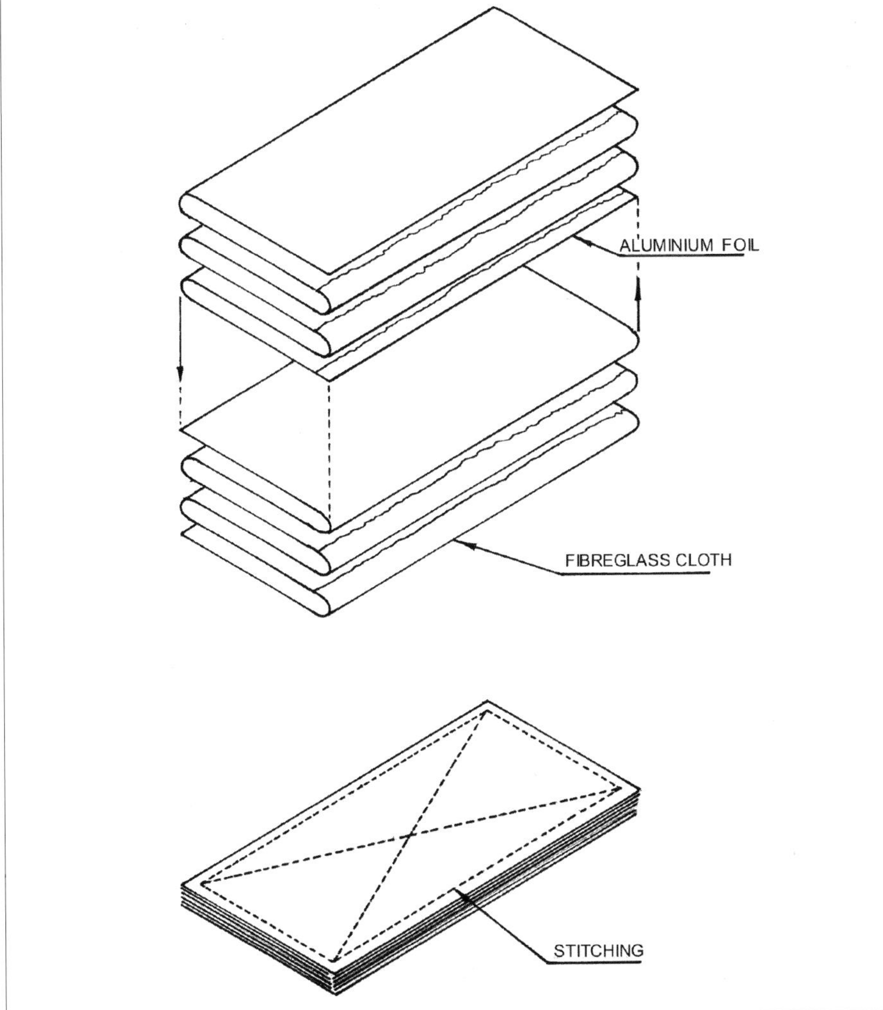

Heavy duty aluminium foil and fibreglass cloth folded over and over, then sewn together, make an ideal heat reflective blanket.

as speaker grilles on an Austin Mini Moke! Although the latter solution *looked* great, it was a complete waste of time because the radio was inaudible above the road noise and the 'A' series engine! The Mirov project turned out to be no different with regard to the use of kitchen utensils ...

The wheels that came with the Mirov were retained to keep as much of the original look of the car as possible. They are of the three-piece, split rim type made by Compomotive, and the five-spoke centres had been painted to match the car. Unfortunately, two of them had missing centre caps, and, because of the old, 1980s wheel design, much trouble was experienced trying to locate new ones of the correct size. The answer came from an unexpected source when my mother suggested that the wheel caps looked like some small aluminium pudding basins she had bought from a local kitchen shop! A quick measure confirmed she was right and four basins were bought (two as spares). After some slight modification, and the application of genuine Soviet red star army badges, they proved ideal and really look the part. Nobody ever guesses their true origin and when the secret is revealed it always raises a smile. So, when stuck for a particular part or solution, remember; the answer might just be in those kitchen cupboards!

5.3. Heat blanket

Commercially available protective heat blanket can be quite expensive, especially if only a small amount is required. This was the case with the Mirov engine compartment when it was realised that the wiring loom passed within 150mm (6in) of the left-hand exhaust manifold. A section of heat reflective blanket measuring about 300 (12in) x 150mm (6in) was all that was needed to wrap around the loom and rectify the situation, so a suitable blanket was made from fibreglass cloth (woven rovings) and heavy duty aluminium foil.

A large piece of foil was folded over and over to give several layers of the required size. The same was done with a piece of fibreglass cloth, folding it over until it was the same size as the foil. Using an industrial sewing machine, the two were sewn together with strong thread around the edge and diagonally across the middle. This produced a cheap and effective heat reflective blanket, which was tie-wrapped over the loom with the foil side outward.

The beauty of this technique is that any shape or size can be tailor-made to suit almost any situation. The only thing to remember is that blanket of this construction should only be used to reflect heat because of the thread not being flame-resistant. If used directly on an exhaust system to keep the heat in, the thread should be omitted and replaced by thin steel wire ties.

The heater circuit bleed points were positioned as high as possible.

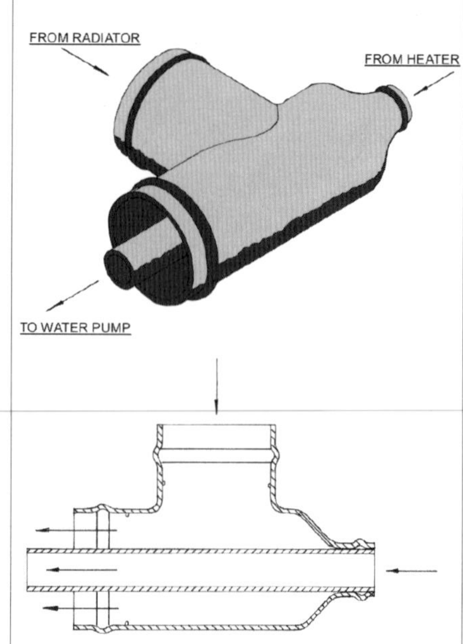

The internal stops were removed from the 13mm (½in) inlet of the 'T' adapter to allow the heater return pipe to exit close to the water pump impeller.

5.4. Bleed points

Previous experience with a mid-engined set-up showed that trapped air in the cooling system can be a problem. The Mirov radiator was fitted in the engine compartment so the original bleed points on the engine dealt with any air in the system, but that still left the heater pipes, which run forward through the tunnel to the dashboard. Dedicated bleed points were installed, made from domestic central heating fittings comprising a screw cap bleed fitting, a 'T'-piece, and two 13mm (½in) soldered in-line connectors.

Domestic plumbing copper fittings make ideal hose connectors and adapters. The pre-soldered type come with a convenient swage around the end.

5.5. Water hose connectors

As well as domestic plumbing bleed points, a number of other fittings can be used. In-line connectors are ideal for joining rubber hoses of all diameters, and 'T' pieces are available in a range of sizes. The pre-soldered variety has a ready-made swage around the end of each fitting, which provides good anchorage for the rubber hoses.

At the back of the Renault V6 engine was some small diameter steel pipework that fed the heater matrix; because the engine was now mid-mounted, this had to be completely remade. This was achieved with 13mm (½in) copper tubing and various 'T' pieces, and in-line connectors.

An electric water pump was fitted to the bottom hose of the water system for maximum cooling efficiency. Part of the fitting procedure involved removal of the mechanical pump impeller for improved flow, which had the unforeseen effect of rendering the heater inoperative, because the return pipe from the heater terminated at the mechanical water pump right in the centre of where the impeller once was, and, by

Here is the 35mm 'T' piece adapter fitted to the water pump inlet to restore circulation in the heater circuit.

removing the impeller, it had effectively stopped the flow of water through the heater circuit.

The solution was to fit a copper 'T piece adapter to the electric pump inlet. The adapter was of the pre-soldered type, to make use of the swages to hold the hoses, and had two 35mm (1⅜in) diameter ends at right angles to each other, the third one 13mm (½in) for the heater hose. Just inside each opening is a pre-formed stop to ensure the copper tubes are not inserted too far into the 'T' piece. The stop inside the 13mm (½in) joint was filed out to allow a copper tube to be pushed right through to finish just proud of the opposite 35mm (1 ⅜in) outlet. This end was then fitted to the pump inlet with a short length of hose so that the 13mm (½in) pipe was as close to the impeller as possible. The other end of the 13mm (½in) pipe was connected to the re-routed heater outlet and the 35mm (1⅜in) inlet to the bottom hose of the radiator. The result is that engine cooling is just as effective as before with the added bonus of a working heater.

5.6. Steering rack extensions

When building kit cars and specials one requirement that regularly crops up is the extension of steering rack track rods to achieve correct suspension geometry and avoid bump steer. The most common solution involves the use of screw-on adapters, which is sound engineering provided everything is well made and fitted correctly. However, if a cleaner look is preferred, or clearance is a problem, a different approach is required.

The Mirov uses the chassis from a UVA M6 GTR kit car, which employs a Mini Metro steering rack fitted with track rod extensions. I had a Metro steering rack but no extensions. I also happened to have a Mk3 Ford Cortina steering rack that had longer track rods; upon removing the rubber gaiters from both racks, I saw that the inboard fitting was identical. So it was a simple matter to swap the Metro track rods for the Cortina ones to achieve the correct rack width and install a pair of Ford Sierra track rod ends to finish the installation.

5.7. Brake & clutch pedal mechanisms

Trying to fit the necessary components into an existing body shell is a much harder exercise than making a body around a fully equipped rolling chassis. Space limitations always contrive to make life difficult, and this was the case with the clutch and brake pedal mechanisms. The solution was to pinch an idea already used widely by the world's car producers to convert many left-hand drive designs to right-hand drive; namely, the use of bellcranks.

Most front-wheel drive cars have the transverse engine fitted slightly to the right of centre, with the gearbox to the left, which leaves ample space to mount the brake servo unit above the latter. When converting to right-hand drive, the servo remains in place and the drive from the pedal is transmitted across the bulkhead by a torque tube, or bellcranks and pull/push rods.

With the Mirov clutch master cylinder mounted directly to the front of the pedal box, there was no room to mount the fluid reservoir above without it poking out of the front panel. A bellcrank was manufactured from

The longer Cortina track rod and Sierra track rod end makes for a neat solution to the extension of the Metro rack.

The clutch bellcrank drops the pedal motion 150mm (6in) and turns it through 90°. M12 bolts provide a trunnion pivot at top and bottom.

The brake bellcrank transmits drive to the side-mounted servo unit in the right-hand wing. The rod ends are secured to the shafts with lock nuts.

welded 1.6mm (16swg) steel to drop the pedal motion by about 150mm (6in) and rotate the drive through 90° to the newly-mounted master cylinder.

The brake pedal motion was transferred backward by a pull rod, and turned through 90° with a bellcrank fitted under the dashboard. From this, a pushrod operated the servo unit mounted on the bulkhead to the right of the windscreen. Both bellcranks had M12 nuts welded to them with bolts passing through that attached to the surrounding structure to act as trunnion pivot points. The operating rods with adjustable spherical bearing ends were all equipped with lock nuts to prevent anything working loose.

The servo unit in the RH wing sits at right angles to the pedal box.

5.8. Electronic speedometer sensor

Another common problem with amateur build vehicles with the advent of the SVA test is speedometer accuracy. If wheel or tyre size is changed with a cable driven speedo, there is a risk of calibration problems. One easy solution is to fit an electronic speedo with a remote sensor which has to be fitted near a driveshaft in order to pick up pulses from magnets attached to the shaft. Attaching the magnets to the shaft can be a problem.

The Mirov has four magnets securely fitted to the left-hand driveshaft joint with a custom-made clamp system. It was made by cutting a 25mm (1in) wide strip of thin steel from the side of an old oil can the length of the circumference of the driveshaft joint. A small press tool was fashioned from a piece of metal the same thickness as the magnets, and a square slightly larger was notched out of the side. A small square of metal identical to a magnet was cut and used to form four equally spaced recesses in the side of the thin steel strip.

The formed strip was then used to trap the magnets around the driveshaft and the whole assembly was retained by 22swg stainless steel locking wire.

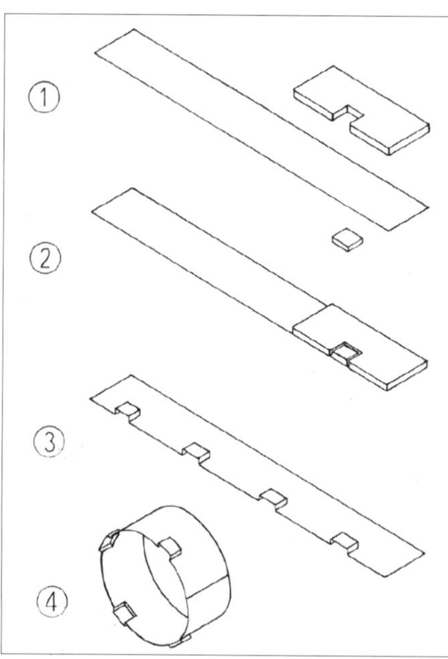

1) A thin strip of steel is cut from an old oil can. 2) Aluminium formers are made. 3) The formers are used to press square housings into the strip. 4) The strip is curved to fit around the driveshaft joint.

Sensor magnets are held securely to the LH driveshaft joint with stainless steel locking wire around the collar.

Chapter 7
Interior

Designing and trimming the interior of a car is an important part of a build because it is the point at which everything comes together to make or break a project, so is worth getting right. At kit car shows I have lost count of the beautiful home built cars I've seen which are let down by a poor interior. This chapter describes how a quality interior can be achieved with minimal skill using basic materials such as wood and metal, finished off with a simple leather covering.

To describe my woodworking skills as marginal would be an overstatement. I once ambitiously embarked on the manufacture of a Hi-Fi cabinet, but had a spot of trouble with the doors; by the time I had finished cobbling the corner joints each door was 6mm (¼in) too narrow. Don't worry if you have little or no woodwork experience as it didn't stop me. Although the Mirov dashboard is mainly wood, the only part of its construction which can be even remotely termed 'cabinet making' is the small glovebox drawer, but even this does not involve any fancy dovetail joints. Modular construction was used for the dashboard and centre console to ease manufacture and trimming, with the added bonus that it would allow good access for future maintenance.

A professional-looking interior need not be hard to achieve.

The Mirov had a completely empty interior; a large blank canvas, upon which everything had to be made from scratch, including the seats. When finished, it was fully carpeted and featured a centre console and wraparound dashboard, all trimmed in a combination of red and black leather and grey suede. The trim was inexpensive to make, as the leather was

The transverse steel box section provided the main support for dashboard construction. Note the rather large heater unit dominating the central space.

bought from car boot sales for less than £30, and all the metal used was scrap offcuts. The contact adhesive was the single most expensive item at £60 (for enough to do the whole interior). Polished aluminium detailing added extra interest, and included a custom-made, illuminated gear knob; a bit over the top, perhaps, but fun to do!

Choosing to use a large heater unit ultimately compromised the final dashboard design, but the end result still belies its basic homemade construction. It is a composite of plywood and aluminium, formed into simple shapes to permit easy covering, and screwed together to produce a complex-looking whole. Even the polished aluminium trim strips were dead easy to incorporate and look fantastic.

1. DASHBOARD

The space in which to accommodate the dashboard was very deep – measuring some 535mm (21in) – due to the pronounced curvature of the windscreen, but was only 1220mm (48in) wide, which did not leave much room for creativity. The components in place before construction began included a vast heater unit and water pipes in the centre, along with the blower motor on the left, and the pedal box, brake bellcrank, steering column, and instrument pod on the right all supported by a transverse steel box section running the full width of the interior. Along the front of the box

An alternative method of forming curved metal channel sections using a pair of wooden formers (1). Securely hold the metal sheet between the formers by clamping in a vice (2). Gently tap over the exposed metal (3) ...

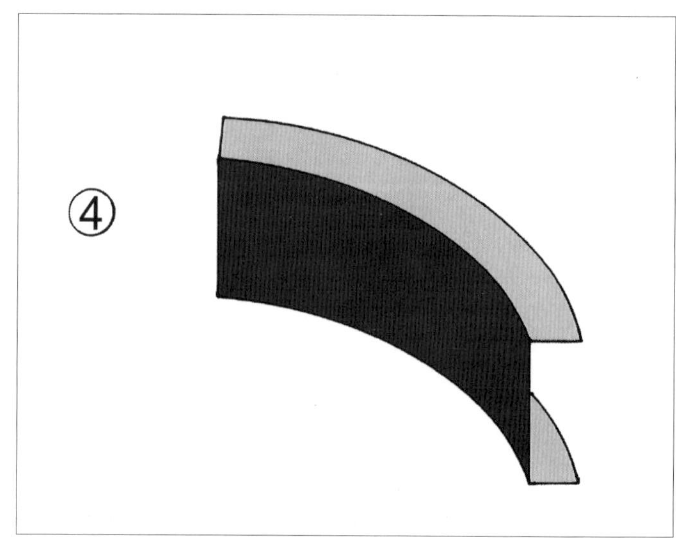

... to obtain a curved channel section (4).

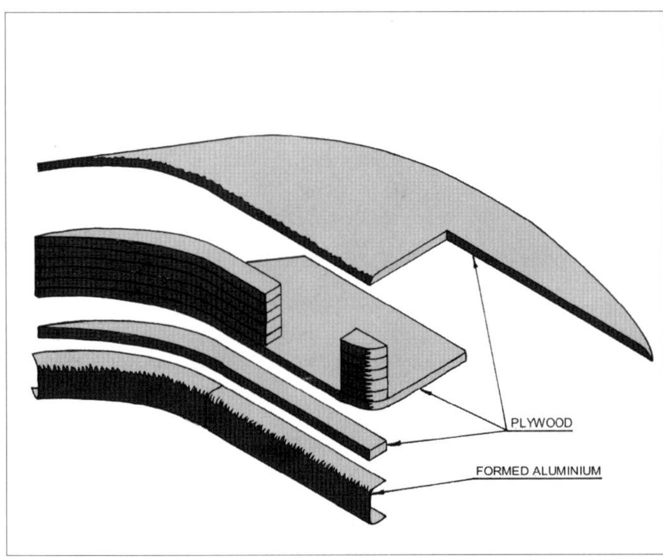

This diagram illustrates the simple laminated plywood construction technique used for the main body of the dashboard.

The main part of the dashboard takes shape. The shallow recess to the left of the CD player was cut to house an aluminium 'Mirov II' badge to ensure it sat flush and conformed to SVA test interior projection requirements.

section were mounted all of the relays incorporated when wiring the car, and on top of the heater unit sat the specially fabricated fibreglass air box for windscreen demisting. All of these parts had a hand in influencing the final dashboard design, and formed the bare bones from which to start.

1.1. Construction

The method of dashboard and centre console construction is best described as very basic indeed; simply a stack of 10mm (⅜in) plywood sections laid horizontally or vertically, glued together and then carved to shape with an angle grinder and sanding disc – very messy but effective, and the easiest way to obtain the necessary shapes.

The wraparound style of the dashboard was roughly sketched out on paper to get an idea of the layout. To start with, aluminium sheet was cut and folded into three 'U' channels large enough to cover the relays fitted on the front of the transverse steel support. The left- and right-hand channels were formed with a stretcher into a curved shape. If a shrinker/stretcher machine is not available to you, a similar result can be achieved by beating the aluminium or steel around shaped wooden formers.

The first layer of 10mm (⅜in) plywood was cut to form the base of the main body of the dashboard, following the curve of the left-hand aluminium channel to achieve a wraparound appearance, and fixed to the top of the transverse steel box section with large, self-tapping screws equipped with spacers. From this the shape of the next section was determined, and the process repeated, each subsequent plywood sheet a slightly different shape and screwed to the previous one. Eight layers made up the main body of the dashboard with a further six making up the shroud over the instruments.

The resultant embryonic dashboard had square edges and stepped features that formed a contour map of the overall shape. The layers were removed from the car and reassembled on the bench to permit sanding and shaping with the metalworker's favourite woodworking tool; an angle grinder fitted with a sanding disc. The desired shape was achieved by sanding off the stepped portions with constant reference to the layers in the plywood to keep everything straight and smooth. To ensure a snug fit some panels – such as the dash top and instrument cowl sections – were shaped on the inside as well. Any low spots were filled with polyester body filler and finished by hand, after which, everything was reassembled in the car to check for a good fit.

Most of the screws holding together the layers were fitted vertically from the top to ease assembly, but

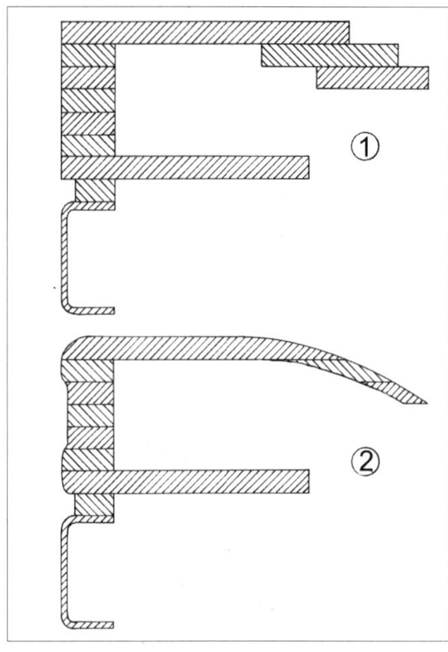

Two cross-sections through the dashboard showing its basic construction before and after sanding and shaping.

care had to be taken to ensure that the screws would still be accessible when the windscreen was eventually fitted. The centre few layers were glued together to form a single unit, and, between this and the single layer that formed the dashboard top, a thin aluminium trim strip with a polished edge was incorporated. Remember to allow for the thickness of the intended

The aluminium-fronted plywood glovebox that slides in and out; small but practical.

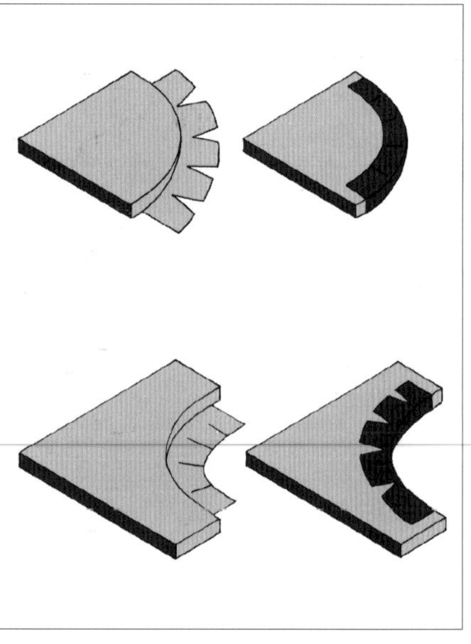

When trimming an external curve it helps to cut small 'V' notches to lose the excess material, and when tackling internal edges cut slits that will open out and help stretch the material.

trim material between the component parts of the dashboard. I didn't and this caused a few minor headaches when trying to line up everything on final assembly.

A basic high-sided tray of plywood was constructed to form the glovebox, and fitted with a curved aluminium front. A finger slot was cut in the base to allow it to be opened easily, covered on the inside by a piece of carpet trim. The entire assembly slides on basic folded aluminium runners fixed to the underside of the dashboard, and is held shut by a magnetic catch.

1.2. Trimming

Because all of the various parts had been kept relatively small and simple in shape, they were not difficult to trim. Each component of the interior was covered similarly with leather secured with contact adhesive or staples. The trick was to keep the covering taut as it was being applied to prevent wrinkles. Some items, such as the aluminium channels, received a thin sponge rubber covering before the leather to give a slightly padded appearance.

Each component was laid onto the reverse side of the leather and drawn around with a ballpoint pen, allowing enough margin for fixing to the back or sides. A combination of scissors and a sharp knife was used to cut out each piece.

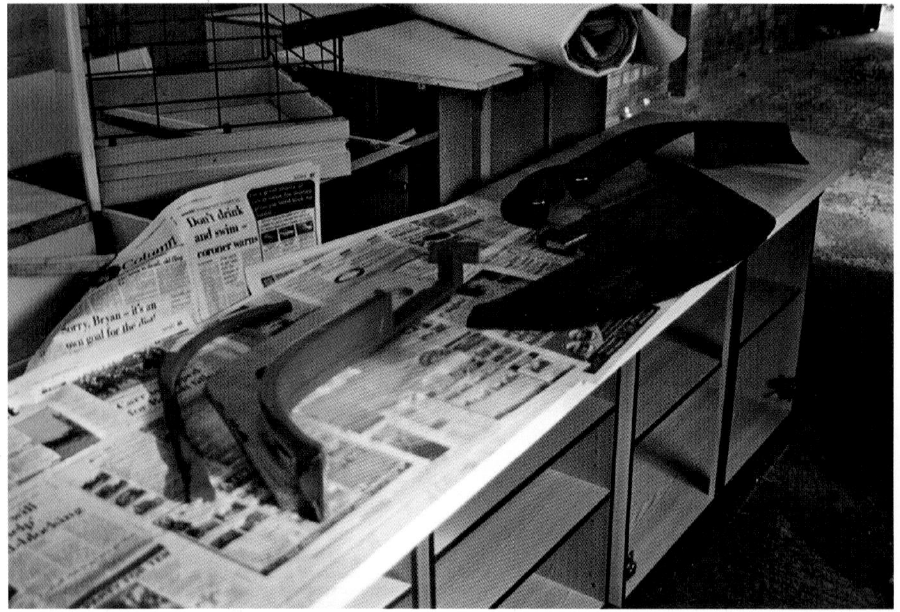

Modular construction made the application of leather trim a fairly simple affair.

The leather was pulled around and fastened at the back or sides of the various sections, and, to assist with this, slits were cut in the glued edges when internal curves were trimmed to help the leather stretch; to help it to shrink when external curves were tackled, small 'V' shapes were cut out of the edges, doing away with the excess material without having to form pleats.

The natural stretch of the suede came to the rescue when covering the instrument shroud, almost all of it being covered in one operation. The underside near the instruments

Assembling the leather-covered sections. The instrument binnacle was recycled from the Renault donor.

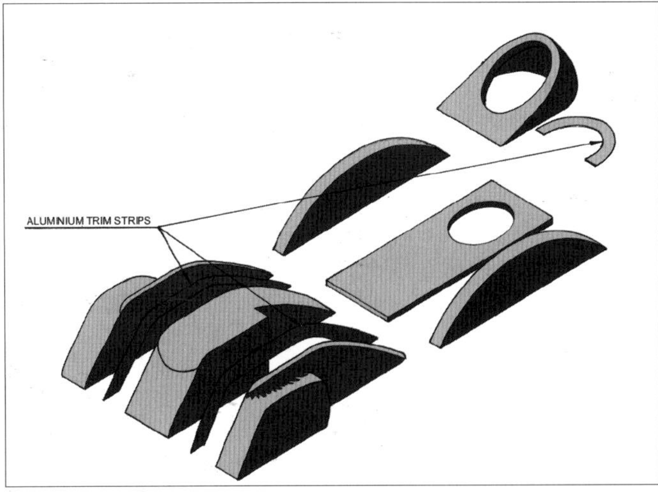

The wood and aluminium component parts of the centre console.

themselves had to have separate small sections added to fill some unavoidable gaps, but these are almost undetectable and do not spoil the final finish.

The top panel of the dashboard had been created with a small bulge in the middle to clear the heater system bleed points. Again, the stretchy grey suede greatly assisted the operation and avoided unsightly wrinkles.

To make the leather hug the contours of the 'Mirov' badge recess on the front panel, a hardboard former was cut to fit exactly and used to clamp the leather into the rebate, after which the edges of the leather were glued around the rest of the panel. It was left overnight until the glue had gone off completely, and when the former was removed the leather stayed closely tailored to the recess contours, which gave the panel a moulded look.

2. CENTRE CONSOLE

The centre tunnel had been kept as low as possible, which meant there was enough elbow clearance to fit some form of centre console, complete with arm rest to cover the handbrake, and allowing access to the seatbelt stalks on each side. A curvy design seemed appropriate, but not too long because the forward part of the tunnel in front of the gear lever had been cut away to make room for a clutch foot rest, and was only 88mm (3½in) high, so that part would require only a covering of carpet.

2.1. Construction

The method of console construction was very similar to that used for the dashboard, except that part of the arm rest over the handbrake was laminated vertically instead of horizontally. All of the plywood was glued together to form a single block which was sculpted to shape with an angle grinder and hand finished with a file and sandpaper. The handbrake emerged from the right-hand side of the front of the block, which sloped back and blended into a short horizontal section, before dropping back down to the tunnel to allow access to the engine cover release lever in the middle of the bulkhead. The seat belt stalks were housed in a recess in each side of the armrest, and held steady with aluminium straps screwed to the tunnel. Once the arm rest was finalised it was cut vertically into three pieces for easy trimming. Screws inserted horizontally from each side held the three vertical sections together,

The simple construction of the centre console can be clearly seen in this picture. The rear section has yet to be cut vertically into three parts.

complete with polished aluminium trim between each section.

Running forward from the arm rest, a separate section was added with a flat plywood base, which extended around the gear lever. Straight sides fashioned from wood with a curved top edge were added to the base to form a sort of tray area where the handbrake lever would live when in the off position, and around the base of the gear lever a wedge-shaped surround was fashioned from horizontally laminated plywood, which provided a fixing point for a polished aluminium gaiter ring.

2.1. Trimming

The centre console was made in seven separate sections screwed together, which allowed for easy covering. Each of the three middle pieces was covered with red leather in a similar manner to the dashboard components, the four outer parts covered with stretchy grey suede. The two outer arm rest blocks sandwiched the red leather centre section separated by polished aluminium trim strips, and were held together with screws inserted horizontally from each side.

3. DOOR PANELS

As mentioned in chapter 5 the door trim panels had already been made in advance by taking a fibreglass moulding off the inner door skins because the shape would have been impossible to replicate from a flat sheet of plywood or hardboard. The six fixing screws were positioned on the front, rear and bottom of each panel so that they would not be visible from inside the car.

The interior door handles, lock plungers, and electric window switches were grouped on the forward lower corners of each door; to permit the door panels to be removed without disturbing these, the corresponding part of each panel was cut out. With the handles and switches removed, some thin, self-adhesive foam rubber was stuck directly to each inner door skin, followed by a covering of red leather fixed with contact adhesive.

The rest of the panel was covered with the same thin foam rubber and two sections of leather – one red and the other black – separated by a piece of grey suede piping.

Large external corners, such as those on the bottom of the door panels, can be tricky to cover with material that has limited stretch, like leather. A good way to tackle these is to first glue the main flat part of leather, and then make one diagonal slit in the corner. Fold down the sides and glue into place, overlapping the excess at the corner. Then, using a sharp knife, cut through both layers of leather along the corner

On the left is the armrest section of the centre console after being cut into three to permit covering with red leather and grey suede. The edges of the polished aluminium trim strips are just visible between them. On the right is the handbrake gaiter, which was eventually replaced with a simple rubber seal.

The forward part of the centre console showing the gear lever gaiter ring and the polished trim strip below it.

The finished centre console in place. Note the cut-out for the seat belt stalk.

The inside of the RH fibreglass door trim panel showing how the leather is cut to assist in the covering operation.

Taking a mould of the inner door produced contoured trim panels that effectively hide the fixing screws from view. They are positioned on the front, rear, and bottom of the door.

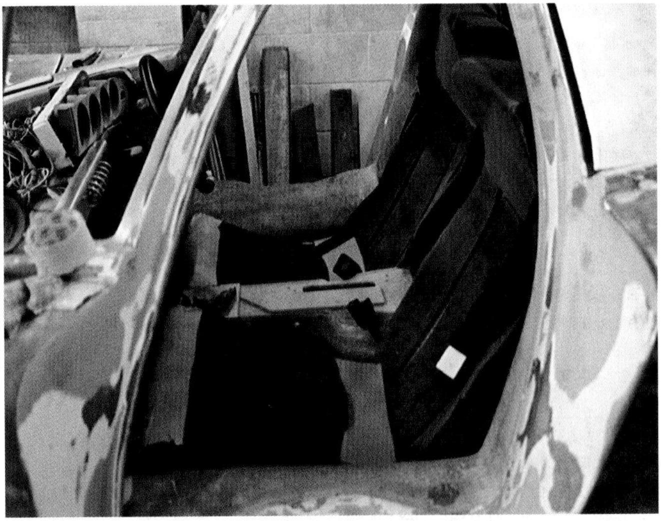

Mocking up the seats with boards and foam rubber to get an idea of size, position, and construction.

to the edge of the panel. Remove the excess piece of leather and gently peel back the covering to reveal the other cut piece and remove. Then, using more glue if required, replace the flaps, which will be an exact fit with each other. The join should be so tight that, to the casual observer, it will be almost invisible.

4. SEATS

Seats should really be very straightforward: choose a pair, buy them, and fit them. Unfortunately, mine had to be designed and built from scratch because the restrictive cockpit dimensions negated fitment of anything else. Experimentation with old foam rubber cushions from aircraft seats and bits of board revealed that I would have to be sitting on the floor with my back almost resting on the rear bulkhead to be comfortable. This actually made the process a lot easier because it meant a self-supporting structure was not necessary. All that was required was a collection of shaped cushions fitted to the rear bulkhead and floor, which, when viewed as a whole, would look like seats.

4.1.Construction

There were two things to bear in mind before beginning: the inertia reels of the seat belts were mounted at shoulder height on the rear bulkhead, so would best be hidden within the structure of the seat back; two fire extinguishers had to be stowed under the front of the seats if possible.

Using the information acquired from sitting in the car and propping up bits of wood and foam cushion on the rear bulkhead, positioning of the backrest was ascertained. It was made from two pieces of 10mm (3/8in) plywood hinged horizontally in the middle, and fixed to the floor of the car with another pair of hinges, all of which had removable sliding pins for easy disassembly. The backrest was screwed to blocks of wood bonded to the bulkhead with resin paste, which allowed for future adjustment, if necessary, via the addition of spacers on the screws.

The upper outboard corner of the backrest was cut away to provide clearance for the seat belt reel and the corner was replaced with an aluminium plate, which had a guide slot, lined with nylon grommet material to prevent chafing, for the belt webbing.

Another pair of hinges with removable pins were bolted to the floor to secure the rear of a plywood thigh support. A block of wood screwed to the bottom of this propped it up at the required height, creating storage space for the fire extinguishers under the front of each seat.

With the plywood sections in place, the basic structure for each seat was complete. A simple design for the cushion arrangement was cut from cardboard, and, after checking the fit, each piece was replicated in plywood and screwed in place.

4.2. Trimming

Further experiments revealed that the seat would be acceptable if covered with 25mm (1in) thick foam rubber on the centre portions of plywood, with fat wedge sections for the side supports. Larger foam pieces were shaped and used for the head restraint and thigh support, which due to their depth and flat sides had to be covered with three pieces of leather, because a single piece could not be persuaded to take up such a shape. The three parts were sewn together on an industrial sewing machine.

Covering all the different cushion bases was simplicity itself. Firstly, the foam was cut to size and glued in place on a base section of plywood, after which a piece of leather cut larger than the base was laid face down on a clean bench. The foam was positioned centrally on the back of the leather with the plywood uppermost.

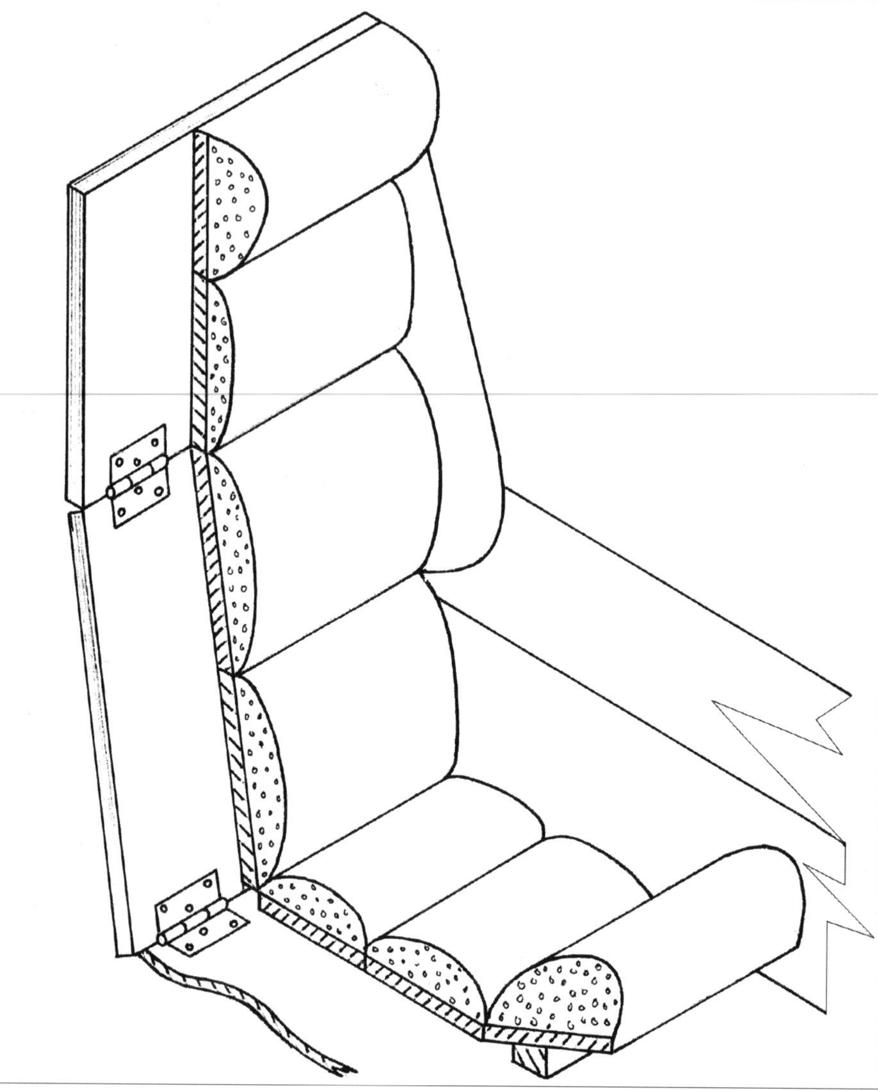

The basic seat construction is revealed in this sectional diagram. Hinged plywood boards are screwed to the floor to form the backrest. Separate plywood sections are simply trimmed with foam and leather, then fitted in position with a combination of screws and hook and loop Velcro fastenings.

The driver's seat takes shape. Note how the seat belt reel is housed within the seat back.

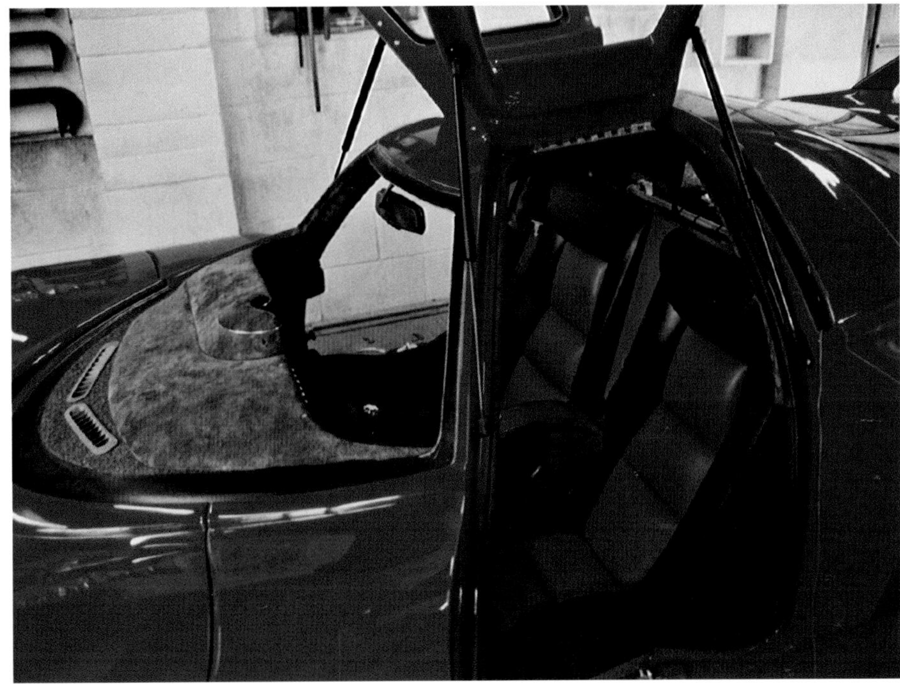

The matt finish of the grey suede is ideal for the dashboard top to eliminate glare and reflection.

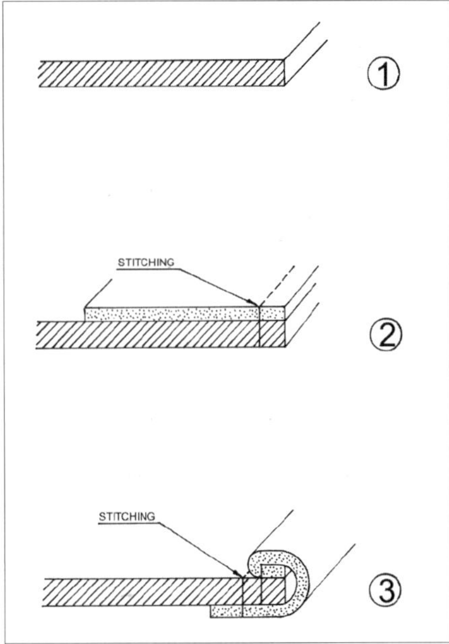

Carpet edges (1) can be bound with leather or vinyl by stitching close to the edge (2), then wrapping around and adding a second row of stitching, which is lost in the carpet pile for a neat finish (3).

The middle of one side of leather was pulled loosely round the back of the plywood and fastened in place with a staple gun. The middle of the opposite side was pulled round firmly and attached in a similar manner, and then the process was repeated for the middles of the other two sides. With the base now securely located, the rest of the leather was pulled round and fastened, always working first one side and then the other to prevent wrinkles. The corners were dealt with by either forming neat pleats or cutting off excess leather, depending on how thick it was.

The process was repeated for each section of seat using the same technique, the only complication being with covering the backrest side bolsters. The bases for these were made from three pieces of plywood that formed a large right angle, one side kinked to match the shape of the backrest.

With all of the cushions covered, it only remained to attach them to the backrest and floor. Because the backrest had been made removable, most of the cushions were attached from behind via short, self-tapping screws, except for the top two which were held in place with Velcro hook and loop fastenings to facilitate access to the backrest securing screws.

The side cushion of the base was secured to the floor with two small aluminium brackets, after which the rearmost base cushion was located with a similar pair of brackets also screwed to the floor. This left a gap for the front base cushion to be wedged in behind the thigh support, and held in place simply by being a very good fit.

The beauty of this method of trimming the seats is that, if any part is damaged, it will be simple to remove and recover it without having to trim the whole seat.

5. CARPETS

It is not hard to carpet a car, just time-consuming to get right. The thing to remember is to work with the material used and not try and force it to do something it does not want to. For instance, do not try and persuade car carpet to form a compound curve; it would really rather not. Limit your

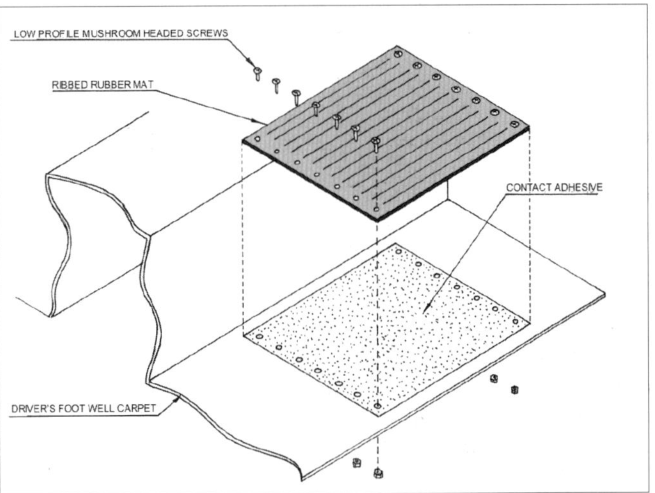

When a rubber heel mat is too thick to stitch in place, an alternative is to use contact adhesive. Shallow-headed bolts ensure the edges do not peel up and add visual interest.

ambitions to simple shapes, which, with care, can still produce pleasing results, and always use proper automotive carpet as it is easier to work with and looks better than the domestic variety.

5.1. Planning

Divide the area to be covered into manageable parts, and try to avoid creating sections that incorporate a number of folds or curves in different directions. The Mirov interior, despite being small, was divided into thirteen parts, six of which were curved surfaces. These were the sills and the front and rear of each door opening, with very tricky junctions formed by the intersection of curves where they met.

Rolls of old wallpaper were used to make accurate patterns of all the required pieces, and much effort was invested in fine tuning them to fit perfectly, which saved time when cutting and fitting the black carpet. Each section was labelled as left- or right-hand, along with its position in the car, some cut oversize to allow joins to overlap and avoid gaps.

Each pattern was placed on the back of a large square of automotive quality carpet and arranged to preclude wastage. After making sure that all of the patterns were the correct way up, they were drawn around with a black permanent marker pen, which showed up well on the grey backing, and then cut out using a sharp knife and a good pair of large scissors.

With all of the carpet cut the two floor sections and tunnel top were singled out to receive red leather edge trim, which would break up the expanse of black.

Several 50mm (2in) wide strips of leather were cut to fit each carpet edge, and attached using an industrial sewing machine. First of all a strip was sewn, right sides together, to the edge of the carpet with a 10mm (⅜in) seam. The free flap of leather was pulled around and secured to the back of the carpet by sewing through the pile close to the original seam. This was repeated for each edge.

To prevent wear of the driver's carpet, a rubber heel mat was added. A square of ribbed rubber proved too thick to attach by sewing so was glued in place with contact adhesive. The front and rear edges were prevented from lifting by securing them with shallow, dome-headed stainless steel nuts and bolts through the carpet.

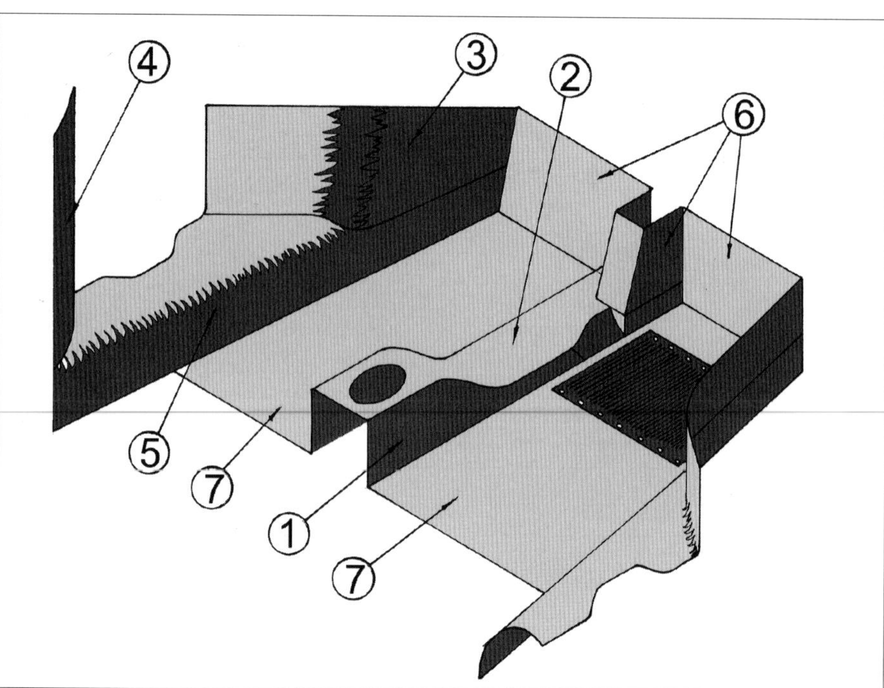

This diagram shows the order in which the interior carpet was fitted to get the overlaps right.

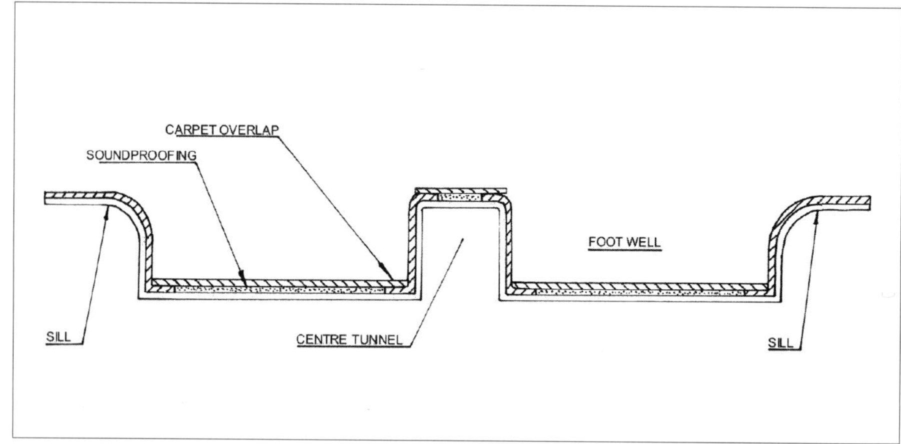

This cross-section through the cockpit area shows how the overlaps are arranged for a neat appearance.

5.2. Fitting

Contact adhesive was used to fix sound-proofing material to the front bulkhead and floors, and the order of carpet installation was dictated by the overlaps. With reference to the diagram at the top of the page, the sides of the front half of the centre tunnel (1) were the first to go in with a generous overlap onto the top of the tunnel, front bulkhead and floors, followed by the tunnel top (2). The sides of the foot wells followed (3), which overlapped onto the front bulkhead and sills. Next to go in were the panels to the rear of each door (4), which also overlapped onto the sills.

The sill carpets (5) came next, their lower edges overlapping onto the floors and front edges on the front bulkhead. The top of the forward half of the sill carpets exactly butted up to the lower edge of the footwell sections (3) to give an invisible join. This left just the two

Red leather edging highlights the plain black carpet.

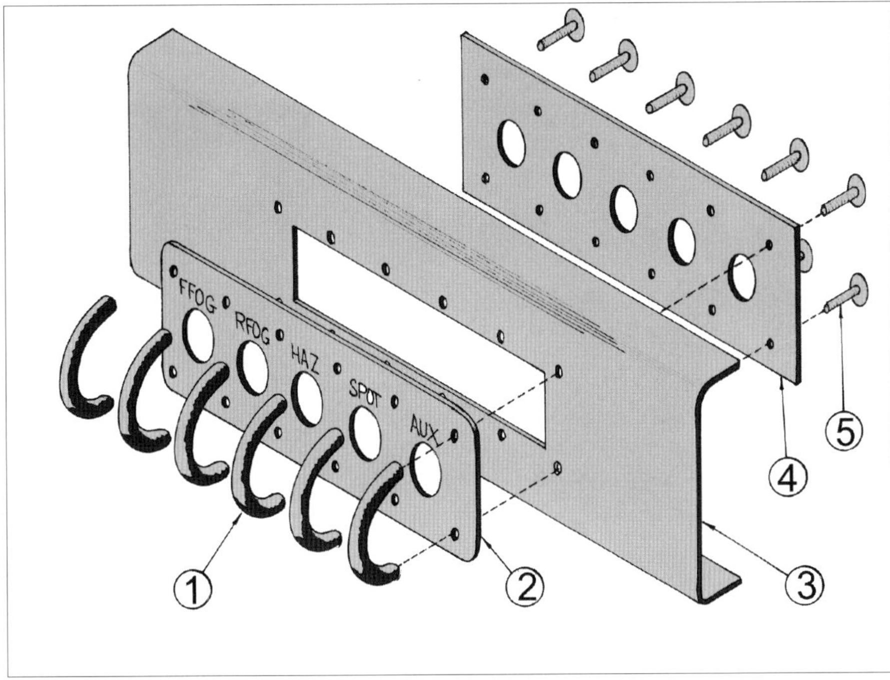

An exploded view of the illuminated switch panel showing the fabricated guard hoops (1), the face panel (2), the aluminium dashboard (3), the translucent green switch mounting panel (4), and the fixing screws (5).

areas of bulkhead at the ends of the footwells (6), which incorporated the clutch foot rest; last to be installed were the two floor mats (7).

Where the carpet abutted the door aperture, it increased the thickness of the door seal flange, which made it virtually impossible to get the seal to fit comfortably. The carpet had to be accurately cut back by 20mm (¾in) to butt up against the seal when fitted. A couple of very narrow gaps, in which the light colour of the fibreglass sill could be seen, were effectively disguised by colouring the sill with a black marker pen.

6. Detailing

It is worth taking the time to attend to a few fiddly details, as it is these that separate a good interior from an outstanding one. They do not have to be as outrageous as an illuminated gear knob, but it is amazing what a touch of polished metal here and there can achieve. Even things like the illuminated switch panel, which can only be appreciated by the driver, should always be considered as it makes the finished car more pleasing to live with. If nothing else, some form of badge or logo does add a touch of class if done well.

6.1. Illuminated switch panel

The only available space to house the required switches was right in the centre of the dashboard on the aluminium channel. Four switches were needed – front fog lights, rear fog lights, driving lights, and hazard warning lights – but, from an aesthetic point of view, a group of five looked better, so an extra one was added and labelled 'aux' for auxiliary.

Switch mounting involved the use of two translucent green plastic panels. The rear one carried the switches themselves, which protruded through five holes in the front panel and enabled them to be backlit. Small, vinyl lettering was applied to the front panel, sprayed silver before the letters were removed, which allowed each switch legend to be illuminated from behind by the same light source that served the switches.

Because toggle switches were being used, they had to be fitted with some form of guard to conform to SVA regulations regarding interior projections. So a series of half hoops were formed from stainless steel tubing using a hand-held pipe bender usually used for brake and fuel pipework. Small rivnuts (a sort of pop rivet with an internal thread) were fixed into each end of the stainless tubes to screw them onto the switch panels from behind. The dashboard aluminium channel had a rectangular hole cut in it, large enough to accommodate the switches. It was sandwiched between the rear panel carrying the switches, and the silver front one with the switch labels, and secured by screws passing from the rear into the rivnuts in the guard hoops on the front to create an invisible fixing.

All that remained was to fix two small bulb holders behind the panel assembly, wire them into the instrument lighting circuit, and the job was done. When on, all of the switch legends light

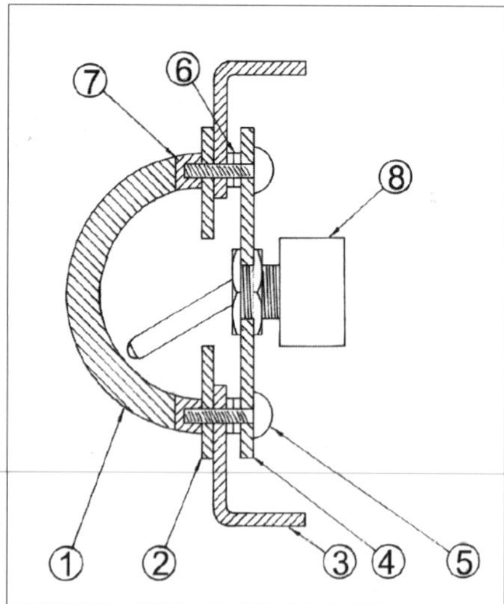

A cross-section of the switch panel installation showing the same features as the previous diagram assembled with spacing washers (6), rivnut inserts (7), and one of the switches (8).

The finished illuminated panel assembly.

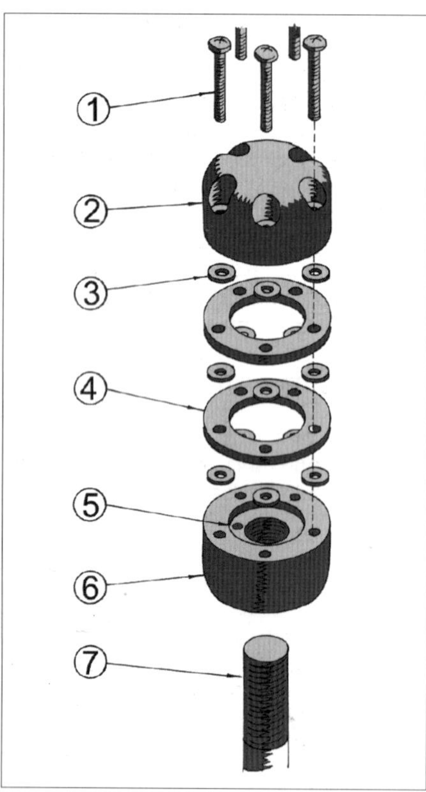

An exploded diagram showing the gear knob construction. The fixing screws (1) pass through the top (2), spacing washers (3) and rings (4) to screw into the base (6). The complete assembly then screws onto the gear lever (7). Note the hole (5) for the power supply wire.

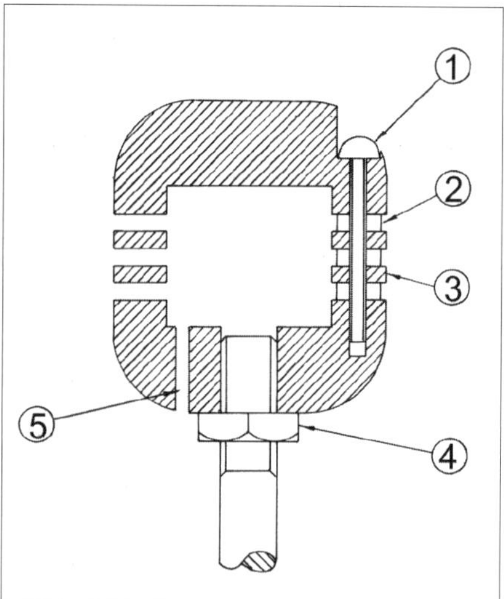

A cross-section of the gear knob assembly showing how the screws (1) pass through the spacing washers (2) and rings (3). The power supply wire hole (5) is located close to the locknut (4) which secures the knob to the lever.

An illuminated gear knob may be a bit over the top. Power supply and earth wires are hidden under the suede gaiter.

up, along with a circle of light around the base of each switch, which looks very stylish and was well worth the effort.

6.2. Illuminated gear knob

This could probably be viewed as a bit over the top, but it is this sort of detail that lifts a home-built interior into a different league – and it's quite easy to make. The entire assembly was made from four pieces of turned aluminium, the base drilled and threaded to screw onto the gearstick. The power supply wire, from the lighting circuit, was fed up through a small hole drilled next to this. Five setscrews recessed into the top held it onto the base, the two parts separated by two aluminium rings and spacer washers to form slots for three green Light Emitting Diodes (LEDs) to shine through. The diodes were soldered in parallel to the end of the supply wire inside the knob and insulated with tape. A loop terminal provided the earth by being trapped between the rings on one of the setscrews. An earth wire from the chassis was clamped to the base of the gearstick with a small hose clip.

Although the full effect of the finished knob is hardly ever seen because the car is rarely driven at night, its manufacture and installation gave me great satisfaction!

6.3. Aluminium trim

The trick when using aluminium for interior trim is to use material thick enough to enable edges and corners to be rounded off, and fixing screws to be countersunk flush to improve the look of the finished component.

A cardboard pattern is the best place to begin when finalising the shape and size of the part required. Remember that components do not have to be round or square; any shape is possible. The Mirov gear lever trim is sort of egg-shaped, and the handbrake is a curved right angle section made with the help of the same shrinker/stretcher machine used for the dashboard. Again, a similar result could be obtained by using wooden formers.

The polished aluminium trim adds to the quality feel of the interior.

The centre portions can be cut out using several different methods, including a jigsaw, chain drilling, hole saws, or even a small tapered reamer used in an electric drill. Whichever method is used to cut and shape the metal, it is the time taken to do the final finishing that produces a quality result. The edges are best rounded off with a file, followed by fine wet or dry paper, then scotchbrite pads, and, finally, metal polish.

The door lock plungers received aluminium trim that was eye-shaped, with forward and backward facing flanges. These were formed by being trapped between two wooden formers and gently beaten over with a nylon hammer.

The polished aluminium trim along the dashboard and centre console was made by cutting sheet to the same

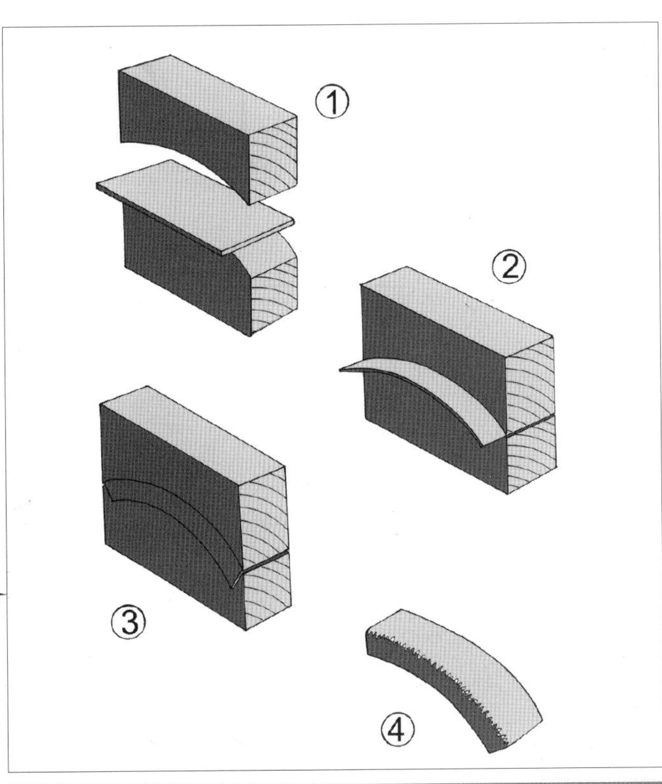

Wooden formers can be used to shape items like the handbrake trim. (1) The aluminium is cut to size and the blocks cut to the required shape. (2) The metal is trapped between the blocks and held in a vice. (3) The flange is then gently tapped over. (4) The resulting angle just needs the slot cutting and final trimming, drilling and polishing.

Even the door lock plungers received polished metal trim.

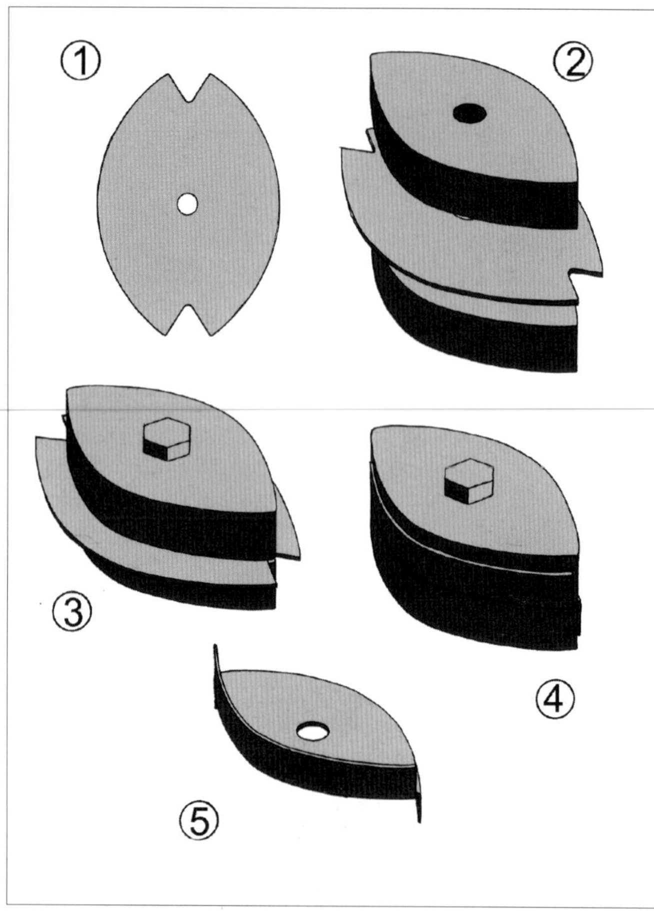

When making odd-shaped metal trim parts using formers such as this door lock plunger surround, it pays to make paper and card templates to establish the correct shape of metal needed to start with. This will ensure that the minimum amount of metal is formed so it will be easier to work and the end result will require very little finishing.

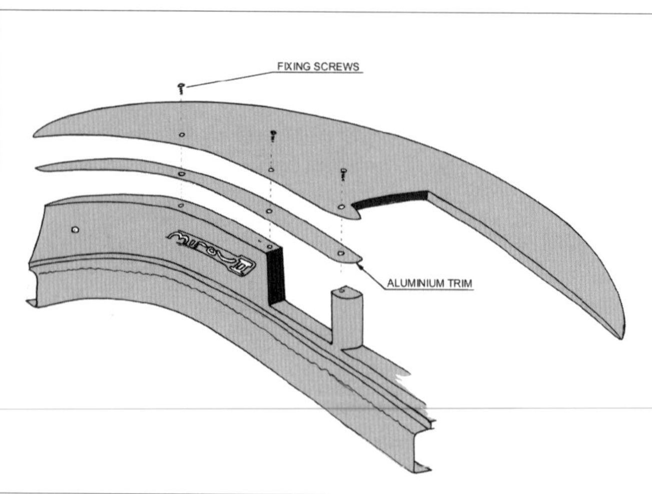

The polished aluminium dashboard trim is trapped between the layers using the three fixing screws for the top panel.

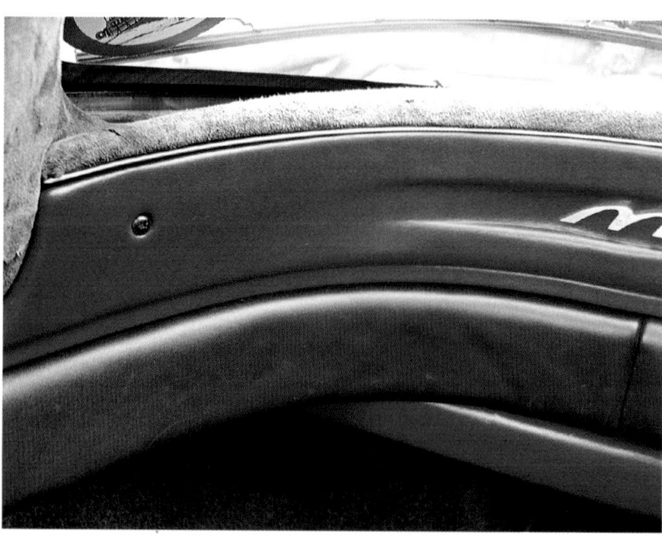

Subtle, but effective: polished aluminium trim sandwiched between the dashboard layers.

profile as the plywood sections they would be trapped between, and then simply polishing the edges before installing them.

6.4. Mirov II logo

The polished aluminium Mirov II logo on the left side of the dashboard is another little touch that lifts the quality of the interior. My father just happens to be an expert with a fretsaw, and cut the lettering from a piece of aluminium using artwork supplied by me. To satisfy the internal projection requirements of the SVA test, a recess was cut in the front of the dashboard to allow the badge to sit flush. The polished aluminium lettering in the leather trimmed dashboard adds to the production car feel I was trying to obtain.

It's all in the detail. 'Mirov II' logo adds a touch of class. It is recessed in the dashboard to ensure compliance with SVA regulations regarding interior projections.

Index

Veloce *SpeedPro* books -

978-1-903706-92-3

978-1-901295-26-9

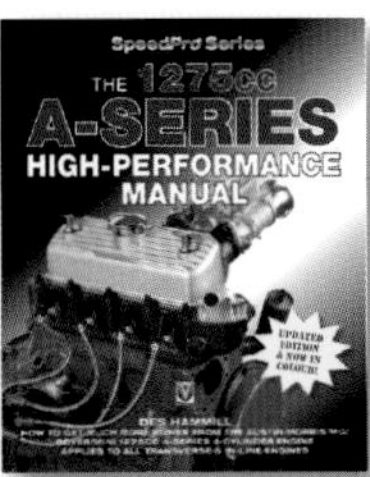

978-1-845840-23-5

978-1-845840-19-8

978-1-845840-21-1

978-1-903706-59-6

978-1-903706-76-3

978-1-904788-78-2

978-1-903706-78-7

978-1-903706-72-5

978-1-903706-94-7

978-1-845840-06-8

978-1-903706-91-6

978-1-845840-05-1

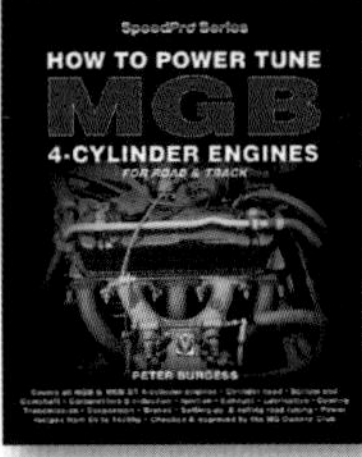

978-1-903706-77-0

978-1-84584-187-4

978-1-904788-93-5

978-1-901295-73-3

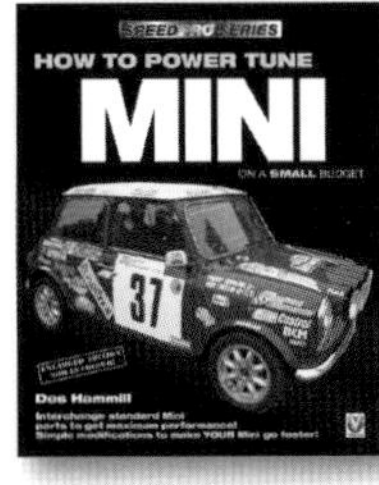

978-1-904788-84-3

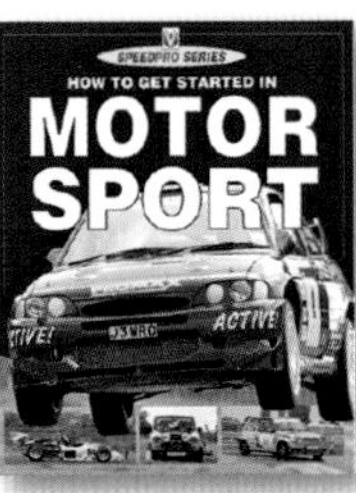

978-1-903706-70-1

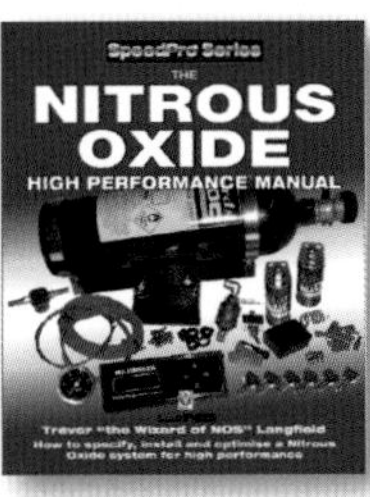

978-1-904788-89-8

978-1-903706-17-6

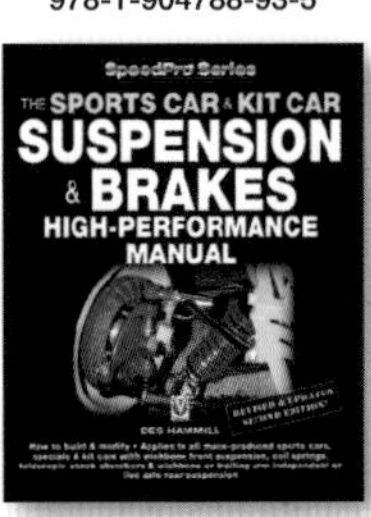

978-1-903706-73-2

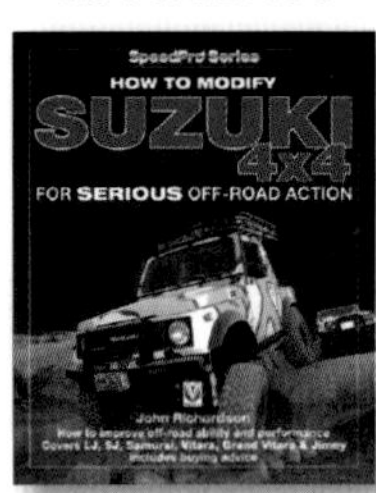

978-1-904788-91-1

978-1-845840-73-0

978-1-904788-22-5

978-1-903706-80-0

978-1-903706-68-8

978-1-845840-45-7

978-1-874105-70-1

978-1-903706-14-5

978-1-903706-99-2

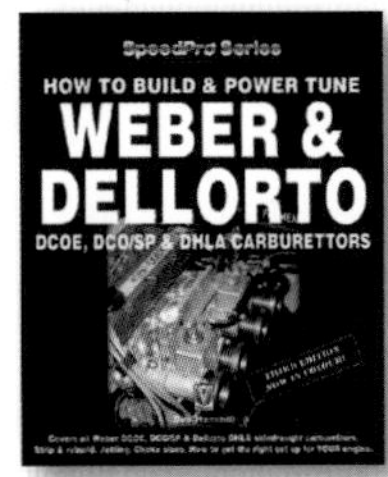

978-1-903706-75-6

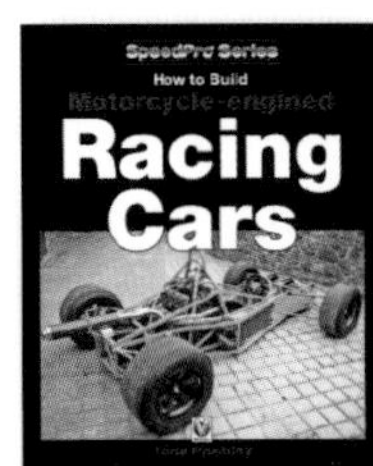

978-1-845841-23-2

978-1-845841-62-1

– more on the way!

Also from Veloce Publishing

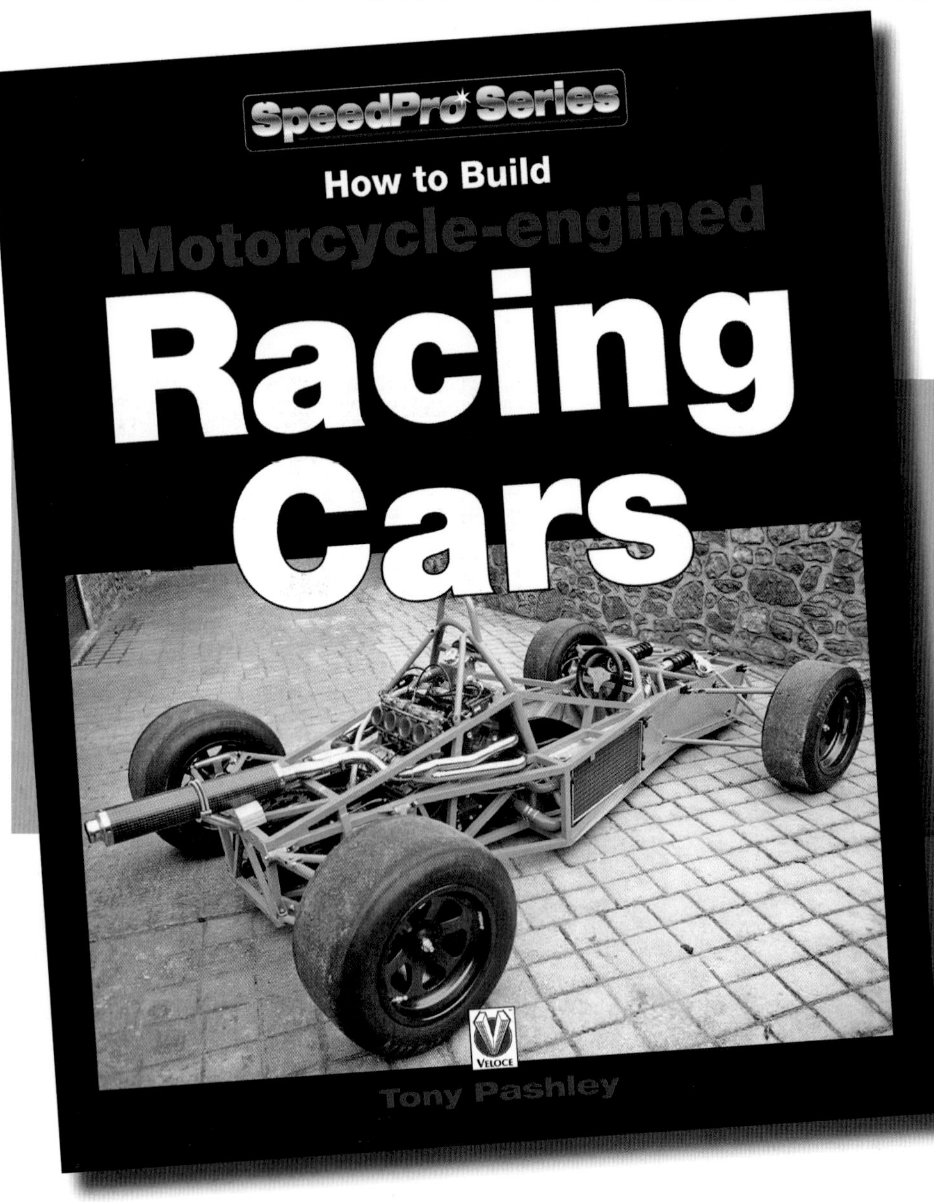

Paperback

128 pages

ISBN: 978-1-845841-23-2

£24.99

Over 400 pictures, mostly colour

- Takes the reader from budget racing car concept to the car's appearance on the racetrack, in easily comprehensible steps
- Ideal for hillclimbing and sprinting activities, plus wider applications
- Discusses suitable motorcycle engine types and how to procure them
- Advice about the associated pitfalls
- Guidance on design, properties and selection of materials
- Construction processes and necessary equipment all described in detail
- Over 200 photos, plus detailed step-by-step instructions and extensive diagrams, make this book a vital addition to any would-be kitcar builder's library

Prices subject to change • P&P extra • For details on these and all Veloce books

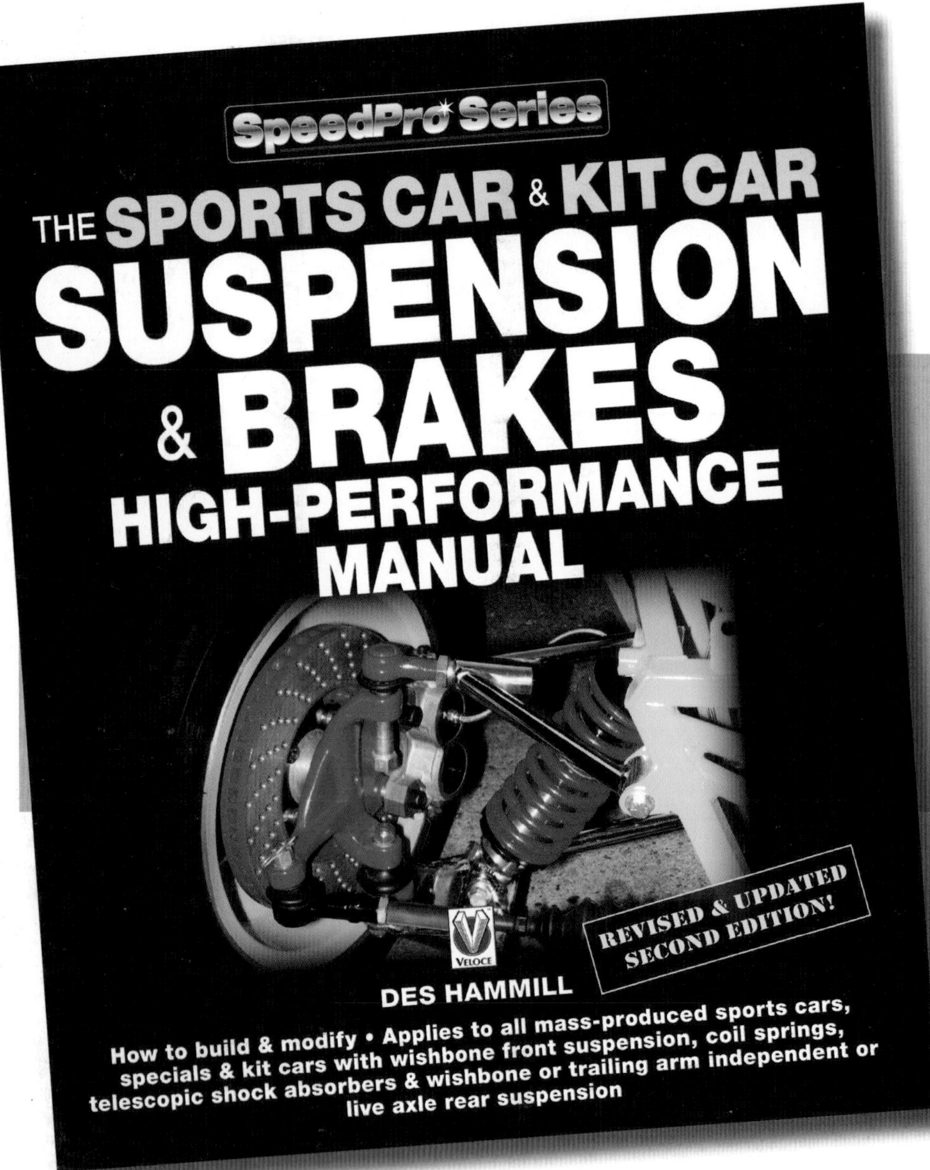
SpeedPro Series
THE SPORTS CAR & KIT CAR
SUSPENSION
& BRAKES
HIGH-PERFORMANCE
MANUAL
REVISED & UPDATED
SECOND EDITION!
VELOCE
DES HAMMILL
How to build & modify • Applies to all mass-produced sports cars, specials & kit cars with wishbone front suspension, coil springs, telescopic shock absorbers & wishbone or trailing arm independent or live axle rear suspension

S320

INFECTIOUS DISEAS[E]

EVOLVING INFECTIONS

prepared for the Course Team by
Michael Gillman and Tim Halliday

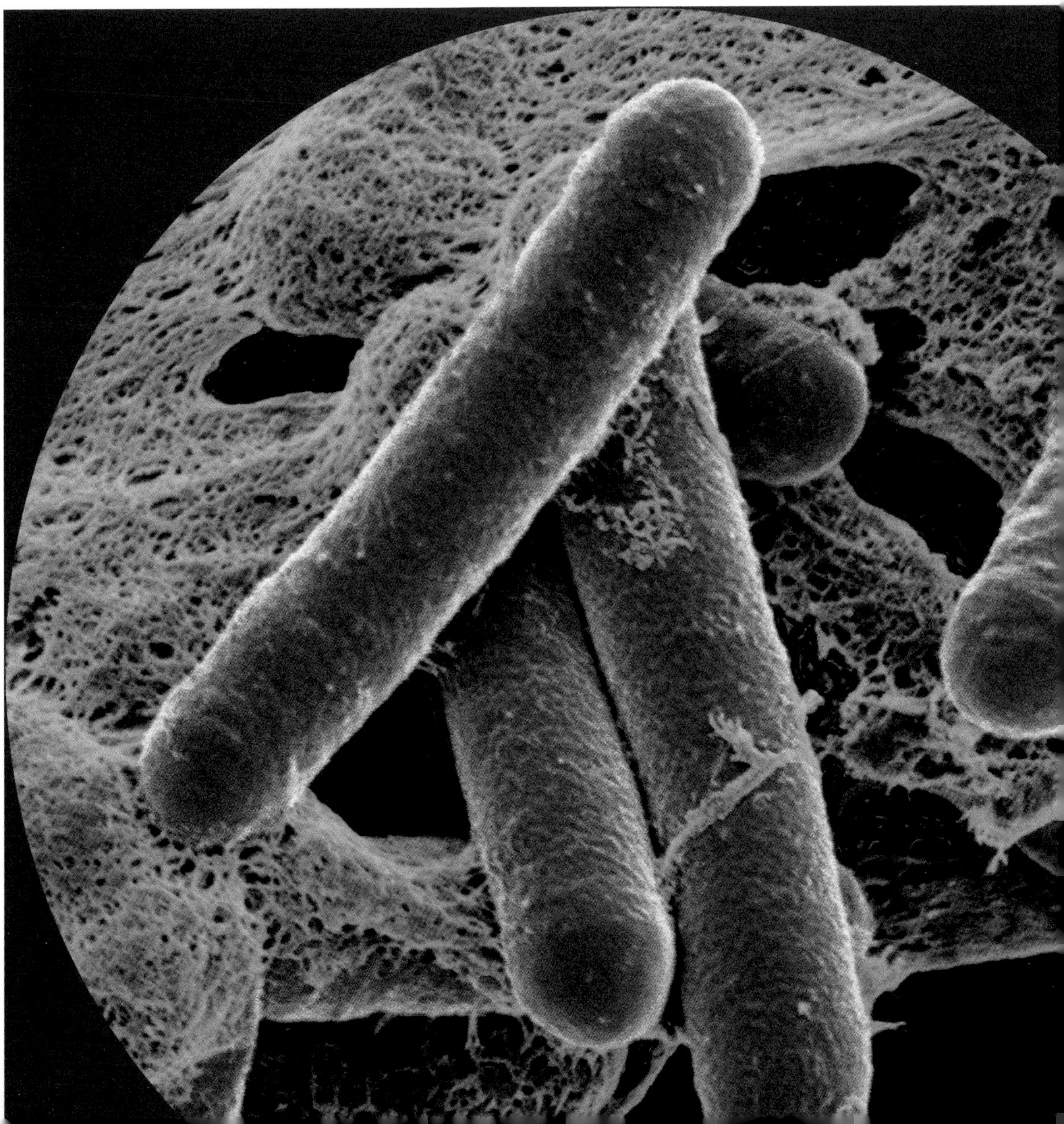

Cover picture: Coloured scanning electron micrograph (SEM) of *Clostridium botulinum* bacteria (blue), the cause of botulism in humans. Botulism is a type of food poisoning caused by the powerful neurotoxin that these bacteria produce.

This publication forms part of an Open University course S320 *Infectious Disease*. The complete list of texts which make up this course can be found at the back. Details of this and other Open University courses can be obtained from the Course Information and Advice Centre, PO Box 724, The Open University, Milton Keynes MK7 6ZS, United Kingdom: tel. +44 (0)1908 653231, e-mail general-enquiries@open.ac.uk

Alternatively, you may visit the Open University website at http://www.open.ac.uk where you can learn more about the wide range of courses and packs offered at all levels by The Open University.

To purchase a selection of Open University course materials visit the webshop at www.ouw.co.uk, or contact Open University Worldwide, Michael Young Building, Walton Hall, Milton Keynes MK7 6AA, United Kingdom for a brochure. tel. +44 (0)1908 858785; fax +44 (0)1908 858787; e-mail ouwenq@open.ac.uk

The Open University
Walton Hall, Milton Keynes
MK7 6AA

First published 2003.

Edited, designed and typeset by The Open University.

Printed and bound in the United Kingdom by the Alden Group, Oxford.

ISBN 0 7492 56591

1.1

THE S320 COURSE TEAM

Course Team Chair

Michael Gillman

Course Manager

Viki Burnage

Course Team Assistant

Dawn Partner

Course Team Authors

Basiro Davey (Books 1 & 7)

Tim Halliday (Book 5)

Paddy Farrington (Book 6)

Michael Gillman (Books 1 & 5)

Hilary MacQueen (Books 2 & 4)

David Male (Books 1, 3 & 7)

Consultant Authors

Eric Bowers (Book 2)

Christine Heading (Book 7)

Laura Hibberts (Books 2 & 4)

Ralph Muller (Book 7)

Editors

Gerry Bearman

Pat Forster

Gilly Riley

Margaret Swithenby

Academic Reader

Mary Manley

External Course Assessor

Bo Drasar

OU Graphic Design

Roger Courthold

Sian Lewis

Video Editing

Wilf Eynon

Michael Francis

CD-ROM Production

Greg Black

Phil Butcher

BBC Production

Martin Kemp

Rights Executive

Christine Brady

Picture Research

Lydia Eaton

Indexer

Jean Macqueen

Course Websites

Patrina Law

Louise Olney

Sue Dugher

CONTENTS

1 SETTING THE SCENE

1.1 Introduction

This book deals with aspects of the ecology and evolution of hosts and their pathogens, the biology of which has been discussed at length earlier in this course and in OU courses that you may have already studied. As background reading to this chapter, you may find it helpful to read Chapters 1 and 4 from S204 Book 4, available on the *Reference* CD. A total of three study hours has been allocated to this chapter with five hours for Chapter 2, four hours for Chapter 3 and two hours for directed reading. Chapter 1 of Book 1 discussed terminology as it relates to organisms that cause infectious disease. As in the rest of this course, we use the word 'pathogen', but you should be aware that 'parasite' is most widely used in the literature to which this book relates.

The outbreak of bubonic plague known as the Black Death killed more than 25 million people, at least one-third of the population of Europe at the time, between 1347 and 1351; the influenza pandemic that swept the world in 1918 killed twice as many people as the First World War; by the end of 2001, an estimated 65 million people worldwide had been infected with HIV, of whom 25 million had died of AIDS-related illnesses. These are statements about the enormous impact that infectious diseases can have on our species, or on human populations. In this part of the course, we make a fundamental shift in the way that we look at infectious diseases, away from their effect on *individuals*, to their impact on *populations* and *species*. This is the realm of the branch of Biology that is called **Ecology**.

The Black Death and the 1918 flu pandemic were significant events in human history. They were also distinct phases in the evolution of our own species and that of the pathogens which cause these diseases. Humans and the pathogens that affect them evolve together, a process called **coevolution** that we will examine in Chapter 2. In the minds of most people, evolution is about the past; we study the evolution of organisms in order to understand how they have come to be the way they are today. Evolution does not, and has not, stopped; however, humans and their pathogens continue to coevolve. As we will discuss later in this book, important features of human pathogens have changed in recent times and, every year, at least one disease that is new to humans emerges. Moreover, the coevolved relationship is a *dynamic* one, with frequent shifts in the relationship between host and pathogen. Most researchers in the field of human disease believe, for example, that there is a high probability that a major flu pandemic will happen again in the near future.

The application of evolutionary theory and analysis to the biology of infectious diseases has four aspects:

1 The analysis of *process*. All organisms are subject to natural selection which, together with other processes, shapes their genotype and phenotype. It is important that we understand the processes that cause both pathogens and hosts to change over time if we are to combat diseases successfully. The process by which hosts and pathogens coevolve is discussed in Chapter 2.

2 The analysis of *relationships*. As humans, we are concerned with knowing if we are more closely related to gorillas or chimpanzees. It is also important to understand the relationships of our pathogens to pathogens of other species and to non-pathogenic organisms.

3 The analysis of *chronology*. Modern genetic techniques provide a powerful tool that enables us to determine both the relationships between hosts or pathogens and when particular pathogens first evolved. The analysis of relationships and chronology is discussed at various points in Chapter 2 and in Chapter 3, Section 3.5.

4 Shaping the *future*. The efforts of humans to control infectious diseases impose selection pressures on pathogens, causing them to change. Whether such changes will make infectious diseases a lesser or a greater threat to humans in the future depends on our correctly understanding how natural selection works. This is discussed in Chapters 2 and 3 and in the directed reading.

Interest in the evolution and ecology of infectious diseases is comparatively recent. It is only in the last 20 to 30 years that medicine has come to appreciate the central biological notion that 'nothing in biology makes sense except in the light of evolution' (Dobzhansky, 1973). During this time, there has also been a major shift in the thinking of biologists about the role of disease in the ecology of animals and plants, a role that has been previously underestimated. Until recently, ecologists assumed that animal and plant populations are regulated by two processes: predation, and competition for food and other resources. It is now realized that infectious disease is a third major cause of mortality for many species and has, therefore, been a major driving force during their evolution. This observation had been made earlier by Haldane for humans over the last 5000 years (Book 3, Section 5.1).

At this point, it is worth exploring the differences between pathogens and predators, two types of +/– relationship (Box 1.1) both of which include examples of coevolved relationships. Predators are adapted to kill their prey and have evolved many specialized characteristics for doing so. In contrast, it is not generally to the benefit of a pathogen to kill its host because, in so doing, it is likely to bring about its own demise; at best, it creates for itself the very uncertain future of having to find a new host. Pathogens are thus not specifically adapted to kill, as predators are, and, when they kill their hosts, this is best seen as a *consequence* of their activity, not as its objective. Because pathogens rarely benefit from the death of their host, it is commonly argued that pathogens should typically evolve towards being less virulent, that is, towards being commensals rather than pathogens. The evolution of virulence is a major preoccupation of evolutionary biologists interested in disease and, in Chapter 2, we will examine the circumstances in which this argument is or is not supported in the living world.

☐ From your general knowledge, do you think that it is realistic to regard predation, competition for food and disease as separate, independent processes?

■ No, this is an unrealistic view. Predators may take as prey those individuals that are weakened by illness or starvation, and it is well known that, for humans, malnutrition may make individuals more susceptible to disease.

This illustrates a major problem facing ecologists studying the impact of infectious diseases on populations of animals or humans: different causes of mortality interact with one another, making it difficult to determine accurately the impact of any one

BOX 1.1 Interactions among species

Six principal kinds of interaction between species are generally recognized: competition, predation, parasitism, commensalism, mutualism and detritivory. These can be categorized according to whether each of the two interacting organisms derives a gain (denoted by a +), incurs a cost (–), or whether there is no impact in fitness terms (0) (see Table 1.1).

TABLE 1.1 A classification of interactions between species.

Interaction	Consequences for species A and B	Comments
competition	0 – or + –	competition in which A competitively excludes B
	– –	competition in which A and B coexist
predation	+ –	includes carnivory, herbivory
parasitism	+ –	A is parasite; B is host
commensalism	+ 0	
detritivory	+ 0	B is dead, so incurs no cost
mutualism	+ +	
neutralism	0 0	

Interactions between animal hosts, such as humans, and microbes fall into three categories. Parasitism is an interaction in which one organism lives in (endoparasite) or on (ectoparasite) another organism, its host, obtaining nourishment at the latter's expense (Book 2, Section 1.1). Typically, the host is not killed by the parasite, but it is harmed to a greater or lesser extent, possibly just by a small blood meal or competition for the host's food. *Where this harm is manifested as a significant amount of damage to host cells, the parasites are referred to as pathogens (disease-causing).* Commensalism (introduced in Book 2) is an interaction in which one organism lives in or on another, its host, at no detriment to the host. Mutualism is an interaction in which two organisms live in a close association, to the benefit of both. Humans have commensal and mutualistic relationships with many microbes, notably the bacteria that live in our guts, some of which may help us digest food.

Parasitism, commensalism and mutualism are all forms of **symbiosis**, defined as the living together in permanent or prolonged association of members (symbionts) of two different species with beneficial or deleterious consequences for at least one of the parties. (Note that some books and papers use symbiosis in the same sense as we have used commensalism and/or mutualism.)

During the course of evolution, it is theoretically possible for a symbiotic association between a host and a microbe to change from one category to another. The endosymbiotic theory for the origin of complex organisms, for example, proposes that mitochondria are the descendants of microbes that first invaded eukaryotic cells as pathogens or commensals and became mutualists.

of them. A researcher may see a lion kill an impala that the researcher has good reason to believe is already sick or malnourished; is the cause of that death predation or disease?

The hypothesis that, while predation may be the immediate cause of death, disease may have played an important role, has been tested in wild populations of Townsend's vole (*Microtus townsendii*). Experimental animals, treated with an anthelminthic drug, were less likely to be killed by predators than non-treated control voles. It is rare to see obviously sick animals in nature and the reason may often be that predators take them at an early stage of illness. If this is so, it goes some way to explain why ecologists have, until recently, underestimated the importance of infectious disease as a cause of mortality in wild animals.

For humans, we can, fortunately, disregard predation as a significant cause of mortality. We cannot dismiss access to resources, nutrition and public awareness/ education, however. The fact that wealthy western tourists can safari in malaria-infested parts of Africa with virtual impunity, thanks to prophylactic drugs, while thousands of indigenous people die in poverty from malaria is a salutary reminder of the crucial role that the uneven distribution of resources among human populations plays in the ecology of infectious disease. Almost all (95%) of new HIV infections occur in the world's poorer countries.

1.2 The importance of infectious diseases of animals and plants to humans

This course focuses on infectious diseases that affect humans but, in this book, frequent reference will be made to diseases of other animals, and occasionally of plants. There are several reasons for this:

1 Diseases of animals provide valuable data for developing general models of the dynamics of infectious diseases that can be applied to humans. There is no reason to suppose that, apart from the socio-cultural dimensions of disease spread, animal diseases differ in any significant way from human diseases (see (2) below). Much current research on human diseases involves developing mathematical models, such as those advanced by the mathematical biologists Roy Anderson and Robert May, and these are largely based on data from diseases of insects and other animals. (Mathematical models are discussed in Chapter 3 of this book and in Book 6.) It is fair to say that the modelling approach to infectious disease has outstripped the collection of hard data. For example, it was shown, over 20 years ago, that a pathogen could theoretically control the population size of its host, but it has yet to be shown that such a situation occurs in nature. Gathering good data on infectious disease in nature is a very complex and time-consuming task, and those seeking to combat disease are heavily reliant on models. For example, the date of the 2001 General Election in the UK was affected by theoretical predictions as to when the foot-and-mouth outbreak of that year would have run its course.

2 Humans share many diseases with other species (Figure 1.1). A recently developed database of human diseases lists 1415 pathogens that cause disease in humans, of which 61.6% also cause disease in other species. The existence of such a large number of multihost pathogens is very important for combating disease because, as we will see later, the fact that a pathogen occurs in another

species can have a profound effect on its ecology and evolution, and therefore on the way that we seek to control it. For example, the control of rabies has to take account of the fact that the rabies pathogen infects domestic animals, such as dogs, and wild animals, such as foxes.

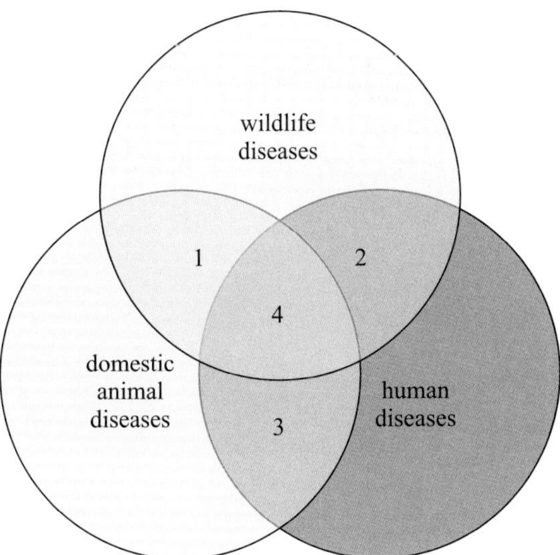

FIGURE 1.1
Overlap among human and animal hosts of infectious diseases. (1) Diseases infecting domestic and wild animals (e.g. canine distemper). (2) Diseases infecting wild animals and humans (e.g. Lyme disease). (3) Diseases infecting humans and domestic animals (e.g. cat scratch fever). (4) Diseases infecting all three (e.g. rabies).

Diseases that can be transmitted from vertebrate animals to humans are called zoonotic diseases or zoonoses (defined in Book 1, Box 1.2). Among diseases that are labelled as 'emerging', that is, that have begun to infect humans in the recent past, 75% are zoonotic. Clearly, other species are an important source of new human diseases. One example is variant Creutzfeldt-Jakob disease (vCJD), which is the human equivalent of bovine spongiform encephalopathy (BSE), or mad cow disease (Book 2, Chapter 4). Another is hantavirus infection, which is caused by a virus transmitted from rodents to humans; humans cannot pass it to one another.

3 Plant and animal diseases can be of enormous economic importance if they affect crops and domestic livestock. Plant diseases destroy about 10% of crops every year worldwide, and the annual bill for fungicides to control plant diseases was estimated in 2001 to be US$6 billion. Moreover, they can have a major impact on food supplies, especially in less-developed countries, and can cause major social disruption.

4 We are living at a time of global ecological difficulties, when biodiversity on Earth is declining rapidly. It is becoming increasingly apparent that infectious disease is often a significant factor in the decline and extinction of plant and animal species. The landscape of Britain and much of mainland Europe was transformed in the 1970s and 1980s by the elimination of elm trees through Dutch elm disease and, at the time of writing (2003), a lethal fungal disease that affects amphibians, called chytridiomycosis (Figure 1.2), is devastating populations of frogs, toads and salamanders throughout the world.

Chytridiomycosis is a tragedy for frogs, and for those people who love them, but is it a cause of concern for humans in general? The answer depends on why frogs and other organisms are being stricken by disease *now*. Disease has undoubtedly

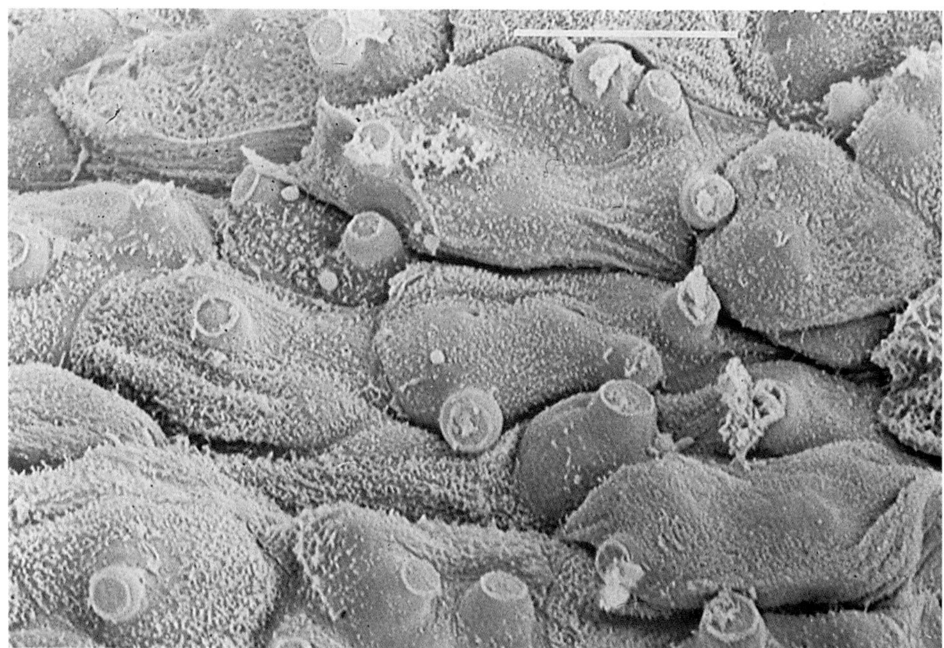

FIGURE 1.2 Scanning electron micrograph of the skin surface from a frog with chytridiomycosis. Fungal discharge tubes are poking through the epithelial surface. (Scale: 10 μm.)

been a fact of life for all but the simplest organisms since the beginning of biological evolution but there is a feeling that major outbreaks, often of apparently new diseases, are becoming more common. There is a problem here, of course; this perception may simply be the result of biologists being much more aware of disease than they were 20 or 30 years ago. It has been suggested, however, that diseases like chytridiomycosis are having a more devastating effect now because the immune system of frogs has been weakened by some other ecological factor, such as pollution, increased UV radiation or climate change. If this hypothesis is correct, then there is a cause for concern among humans, because such factors may be compromising our immune systems too.

Interactions between pathogens and their hosts are complex and, if we are to understand them, we need to get to grips with many aspects of the lives of both protagonists. The following section introduces, explains and defines important terms relating to the life histories and life cycles of host and pathogen. Many of them may be familiar to you, but be prepared to find some terms used in different ways from those you have encountered before.

1.3 Life histories and life cycles

All organisms have a **life history**, which is characteristic for a given species, and which refers to the temporal patterning of four aspects of life: birth, growth, reproduction and death. Some organisms reproduce only once in their lives and are said to be semelparous; organisms that breed several times are iteroparous. The human life history can be summarized as follows: birth followed by growth to about 16 years of age followed by iteroparous reproduction until about age 40 (for females), then post-reproductive life (a feature we share with very few other species) and finally death at around 70 years or much later in many countries from the late twentieth century onwards. In humans, as in most animals, growth slows down or ceases altogether when reproduction begins, a point to which we will return. The study of life histories is primarily concerned with the relative durations and frequency of birth, growth and reproduction and how organisms allocate food and other resources to these activities.

The term 'life history' does not mean quite the same thing as 'life cycle'. The life cycle of a species refers to the particular sequence of phases an individual of that species passes through from birth. Life cycles of several pathogens were described in Book 2 (e.g. Figures 7.1 and 7.19).

There is one other important feature of life cycles that is especially relevant to interactions between hosts and pathogens. This is the movement or transmission of pathogens between hosts. Individuals of many non-pathogenic species make short- or long-distance migrations once or more during their lifetimes. For pathogens, migration between hosts, often occurring at fixed points in the life cycle, is an occupational hazard. The pathogen and its offspring must find new hosts or the population will become extinct. The process of transmission of pathogens between hosts is discussed in detail in all three chapters.

1.3.1 Host life histories and life cycles

Within a host or pathogen species, there is typically much variation in all life history parameters. We know this from our own experience of humans; some individuals reach sexual maturity earlier than others, some live longer than others, etc. Some of this variation is environmental; for example, in developed countries, improved nutrition has lead to earlier sexual maturity. There is also a genetic component to life history variation, which is of great evolutionary significance, as we will see later.

Natural selection shapes the life history of a species so as to maximize individual **fitness** (see Box 1.2). Since fitness is defined in terms of reproductive success, this statement may appear to suggest that all organisms should go all out for reproduction as early in their lives as possible. This, clearly, is not the case; many animals, including humans, do not start breeding until they are quite old. An important factor here is body size. For many female animals, reproductive success (i.e. the survival and number of her offspring) is related to their body size, so that delaying breeding allows growth to a size that optimizes reproductive success. There is a **trade-off** to be considered here, however. The longer a female delays breeding, the greater is her risk of dying first.

BOX 1.2 Fitness

Fitness is a very important concept in evolutionary biology, but its precise definition and measurement are problematic. In host species, it refers to individuals and is a measure of reproductive success, defined as the number of their genetic descendants. It is a relative measure, the most fit individual in a population being assigned a fitness of 1, and all other individuals a fitness of less than 1; such measurements are made under natural conditions. It is thus a measure of relative success resulting from natural selection. In many studies, the number of genetic descendants is measured as the number of first-generation progeny (children) but, ideally, it should be measured over more than one generation to include grandchildren, great-grandchildren, etc. There are very few studies of wild animals or plants in which fitness has been measured over more than one generation and, in general, biologists have to settle for the number of first-generation progeny, and make the assumption that this is a good estimate of 'true' fitness.

Determining the reproductive success of individual pathogens is clearly extremely difficult and the concept of fitness is applied to pathogens in a quite different way. It usually refers to a specific strain and is measured as the number of new infected hosts that result from infection within a single host.

Trade-offs in the host between defence, survival and reproduction

The concept of a life history trade-off is central to understanding the life history of both hosts and pathogens. An organism acquires resources during its life that it has to allocate, as nutrients and energy, either to growth and survival (called somatic effort) or to reproduction (reproductive effort). In many animals, including humans, resources are allocated entirely to somatic effort until body size is sufficient to allow successful reproduction, at which point resources are allocated to reproduction. As a result, growth in most animals ceases or slows down considerably at the onset of reproduction.

In iteroparous species, there are important trade-offs between current and future reproduction. In human females, for example, giving birth to twins may seem to be adaptive because, potentially, it doubles reproductive success. If resources are scarce, however, both babies may die, whereas a single baby might have survived, or, if one twin dies, the survivor might turn out to be smaller and weaker than a single baby would have been. An additional cost of having twins in a low-resource environment may be that it delays the time at which the mother is able to give birth again. The fact that twinning, which has a genetic basis, is rather rare in humans suggests that, over most of human history, it has been more adaptive to have one baby at a time. In trade-off terms, current reproductive effort is constrained to enhance future reproductive success.

An important component of somatic effort is defence against infectious diseases. If they are to survive to breed, host animals must allocate resources to maintaining an immune system as well as to growth, survival and reproduction. Here evolutionary biologists and ecologists face a problem, as it is not at all clear how much it costs, in comparison to growth and reproduction, to maintain an effective immune system. Generally, it is assumed that the resource costs are high, but this is not based on direct measurements and there are some biologists who question the assumption that maintaining an effective immune system is costly.

Table 1.2 presents the results of some animal studies that appear to support the hypothesis that the costs of maintaining immune defences are high, and that they are traded off against reproductive effort.

- ▢ What other interpretation might be placed on the evidence that red grouse females treated with the drug that eliminates helminth parasites rear more young?

TABLE 1.2 Evidence for a trade-off between reproductive effort and immunocompetence.

Species	Evidence	Interpretation
great tit (*Parus major*)	parents with experimentally enlarged broods have higher pathogen loads	increased reproductive effort leads to reduced immunocompetence
bighorn sheep (*Ovis canadensis*)	lactating ewes have higher pathogen loads than non-lactating ewes	lactation diverts resources from the mother's immune system
	ewes rearing sons (which are larger) have higher pathogen loads than ewes rearing daughters	sons require more resources than daughters
red grouse (*Lagopus lagopus*)	females treated with a drug that eliminates helminth parasites rear more young	reducing the need to mount an immune response releases resources for reproduction

It may be nothing to do with the immune system. It could be that the parasites compete for host resources or have some other effect that indirectly affects reproduction. It may also be that the drug has an effect on the reproductive system.

While results such as these are highly suggestive, they are not conclusive. Reproduction involves sex hormones that, as we will see below, have direct effects on the immune system. As a result, changes in immunocompetence during reproduction may not simply be due to animals redirecting resources from immune defence to reproduction.

Anyone who follows sport is likely to be puzzled by the frequency with which prominent athletes fall ill. After all, exercise is generally assumed to make a person healthier. Highly trained athletes do show a higher than normal incidence of mild to severe illness. One explanation for this is that very high levels of training involve a trade-off, with resources being diverted from the immune system. It is more likely, however, that the effect is hormonal. Athletes are often also under severe stress to win and stress induces elevated levels of hormones such as cortisol which affect the immune system. The causal basis of these effects is not important to us here; what is important is that high investment, either in reproduction or in physical exercise, may incur a cost in terms of reduced immunocompetence.

Age-specific susceptibility to infection

An aspect of host life history that is particularly relevant in the context of infectious disease is age-specific susceptibility to infection. In humans, children and the elderly are at higher risk of contracting infectious diseases, but for very different reasons. Babies may be protected against many diseases by antibodies transferred from the mother via the placenta prior to birth, but this passive protection falls rapidly (Figure 1.3). As infants are exposed to pathogens, they develop their own antibodies but, until these have built up to adult levels, children are more susceptible to infections than adults.

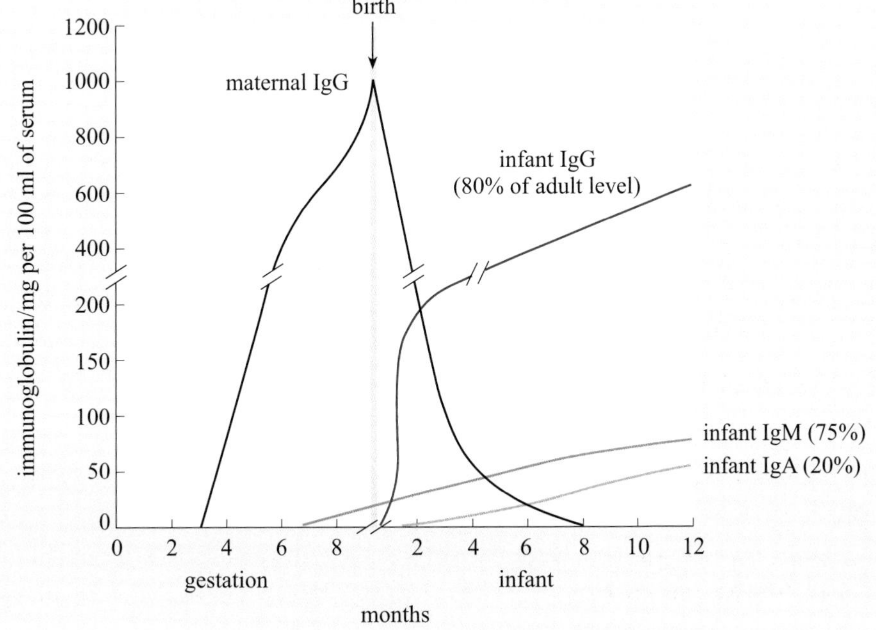

FIGURE 1.3 Levels of antibodies in the circulation of the human fetus in the first year after birth. The figures in brackets after each immunoglobulin class are the percentage of adult levels of that antibody in infants at one year of age.

In birds, mothers similarly protect newly hatched chicks by depositing immunoglobulin G (IgG) in egg yolk. They also deposit carotenoid pigment, which makes egg yolk yellow, orange or red; this protects IgG from the harmful effects of free radicals.

In elderly people, reduced immunocompetence is but one of many aspects of deteriorating function associated with ageing and is called senescence. As a result, diseases like influenza and pneumonia are more frequent and/or more severe among the elderly. There is considerable debate about the evolution of ageing that essentially addresses the question: why has natural selection not produced organisms that do not age? The simple answer is that it cannot. Many genes are age-specific in their action, an obvious example being those controlling morphological and other changes at adolescence. Alleles that cause any kind of deterioration before an organism has reproduced will tend to be eliminated by natural selection, because individuals carrying them will have reduced reproductive success. Alleles that cause deterioration later in life, however, cannot be eliminated because they have already been passed on. Thus a major cause of senescence, including the reduced effectiveness of the immune system, is the cumulative effect of late-acting alleles.

Pity the poor male?

A common finding from the analysis of animal life histories is that males suffer higher mortality and, consequently, have lower average longevity than females. There are very few species in which mortality is higher in females. This effect is seen in humans and is attributable to several factors (Figure 1.4). Males lead more hazardous lives than females and are more likely to be murdered or die through accidents, effects that become apparent at puberty. In addition, from the age of about 25, men are more likely to die as a consequence of infectious disease.

Comparative studies across mammals suggest that this effect is related to **sexual dimorphism** in body size; in the majority of mammals, males are larger than females. Sexual dimorphism is relatively slight in humans but is very large in some mammals; for example, mature elephant seal (*Mirounga angustirostris*) bulls weigh three times as much as females. An analysis covering 355 species of mammals revealed that there is a strong association between male-biased parasitism and the degree of sexual dimorphism in body size. Species in which males are very large carry relatively higher pathogen loads.

Correlational data are highly suggestive, but are not conclusive evidence of a causal relationship. Ideally, experimental data are required. Soay sheep (*Ovis aries*) living on St. Kilda, Scotland have been studied over many years. Soay rams are much larger than ewes, have an average annual mortality rate twice that of ewes, and have significantly higher rates of infection with gastrointestinal nematodes. Experimental removal of these pathogens (using drugs) from yearling males and females eliminated the male-biased mortality, confirming that pathogens are the cause of sex-biased mortality in these sheep.

There are a number of possible explanations for higher pathogen loads in males, none of which mutually excludes any of the others:

(i) Larger animals present a larger 'target' and so are more likely to be found by pathogens.

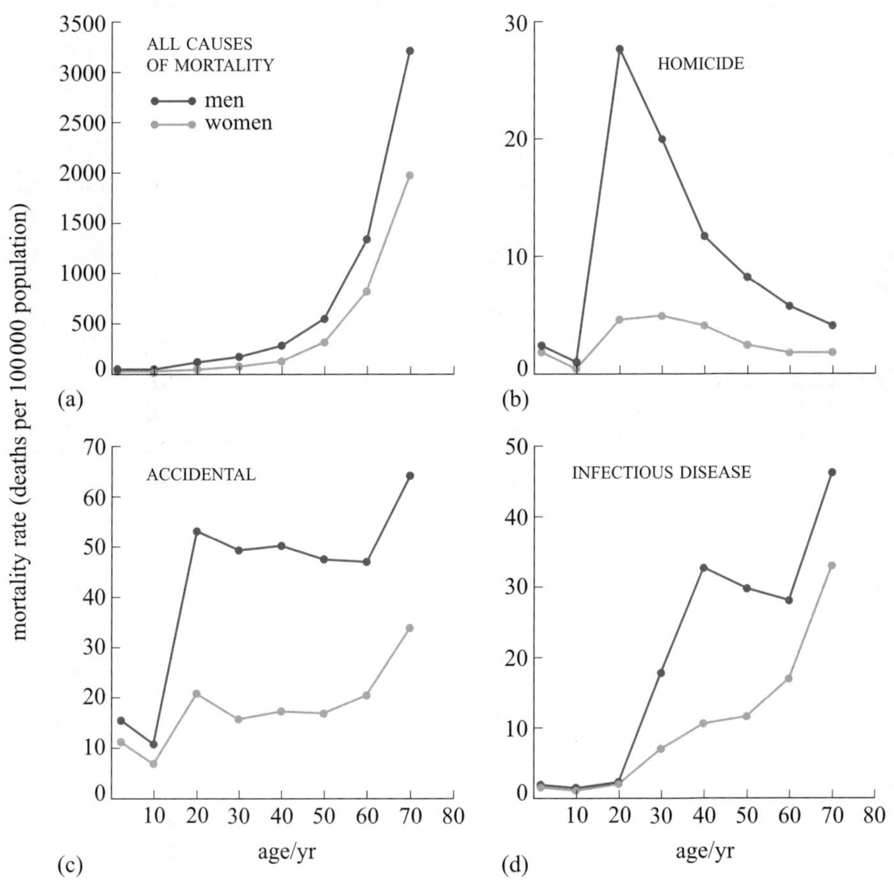

FIGURE 1.4
Sex differences in human mortality.
(a) Mortality rate in males is higher than in females from puberty onwards.
(b) Mortality due to homicide.
(c) Mortality due to accidents.
(d) Mortality due to infectious disease.
(*Note:* the data do not extend beyond 70 years of age.)

(ii) Size being related to age, larger animals will generally be older and thus have had more opportunity to be infected by pathogens.

(In relation to (i) and (ii), there is a positive correlation, across species, whereby larger and longer-lived species are host to a greater number of pathogen species.)

(iii) Males engage more in activities that expose them to pathogen infection, such as fighting.

(iv) For a male to grow large, he has to direct resources away from other functions, including immune defence. In other words, there is a trade-off between immune defence and growth.

(v) Increased male body size at sexual maturity is, in part, a response to increased testosterone levels. Testosterone has a suppressive effect on the immune system.

Whatever the reasons, a large number of studies of animals have shown a positive relationship between male reproductive effort and pathogen loads. Males pay a high price, in health terms, for reproductive success. The association between sex and pathogens has a number of interesting ramifications that we will explore in Chapter 2.

1.3.2 Pathogen life histories and life cycles

The life histories of pathogens are very different from those of their hosts. But, as you will be aware from previous books and case studies, there is a bewildering diversity of pathogen life histories. In some cases, longevity may be very short, perhaps less than an hour. In these organisms, e.g. some bacteria, growth may be very rapid. Furthermore, bacteria do not die under normal circumstances unless due to accident or infection by phages – they just divide! In contrast, some individual pathogens may live for months or years in their host. There is also a wide range in the numbers of offspring produced.

Following its entry into a host (infection), the pathogen finds its way to its preferred home within the body. There are two important variables related to this phase of the pathogen's life cycle:

1 The **latent period**. This is the time period from infection until the host begins to release the pathogen's progeny, i.e. until the host becomes infectious (Figure 1.5).

☐ What is the distinction between latent period, as described here, and latent infection, as described in Book 1, p. 21?

■ A latent infection is one in which a pathogen may be hidden in the host without causing disease symptoms (we refer to this as the dormant period below, to avoid confusion with the latent period as defined here).

2 The **incubation period**. This is the time period from infection until the host begins to show symptoms.

The latent period is always shorter than the incubation period; in other words, the host can pass on the disease before it has developed symptoms (Figure 1.5).

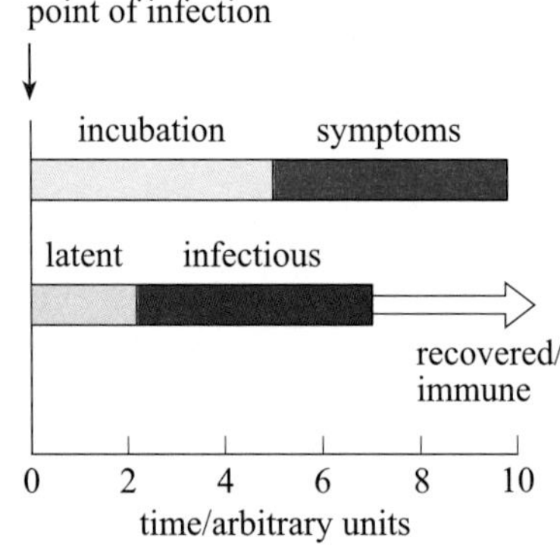

FIGURE 1.5
The relationship between incubation, latent and infectious periods of a pathogen. Note that the infectious period and the duration of symptoms of disease are not necessarily synchronous.

Another variable that is important to know for preventing the spread of a disease is its **infectious period** (Figure 1.5). This is the time for which, following infection and the latent period, a host can pass on the disease. For measles-infected individuals, it is six to seven days; for HIV/AIDS individuals, it is several years.

Every organism, be it host or pathogen, has a characteristic **generation time**, defined, for a sexually reproducing species such as humans, as the average span of time between the birth of parents and birth of their offspring. For humans, this is around 20 years; for our pathogens, it can be much shorter. Bacteria can vary in fission time from 12 minutes, through 30 minutes for *E. coli* in the gut, to days for the leprosy-causing bacterium (*Mycobacterium leprae*).

☐ Recall from Book 2 the characteristic generation time of the smallpox virus (Figure 3.15).

■ At least 6 to 25 hours (DNA replication and morphogenesis, Figure 3.15).

In other pathogens, such as the protoctists or helminths, the life cycle is indirect, i.e. occurring in more than one host or host and vector. In these cases, the generation time has to be measured across all the hosts from one stage to the completion of the same stage in the next generation.

☐ What is the typical generation time of filarial roundworms (Book 2, Figure 7.19)?

■ The pathogen spends 10–14 days in the insect vector and anywhere from 3 to 12 months in the human host. Therefore, generation time may be from 3.5 to 12.5 months.

Finally, whether or not an infection leads to illness may depend on the number of pathogens that enter the body at the time of infection. For hepatitis B, one virion can cause illness; for other diseases, a large number may be required. For example, *E. coli* 0157 requires about 10–500 individuals, *Salmonella* requires anywhere between 100 to 10^7 (dependent on the strain) and for *Giardia*, 10 cysts are required for infection. In discussing this issue, it is important to distinguish between the actual number required for infection versus the higher probability of infection due to high numbers of pathogens.

☐ Recall from the *Cholera* Case Study the typical number of vibrios per host required to cause cholera.

■ 10^8, i.e. 100 million.

This variable is called the **infectious dose**, and is sometimes expressed as the **ID_{50}**, which is the number of pathogens required to make 50% of infected hosts ill. ID_{50} values are determined experimentally, by injecting different doses of pathogen into susceptible animals. Knowing the infectious dose of an organism is important in treatment and control, e.g. determining the level of hygiene that is required to prevent its spread. For a disease like winter vomiting, with a low infectious dose of 10 to 100 virions, very high standards of disinfection are required.

Table 1.3 presents data on the range of variation in these life cycle and host response variables that occurs among the pathogens featured in the case studies in this course.

TABLE 1.3 Values for the life cycle and host response variables of the case study pathogens in humans.

Disease	Influenza	Malaria	Cholera	Syphilis	TB	AIDS
pathogen	orthomyxoviruses	*Plasmodium* sp. (protoctist)	*Vibrio cholerae* (bacterium)	*Treponema pallidum* (bacterium)	*Mycobacterium* (bacterium)	HIV
latent period (L)	1+ days	21 days*		up to 4 months		1–2 months
infectious period (I)	3–4 days	1 to 3 years	less than 2 weeks	up to 4 years	months or years†	
incubation period	1+ days	12 days to 30 days	usually 2–3 days	9–90 days (average 3 weeks)	4–12 weeks	up to 10 years
duration of symptoms	7–10 days usually	maximum of several years from dormant pathogens in liver cells	about 48 hours	months or years	months or years†	several years
infectious dose (no. of organisms)	800	10	10^8	60	not known	uncertain

* See Chapter 3. † Depends on reactivation.

- ☐ Describe the range of variation in the life cycle parameters in Table 1.3.
- ■ In all cases there is enormous variation, especially in the infectious period and duration of symptoms, where the range is from a few days to years – this probably represents up to three orders of magnitude variation (less than 10 to more than 1000 days).

Once established in the host, the pathogen begins to reproduce and it is the host's response to this that usually triggers symptoms. Pathogens vary in the extent to which they spread through the body at this stage. Diseases like influenza usually remain confined to the respiratory tract, but others, like HIV and syphilis, spread to many different parts of the body.

1.3.3 Transmission

We have mentioned the importance of transmission between hosts in the life histories of pathogens. Once outside the host, there are various routes by which pathogens find their way to new hosts. In all of the following discussion, we will consider horizontal routes of transmission.

- ☐ Recall from Book 2, Section 1.5 the routes of transmission.
- ■ The routes listed were via the air, by direct person-to-person contact, by invertebrate vectors, by inanimate objects (fomites) and via food or water.

Examples of these routes of transmission are given in Figure 1.6.

Let us put these routes of transmission into three categories. First, transmission via the abiotic external environment, without involving other organisms, that may be through the air via mucus droplets (colds, influenza), via water bodies or inanimate objects. In these cases, direct contact between hosts is not necessary, although close proximity may increase the likelihood of transmission. Secondly, direct contact between hosts, e.g. diseases that are sexually transmitted (syphilis and other venereal diseases). These pathogens are generally unable to exist outside the host (e.g. *Treponema pallidum*). In contrast, some pathogens transmitted via the abiotic environment can last for months or years outside the host, aided by entering a resistant phase.

- ☐ Recall from Book 2 an example of a pathogen that survives in the soil as an endospore.
- ■ The bacterium that causes anthrax, *Bacillus anthracis*.

In the case of anthrax, transmission time may be decades. The third type of transmission is by an invertebrate vector, several of which you have already encountered in this course, including mosquitoes and ticks. Again, the time spent in the vector may be considerable and, in all cases, is of a minimum duration to allow particular stages of development to occur. For example, *Plasmodium falciparum* needs to spend about 10 days in its mosquito vector in order to complete that stage of its life cycle. This represents an important difference when compared to the transmission modes of diseases via the abiotic environment, where usually no development takes place, and certainly not a different set of developmental stages to that in the host(s). For example, although the endospore of *Bacillus anthracis* is a different developmental stage, the development happens in the vegetative cell (in the

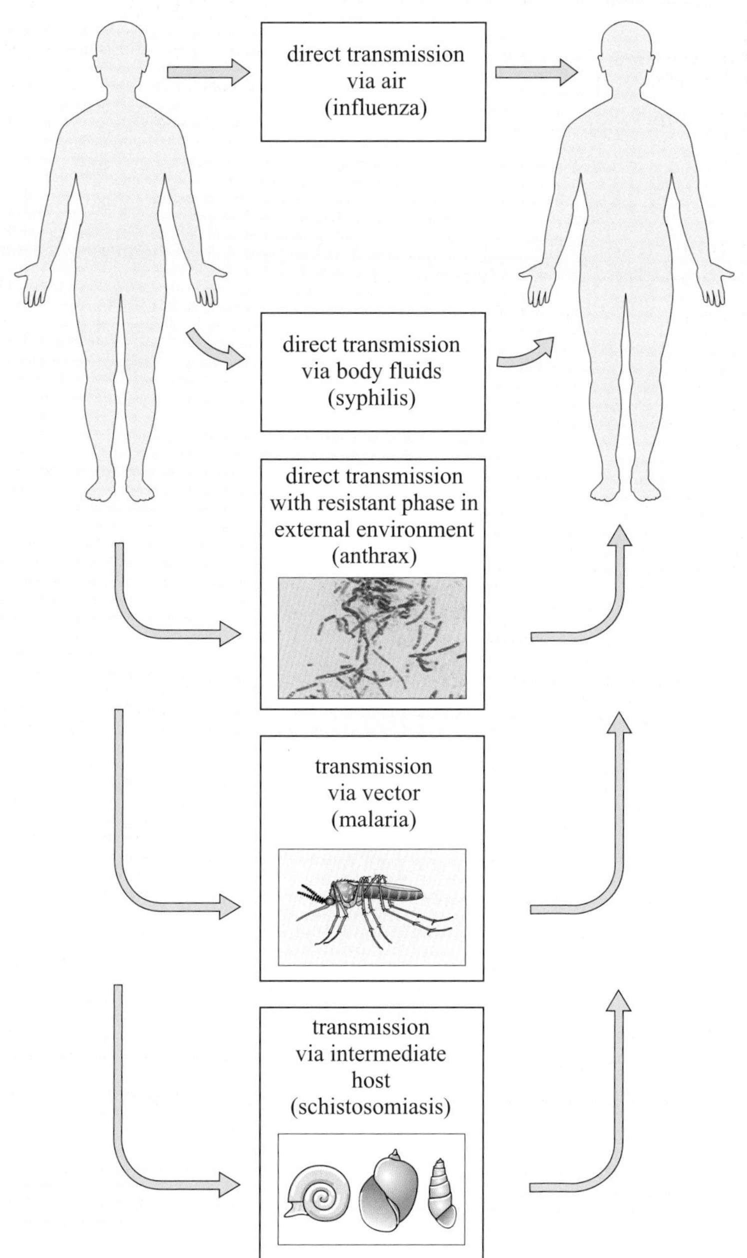

FIGURE 1.6
Examples of routes of disease transmission associated with direct or indirect life cycles.

host) before release into the abiotic environment. However, there are exceptions, for example, hookworms live free in the soil and develop from eggs to infective larva. They then develop into adults in the host (Book 2, Section 7.5.1).

Most tapeworms and flukes spend part of their life cycle in an intermediate host, such as a pig or aquatic snails.

- ▢ Recall from Book 2, Figure 7.1 the methods of transmission between the intermediate and human host.

- The method of transmission is via the abiotic environment, e.g. water or soil. In some cases, movement through the water is aided by swimming towards the next host.

Transmission is a risky process from a pathogen's perspective and, for many diseases, may offer humans the best opportunity to combat a disease. But how can we measure the efficiency of transmission? In Book 6, you will find extensive discussion of aspects of the efficiency of transmission of a pathogen. From both an ecological and epidemiological perspective, we are interested in the number of pathogens transmitted for a given number of pathogens in the infected host. Thus, if an infectious host has 1000 pathogens, what number are able to find a new susceptible host? In other words, what is the probability of successful transfer of pathogens from an infectious to a susceptible host? To determine this, we need to identify two components of transmission.

The first component is the predictability of transmission events. Transmission via the abiotic environment is highly predictable – air, water or soil is usually present around an infectious host. In contrast, transmission by host–host contact is far less certain, although some pathogens increase their chances by exploiting the sexual behaviour of their hosts. Transmission by vectors probably lies somewhere between the two extremes of abiotic and direct contact. Biting mosquitoes are widespread and bite with high and predictable frequency.

The second component is the efficiency with which transmission occurs if the susceptible host encounters the pathogen. Direct contact between hosts offers a highly efficient transmission route for pathogens. The same is true of vectors, especially biting mosquitoes that are able to seek out the peripheral blood supply of the host. In both these cases, the pathogen never has to pass out of the host's or vector's circulatory systems. Transfer via the abiotic environment is far less efficient, because the pathogens disperse within the water body, air or soil. As mentioned above, this is where high densities of the host, such as occurs with TB cases, or use of the same body of water, can dramatically increase efficiency of transmission.

- ☐ Give an example from the *Cholera* Case Study of how use of a particular water supply led to high transmission of the cholera pathogen.

- ■ The study by John Snow in 1854 of the outbreak of cholera around the Broad Street water pump (*Cholera* Case Study, p.6).

Another example was given in Book 2, Figure 7.10, where the prevalence of schistosomiasis was higher for communities living closer to infected rivers. Understanding the routes of transmission and their chances of success are vital in strategies for controlling infectious diseases. Changes in public hygiene have played a major role in control of diseases such as cholera by reducing the effectiveness with which pathogens are transmitted from host to host. In Chapters 2 and 3, we will consider the control of vector-borne diseases by breaking the routes of transmission.

1.3.4 Do pathogens have distinct life-history strategies?

Faced with the enormous range of pathogen life histories (exemplified by the range of values in Table 1.3) and the great variety of routes of transmission, it is tempting

TABLE 1.4 A way of categorizing pathogen life-history strategies.

		Within-host variables		
	minimum duration in host	short (<10 days) § (none)	medium (>10 days) (moderate)	long (>30 days) (complex)
Between-host (transmission) variables	abiotic environment (air, soil, water)	(i) influenza, cholera		TB*
	vector		(ii) malaria	
	host-to-host contact			(iii) syphilis, HIV, TB†

* *Mycobacterium tuberculosis*.

† *Mycobacterium bovis*.

§ level of countermeasure against host defence

to conclude that all possible manner of pathogen existence has been exploited and all we can do is simply document that variation. However, ecologists and evolutionary biologists always attempt to seek patterns in the variation (possibly in vain!) and we are no exception on this course. Seeking such patterns is helpful not only in considering how pathogens may evolve and interact with hosts, but also in ordering our thoughts about host–pathogen interactions. We can then discuss these ideas as we progress through the book.

We noted in Table 1.3 that the pathogens appeared to fall into several categories with respect to *within-host* variables, such as incubation period. Similarly, we have also recognized three different categories of transmission that can be referred to as *between-host* variables. If there is some relationship connecting within-host and between-host life-history parameters, then we may be able to recognize distinct life-history strategies. One possible relationship is summarized in Table 1.4.

According to this view, we can place our case-study pathogens, with the partial exception of TB, into one of three categories (i–iii). In the first case (i), exemplified by influenza and cholera, the pathogen reproduces very rapidly in the host and moves on to another host before the infectious host's immune system has had time to develop an effective response.

- ☐ Recall from Book 1, Figure 2.2, the delay in response of the host immune system to a typical influenza virus infection.

- ■ Antibodies begin appearing by day 3, which is also the onset of virus particle transmission from the host.

Thus for strategy (i), there is no selection pressure favouring countermeasures against the host defence. Viral particles or bacteria that evade or protect themselves against the host defence are not predicted to have a higher fitness than those that do not have such protection. However, it is predicted that these pathogens need to reproduce rapidly so that large numbers of pathogens can be generated quickly (within 3–4 days) in a single host. Large numbers are required because they are transmitted via the abiotic environment.

At the other extreme is the strategy of stealth and evasion ((iii) in Table 1.4). These pathogens, such as HIV and *Treponema pallidum*, succeed by resisting the immune response of their hosts. In the case of HIV, this is also combined with high rates of production of virions in an infected person. TB is a special case because it can fit into one of two categories, depending on the route of transmission. TB can be transmitted by water droplets through the air or via infected milk (*M. bovis*). In the latter case this is essentially a host-to-host contact, which puts it into category (iii).

- ☐ Can you recall from the *Tuberculosis* CD some of the complex countermeasures of *Mycobacterium* sp. against the host defence, which help it to persist in the host?

- ■ It is able to enter a dormant state in the host, within local foci in the lungs, and in macrophages. Its waxy cell wall helps protect it from the immune response, e.g. by its possession of the glycolipid LAM. This biomolecule confers various protective properties against hosts, including the delay of production of TNF-α in host macrophages, thereby delaying destruction of the macrophage within which the bacterium can persist. (See *Tuberculosis* CD, 'Immunology' CD screen 19 and Book 2, p. 28.)

Mycobacterium tuberculosis also has similarities to *Treponema pallidum* in that it does not persist for long in the abiotic environment, being broken down by UV radiation. This, combined with its dispersal in water droplets, is why transmission is most frequent in dark, humid, overcrowded areas.

Another example of a type (iii) strategy microbe is the virus herpes simplex that causes cold sores. This organism lives for years in its host, being dormant for long periods and only occasionally being infectious. Herpes simplex lives in the nervous system, where it is safe from attack by the host's immune system; the host cannot afford to damage its own nervous system by mounting a full immune reaction.

Some species of *Plasmodium* and *Trypanosoma* can also be long-lived in their host, evading their immune system by repeatedly changing their surface molecules. A detailed account of this is given for *Trypanosoma brucei* in the *Immunology* CD.

In the search for pathogen life-history strategies, we are not just looking for examples of combinations of variables to go into Table 1.4. We are also looking for empty cells in the table that will indicate strategies that are not viable options for pathogens. For example, from Table 1.4 we do not have amongst the case studies an example of a pathogen that has transmission by direct host–host contact but that has a duration in the host of less than 10 days.

- ☐ Why do you think this may not be a viable option for pathogens?

- ■ Because the direct contact between hosts would not be sufficiently frequent for transmission of pathogens. Pathogens in one host would have too low a probability of being transferred to another host, and therefore become extinct.

We will need to test this prediction with other pathogens (starting with Question 1.4 at the end of this chapter).

1.4 Biodiversity

> At the present time, scientific estimates of the number of living species on Earth, including microbes, range from 1.4 million to 200 million. This laughable range means we are simply clueless about the number, let alone types, of living creatures on Earth.
>
> (*All Species Inventory*, 2002)

In view of all the media hype about the advances in Biology over the past 100 years, it is sobering to be reminded of how ignorant we still are about such a fundamental aspect of the subject as the number of species on Earth. In fact, this is just one aspect of the term 'biodiversity' which also relates to the genetic and ecosystem levels of diversity. Modern technologies are helping to elucidate these two levels of diversity. Pertinent to this course, by the end of 2002, molecular biology had provided the genome maps of *Plasmodium falciparum* and one of its vectors, *Anopheles gambiae*. Remote sensing (using satellite systems) analysed via geographic information systems are also helping at the ecosystem level of diversity, e.g. in describing the rate of spread of an infection.

Whilst we do have reasonably accurate figures for some components of biodiversity, our greatest area of ignorance concerns microbes. We know there are about 40 000 vertebrate species, of which about 4600 are mammals and about 8800 are birds. We also know that a high percentage of all described and named species are insects (750 000), of which about 300 000 are beetles. In contrast, it is estimated that the 4000 species of bacteria described to date represent only 0.1% of all bacteria species. More recent estimates suggest this may be a serious underestimate. For example, it was estimated that 30 g of soil, taken from a Norwegian forest, contained 500 000 species of bacteria. Microbial diversity increases towards the equator, thus this value is expected to be much higher in the tropics. The percentages of described 'species' are somewhat higher for viruses (1%), fungi (5%) and protoctists (40%).

There is a serious problem when it comes to estimating the biodiversity of microbes. It is not clear what constitutes a species; indeed, the species concept as applied to multicellular organisms may not be appropriate for microbes.

☐ Based on information from Book 2, why may the species concept not be appropriate for microbes?

■ Two major reasons for this are: first, that sexual reproduction, which is central to the biological species concept, does not occur in many microbes; and secondly, that very different microbe 'species' can exchange genetic material with one another (see Box 2.2 on mobile genetic elements in Book 2).

How many of these diverse microbes are pathogens? You read earlier that 1415 human pathogens have been described, of which 62% are also symbionts of other species. This means that there are around 540 pathogens that are exclusive to humans. If all 4600 species of mammal have only half that number, there are over one million species of mammalian pathogens in the world that are exclusive to their hosts, and an even larger number that can move between hosts. Human zoonoses do not only come from mammals; a number of diseases, such as West Nile virus, come from birds.

Does any of this matter? Yes, it does, for three main reasons:

1 As mentioned above, around 70% of recently emerged human diseases are zoonotic. This suggests that there may be an extremely large number of pathogens that might find their way into humans in the future.

2 Other species are a major source of drugs to combat disease. Of the top 10 prescription drugs used in the USA until 1995, nine were based on natural plant products. Plant diversity is relatively low in the USA, and other parts of the world, especially the tropics, are likely to be a richer source of new pharmaceuticals. Some frog species secrete compounds in their skin that kill bacteria and viruses, a sensible adaptation for animals living in dirty water. Such sources of compounds that humans might be able to use to combat disease are largely unexplored and there is a serious danger that the loss of biodiversity may eliminate such sources before they have been discovered.

3 The number of pathogenic microbe species is minuscule compared with the overall biodiversity of microbes. The numbers of microbes that live in a human body exceed the number of human cells by at least two orders of magnitude (10^{14} versus 10^{12}). Large numbers of microbes, whatever their environment, leads to intense competition for resources, and microbes are engaged in a constant struggle for existence with one another. One of their adaptations in this struggle is the production of chemical agents that attack, incapacitate or kill other microbes; these are what we call antibiotics. When we attack parasitic microbes with antibiotics, we are using a strategy that microbes have been employing among themselves for millions of years. We should not be surprised, therefore, that microbes can evolve resistance to antibiotics, a topic we return to in Chapter 2, Section 2.6.

Summary of Chapter 1

1 Study of ecology and (co)evolution of infectious disease shifts the emphasis away from individual hosts or pathogens to populations and species.

2 Disease has only recently been widely recognized as an important contributor to mortality in many species, relative to the contributions from predation and competition.

3 Plant and animal diseases are relevant to humans as models of disease, because they have pathogens in common with humans and due to their economic importance and effect on biodiversity.

4 Both pathogens and hosts have characteristic life histories and life cycles which describe, respectively, general and specific features of birth, growth, reproduction, migration (transmission) and death.

5 Hosts may trade-off infectious disease defence (e.g. maintenance of a potentially costly immune system) against growth and/or reproduction.

6 Host organisms of different sex and different stages of their life history may have different levels of susceptibility to infection.

7 Life cycles of pathogens show a wide range of latent, incubation and infectious periods. Other key variables, which may be difficult to measure, are generation time and infectious dose.

8 Pathogen life histories can be categorized according to routes of transmission (between-host characteristics) and duration in hosts (within-host characteristics).

9 Microbial diversity, an important component of biodiversity, is high and poorly established. This, combined with the overlap of human and animal hosts, creates uncertainty for predictions of future patterns of disease.

Learning outcomes for Chapter 1

When you have studied this chapter, you should be able to:

1.1 Define and use, or recognize definitions and applications of, each of the terms printed in **bold** in the text. (*Questions 1.1, 1.3*)

1.2 Give reasons why the study of diseases in plants and non-human animals are important for humans. (*Question 1.2*)

1.3 Show how an understanding of trade-offs between survival, defence and reproduction sheds light on host–pathogen interactions. (*Question 1.5*)

1.4 Give examples of age-specific and sex-specific responses to disease. (*Question 1.5*)

1.5 Describe the main (generalized) stages of the pathogen life cycle and the responses of the host. (*Question 1.3*)

1.6 Categorize the types of transmission and discuss their relationship to within-host variables. (*Question 1.4)*

1.7 Discuss the importance of biodiversity to human–pathogen interactions. (*Question 1.2*)

Questions for Chapter 1

Question 1.1

In this course, we have chosen to use the term pathogen in preference to parasite. Provide a short account of reasons for and against such an argument.

Question 1.2

Give two examples of human diseases that require the study of diseases in other organisms. Provide a brief justification for your choices.

Question 1.3

Summarize the life histories of human hosts and their pathogens. What, if any, are the fundamental differences between the two life histories?

Question 1.4

Where do the following diseases fit into the scheme of Table 1.4? Do they provide support for recognizable pathogen life-history strategies? You may have to refer back to Book 2 for some of the details.

Cryptosporidium, *Trypanosoma brucei*, filarial roundworms, herpes simplex, schistosomes and transmissible spongiform encephalopathies (TSEs).

Question 1.5

Describe one example of a host life history trade-off involving defence against pathogens that is likely to change with host age.

2 COEVOLUTION OF HOSTS AND PATHOGENS

Tadpoles of the North American green frog (*Rana clamitans*) are parasitized by a trematode (*Echinosterma* sp.), the dispersal phase of which (cercariae) enter via the tadpole's cloacal opening and invade its kidneys. In a sample of 200 tadpoles, 97% had pathogens only in the right kidney. This lateral bias by the pathogen ensures that its tadpole host, which can survive the destruction of one kidney, but not both, does not die, to the benefit of both host and pathogen.

Lizards are often parasitized by ticks and mites, which tend to cluster around the host's eyes and ears and in skin folds, to the irritation of their host. The Spanish lizard *Psammodromus algirus* has a little pocket of skin on each side of its neck that provides an ideal home for the tick *Ixodes ricinus*. Unless the number of ticks on an individual lizard becomes very high, they remain mostly in the pouches, leaving other parts of the host tick-free.

These and numerous other examples illustrate the intimacy that characterizes many coevolved relationships between hosts and their pathogens. As emphasized in Chapter 1, pathogen–host relationships are fundamentally different from predator–prey relationships in that both partners generally have a shared interest in the host's survival. As a result, adaptations have evolved in hosts, which cannot avoid pathogens, that mitigate their adverse effects. For their part, many pathogens have evolved adaptations that reduce the threat they pose to the health and survival of their host. However, the pathogens with which we are concerned in this course make people very sick and often kill them. Why are some pathogens benign and others lethal? In this section, we examine aspects of the life history and ecology of pathogens and hosts that favour the evolution of coexistence and consider whether it is the inevitable evolutionary outcome of all pathogen–host associations.

2.1 What is coevolution?

Coevolution, introduced in Chapter 1 and Book 2, Section 7.6, is a word that is widely used in evolutionary biology, often rather loosely, in the context of intimate relationships between species, such as between plants and the insects that pollinate them. Strictly defined, coevolution refers to relationships in which the evolution of a particular trait in one species has led to the evolution of a particular trait in another. For example, in the context of infectious diseases, the evolution of the ability of a host to detect and respond to an infecting pathogen at an early stage has lead, in many pathogens, to the evolution of adaptations that enable it to evade host defences. In Chapter 3, we will discuss how coevolution has led to increased specialization.

There are three contrasting models of how hosts and pathogens can coevolve:

1 ***Mutual Aggression***. Host and pathogen are engaged in an evolutionary 'arms race', with each species continually evolving in an aggressive manner toward the other (this was the example of coevolution given in Book 2, Section 7.6). In the pathogen, selection favours greater exploitation of the host; in the host, selection favours more effective exclusion of the pathogen.

2 ***Prudent Pathogen***. Selection in the pathogen favours traits that limit the harm it does to the host. As a result, the host and pathogen survive longer. From the host's point of view, it can invest fewer resources in defence and so comes to tolerate the pathogen. Note that this model assumes host defences against pathogens are costly, an assumption to which we will return.

3 ***Incipient Mutualism***. Pathogen and host not only evolve towards doing one another less harm, but also evolve ways to benefit one another.

These three models are well illustrated by the many microbes that make up the normal flora that live on and in animals, particularly in the gut. The number of individual microbes that make up the normal flora is enormous. The majority of these microbes appear to have no harmful or directly beneficial effect on their host and so illustrate the Prudent Pathogen model. For some animals, notably ruminant mammals such as cows, certain species of bacteria play a vital role in breaking down specific components of food, such as cellulose, which the host cannot digest itself. Such bacteria are mutualists, and if evolved from pathogens, illustrate the Incipient Mutualism model. Occasionally, the gut may be infected by a harmful microbe, such as *E. coli* 0157 or *Salmonella*, which can kill its host; these exemplify the Mutual Aggression model.

2.2 Variation and reproduction

When a pathogen infects a human population, it is immediately apparent that there is a great deal of variation among individual hosts. Some do not become ill at all, some are only mildly affected, some are very ill indeed and others may die. The causes of this variation are many and varied. Some individuals are just lucky and do not get infected; some receive a larger dose of pathogen than others; some are more susceptible than others to the pathogen. Variation in susceptibility may reflect variation in exposure to the disease earlier in life, it may be due to overload of an individual's immune system as caused by a number of superimposed infections compounded by poor diet, or it may have a genetic basis. In this section, we are primarily concerned with genetic variation, both among hosts and among pathogens; it is the interplay between host and pathogen genotypes that provides the basis of their coevolution.

Genetic variation is the fundamental basis for evolution by natural selection. If there is no genetic variation in a character, it cannot evolve. In this section, we will explore the nature and sources of genetic variation in hosts and pathogens. A major source of variation is reproduction and so we will also consider the nature of reproduction in the two partners in their coevolved relationship.

2.2.1 Variation and reproduction in hosts

The development of new techniques for analysing genomes has made it possible to quantify the genetic basis of variable susceptibility to infectious diseases. For example, 12 genes have been identified that contribute to susceptibility or resistance to malaria in humans. For large, complex organisms such as humans, the major source of genetic variation is sexual reproduction. Many organisms reproduce asexually, either facultatively or obligately, and we will consider the significance of this in relation to infectious disease later. During sexual reproduction, meiosis and syngamy (fusion of gametes from different parents) involve genetic reassortment and recombination, as a result of which offspring have unique genotypes. Other sources of genetic variation are mutation and, at the level of populations, genetic drift.

Genetic mutations occur spontaneously, but mutation rates are accelerated by a variety of environmental factors such as chemical pollutants and increased radiation, e.g. radioactivity and UV-B. Few mutations are expressed phenotypically; many are eliminated by DNA repair mechanisms, others are eliminated by natural selection during development, while others are recessive and not expressed in diploid or polyploid organisms. Nevertheless, in organisms with large genomes, such as humans, every individual carries a small number of novel mutations.

Genetic drift is a factor in small, relatively isolated populations of a species. Such populations contain a random sub-set of all the alleles in the genome of that species. Genetic drift is an important factor in many aspects of host–pathogen coevolution. For example, small, isolated populations of humans and other vertebrate animals are often more susceptible to a particular disease because, by chance, they lack alleles protecting that species against that disease. It may also be important, as we will see later, in the evolution of pathogens.

Contemporary host populations show enormous genetic variation that is the result, not only of mutation, drift and reproduction, but also of natural selection. The genome of a species is the result of generations of natural selection and reflects its evolutionary history. This is very apparent in the context of infectious disease. In humans, a genetic basis for variation in susceptibility to infectious diseases has been revealed by a variety of techniques. The frequency of some susceptibility alleles shows a very strong association with disease. For example, alleles associated with immunity to malaria are much more common in Africa, which has long been exposed to this disease, than in other parts of the world that have no history of exposure to it (see *Immunology* CD2 'Malaria' lecture).

☐ Recall from Book 3 an example of genetic variation related to historical variation in malarial incidence.

■ The high frequency of HLA-B35 alleles in lowland areas of Sardinia where malaria was (historically) more frequent (Chapter 5, Section 5.1).

In contrast, alleles that influence the infectivity of HIV, a very recent disease, are expected to be much less common in the human population. In Book 3, we described how the allele called CCR5Δ32 provides low or high protection against AIDS, depending on whether it is in the heterozygous or homozygous state. These alleles are predicted to increase in frequency, because they prolong survival during peak reproductive years. In fact, this allele frequency is about 10% in Caucasians, which is more common than most alleles that affect malaria susceptibility. It is not known why CCR5Δ32 should occur at such a high frequency. The mutation itself does not seem to be deleterious to the immune system, since other linked genes can carry out the functions of this particular chemokine receptor. We can speculate that either (1) it is a duplicate gene that has arisen by chance; until now it has been evolutionarily neutral and has coincidentally been common in the gene pool, or (2) it is linked to a gene which has a definite evolutionary advantage – possibly another chemokine receptor.

The most highly variable part of the genome of humans and other mammals is the major histocompatibility complex (MHC), introduced in Book 3, of which HLA-B35 is one variant. The MHC consists of a small number of linked genetic loci that code for human leucocyte antigens (HLAs). Six loci are commonly recognized, called HLA-A, -B, -C, DP, DQ and DR. These loci are highly polymorphic and an ever-increasing number of alleles are being identified. The number of alleles known by late 2002 was 206 at HLA-A, 403 at HLA-B, 92 at HLA-C and 400+ at HLA-D. Such levels of genetic polymorphism are far greater than anything known for other parts of the human genome. At most loci in the human genome, the number of alleles is in single figures. Different human populations have different MHC allele frequencies, presumably reflecting the history of diseases to which that population has been exposed (Figure 2.1).

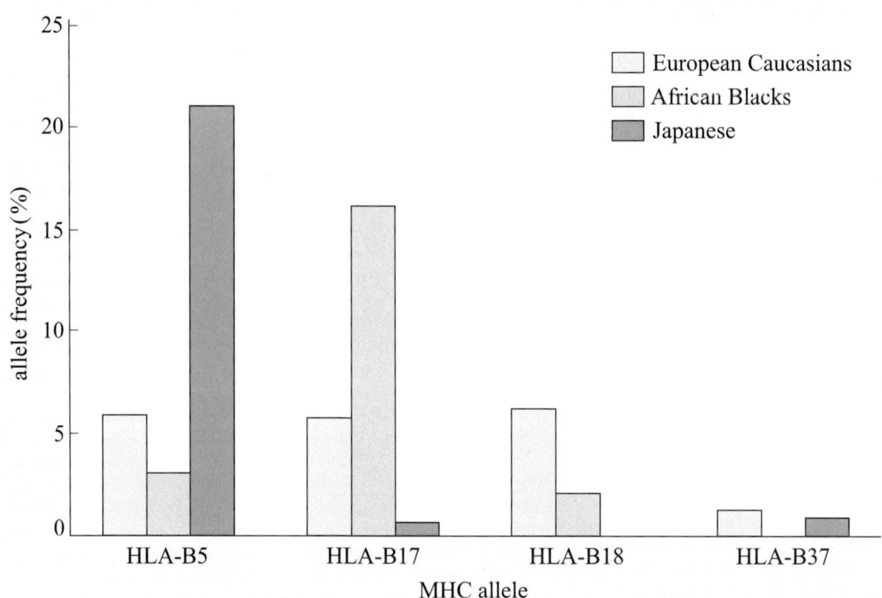

FIGURE 2.1
Percentage allele frequency for selected MHC variants in different human populations.

The MHC was originally discovered in the context of graft rejection. Tissue grafts are much more likely to be successful when donor and recipient have very similar MHC genotypes, and this is more likely when they are close relatives. Genetic variation in the MHC is interpreted as an adaptation against pathogens; over a number of progeny, it allows recognition by the immune system of a wide range of pathogens (see Book 3, Chapter 5). A consequence of the very high levels of variation that exist at MHC loci is that there is a great deal of variation in the effectiveness with which individuals respond to specific pathogens.

If genetic variation in the MHC is an adaptation against pathogens, then we would expect to find hosts to be more susceptible to pathogens if, for some reason, that genetic variation is reduced.

- Can you suggest a process that tends to reduce genetic variation?

- Inbreeding. Frequent matings among close relatives lead to a reduction in heterozygosity, i.e. reduced genetic variation.

This hypothesis has been tested among free-ranging Soay sheep living on the Scottish island of St. Kilda. Because the size of the sheep population is restricted by the small size of the island, the level of inbreeding is quite high. The study revealed that, in winters when particularly severe weather caused high mortality, the sheep that died had higher levels of intestinal nematode pathogens and were also more inbred than those that survived. What is unclear is the extent to which the homozygosity or the increased parasite burden (possibly caused by the former) contributed to the lower survival.

The very high levels of variation that exist at loci associated with immune defence are paradoxical. Infectious disease exerts strong selection on host populations and the usual outcome of strong selection is very low levels of genetic variation. However, in this case we should not consider 'infectious disease' as a single entity. Each infection is different and requires a different means of recognition (antigen presentation) and response. Consequently, different pathogens select for different genes and therefore promote diversity. The severity of specific disease outbreaks also varies from generation to generation. As a result, strong selection by one pathogen is not sustained for long enough to drive alleles related to that disease to fixation. The 'selective environment' presented by disease is constantly shifting and much of the genetic variation we observe among hosts reflects the exposure of past generations to infections.

There are a number of other factors that may promote high genetic variation in hosts, including:

1. Pathogens selectively infect commoner genotypes so that rare genotypes escape infection and thus tend to increase in frequency. For example, rare genotypes of the New Zealand snail *Potamopyrgus antipodarum* largely escape infection by the trematode *Microphallus*.
2. A number of species, including humans, have been found to mate preferentially with partners who are different from them at MHC loci (a mating pattern called disassortative mating). This increases heterozygosity at MHC loci. Experimental studies using mice provide evidence that MHC heterozygosity is adaptive. Mice were exposed to multiple strains of *Salmonella* and a single strain of *Listeria* in large population enclosures. MHC heterozygous mice had greater survival and higher body weight than homozygous mice.
3. Selection, as in the case of the Soay sheep described above, may act against homozygous individuals.
4. Migration of individuals from one part of a host's range to another introduces novel alleles into local populations. People are particularly mobile hosts and levels of genetic variation in human populations due to migration are thought to be very high.

As a result of all these factors, the human genome is far from static over time; indeed, in terms of allele frequencies in local populations, it is in a constant state of flux.

> Genomes change. Different versions of genes rise and fall in popularity driven by the rise and fall of diseases. ... The genome that we decipher in this generation is but a snapshot of an ever-changing document. There is no definitive edition.
>
> (Ridley, 1999)

Because humans reproduce sexually, we tend to assume that sexual reproduction is the 'normal' way to reproduce. It is, however, only one of many reproductive mechanisms found among animals and plants and its evolution is a matter of continuing debate among evolutionary biologists. This debate arises because sexual reproduction is metabolically very costly, for reasons we cannot explore here. To offset these costs, sexual reproduction must confer some very significant advantage.

> Sex must be important, simply because reproducing in this eccentric way is so expensive. By becoming involved with a male, a female dilutes her genes with those of someone else who does rather little to ensure that they survive. Even worse, she produces sons who go in for the same selfish behaviour. To balance this enormous cost, sex must have some hefty advantages for genes if not for their products – and it does; for a sexual world has conquered death.
>
> (Jones, 1999, p. 272)

Jones is referring to the capacity of sexual reproduction to act as a filter of germ cells that eliminates the majority of mutations before they can be passed on to progeny. But this is only one reason why sex is advantageous. It is widely accepted that another important advantage is that the genetic recombination that results from sex enables a species to counteract pathogens that cause infectious disease. Evidence that pathogens may play a role in determining the reproductive mode of hosts comes from studies of the freshwater snail *Potamopyrgus antipodarum* in New Zealand lakes. Individual snails are either male or female, unlike many snails that are hermaphrodites, but females are capable of a form of asexual reproduction called parthenogenesis (meaning 'virgin birth'). Some populations consist entirely of females and so must reproduce asexually; others contain as many as 40% male individuals, and so have the potential for sexual reproduction. A comparison of 66 snail populations revealed a strong tendency for males to be more frequent in locations that were heavily infected by parasitic trematode flatworms (Figure 2.2). This suggests that sexual reproduction is favoured in snail populations where pathogens are abundant.

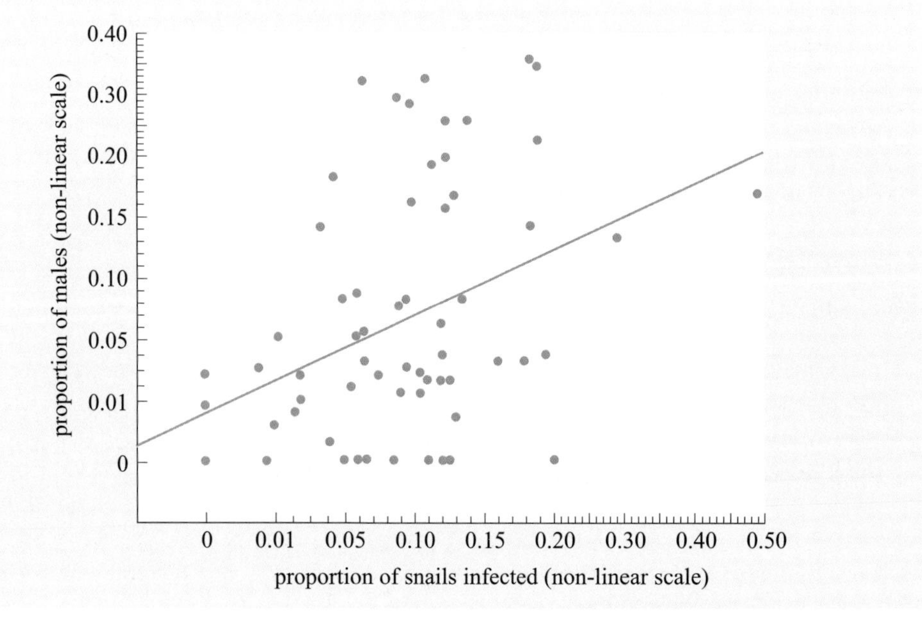

FIGURE 2.2
The relationship between the frequency of males in each population of host snails (*Potamopyrgus antipodarum*) and the proportion infected with parasites.

Sexual reproduction is a complex process that confers many diverse benefits on individuals, but which also incurs many diverse costs. Its role in generating genetic variation as a defence against disease is only one benefit. An important cost is that it provides a very reliable and efficient means of transmission for pathogens, a topic to which we return in Section 2.5. An interesting benefit, relevant to infectious disease, is the opportunity it provides for individuals to mate preferentially with apparently disease-free partners.

2.2.2 Variation and reproduction in pathogens

Like hosts, pathogens show genetic variation that results from mutation and drift, but they vary in terms of the amount of variation resulting from reproduction. Typically, viruses and bacteria reproduce asexually, but protoctists and invertebrate pathogens possess various forms of sexual reproduction that increases genetic variation, as it does for hosts. For example, many tapeworms, which have a very small chance of encountering a mate, may be self-fertilizing hermaphrodites. A survey of pathogens found that sexual reproduction is more common in parasitic species than it is in closely related non-parasitic species and models of coevolution suggest that, under certain conditions, sexual reproduction is adaptive for pathogens.

Although most bacteria do not engage in sexual reproduction, there is increasing evidence that they achieve higher levels of genetic recombination than has generally been assumed. A review of reproductive mechanisms among pathogenic protoctists suggests that most can reproduce sexually, thereby rapidly generating genetic variation, and clonally (i.e. asexually), thereby stabilizing successful genotypes. The mechanisms that cause a protoctist pathogen to switch from one reproductive mode to another are not known.

As we saw in Book 2, a source of genetic variation that sets viruses and bacteria apart from other pathogens is **horizontal transfer** of genes from a variety of sources. Viruses can acquire genes from other viral strains and from host cells. Bacteria can incorporate into their genomes a variety of genetic elements, including plasmids, phages and transposons that may be derived from their environment or from bacteria of other strains or 'species' (Book 2, Box 2.2). The details of these mechanisms are beyond the scope of this book; the significant point is that viruses and bacteria have many ways of acquiring genes from a variety of sources, and thus have the capacity for generating a very high level of genetic variation.

Of particular interest in the context of host/pathogen relationships are genetic elements called pathogenicity islands (PAIs).

- ☐ Recall from Book 2, p. 33, the definition of pathogenicity islands.

- ■ Particular regions in the bacterial genome that code for virulence factors.

PAIs are large regions of a bacterial genome that are present in the genomes of pathogenic strains but absent from the genomes of the same or related non-pathogenic bacterial species. They are transferred horizontally among bacteria and identical PAIs have been found in bacteria that cause different diseases. They can influence the virulence of a bacteria in a variety of ways, for example, by coding for toxin production (see Section 2.3 for discussion of virulence). PAIs have only recently been discovered and important questions about them are still to be answered, such as: where do they come from and what kind of selective processes are involved in their transfer?.

Largely as a result of the development of modern molecular techniques, biologists are now much more aware of the extent, and the causes, of genetic variation in pathogens than they were some 20 years ago. Previously, pathogens were assumed to conform to a 'clonal model' in which a successful strain could spread through a host population, reproducing asexually, and remaining little changed genetically. It is now realized that, in many pathogens, new strains can appear very frequently because they have ways of generating genetic variation that had not previously been appreciated (see above). One consequence of this is that a single host individual may be host to more than one pathogen strain at the same time. Such within-host variation has important consequences for the severity of illness experienced by hosts. Experimental studies have compared the effect of injecting mice with *Plasmodium* cultures of single and of mixed genotypes. The immune response that mice have to mount against mixed genotype pathogens is more costly and they suffer more severe sickness than when injected with a single genotype. More significantly, the occurrence of within-host variation has completely altered the way in which biologists now view the evolution of a very important aspect of pathogens – their virulence (Section 2.3).

As the number of pathogens whose genomes have been sequenced increases, it becomes apparent that some microbes are more variable than others. Very high levels of genetic variation have been found among samples of *Escherichia coli*, *Helicobacter pylori* and *Staphylococcus* sp., but very little variation has been found among samples of *Mycobacterium tuberculosis*. In contrast to the other species, the genome of *M. tuberculosis* shows very little evidence for the acquisition of new alleles by recombination or by horizontal transfer. High variation is related to pathogen versatility; some *Staphylococcus* species, for example, cause many kinds of disease in many different host species.

2.2.3 HIV

The capacity of pathogens to generate very high levels of genetic variation is strikingly illustrated by HIV. You will recall that HIV is an RNA virus. RNA is intrinsically less stable than DNA, both because it breaks more often and because DNA can be repaired using a complementary strand absent in RNA.

- ☐ Recall from Book 2 the peculiar feature of RNA replication in HIV (e.g. see Section 3.3.2).
- ■ HIV is a retrovirus which means that DNA can be produced from its RNA template using reverse transcriptase.

Reverse transcriptase has a high error rate, leading to base substitutions, insertions or deletions (see Screen 49 on the 'Biology of HIV' in the *HIV/AIDS* CD-ROM). The consequence is that on average there is about one mutation per genome in every replication cycle. Furthermore, recombination may occur between the two RNA strands in the HIV virus.

- ☐ What do you predict is the consequence of the high mutation rate and the recombination between strands?

■ It will lead to high genetic variation in the virus.

Because HIV is able to replicate very rapidly, the genetic diversity is apparent even within a single host.

□ Can you recall another feature of HIV that is particularly relevant here?

■ It has an extremely long period of infectivity, which can be as much as 10 to 15 years. Therefore, HIV has a very long time within a host in which to reproduce and generate variation.

When HIV infects a person, it reproduces and migrates to different parts of the body, especially to the lymph nodes. As a result, several sub-populations are formed which are largely physically isolated from one another. This situation is very similar to the distribution of many animals and plants in fragmented landscapes and, in the language of ecology, is called a **metapopulation** (a population of populations). Each sub-population may differ genetically from the others from the start, because of genetic drift, and, as reproduction proceeds, sub-populations tend to diverge more and more over time. A genetic analysis of HIV samples taken from different parts of a single dead person's body revealed very large genetic differences between different sub-populations (see the *Immunology* CD2 lecture 'HIV'). These genetic differences revealed are greater than those that separate humans from chimpanzees; the latter having evolved over 5 to 10 million years. Genetic variation is much greater in HIV-1, which also has a much wider geographic distribution, than in HIV-2. Twenty-four distinct genetic forms, or 'quasispecies' of HIV-1 had been identified by 2002.

This example raises an important general point about the nature of the environment that hosts provide for pathogens. It has been suggested that to many pathogens 'we and other mammals ... are little more than soft, thin-walled flasks of culture media' but, in reality, the host environment is much more diverse. A large, complex organism like a human provides a very varied environment for a pathogen, which can be regarded as a number of 'habitats' or habitat patches. Most pathogens are specialized to colonize only one habitat (e.g. the influenza virus colonizes the respiratory tract), but some can colonize several habitats. The colonization of different parts of a host's body by a pathogen has two important potential consequences:

1 As in the example of HIV described above, it can lead to the pathogen population forming a metapopulation structure with consequent considerable genetic variation.

2 A particular pathogen may have very different effects on its host, depending on which part it has colonized. For example, *Neisseria meningitidis* is typically a commensal inhabitant of the upper respiratory tract, but is a highly virulent pathogen when it crosses into the brain, causing meningitis.

2.2.4 Conclusion

We have noted that coevolution between hosts and pathogens is a process in which each partner is adapted to counteract the adverse effects on it caused by the other. This is a process that may never reach a stable or static outcome.

- ☐ What is the hypothesis that suggests that coevolved organisms are in a state of continuous evolution?
- ■ The Red Queen hypothesis (Book 2, Section 7.6).

Thus, both partners are constantly generating genetic variation. For either partner to continue to exist, it must continually counteract the genetic changes that arise in the other. An important feature of the coevolutionary relationship between hosts and pathogens is that it involves partners that differ, sometimes markedly, in the mechanisms that each possesses for generating genetic variation. They also differ markedly in another important respect – generation time. Because genetic variation largely arises from, and can only be passed on during, reproduction, it follows that the rate at which an organism can generate new genetic variants depends on its rate of reproduction, which is determined by its generation time. Humans have a generation time measured in years; many pathogens have generation times measured in hours or a few days. It follows that pathogens can, potentially, generate new genetic variants at a much higher rate than their hosts.

Summary of Sections 2.1 and 2.2

1. Three models of host–pathogen coevolution are presented: Mutual Aggression (host and pathogen engaged in arms race); Prudent Pathogen (pathogen evolves towards doing less harm to host) and Incipient Mutualism (where pathogen and host come to benefit each other).
2. Genetic variation amongst hosts is one reason for variation in susceptibility to infection. This is illustrated by alleles associated with malaria defence and infection with HIV. The most variable region of the mammalian genome is the major histocompatibility complex (MHC).
3. Genetic variation in hosts may be decreased by inbreeding, which may reduce resistance to disease. Conversely, genetic variation in hosts may be increased by pathogens due to selective infection of commoner genotypes, preferential mating with partners with different MHC loci, temporal variation in the pathogen environment and selection against homozygotes.
4. Genetic variation in pathogens is generated, as in the hosts, by sexual reproduction (amongst protoctists and invertebrate pathogens) and, unlike the hosts, by horizontal transfer of genes (bacteria and viruses). A single host may possess several pathogen strains at one time, exemplified by HIV. Pathogens vary greatly in their genetic variation (e.g. high in *Staphylococcus aureus* and low in *Mycobacterium tuberculosis*).
5. HIV provides a good example of a pathogen that has high genetic variation both within and between hosts. The variation is generated by copying errors by reverse transcriptase and recombination between the RNA strands. This variation is realized within hosts due to the rapid replication of the virus and may be patchy due to the movement of the viruses to different parts of the host, creating a metapopulation structure.
6. The relatively short generation times of pathogens and their high capacity for genetic variation pose a major problem for hosts with long generation times.

2.3 The evolution of virulence

The mechanisms that determine the virulence of a particular pathogen, and the evolutionary factors that determine how virulent it is, are topics of considerable interest.

- ☐ Recall from Books 1 and 2 the meaning of virulence.
- ■ In Book 1, it is a bold term with a concise definition concerning ability to establish an infection. In Book 2, virulence is described as a measure of the ease with which an organism is able to cause damage and disease in host tissues. Bacterial products that contribute to virulence are termed virulence factors.

Thus, the term virulence is being used to cover both the ease with which an infection is established and the degree of damage. Elsewhere, the former definition of virulence is sometimes replaced by the term **infectivity**, which refers to the capacity of a pathogen to infect new hosts, rather than the harm that it does to its host.

Once the pathogen has been transmitted, a major factor determining the virulence of a pathogen is its reproductive rate, as it is by reproducing in host cells that pathogens establish infection and cause damage to host tissues. In other words, virulence can be regarded as 'collateral damage' of pathogen reproduction. This is an important point about the pathogen–host relationship and is crucial for understanding the evolution of virulence. Unlike predators, pathogens are generally not specifically adapted to kill their hosts, but may be adapted to reproduce rapidly. To understand the evolution of virulence, therefore, we need to consider how natural selection acts, not on virulence *per se*, but on characteristics such as the reproductive rate of a pathogen. This raises an important point about the analysis of evolutionary processes, which was emphasized by the late Stephen Jay Gould. Just because a particular character of an organism, such as the virulence of a pathogen, is of interest to us, it does not follow that it is a character that has been subjected directly to natural selection. It may either be a combination of traits or it may be the result of 'coincidental evolution' resulting from natural selection acting on another character. For example, bacteria such as *Clostridium botulinum*, which causes botulism, and *C. tetani*, which causes tetanus, produce powerful toxins that attack the nervous system, making them very dangerous to humans. Neither pathogen is transmitted from human to human; both are better regarded as soil-living bacteria that can infect humans. (Neonatal tetanus is a major global problem, causing about 500 000 deaths per year.) It is thus likely that their toxins have evolved in the context of their normal, soil (or sausage!) -living existence and that their pathogenicity in humans is coincidental.

All other things being equal, natural selection favours those pathogen strains that reproduce most rapidly because they leave more progeny. There are circumstances, however, in which slower pathogen reproduction is favoured by natural selection because the host lives for longer. There is thus a trade-off between rapid reproduction and host survival, that is between high and low pathogen virulence.

The above definitions of virulence of a pathogen are useful as qualitative descriptions but need to be quantified for formulating mathematical models of the epidemiology or evolution of disease. In studies using animals, the virulence of a pathogen is expressed as its lethal dose (LD_{50}), the number of microbes required to kill 50% of infected hosts. In human studies, it is expressed as the case fatality rate, the number of infected individuals who die divided by the number of individuals infected, usually expressed as a percentage. The case fatality rate of diarrhoeal diseases is 5 or 6% (death rates in children are much higher), cholera 5–50% (depending on treatment) and AIDS at least 90%. These definitions measure virulence in terms of host mortality, and thus provide convenient, explicit and quantifiable measures that can be used in mathematical models. They ignore, however, many aspects of the harm that pathogens do to their hosts that do not involve death, but which can be considered to be aspects of virulence, such as how incapacitated does a host become.

When thinking about the evolutionary biology of infectious diseases, we need to define virulence in terms of host fitness; the virulence of a pathogen is the reduction in the fitness of a host that results from infection by that pathogen. This definition is also problematic for two reasons. First, fitness is very difficult to measure and, secondly, as emphasized in Section 2.2, individual hosts vary considerably in their response to infection by a particular pathogen, which creates a problem for all definitions of virulence. Virulence is not a fixed property of a given pathogen but is a dynamic property of the interaction between host and pathogen, changing over time. For example, syphilis in Europe may have been a much more severe disease in the 16th century, killing people within months rather than years.

- ☐ What problem for this interpretation is highlighted by the *Syphilis* Case Study?
- ■ It raises the debate as to whether 'the Great Pox' was actually syphilis or another disease or even a cocktail of diseases (possibly including syphilis).

Scarlet fever, caused by the bacterium *Streptococcus pyogenes*, was a disease with a very high case fatality rate in the late 1800s, killing very large numbers of children, but by the 1930s and 1940s it had become a relatively mild childhood disease. This may in part have been due to its development of effective treatments. Influenza is the best-known example of a disease in which periodic outbreaks are caused by the emergence of especially virulent viral strains, the most recent being the 1918 pandemic (Book 1, Chapter 2).

FIGURE 2.3
Rabbit infected with the *Myxoma* virus.

The idea that some diseases may have been more severe in the past is often used as evidence that there is a general evolutionary trend by which virulent pathogens become more benign. Further evidence for such a process comes from the history of myxomatosis in Australia, a rare example in which evolutionary change in a disease was directly observed over several years. The *Myxoma* virus is indigenous to South America, where it causes a non-lethal disease in rabbits. In 1950 it was introduced to Australia in an attempt to control massive populations of rabbits, themselves introduced from Europe. A flea-borne pathogen, the *Myxoma* virus caused an epidemic that killed 99.8% of rabbits (Figure 2.3). A second epidemic killed 90% of the rabbit generation that resulted from the survivors of the first, but a third epidemic killed only 50%. This rapid change was due in part to a decrease in the virulence of the virus, in part to rapidly evolving immune defences among the rabbits. So prevalent is the idea that pathogens generally evolve from being very virulent towards being benign that it has been referred to as the 'conventional wisdom'. The emphasis of much of the recent literature in this area is to challenge this view, and to identify the circumstances in which it is and is not true.

Venereal syphilis is an example of a disease that may have evolved from one of two milder diseases – pinta and yaws. There is fairly general acceptance that pinta and yaws existed among humans long before syphilis evolved. One theory for the origin of syphilis is that it followed the early transition of human societies from a purely rural existence to urban life. One suggestion is that the pathogen evolved into a venereal pathogen when the wearing of clothes reduced the frequency of the skin-to-skin contact by which yaws and pinta are transmitted. As a result, a mild disease of children evolved into a severe disease of adults.

- Based on the pathogen life-history strategies in Table 1.4, what would you predict about the duration of yaws and pinta in the host if the frequency of skin-to-skin contact is higher than for syphilis.

- The pathogens of these species would be expected to have shorter durations in the host. This appears to be true, although yaws may remain in the host for up to 10 years (pinta has a much shorter duration in the host).

Another example is provided by detailed genetic analysis of the plague pathogen *Yersinia pestis*, that suggests it evolved from the much less virulent *Y. pseudotuberculosis*, a human enteric pathogen. However, we need to be wary about distinguishing between evolution of new strains or species with increased or decreased virulence and evolution of more or less virulence within a strain or species.

In Book 2, it was noted that the virulence of bacteria is determined by a number of specific aspects of its biology, called virulence factors, often determined by genes derived by horizontal transfer. These virulence factors include the effectiveness of the bacterial pathogen in penetrating host cells, how successfully they evade their host's immune system, and their ability to obtain essential nutrients, particularly iron, from its host. (Such arguments about virulence factors can also be applied to pathogens other than bacteria.) A recent discovery suggests that at least one virulence factor, colonization of the host, can change very rapidly. Cultures of the cholera pathogen *Vibrio cholerae* collected from pond water are less infectious than cultures collected from human faeces; passage through the gut of a human host induces a change in the bacterium that makes it more infectious. This change involves the activation of *V. cholera* genes that are not expressed in pond water. In experiments using mice as hosts, cholera bacteria collected from human faeces were 700 times more infectious than bacteria collected from laboratory cultures. This hyperinfectivity lasts for at least five hours in pond water, but disappears in bacteria kept for 18 hours in the laboratory. The mechanism underlying hyperinfectivity may help explain why it is that cholera epidemics spread very rapidly.

Finally, it is important to consider that the virulence of a pathogen with respect to a particular host depends on whether or not that pathogen has alternative hosts. For such pathogens, it may be entirely inappropriate to consider virulence with respect to humans as being subject to natural selection in humans at all. Some of the deadliest human infectious diseases are caused by pathogens whose natural hosts are other mammals or birds, e.g. Ebola fever and hantavirus. For these diseases, virulence in humans appears to be much greater than it is in their non-human hosts and is best regarded, not as an adaptation by a pathogen to human hosts, but as a by-product of its coevolution with its non-human hosts.

> A truly successful pathogen is commensal, living in amity with its host, or even giving it positive advantages … A pathogen that regularly and inevitably kills its hosts cannot survive long, in the evolutionary sense, unless it multiplies with tremendous rapidity.
>
> (Mr Spock, *Star Trek 2*)

Summary of Section 2.3

1 Virulence has been defined as both the ease with which an infection is established and the degree of damage. The best definition from an evolutionary point of view is effect on host fitness, but this is difficult to measure.

2 Virulence can be thought of as collateral damage of pathogen reproduction. As such, evolution of virulence may be misleading and we should be considering evolution of reproduction rates.

3 Quantitative definitions of virulence include lethal dose and case fatality rate.

4 Conventional wisdom is that pathogens evolve from more to less virulent. However, there are counter-examples, especially in the initial stages of pathogen evolution (e.g. *Yersinia* species). What is certain is that virulence factors may change rapidly, e.g. as in cholera.

2.4 Manipulation of hosts by pathogens

2.4.1 Introduction

Crickets are terrestrial animals that normally avoid water. Individuals infected with hairworms (genus *Nematomorpha*), however, hurl themselves into ponds and streams, where they are eaten by fish. This is but one example of manipulation of host behaviour by a pathogen. The host's behaviour is maladaptive for itself but is adaptive for the pathogen; in this example, fish are the final hosts and crickets an intermediate host for the pathogen. Many examples of **host manipulation** involve pathogens with complex life cycles, in which it is the behaviour of an intermediate host that is manipulated in such a way that the chances of the pathogen's life cycle being completed are increased (see Table 2.1 and Figure 2.4).

☐ Recall from Book 2 an example of manipulation of hosts by pathogens.

■ The liver fluke *Dicrocoelium dendriticum* that affects the behaviour of its intermediate ant host (Book 2, Chapter 7).

TABLE 2.1 Manipulation of hosts or vectors by parasites/pathogens.

Host or vectors	Parasite/pathogen	Nature of manipulation
beetle, *Tenebrio monitor* (final host is rat)	tapeworm, *Hymenolepis diminuta*	infected beetles invest less in reproduction and consequently survive longer (40% increase in survival time in females, 25% in males)
mammals	rabies virus	infected host develops rabid behaviour, which includes intense salivation and tendency to bite other animals
snail, *Succinea* (final host is bird)	trematode, *Leucochloridium macrostomum*	parasite sporocysts invade snail's tentacles, causing them to swell, making snail very conspicuous to birds and thus more likely to be eaten (see Figure 2.4)
banded killifish, *Fundulus diaphanus* (final host is bird)	digenean trematode, *Crassiphiala bulboglossa*	parasitized fish are hungry, move to periphery of shoal to find food, more likely to be eaten by birds
mosquito	malaria pathogen, *Plasmodium* sp.	infected mosquitoes continue feeding throughout the night, whereas uninfected ones do not; as a result, infected mosquitoes bite more hosts

FIGURE 2.4
Manipulation of its host by a pathogen. The snail (*Succinea*, top left) is the intermediate host of the bird trematode *Leucochloridium macrostomum*. Reproduction in the snail produces large sporocysts (lower left) that migrate into the snail's tentacles, making them very swollen (lower right). These are very conspicuous (top right) to birds which bite them off the snail, thus becoming infected.

Pathogens affect the physiology and behaviour of their hosts in a variety of ways. In the context of human diseases, these changes, such as sneezing or diarrhoea, are generally regarded as symptoms. There are three ways of looking at these:

1 they are incidental consequences of infection, and are of no functional significance to either host or pathogen;

2 they are adaptive, defensive reactions to infection by the host;

3 they are changes in the host caused by pathogen manipulation and are adaptive for the pathogen, e.g. in aiding transmission.

Categories 2 and 3 are not mutually exclusive – it is possible for a change in a host to be adaptive for the host and to be adaptive for a pathogen (see below).

The possibility that symptoms of disease may be adaptive responses on the part of the host belongs to an area of biology called evolutionary medicine, which was pioneered by Randolph Nesse and George Williams. This takes the view that symptoms of disease such as pain, coughing, nausea, vomiting, diarrhoea and fever are defensive responses by the host that reduce the impact of infection. Vomiting and diarrhoea are mechanisms that eliminate pathogens from the body quickly; fever changes the host's body temperature in a way that favours the host's defence systems over the pathogen.

This way of viewing the world of infectious diseases raises a lot of interesting ideas but is fraught with pitfalls. A problem with evolutionary theory is that it can be used to explain everything by applying the general argument that 'if it exists it must be adaptive'. This does not advance our scientific understanding. Explanations that invoke adaptation should be regarded as hypotheses that can be rigorously tested. If we wanted to test the hypothesis that vomiting is an adaptive response to infection, for example, we would need to find a way of preventing it and then seeing if subjects become more ill as a result. There have been very few rigorous tests of ideas put forward under the heading of evolutionary medicine and so, for the present, it is best regarded as an interesting alternative way at looking at some aspects of infectious disease.

2.4.2 *Wolbachia*

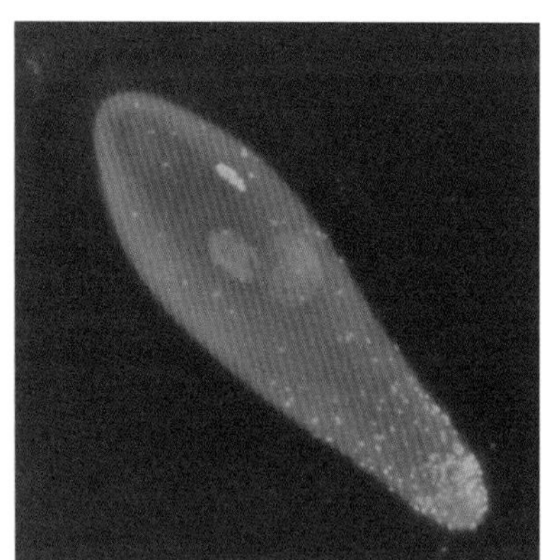

FIGURE 2.5
Electron micrograph of *Wolbachia*.

A remarkable form of host manipulation by symbiotic microbes is shown by rickettsial bacteria of the genus ***Wolbachia***. These infect arthropods and nematode worms (and may infect other invertebrate species) and are primarily transmitted vertically in the cytoplasm of host eggs, but can also be transmitted horizontally, sometimes between host species. In line with the general prediction that vertically transmitted symbionts will be benign or mutualistic, they are generally not virulent and, indeed, there are cases where they enhance host fecundity. However, the fact that they are transmitted exclusively through host females means that they are very hostile to males of host species. Some *Wolbachia* species kill male host embryos, others render sperm incompatible with uninfected eggs and others cause males to become females. In some host species, normally sexually reproducing females become parthenogenetic as a result of *Wolbachia* infection, rendering host males redundant.

Research into *Wolbachia* is at such an early stage that it is not clear how diverse it is, in terms of numbers of 'species', nor how wide is its range of hosts. In 1997 it was estimated to be present in 15 to 20% of all insect species, but by 2001 it was thought to be present in 75% of all arthropods! Although usually benign, at least to female hosts, some forms of *Wolbachia* are highly virulent. A strain found in *Drosophila*, charmingly called 'popcorn', becomes active as its host reaches maturity and kills it before it reproduces.

Research into *Wolbachia* has increased greatly in recent years, much of it driven by the possibility that *Wolbachia* could be used as a means to control insect pests, including disease vectors. For example, research is currently under way to see if *Wolbachia* can be used to control tsetse flies.

The human disease river blindness (onchocerciasis) is caused by the insect-borne nematode *Onchocerca volvulus* (Book 2, Section 7.5.2). It has recently been discovered that the immune reaction in the cornea that leads to blindness is not due to the nematode itself, but to endosymbiotic *Wolbachia* in the nematode. Treating the nematode with antibiotics eliminates the *Wolbachia*; it no longer causes blindness and, furthermore, becomes sterile.

2.4.3 Fever

Increased body temperature is a common symptom of infectious disease. There has long been a debate as to whether fever is an example of host manipulation by pathogens or is an adaptive response by the host. This question has been addressed experimentally in reptiles, and mammals, such as rabbits. Reptiles are ectotherms, meaning that they acquire body heat from their external environment, moving to warmer places to raise their body temperature; mammals are endotherms, generating heat internally. With reptiles, it is relatively easy to experimentally change their body temperature, by simply controlling the temperature of their environment. Several studies of this kind have shown that the survival of infected animals is increased if their body temperature is raised. With mammals, the most commonly used experimental approach is to suppress the physiological responses that cause fever; many such studies have shown that this procedure reduces the survival of infected animals.

At one time, it was thought that fever acts as a defence against infection by suppressing bacterial or viral reproduction, but this is not usually the case. Rather, it seems to enhance certain aspects of the host's immune response, e.g. increasing the rate of lymphocyte division. In particular, it acts synergistically with the host's physiological mechanisms that reduce the amount of iron circulating in the body. Iron is vital for microbe reproduction and denying them access to it reduces their reproductive rate.

Views on the importance of host manipulation as an outcome of the coevolution of hosts and pathogens are varied, and have shifted over the years. Examples like those listed in Table 2.1, which mostly relate to the manipulation of intermediate rather than final hosts, lead some researchers to see manipulation as a general characteristic of pathogens. A detailed analysis of the literature by Poulin, published in 2000, however, showed that the concept of host manipulation was a 'weakening paradigm'. On the other hand, it appears that the concept of host manipulation is staging a revival, primarily as the result of new discoveries about the very intimate ways in which pathogens interact, at a sub-cellular level, with their hosts. These ways include the process of apoptosis (Book 2, p. 81) in which the response of hosts to infection is to selectively kill off infected cells. As might be predicted from coevolution, some pathogens can prevent this threat to their survival by switching apoptosis off, for example, cytomegalovirus (CMV).

Summary of Section 2.4

1 There are three interpretations of changes in host behaviour and/or physiology due to pathogens. First, as incidental consequences of pathogens, secondly as adaptive defensive reactions by the host and thirdly as changes which favour the pathogen, e.g. in transmission.

2 *Wolbachia* bacteria manipulate their invertebrate host species by killing or harming males or removing the need for males by causing females to reproduce parthenogenetically.

3 The role of fever as either host manipulation or adaptive response of hosts has been tested experimentally. These studies have shown that fever increases host survival, probably by enhancing the immune response.

2.5 Evolution of transmission mechanisms

In Chapter 1, we emphasized the importance of transmission of pathogens in its relationship to within-host processes (Table 1.4), recognizing three routes of transmission. In this chapter, we have also discussed the importance of transmission with regard to virulence. It is therefore appropriate to spend some time discussing evolutionary aspects of transmission, focusing on two of the transmission types in Table 1.4: host-to-host contact and vectors. This will set the scene for discussion of related ecological aspects of transmission in Chapter 3.

2.5.1 Sexually transmitted infections

Sexually transmitted infections (STIs) are caused by pathogens whose principal means of transmission from one host to another is sexual intercourse by the host. This is a somewhat loose definition; some STIs can be transmitted in other ways (e.g. HIV by sharing hypodermic needles or blood transfusion). In addition to horizontal transmission during sex, many STIs are also transmitted vertically, either to the foetus in the uterus, or during birth, as the baby passes through the infected vagina. Whilst more than 20 pathogens may be transmitted during sex in humans (WHO Department of HIV/AIDS), we are only beginning to appreciate the diversity of STIs among other host species (see below).

Examples of the diversity of human STIs are given in Table 2.2. They typically cause chronic symptoms (see definition in Book 1, p. 21), for reasons we will explore, and, with the exception of HIV, cause relatively low mortality. WHO estimated that 174 million new cases of three STIs, gonorrhoea, syphilis and trichomoniasis, occurred worldwide in 1999 in men and women aged 15 to 49 years (WHO Department of HIV/AIDS). At the end of 2001, 40 million people were infected with HIV, with 5 million new cases occurring in 2001 ('HIV' lecture on the *Immunology* CD2). STIs are a major cause of infertility in women and when transmitted vertically to infants they often have much more serious effects than they do in adults. They are also associated with a greatly increased risk of HIV infection: people with gonorrhoea have a three-fold increased risk of contracting HIV, people with syphilis a four-fold increased risk (see *Syphilis* Case Study). The causal basis of this effect is not fully understood but is likely to involve several factors; for example, the genital lesions caused by STIs may make people more likely to be infected by HIV.

It is not surprising that many pathogens exploit host sexual activity as a means of transmission; it is a very intimate form of contact, ensuring reliable transmission and, for many species, it is the only context in which hosts come close enough for transmission to occur.

☐ What other advantage does transmission by sexual contact provide for the pathogen?

TABLE 2.2 Sexually transmitted infections of global importance.

Disease	Pathogen	Incidence*	Comments
syphilis	spirochaete bacterium *Treponema pallidum*	estimated 24 million new cases worldwide in 1999	can cause abortion, premature delivery, stillbirth; other symptoms detailed in *Syphilis* Case Study
gonorrhoea	coccal bacterium *Neisseria gonorrhoeae*	estimated 62 million new cases worldwide in 1999	common cause of pelvic inflammatory disease with subsequent risk of infertility; vertical transmission to infants causes blindness
genital herpes	herpes simplex virus 2 (HSV2)	approximately one-fifth of US adult population infected in late 20th century	closely related HSV1 causes oral herpes (cold sores)
AIDS	HIV	estimated that about 5 million new cases occur worldwide every year	see *HIV/AIDS* Case Study
chlamydia	bacterium *Chlamydia trachomatis*	estimated 92 million new cases worldwide in 1999	common cause of pelvic inflammatory disease with subsequent risk of infertility; vertical transmission causes conjunctivitis, blindness, pneumonia in infants
trichomoniasis	flagellate protoctist *Trichomonas vaginalis*	estimated 88 million new cases worldwide in 1999	affects women; men are asymptomatic carriers; associated with premature birth and low birth weight; may facilitate spread of HIV
candidiasis (thrush)	yeast *Candida albicans*	extremely common	see Book 2, p. 117

**Source:* WHO Department of HIV/AIDS.

- It guarantees transmission to another member of the same species (normally!), i.e. it provides host specificity.

Thus there is little or no opportunity for STIs to be transmitted between species. As a result, STIs are typically species-specific and we do not have to consider other host species in the context of controlling them.

STIs share a number of features that can be understood, in evolutionary terms, as adaptations by the pathogens to their mode of transmission. They have a long incubation period and latent period. They typically do not cause debilitating illness, except in very late stages of infection. The host does not develop immunity to them and so can be repeatedly infected.

Consider the host/pathogen relationship from the perspective of a venereal pathogen. The ideal host would be one that mates frequently and with many partners; such host behaviour would maximize its transmission to new hosts. In the real world, however, most hosts do not conform to this ideal. For many species, mating is a rare event and may occur only at certain times of year. There are many species that mate quite often, but do not often change their sexual partner. This is important from the standpoint of a venereal pathogen, because its fitness depends on the number of new hosts infected. In general, therefore, the interval between infection of a new host and that host mating with a new partner is long, much longer than that between catching a cold and starting to sneeze. Were a venereal pathogen to cause a debilitating, acute illness, it would severely reduce its chances of being transmitted to new hosts. Theoretical studies have suggested that, if a venereal pathogen reduces the mating success of its host, selection will favour strains of the pathogen that have reduced virulence. The optimal strategy for a venereal pathogen is thus to minimize the damage it does to its host for as long as possible. Consequently, it has to evade rather than seek to outpace its host's immune defences (see the discussion on pathogen strategies in Chapter 1).

Evasion of host defences involves two possible strategies: finding a place where the immune response is relatively weak, and becoming less detectable by the host's immune system. The genital tract of a female host is a potentially safe place for a pathogen because the host cannot afford defences so effective that they destroy sperm. Herpes viruses, including herpes simplex and herpes zoster, invade the nervous system of their host, a relatively safe site because the host cannot afford to damage nerve cells by mounting a vigorous immune response. There they remain dormant until the host's immune system is compromised by stress or illness. HIV incorporates itself into the cells of the host's immune system. The syphilis bacterium sheds the surface molecules that enable its host to recognize it, and the gonorrhoea bacterium changes its surface molecules so frequently that the host immune response does not catch up. Interestingly, the pilus genes of *Neisseria gonorrhoea* are one of the few places where introns occur in prokaryotic genes. The presence of introns introduces the possibility of varied splicing patterns which may contribute to variation of the *N. gonorrhoea* surface.

Related to the essentially 'stealthy' nature of sexually transmitted pathogens is the fact that many infected people present no symptoms; they are nonetheless able to transmit STIs to others. For example, 70 to 75% of women and 50% of men infected with *Chlamydia trachomatis* are symptom-free; 80% of women and 10% of men infected with gonorrhoea are asymptomatic (WHO Department of HIV/AIDS). This makes efforts to control these diseases very much more difficult.

- ☐ In the context of transmission, how would you interpret the subtle symptoms of first stage syphilis?

- ■ This helps transmission by not affecting host sexual behaviour and the pathogen not being detected by the host or potential mates.

It has been suggested that venereal pathogens might have evolved mechanisms by which they manipulate their hosts to mate more often or with more partners. In humans, promiscuity and the incidence of STIs are correlated but there is no reason to suppose that the causal basis of this correlation is anything other than that promiscuous behaviour increases the risk of infection. A few studies of animals have sought evidence that venereal pathogens cause more promiscuous behaviour but none has yet demonstrated such an effect.

Given the enormous variation among animal species in terms of how frequently they mate and, more importantly, how many mating partners they have, comparative studies would provide valuable insights into the impact of these variables on the evolution of host/venereal pathogen relationships. The information that is available for animal STIs has been reviewed by Sheila Lockhart and colleagues. They documented over 200 diseases, spread across a wide diversity of host species and involving a wide variety of pathogens. Among mammals, STIs, in comparison to other diseases, typically cause low mortality, are long-lived in their hosts, invoke relatively weak immune responses, have a narrower range of hosts and show less fluctuation in prevalence over time. This agrees with the observations for human STIs.

Detailed studies have been made of two STIs of the familiar two-spot ladybird (*Adalia bipunctata*). The fungus *Hesperomyces virescens* appears to affect ladybirds only in urban habitats and has been studied in London. Samples of ladybirds taken along transects running north to south and east to west across London show that its prevalence reaches a peak, at 50%, near Euston railway station (Figure 2.6). One possible explanation for this distribution is that higher temperatures in central London increase activity in ladybirds, enabling them to mate more often, and thus with more partners, than in rural habitats.

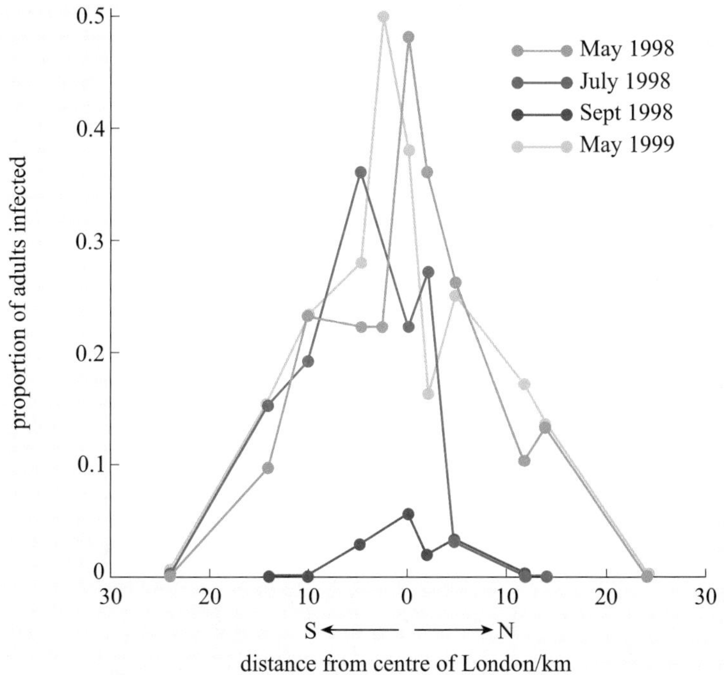

FIGURE 2.6
Prevalence of sexually transmitted disease in ladybirds.

The epidemiology and control of STIs are subject, perhaps more than other diseases, to powerful social factors. First, the social stigma attached to STIs makes infected people very reluctant to report them. Secondly, programmes to control STIs involve intense initiatives to educate people, to improve reporting rates and to carry out contact tracing. Such measures tend to collapse at times of social disruption. There has been a massive increase in the incidence of STIs in Eastern Europe following the break-up of the USSR. Major outbreaks of STIs also occur at times of war; additional factors here are the close association between soldiers and prostitutes and the propensity of invading armies to commit rape.

2.5.2 Vector-borne diseases

You have already studied some of the important infectious diseases of humans transmitted by vectors (see Table 2.3). A vector is a living creature that can transmit infection from one host to another. While vectors are normally considered in the context of transmission from one human host to another, they can also transmit pathogens between different host species and are thus a factor in zoonotic diseases (see Box 1.2 in Book 1). Historically, vector-borne diseases, including malaria, dengue fever, yellow fever and plague, were probably responsible for more human disease and death in the 17th century through to the early 20th century than all other causes combined (although respiratory infections and diarrhoeal diseases, especially amongst babies, may have been as important). The evolutionary biology and ecology of vector-borne diseases is much more complex than that of directly transmitted diseases, because it involves an interaction between three, rather than two partners. We have to consider not only the relationship between pathogen and final host, but also that between pathogen and vector and that between vector and final host.

TABLE 2.3 Arthropod vectors of medical importance.

Arthropod	Diseases transmitted
mosquitoes	malaria, dengue fever, filariasis, yellow fever
sandflies	leishmaniasis, sandfly fever
other flies	trypanosomiasis, onchocerciasis
fleas	plague, rickettsial infection
ticks	relapsing fever, rickettsial infection, Lyme disease
mites	rickettsial infection
lice	relapsing fever, typhus

Insect vectors have been described as ‘flying syringes’, the implication being that they provide a very reliable mode of pathogen transmission, regardless of the mobility of the human host and one which, moreover, evades many of the host’s first-line defences.

Because vector-borne pathogens are dependent on their vector to transmit them to new hosts, it is widely assumed that it is in their best interests not to harm the health of the vector. Insects have complex immune systems, similar in some ways to those of mammals (although insects lack lymphocytes and antibodies) that defend them against pathogenic microbes. Recent research has shown how the insect vector’s immune systems respond to the pathogens they carry. For example, mosquitoes mount an immune response to malarial pathogens, indicating that they are not simply passive in transmission. In response, vector-borne pathogens are covered by surface coats that not only protect them from the vector’s immune system, but which also interact with specific vector tissues to find those sites in the vector’s body where development and reproduction of the pathogen take place. Overall, the question of whether or not malaria pathogens have a harmful effect on their mosquito vectors remains unresolved. The number of studies that have found evidence of detrimental effects is roughly equal to the number that have not. A number of harmful effects of malaria pathogens on mosquitoes have been identified, including tissue damage, loss of protein and glucose to the benefit of pathogens, and an increased risk of death resulting from the fact that infected mosquitoes feed more often and may be more easily swatted!

To be successfully transmitted by a vector, a pathogen must be able to evade or resist defensive responses to it that are made by its vector. Thus, pathogens must acquire adaptations that enable them to be vector-borne. We noted in Section 2.3 that the plague bacillus *Yersinia pestis* evolved relatively recently from *Y. pseudotuberculosis*, which causes a relatively mild food- and water-borne gut disease. Genetic comparison of these two bacteria has revealed that *Y. pestis* differs from *Y. pseudotuberculosis* by the inclusion in the former of two plasmids. One of these codes for an enzyme that protects the bacillus from digestion by its rat flea vector. This ability to be transmitted by a vector may have favoured the evolution of more virulent forms of *Yersinia*, and thus the emergence of plague.

The fact that vectors are not simply passive carriers of pathogens, but have a complex interaction with them, is very important for the development of new control measures for diseases such as malaria. Current efforts to control malaria are hampered by the evolution of drug resistance in *Plasmodium*, the evolution of insecticide resistance in mosquitoes and the lack of an effective vaccine. A potentially effective new tool is to use genetic modification to strengthen the response of mosquitoes to *Plasmodium*. Such genetic modifications have already been achieved, in the laboratory, to produce mosquitoes that are relatively inefficient at transmitting the malaria pathogen. Transferring this technique to the field is fraught with problems however, not least because of public and scientific concerns about the possible long-term effects of releasing genetically modified organisms into the wild.

Recent evidence suggests that the rodent malarial pathogen *Plasmodium berghei* itself limits the degree to which it infects its mosquito vector *Anopheles stephensi*. Only a small proportion of the gametocytes that enter the mosquito's midgut after a blood meal survive. The midgut is a hostile environment for the gametocytes but more than 50% die naturally by apoptosis or programmed cell death. This appears to be an adaptation on the part of the pathogen that limits the burden that it imposes on its mosquito vector. Most significantly, it offers an interesting avenue of research into new ways to control malaria; if mechanisms that can increase the proportion of pathogens that undergo apoptosis can be found, then malarial proliferation in mosquitoes might be reduced.

Some vector-borne diseases are emerging or resurging for a complex variety of reasons. These include urbanization, deforestation and changing agricultural practices, but a major reason is the evolution of drug-resistant pathogen strains and of pesticide resistance in vectors. There are also alarming predictions about the long-term effects of climate change; global warming, it is argued, will cause vectors to expand their range, bringing malaria to temperate regions where currently it cannot survive. The data currently available on the impact of climate change on vector-borne diseases are inconclusive. This should be seen as 'absence of evidence', rather than as 'evidence of absence' for such an effect.

Some emerging infections of humans are primarily diseases of animals that have become more common in recent years because humans have increased their frequency of contact with their vectors. Tick-borne encephalitis and Lyme disease (Book 2, p. 55 and Figure 2.7) have increased in northern temperate regions, including Europe and North America, since the 1980s because of greater human contact with the ticks that transmit them. The incidence of Lyme disease has

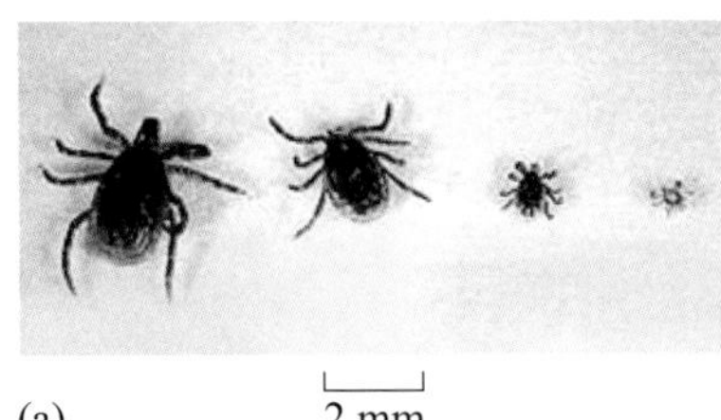

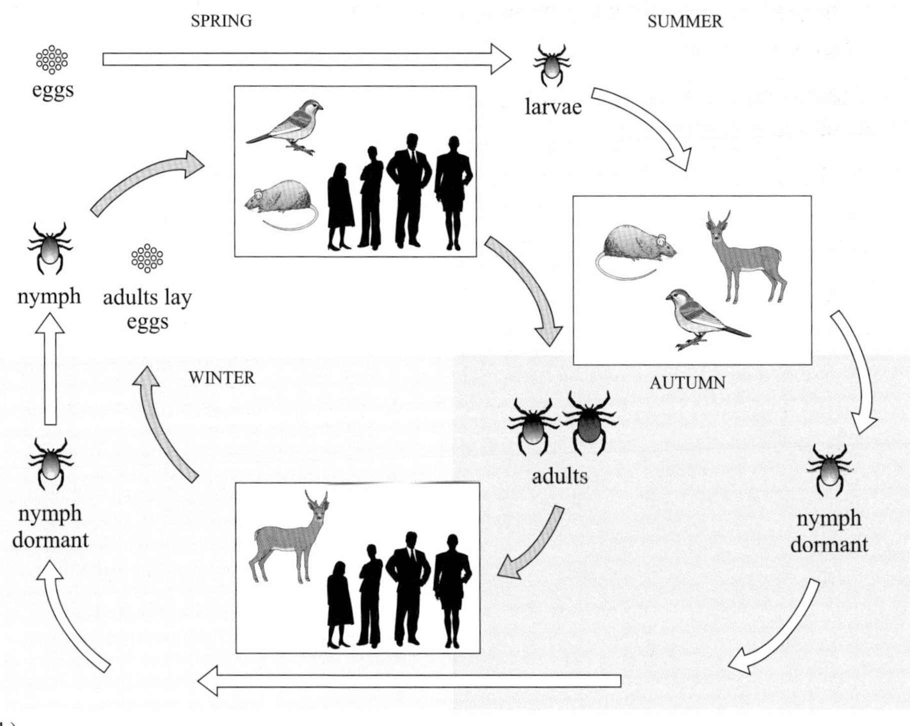

(a) (b)

FIGURE 2.7 (a) *Ixodes* sp.: from left to right, adult male and female; two immature stages. (b) The two-year life cycle of a deer tick located in a north-eastern state of the United States. Life cycles may vary slightly for other ticks in different regions of North America. Adult female ticks lay eggs on the ground in early spring. By summer, eggs hatch into larvae. Larvae feed on mice, other small mammals, deer, and birds in the late summer and early autumn, moult into nymphs, and then are dormant until the next spring. Nymphs feed on rodents, other small mammals, birds and humans in the late spring and summer and moult into adults in the autumn. In the autumn and early spring, adult ticks feed and mate on large mammals (especially deer) and bite humans. The adult female ticks then drop off these animals and lay eggs in spring, completing a two-year life cycle.

increased steadily since its discovery in the USA in 1975. In the eastern USA, a lot of farmland has fallen into disuse, encouraging an increase in populations of wild deer, which carry *Ixodes* ticks; humans pick them up from long grass where deer have been grazing.

Finally, the fact that vectors can transmit pathogens between different host species raises the possibility that they have been responsible for the transfer of animal diseases to humans. For example, the blood-sucking stable fly (*Stomoxys calcitrans*) is capable of transmitting HIV and, because it feeds on the carcases of dead apes offered for sale as 'bush meat' in African markets, as well as humans, it may have been the agent that passed HIV from primates to humans.

Summary of Section 2.5

1 The evolutionary aspects of two types of transmission are discussed in detail – transmission by host-to-host contact through sexual activity and transmission by vectors.

2 Sexually transmitted infections (STIs) are caused by viruses, bacteria and fungi and affect large numbers of people worldwide and generally cause chronic infections.

3 STIs are host-specific with the pathogen adopting a strategy of stealth and/or evasion in the host.

4 There is no evidence that sexually transmitted pathogens manipulate their hosts to increase promiscuity.

5 Studies across a wide range of animal species support the idea of STIs as diseases of low mortality (with the exception of HIV), caused by long-lived pathogens with a narrow host range and eliciting weak immune responses.

6 Insect vectors are effectively flying syringes, providing a reliable means of transmission.

7 The immune systems of insect vectors provide defence against the pathogens they carry. In response, the pathogens protect themselves against the vector's immune system.

8 Genetic modification of the insect vector and the discovery of pathogen-induced apoptosis offers hopes of novel methods for controlling malaria.

9 There are various reasons for emerging or resurging vector-borne diseases, including urbanization, deforestation, evolution of drug-resistant pathogens and pesticide-resistant vectors and possibly climate change.

2.6 The evolution of resistance to antibiotics and drugs

Material on antibiotic resistance, particularly the underlying molecular mechanisms involved, is available in S204, Book 4, Chapter 7 (*Reference* CD-ROM). Also see Book 2, pp. 30–31 for background information on antibiotics.

There is no more striking illustration of the power of natural selection to bring about phenotypic and genotypic change, and to do so very rapidly, than the evolution of bacterial resistance to antibiotics and wider drug resistance in pathogens (introduced in Box 1.4, Book 1). This includes pathogenic fungi that have evolved resistance to antifungal drugs, for example, *Candida* species and drug resistance in *Plasmodium* species.

- ☐ Recall from Book 1, Chapter 1 an example of antibiotic resistance in the bacterium *Staphylococcus aureus*, the most prevalent cause of surgical site infection.

- ■ Resistance to the antibiotic methicillin, giving rise to methicillin-resistant *Staphylococcus aureus* (MRSA). A survey in 1997–1999 (Table 4.1, Book 1) revealed 61% of such infections were caused by methicillin-resistant strains. Antibiotic resistance is predicted to be a major cause of hospital-acquired infections.

As a result of these evolutionary changes, many of the chemical compounds developed to control pathogens, of which so much was expected 50 years ago, are now totally ineffective. Furthermore, many of the most pathogenic microbes that threaten human health have evolved defences against everything that has been developed to control them. These 'superbugs' pose a major threat to people throughout the world, who are now dying of diseases that could previously be cured.

> The use of antibiotics by humans can be seen as an evolutionary experiment of enormous magnitude, a window from which to view not-quite-natural selection operating in real time. Within 50 years, the number of species and strains of pathogenic and commensal bacteria resistant to antibiotics and the number of antibiotics to which they are resistant has increased virtually monotonically worldwide.
>
> (Anderson and Levin, 1999.)

Pathogenic microbes would very likely have evolved some level of resistance to antibiotics even if they had been used in the most prudent way possible. Indeed, evidence from bacterial collections suggests that antibiotic resistance pre-dates antibiotics! This antibiotic resistance may involve selection of pre-existing traits. The problem has been made much worse, however, by the misuse of antibiotics on a massive scale. In the EU and USA alone, it was estimated in 2002 that 10 000 metric tons of antibiotics are used each year. These have not been used exclusively to directly combat human diseases. It has been estimated that up to 75% of antibiotic use has been of doubtful value in terms of treating human disease (Table 2.4). Only 50% of antibiotic use is to treat illness in people; the other 50% is used in agriculture, to counter animal diseases, as prophylactics and as growth promoters. While the benefits and costs of some of these uses is a matter of debate, there can surely be little doubt that some uses of antibiotics defy common sense. In some parts of the world, antibiotics are sprayed on fruit trees, or poured in large quantities into salmon hatcheries. The major problem with these agricultural uses is that antibiotics get into the soil and into ground water, leading to the evolution of antibiotic resistance in a myriad microbe species that are not pathogens, but which provide a source of resistant genes for those microbes that are.

TABLE 2.4 Summary of uses of antibiotics.

Where antibiotics are used	Types of use	Questionable use
humans (50%)	hospitals (20%) community (80%)	20–50% unnecessary
agriculture (50%)	therapeutic (20%) prophylaxis/growth promotion (80%)	40–80% highly questionable

Antibiotics fed to cattle pass into their faeces, which are then spread as slurry over fields. Even in Switzerland, where the use of antibiotics as growth promoters is prohibited, sulphonamide drugs, which do not degrade quickly, occur in the soil at concentrations up to 1 kg per hectare. It was thought that resistant bacteria mostly passed from livestock to humans via contaminated meat, but the soil, which contains vast numbers of bacteria, may be a more significant route. From the soil, resistant bacteria can get into ground water and from there can be widely spread.

Some outbreaks of human disease have been shown to be caused by pathogens that have evolved drug resistance in an agricultural environment. In 1998, a serious outbreak of *Salmonella* poisoning in Denmark was caused by a drug-resistant strain traced back to a single pig farm. Earlier incidents such as this led to the banning of the use of some antibiotics as growth promoters in livestock in the UK and Europe in the 1970s onwards, but the unrestricted practice still continues in the USA. There is strong evidence that agricultural antibiotic use generates populations of antibiotic-resistant bacteria that contaminate animal-derived food products. These interact with the commensal bacteria in the human gut and speed up the evolution of antibiotic-resistant strains in the human gut flora.

The inappropriate use of antibiotics is not confined to agriculture. There is widespread misuse in the treatment of human disease. In particular, antibiotics are often prescribed for viral illnesses, against which they are ineffective. Even when used, appropriately, against bacterial infections, antibiotics have harmful side-effects. When used inappropriately, as well as being useless, we are left only with their harmful effects.

- ☐ What adverse effects would you expect antibiotics to have on humans?
- ■ (a) Antibiotics attack the commensal microbes in a body. A common side-effect of antibiotics is diarrhoea, caused by disturbance of the gut flora.

  (b) Antibiotics encourage the evolution of antibiotic resistance in commensal bacteria. These are then yet another source of drug-resistant genes for pathogenic bacteria.

Antibacterial agents are increasingly appearing in the homes of entirely healthy people and include household cleaning agents, soaps, detergents, hand lotions and, bizarrely, toothbrushes and chopsticks. Such products feed an obsession for a 'germ-free environment' but they carry considerable risks. Not only do they add to the ubiquity of antimicrobial compounds, favouring the evolution of resistant bacterial strains, they may alter a person's commensal microflora, possibly leading to a greater incidence of allergies in children. Moreover, the normal development of the immune system requires the presence of microbes – host animals raised in a bacteria-free environment have vestigial lymphoid organs.

The genetic changes underlying the evolution of resistance to antimicrobial compounds vary from one pathogen to another. While many pathogens acquire resistant genes by horizontal transfer, resistance in the TB pathogen *Mycobacterium tuberculosis* emerges, within individual hosts, by mutation. This variation has profound implications for the development of strategies to combat drug resistance. For TB, the problem has to be addressed at the level of the individual patient; for other diseases, it is a population-level problem.

The within-host population structure of a pathogen may affect its response to antibiotics. A study of a single patient suffering from multiple liver cysts infected with *E. coli* revealed that long-term treatment with a variety of antibiotics led to the evolution of several drug-resistant *E. coli* strains. As discussed earlier, the body of a host is not a single, homogeneous environment for microbes, but consists of a number of 'habitats', in which microbial evolution can proceed independently.

The evolution of drug resistance has been a major problem in malaria control over many years and has led to the development of a succession of new drugs to replace those that have lost their effectiveness. Resistance of *Plasmodium* species to drugs has evolved at very different rates, depending on the drug and its date of introduction (Figure 2.8).

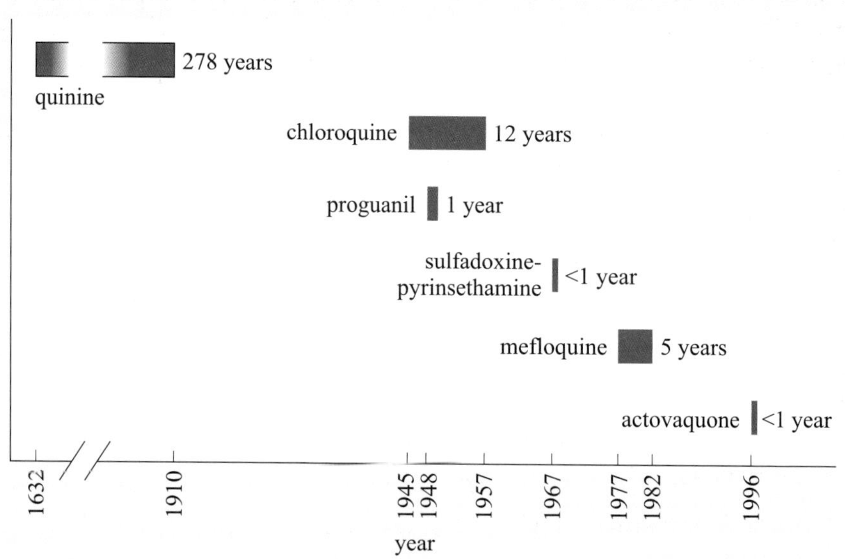

FIGURE 2.8
Variation in the effective life of antimalarial drugs. Purple horizontal bars show, for a succession of drugs, the time from its introduction to the first reports of resistance to that drug. For example, mefloquine was first used in 1977 and resistance to it was first reported in 1982.

For several of these drugs, genetic analyses have identified the alleles that confer resistance in *Plasmodium*. These provide a useful tool for determining the geographic distribution of resistant alleles, so that an appropriate drug can be used in a given area, and for detecting drug resistance in a given area at an early stage.

An interesting question that can be asked in relation to the evolution of drug resistance in pathogens is whether the process can be reversed. Given that drug resistance has evolved by natural selection partly in response to the widespread use of antibiotics, if such use were stopped or greatly reduced, would natural selection reverse the process, and eliminate drug-resistant strains? We would expect it to do so if drug resistance is a costly adaptation for pathogens.

- Suggest a possible reason for any cost to the pathogen.

- Many drug-resistant genes are encoded in plasmids. Gaining and maintaining a plasmid entails replicating extra DNA. Additionally, if drug resistance involves novel enzymes, their synthesis could be an additional metabolic cost.

This question has been addressed experimentally by making drug-resistant strains of bacteria compete, in cultures or in laboratory animals, with non-resistant strains. If drug resistance incurs a fitness cost, such as a reduced reproduction rate, the non-resistant strains should out-compete the resistant strains. Most of such studies suggest, first, that the costs of resistance are modest and, secondly, that microbes counteract them by acquiring ameliorating adaptations rather than by losing drug resistance. It seems that we cannot look to natural selection to get us out of the mess that we have got ourselves into!

The evolution of drug resistance shows a similar temporal pattern in both clinical and community contexts. Following the introduction of a new antibiotic, the frequency of resistant bacterial strains is low for some time, but then increases rapidly to an equilibrium level at less than 100%. Mathematical models, based on data from actual recent occurrences of drug resistance, suggest the rate of increase is greater and the equilibrium frequency higher when the volume of drug use is higher. Thus, the volume of drug use has a direct effect on the rate of evolution of drug resistance. This suggests that, first, the evolution of drug resistance may be prevented by using drugs conservatively and, secondly, that it can be slowed down if drugs are withdrawn as soon as resistance to them is detected.

Summary of Section 2.6

1 The evolution of antibiotic resistance has been rapid and a major cause for concern in hospital-acquired infections.

2 The scale of antibiotic resistance has been increased by widespread misuse of antibiotics, due to overprescribing, patients not completing their treaments, agricultural applications and use of antibacterial agents in domestic cleaning products.

3 Even when correctly prescribed, antibiotics can generate harmful side-effects due to disruption of the commensal gut flora.

4 Genetic change causing antibiotic resistance may be due to horizontal transfer or mutation.

5 The rate of evolution of drug resistance in *Plasmodium* species has depended on the type of drug. In general, the volume of drug use determines the rate of evolution of resistance.

6 Experimental studies of competition between drug-resistant and wild-type strains indicate that natural selection is unlikely to favour the wild type in an environment free of antibiotics.

Learning outcomes for Chapter 2

When you have studied this chapter, you should be able to:

2.1 Define and use, or recognize definitions and applications of, each of the terms printed in **bold** in the text.

2.2 Describe the three models of coevolution and give examples of two of them. (*Question 2.1*)

2.3 Provide examples of genetic variation in hosts due to coevolution with pathogens and describe genetic variation and its causes in a named pathogen. (*Question 2.2*)

2.4 Provide definitions of virulence and discuss the evidence for the evolution of increasing or decreasing virulence. (*Question 2.1*)

2.5 Discuss mechanisms of host manipulation by pathogens and provide examples for humans and invertebrates. (*Question 2.3*)

2.6 Give examples of the diversity and the threats posed by STIs and discuss the strategies adopted by sexually transmitted pathogens. (*Questions 2.2 and 2.3*)

2.7 Give examples of the diversity of vector-borne diseases, the interactions between pathogen and vector and implications for control of insect vectors. (*Question 2.5*)

2.8 Describe the rates of evolution of antibiotic or drug resistance and discuss reasons for the extent of antibiotic resistance. (*Question 2.4*)

Questions for Chapter 2

Question 2.1

Which of the three models of coevolution predicts a reduction in virulence? Give a short justification for your answer.

Question 2.2

Briefly contrast the importance of sexual reproduction to genetic variation in hosts and pathogens.

Question 2.3

To what extent can STIs be considered as an example of host manipulation by pathogens?

Question 2.4

Based on the information in Section 2.6, write a short set of guidelines for the appropriate use of antibiotics.

Question 2.5

Insects are divided into separate orders, which include flies (Diptera), beetles, (Coleoptera) and butterflies and moths (Lepidoptera). Name the insect order that contains most vectors of human disease. Give one reason why this order of insects has so many vectors.

3 ECOLOGY OF DISEASE

3.1 Patterns of pathogen and host range and abundance

In Chapter 1, we noted that Ecology (and Evolution) extends our consideration of disease from individuals to populations and species. A major set of questions asked by ecologists is how patterns of range (defined below) and abundance of populations of organisms change in time and space. Changes in population abundance in time and space are known as **population dynamics**. Once such patterns are described, we can begin to elucidate the underlying processes that give rise to these patterns. In this section, we will introduce some of the patterns of range and abundance of pathogens and their hosts.

3.1.1 Patterns of range

You have already encountered a variety of **geographical ranges** relevant to infectious disease, defined as the full geographical extent of the organism under consideration; for example, the geographical range of the three major species of *Schistosoma* that cause schistosomiasis (Book 2, Figure 7.7). Whilst it is obvious that the pathogen cannot have a larger range than its host, in fact, in many cases, it has a much smaller range. Contrast the geographical range of the malaria pathogen (Figure 3.1) with the distribution of the human hosts who live in all but the most extreme environments on Earth.

FIGURE 3.1 Changing geographical range of malaria. In 1946, the high risk range was all three coloured areas; by 1966, it was down to the yellow and brown areas; and by 1994 it was only the brown areas.

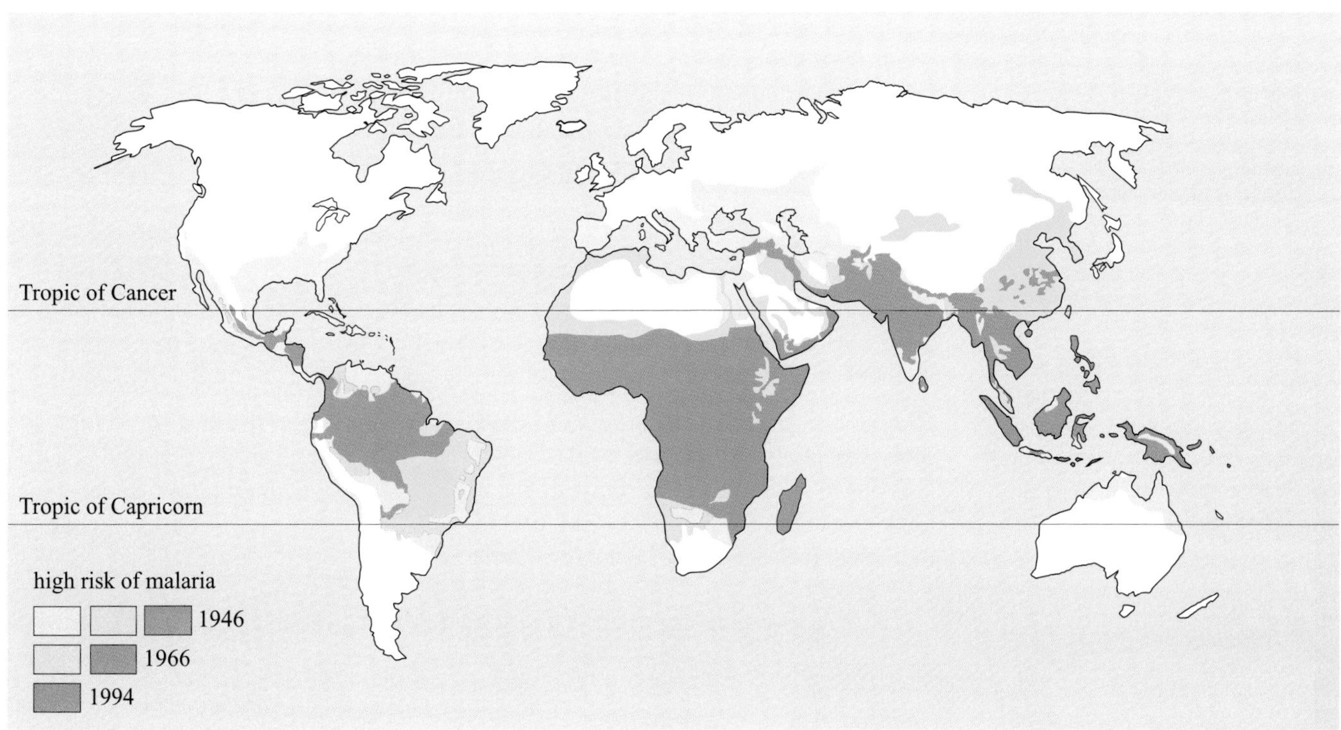

Not only is the pathogen range much smaller than that of the host, it may also be appreciably smaller than that of the vector. (Recall from the *Malaria* CD-ROM that there are about 70 species of *Anopheles* that can act as vectors.) For example, there are several species of *Anopheles* living in Britain. They share the habitat characteristics of their tropical relatives: one species breeds in brackish waters, one in inland fresh-water and one in water-filled tree holes. The difference in range size between pathogen and vector may not always have been so great. Up until the end of the nineteenth century, there was still indigenous malaria (ague) in the coastal regions of Britain. Thus range areas are themselves dynamic (Figure 3.1).

- ☐ With reference to Figure 3.1, what are the present-day limits of the range of the pathogens that cause malaria?
- ■ The limits of the pathogen range are roughly between the Tropics of Cancer and Capricorn, i.e. malaria is now primarily a tropical disease with some areas of high risk in northern subtropical areas, e.g. northern India.

- ☐ How did the range of the malaria pathogens change from 1946 to 1994?
- ■ The range contracted, especially from the northern limits in the southern United States, Mediterranean Europe and parts of the ex-Soviet Union.

This contraction in range has left areas of the world with the nuisance of biting mosquitoes or related flies, but no longer the threat of malaria (such as in the coastal regions of Britain).

3.1.2 Patterns of abundance

It should be apparent to you already that assessing pathogen abundance is extremely difficult. Book 1 introduced a variety of measures of disease abundance that are developed further in Book 6.

- ☐ Are measures of abundance of cases of disease, such as prevalence or incidence, also measures of pathogen abundance?
- ■ Indirectly, as they are measures of the number of human hosts affected by a particular pathogen.

Numbers of infected human hosts may be closely correlated with abundance of pathogens. But they may also be grossly misleading, for example, if the numbers of pathogens per human host are highly variable, or if many pathogens live outside the human host, e.g. in the external environment, in vectors or in intermediate hosts.

Consider the problem of variation of pathogen abundance in the host. A useful way of expressing the abundance of the pathogen is with respect to its relative abundance in different host individuals, in other words, its distribution amongst the host individuals. This is especially useful for larger pathogens, where the number of individual pathogens per host shows a characteristic pattern (Figure 3.2).

- ☐ How is the abundance per host represented in Figure 3.2?
- ■ As the worm burden, i.e. the number of worms per host.

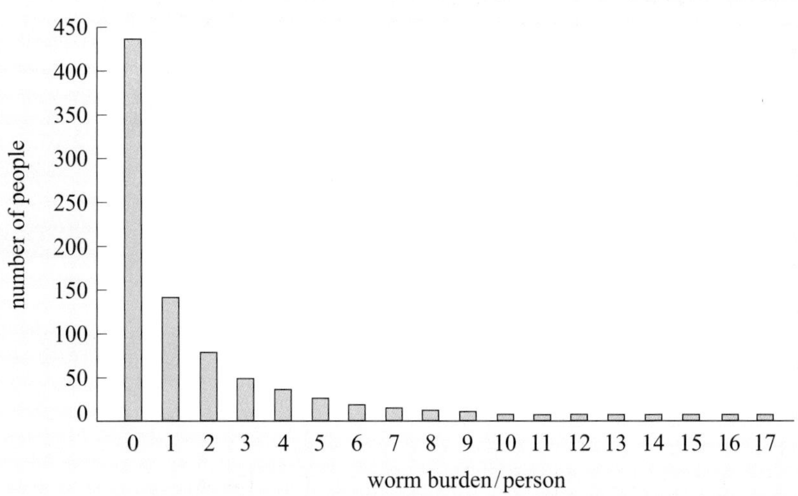

FIGURE 3.2 The frequency distribution of the human roundworm (*Ascaris lumbricoides*) in a rural population in Korea.

- ▢ From the data presented in Figure 3.2, what conclusion can you draw about the distribution of *Ascaris lumbricoides* in the host population?
- ■ The majority of the host population is uninfected by the pathogen whilst a few hosts carry the majority of the worms.

We have already seen an example of this distribution in Book 2 with reference to hookworms (p. 134), showing that a few individuals carry a heavy worm burden, whilst many individuals have no or very few worms.

- ▢ Recall from Book 2 the name given to this type of distribution amongst hosts.
- ■ This kind of distribution pattern is referred to as a clumped or overdispersed distribution. It is also referred to as an aggregated distribution. All three names refer to the large number of pathogens in a small number of hosts.

The **aggregated distribution** or pattern of relative abundance is one of three types of pattern met in ecological (and other biological) studies (Box 3.1). If we were to consider the patterns of malaria pathogen abundance, then, as with the geographical range, we would also need to consider the abundance of the pathogen in the vector. Indeed, for a full appreciation of the abundance of pathogens, we need to consider patterns of abundance within the host, within intermediate hosts or vectors and, in some cases, the abiotic (non-living) environment. Fortunately, understanding the dynamics of disease does not usually depend on a complete assessment of pathogen abundance. This will be illustrated in Section 3.2 and in Book 6.

BOX 3.1 Regular, random and aggregated patterns of abundance

Organisms can be distributed in various ways in space. This may include the distribution (pattern of abundance) of organisms in different habitats or different parts of the same habitat. With pathogens, we consider the patterns of abundance amongst hosts (see main text). In other branches of biology we might consider, for example, the patterns of abundance of cells on a microscope slide. Three common patterns of abundance are random, regular and aggregated. These patterns can be visualized in two ways. First, as the distribution of organisms (such as pathogens) in a grid of habitat patches (such as host organisms), and secondly, as a histogram of the frequency of habitat patches or hosts occupied by different numbers of organisms (e.g. Figure 3.2).

A regular pattern is characterized by an equal number of pathogens in each host. In an aggregated pattern, there is a relatively high frequency of hosts with few pathogens and a low frequency of hosts with a high number of pathogens (see example in main text). In this case, the mean number of pathogens per host is not helpful in describing the abundance of a pathogen. A random pattern lies somewhere between regular and aggregated.

An important distinction here is between the aggregation of the pathogen in the host and the distribution (and possible aggregation) of the host. The latter can be described in the same way as aggregation of pathogens (Box 3.1) except that now the grid is composed of units of geographical space amongst which the humans (or other hosts) are divided. This means that some areas may have a much higher human **population density** than other areas. Population density, defined as numbers per unit area or, in the case of pathogens, numbers per host, is an important variable in population dynamics. Humans are often highly aggregated in space, especially in developing countries (Figure 3.3). A feature of some of the major historical and contemporary diseases, such as plague, cholera, HIV and TB, is their high prevalence amongst aggregated host populations due to enhanced rates of transmission.

FIGURE 3.3
An example of aggregated pattern of abundance of human hosts in space.

We will now move on to consider some of the *processes* giving rise to these observed patterns of range and abundance.

Summary of Section 3.1

1 Changes in population abundance in time and space are referred to as population dynamics. Geographical ranges, comprising the full range of a species, are also dynamic.

2 The geographical range of the malaria pathogens, has declined in the last century and is now largely confined to tropical regions.

3 Prevalence of disease may be a misleading description of pathogen abundance. Similarly, mean pathogen abundance may be unhelpful in describing the distribution of pathogens amongst hosts. Aggregated distributions of pathogens (especially larger species) are well known.

4 Hosts may also be aggregated in space, with the resulting high population densities favouring the transmission of certain pathogens.

3.2 Population dynamics of host and pathogen: an example of a compartmental model

The previous section on patterns of abundance introduced us to the idea that we can identify a series of places (including various categories of host) in which the pathogen can exist (and various places where they do *not* exist). We will refer to these places as **compartments**. At a particular point in time, individual hosts can be categorized into one of four compartments, which were introduced in Book 1 and Chapter 1 of this book:

- susceptible – not yet infected by the pathogen;
- infected but latent (i.e. non-infectious);
- infectious;
- recovered and immune.

(It may also be that individuals do not become immune or they do not recover.)

An individual host can pass through all four stages, i.e. at different times the host may contribute to each of the four compartments, or can die from the disease. The duration of the second and third stages is determined by the latent and infectious periods characteristic of the disease (see Chapter 1).

If we can determine the abundance of the hosts representing each of the compartments at one point in time and the rate at which the hosts flow between compartments, then we can begin to model the population dynamics of the pathogen and host (models of human diseases were introduced in Chapter 1 – the concept of mathematical modelling and the rationale for modelling is discussed in Book 6, Section 2). These models help us to understand why some pathogens spread rapidly through a host population whilst others remain at more or less similar values or decline. Such knowledge will be extremely useful when we come to consider ways of combating a disease.

So let us start building a compartmental model using the example of malaria and following the categories of host identified above. We have purposely chosen a complex example in order to illustrate the ecological and biological issues. However, it is an example with which you are (hopefully!) familiar from the CD-ROM introduced in Book 1. This example immediately creates a new level of complexity as we have a human host and an insect vector giving rise to eight compartments (Table 3.1).

TABLE 3.1 Organization of compartments for a model of the dynamics of malaria.

Category	Human host compartment	Insect vector
pathogen-free (susceptible)	a	b
pathogen-infected (latent)	c	d
pathogen-infected (infectious)	e	f
recovered	g	h
total	a+c+e+g hosts	b+d+f+h insect vectors

We will use this compartmental model to explore the dynamics of the malaria host–vector–pathogen interaction, i.e. how numbers in the different compartments change over time. For example, we might ask, under what conditions and how rapidly would a malaria infection spread through a human population? Let us attempt to answer this question using the compartmental model. Imagine the scenario of an isolated village with resident populations of 99 humans and 1000 female mosquitoes who are all free of *Plasmodium* infection. We will assume that humans of different age and gender are equally likely to be infected with the malaria parasite (we will need to make many such, potentially unrealistic, assumptions). We will also assume that the mosquito population is more or less constant regardless of the presence of malaria; in fact, we will assume there are always 1000 female mosquitoes in the village. Now imagine that a single recently infected human enters the village. We will designate as the beginning of day 1 the point in time that the recently arrived human becomes infectious (and before he or she is bitten by a village mosquito). The values in the compartments for start of day 1 are given in Table 3.2.

TABLE 3.2 Start of day 1: newly arrived human becomes infectious.

Category	Human host compartment	Insect vector (females)
pathogen-free (susceptible)	99	1000
pathogen-infected (latent)	0	0
pathogen-infected (infectious)	1	0
recovered	0	0
total	100	1000

We will need to gather some more data and make a few more assumptions before we proceed. It is valuable to list these in order to see how far our model might depart from reality and to note the variability that is inherent in the malaria host–vector–pathogen system.

Assumptions

- no previous history of malaria in village;
- all hosts are equally susceptible;
- there are always about 1000 female mosquitoes in the village;
- infected human arriving at the beginning of the infectious period.

Data required to proceed with the dynamic compartmental model include:

- length of life and survival of mosquito;
- number of people bitten per day;
- duration of components of life cycle of the pathogen.

The required data are highly variable and depend on the species of pathogen and mosquito and the geographical location under consideration. However, epidemiologists have gathered a lot of related data that may be useful. Let us attempt to tease these data out from the epidemiological data on the *Malaria* CD (you do not have to refer to the CD here, but you may wish to follow up some of the details below).

How long does the mosquito live?

Female mosquitoes have a daily mortality rate of between 5 to 25%. In other words, somewhere between 95% (0.95) and 75% (0.75) of female mosquitoes survive until the next day. This means that if we start with 1000, there will be somewhere between $1000 \times 0.95 = 950$ and $1000 \times 0.75 = 750$ remaining after one day (this ignores recruitment of new mosquitoes – you will see the reason for this later).

☐ What is the maximum and minimum number after two days?

■ Maximum after two days $= 950 \times 0.95 = 902.5$ or $1000 \times 0.95 \times 0.95$
Minimum after two days $= 750 \times 0.75 = 562.5$ or $1000 \times 0.75 \times 0.75$.

This can be expressed as a simple equation to give the number of mosquitoes alive after n days, given an initial number of mosquitoes:

$$\text{no. of mosquitoes alive after } n \text{ days} = \text{initial no. of mosquitoes} \times (\text{fraction surviving})^n \qquad \text{(Eqn 3.1)}$$

☐ Using Equation 3.1, what would be the number alive after 3 days if the daily survival rate was 0.9 and the initial number was 1000?

■ Number alive after 3 days $= 1000 \times (0.9)^3 = 1000 \times 0.729 = 729$.

These values can be incorporated into the dynamic compartmental model. After every day, we can multiply the number of mosquitoes by the survival rate. We will need to do this because we want to track the abundance of the infected mosquitoes. Appropriate values of daily survival rate will be chosen below.

How many people are bitten per day?

Female mosquitoes mostly feed every 2 to 4 days. We also have to take into account the preferences for humans. *Anopheles gambiae* feeds on average once every two nights and prefers feeding on humans whereas *Anopheles culicifacies* feeds once every three nights but feeds predominantly (about 80% of the time) on cattle with only about 20% of feeds on humans. This information can be used to calculate a **daily bite rate** of humans by female mosquitoes.

- ☐ For these two species, what is the (average) daily bite rate on humans?

- ■ *Anopheles gambiae*: 0.5 (assuming 100% feeding on humans)
Anopheles culicifacies: 0.33×0.2 (20% preference for humans) = 0.066.

In our compartmental model, we will work with an average daily bite rate of 0.2, i.e. somewhere between the rates for *A. gambiae* and *A. culicifacies*.

Duration of components of life cycle of pathogen

This information is needed in order to determine the length of the latent and infectious periods in both the human and the insect vector. Not all of this is directly accessible from the *Malaria* CD-ROM. The following information is taken from the CD-ROM and other sources and refers to *Plasmodium falciparum* unless stated otherwise.

Gametogenesis of *P. falciparum* in the mosquito takes about 18–24 hours and sporogony is about 9–10 days (Figure 3.4, stages E and F), longer for other *Plasmodium* species. Thus, it is reasonable to assume that the minimum time for a mosquito to become infective after biting an infected human and itself becoming infected is about 11 days. This is the duration of the latent period in the mosquito. Sporozoites can remain in the mosquito salivary gland(s) for up to 59 days. This means that once a mosquito has become infective it is highly likely to remain infective until it dies.

- ☐ Why is the mosquito *highly likely* to remain infective until it dies?

- ■ Because even with a high daily survival rate of 0.9, the probability of being alive after 59 days is $0.9^{59} = 0.002$, i.e. a very small number.

In humans, passage of the sporozoites through the blood system to the liver (stage A, Figure 3.4) is quite rapid. After 45 minutes, most sporozoites will have left the blood. Hypnozoites usually remain in the liver from 9 to 16 days (stage B) – although some may remain there much longer. The time from schizont to gametocyte is about 48 hours and gametogenesis takes between 10 to 12 days. The minimum duration of the latent period in humans is therefore about $9 + 2 + 10 = 21$ days. We will assume for convenience a latent period in humans of 22 days (i.e. twice the latent period in the mosquito). The delays that occur in the liver mean that humans may remain infective for many weeks following the latent period. There may also be dormancy and reactivation of the pathogen (see Section 3.3).

Now we return to the compartment model and see what happens after the point in time when the infected human became infectious. After one day, we expect that each female mosquito will have bitten 0.2 humans (on average!). Therefore, a total of $1000 \times 0.2 = 200$ humans will have been bitten. As there are only 100 humans, this means that every human is bitten twice each day by different mosquitoes. This bite rate will remain constant as long as there is no change in the number of

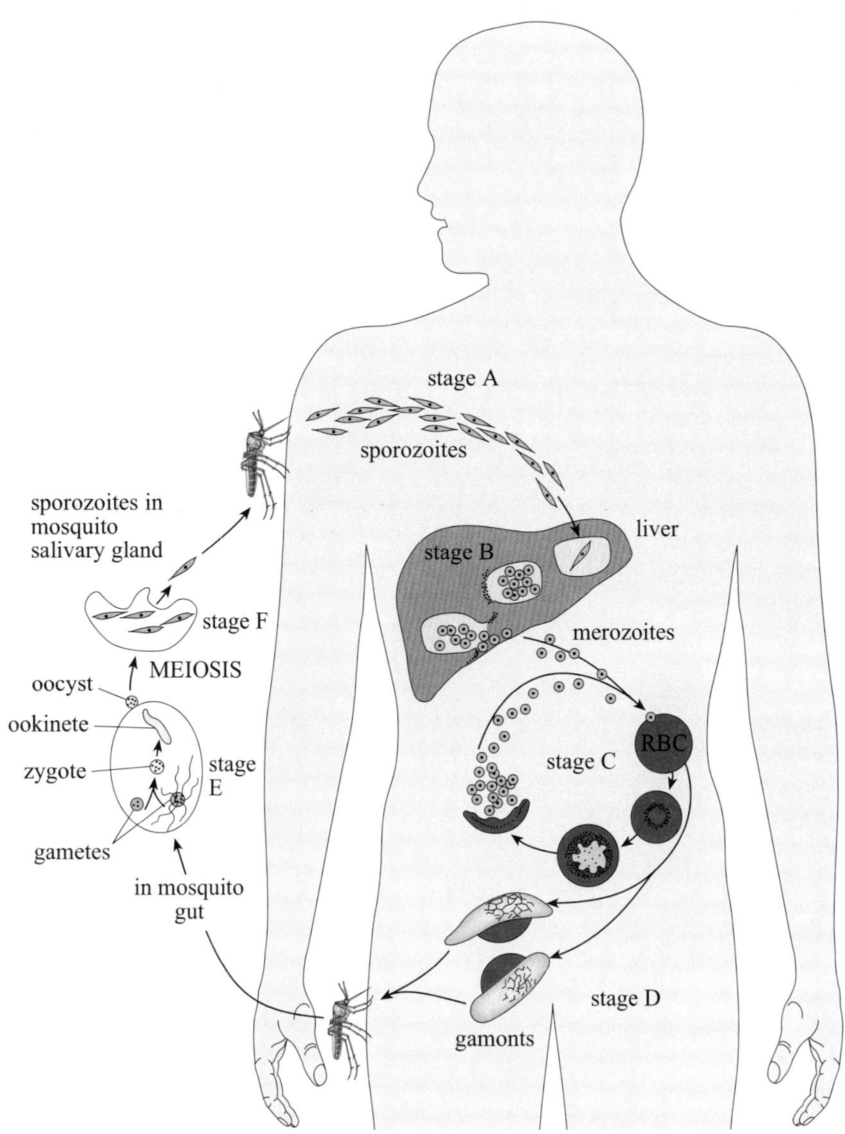

FIGURE 3.4
Plasmodium falciparum life cycle. The durations of stages are given in the text.

humans and female mosquitoes (and the assumptions of the model hold). As one of the humans is infective, at the end of one day, two of the mosquitoes have become infected (assuming that the bite results in successful transfer of the pathogen). So at the end of day 1 we have the situation in Table 3.3.

TABLE 3.3 Compartmental model at the end of day 1.

Category	Human host compartment	Insect vector (females)
pathogen-free (susceptible)	99	998
pathogen-infected (latent)	0	2
pathogen-infected (infectious)	1	0
recovered	0	0
total	100	1000

At the end of day 2, two more mosquitoes have become infectious. Assume that the infected human remains infectious in the village for two days (for simplicity assume that the infectious human leaves the village after two days). There will now be four infected mosquitoes. Now, let us move on to the end of day 11. We can estimate the number of infected mosquitoes alive after 11 days using Equation 3.1:

$$\text{no. of infected mosquitoes after 11 days} = 2 \times (0.9)^{11} = 2 \times 0.314 = 0.628.$$

We also have the two mosquitoes that were infected on day 2. The number of these alive at the end of day 11 is $2 \times (0.9)^{10} = 0.697$. Note that we are also assuming that the females that became infected were newly emerged individuals. These data are now entered into the compartmental model (Table 3.4).

TABLE 3.4 Compartmental model after 11 days.

Category	Human host compartment	Insect vector
pathogen-free (susceptible)	99	1000 – 1.325†
pathogen-infected (latent)	0	0.628 + 0.697 = 1.325
pathogen-infected (infectious)	0	0
left village*	1	n/a
total	100	1000

*Note that the recovered category has been replaced by an emigration category – we have assumed that the infected human left the village after two days.

†Recall the assumption that the female mosquito population stays at 1000. In fact, the number of susceptible mosquitoes will not affect the model (as long as the number is large).

At this point, you may be wondering about the legitimacy of using fractions of mosquitoes and fractions of humans! For a general mathematical model, this is not a problem. The interpretation in these cases can be the probability that a mosquito or human is alive as opposed to the actual number of mosquitoes or humans. It can then be applied to a problem with, e.g., 10 000 or 100 000 humans. We have to be more careful with specific models that are applied to real populations of a certain size, especially where the number of individuals is small.

On day 12, we move into a new dynamic phase in which the first infected mosquitoes become infectious. For simplicity, let us treat the mosquitoes infected on day 1 and day 2 as becoming infectious on the same day and that they have the abundance calculated at the end of 11 days. The number of humans bitten by the infectious mosquitoes on day 12 is therefore 1.325×0.2 (bite rate) $= 0.265$ (Table 3.5).

TABLE 3.5 Compartmental model on day 12.

Category	Human host compartment	Insect vector
pathogen-free (susceptible)	99 – 0.265 = 98.735	1000 – 1.325
pathogen-infected (latent)	0.265	0
pathogen-infected (infectious)	0	1.325
left village	1	n/a
total	100	1000

As the mathematics rapidly becomes complicated, we need to make some simplifying assumptions that will allow us to continue making predictions about the population dynamics without qualitatively affecting the model. One simplifying assumption is that the infectious mosquitoes only bite over two days (days 12 and 13). (This may be an overestimate, as any one mosquito only needs to feed every two to four days. On the other hand, an infected mosquito only transfers about 10% of its sporozoites in one bite.) Therefore, we need to calculate the number of humans bitten by the infectious mosquitoes on day 13:

no. of day 1 infectious mosquitoes surviving = $2 \times 0.9^{12} = 2 \times 0.282 = 0.564$

no. of day 2 infectious mosquitoes surviving = $2 \times 0.9^{11} = 2 \times 0.314 = 0.628$

total no. of infectious mosquitoes on day 13 = 1.192.

The number of humans bitten by infectious mosquitoes on day 13 is therefore 1.192×0.2 (bite rate) = 0.238 (Table 3.6), giving a total of 0.503 infected humans.

TABLE 3.6 Compartmental model on day 13.

Category	Human host compartment	Insect vector
pathogen-free (susceptible)	99 – 0.503 = 98.497	1000 – 1.192
pathogen-infected (latent)	0.265 + 0.238 = 0.503	0
pathogen-infected (infectious)	0	1.192
left village	1	n/a
total	100	1000

After day 13, we are assuming that the infectious mosquitoes have died. So on day 14 we have the situation in Table 3.7.

TABLE 3.7 Compartmental model on day 14.

Category	Human host compartment	Insect vector
pathogen-free (susceptible)	98.497	1000
pathogen-infected (latent)	0.503	0
pathogen-infected (infectious)	0	0
left village	1	n/a
total	100	1000

☐ How long will the compartment values remain the same as day 14?

■ Until the first newly infected human becomes infectious, which is 22 days after first being bitten by an infectious mosquito. This occurred on day 12 so the first newly infected human becomes infectious on day 34.

Let us assume that humans infected on days 12 and 13 become infectious on day 34. Day 34 will be like day 1 when the infectious human arrived in the village. On day 1, there was one infectious human who got bitten by two mosquitoes. The difference on day 34 is that there are 0.503 humans who are infectious (Table 3.8).

TABLE 3.8 Compartmental model on day 34.

Category	Human host compartment	Insect vector
pathogen-free (susceptible)	98.497	1000
pathogen-infected (latent)	0	0
pathogen-infected (infectious)	0.503	0
left village	1	0
total	100	1000

- ☐ Contrasting Table 3.8 with Table 3.2, what do you predict will happen to the pathogen?

- ■ The pathogen population is not likely to be sustained in the village because 0.503 is less than 1.

We have reached an important conclusion about the dynamics of the pathogen. Under this scenario, the pathogen population is predicted not to persist in the host population (the village). Indeed, we would predict that it would eventually go extinct.

So, under what conditions might the pathogen population increase? A useful quantity to calculate would be the minimum requirements for one or more infectious persons on day 34. To do this we have to look at each of the variables to see which, if any, might naturally alter and therefore can be changed in the model to favour increase in the pathogen population. This will be a useful exercise when we come to think of ways of controlling malaria (as opposed to looking at ways in which it might increase!).

- ☐ Suggest two ways in which the abundance of the pathogen might be increased in the village following infection.

- ■ An increase in the daily bite rate and an increase in the number of times the first infected person is bitten (by higher bite rate and/or by longer exposure before isolation or leaving the village).

We have not considered pathogen life cycle, which is already at minimum duration, and mosquito survival, which is already high. Let us take the daily bite rate (b) as the variable to investigate. In order to determine the requirement for a minimum of one infectious person on day 34, we need to solve the following equation:

1 infectious person on day 34 = (no. of infectious mosquitoes surviving from day 1 to 12 (1.325, see Table 3.5) × bite rate, b) + (no. of infectious mosquitoes surviving from day 2 to 12 (1.192, see Table 3.6) × bite rate, b).

This can be written as an algebraic equation (see Book 6, Box 3.2 if you need help in manipulating equations):

$$1 = (1.325b) + (1.192b)$$

$$1 = 2.517b$$

$$b = 1/2.517$$

$$b = 0.397$$

For convenience let us take b as 0.4.

(Note that if the mosquitoes only bite once, then we have $1 = 1.325b$, i.e. b is 0.75.)

- ☐ Is this value of bite rate (0.4) unrealistically high?
- ■ No, it is less than that recorded for *Anopheles gambiae* (0.5).

If b is greater than 0.4, then the pathogen population will increase in the host population. If b is less than 0.4, the pathogen population will decline. The daily bite rate value of 0.4 is therefore a threshold for persistence of the pathogen.

So, if all the other variables of the model are held at the assumed values (and the general assumptions of the model hold), daily bite rate represents an important controlling variable on the success of the pathogen.

- ☐ Considering the potential control of the disease, how could daily bite rate be decreased below the critical value of 0.4?
- ■ One straightforward method is to use nets over beds or hammocks, coinciding use with the peak biting times (early evening). Use of mosquito repellents can also dramatically reduce the frequency of bites.

Development of this model has been helpful in showing the difficulties of working with complex host–pathogen systems and the potential predictive power of mathematical models of disease (see Box 3.2). This is especially important for a disease that continues to kill at least one million people per year. The modelling is further justified on two grounds. First, the role of mosquitoes (and daily bite rate) in a number of globally important diseases in addition to malaria (such as dengue, Figure 3.5, yellow fever and filariasis – see earlier discussion in the course, e.g.

BOX 3.2 Sir Ronald Ross and the history of mathematical models of malaria transmission

Construction of mathematical models to understand the dynamics of malaria first began in the early 20th century with the pioneering work of Sir Ronald Ross (1857–1932). In the late 1890s, he had demonstrated the life cycle of the malarial parasites in mosquitoes, thereby confirming the role of the vectors in the disease. Ross dedicated much of his subsequent working life to understanding ways to control malaria. He undertook field work in many parts of the world including the Middle East and West Africa and developed mathematical models of malaria epidemiology, published in a series of works from 1906 to 1916. He not only sustained a wider interest in mathematics but also received critical acclaim for his poetry! Ross's contribution was recognized in a series of awards, including the Nobel Prize, and many aspects of modern epidemiological models of malaria transmission have their roots in his work. The *Malaria* CD-ROM gives examples of epidemiological models (e.g. Screens 30 and 34 of the 'Epidemiology' tutorial). You are not expected to study these, but you may find them interesting, especially after studying Book 6, as the 'professional' version of the model described in this chapter.

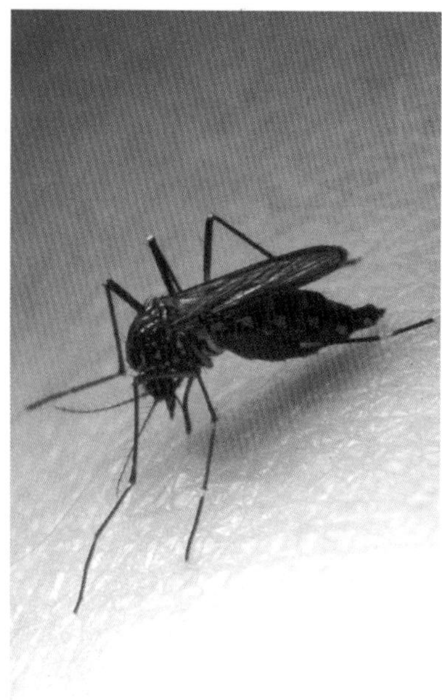

FIGURE 3.5
A dengue mosquito biting.

Section 2.5 of this book and Book 2, Section 7.5.2). Secondly, the concept of pathogen populations increasing or decreasing in host populations is developed and generalized to all diseases in Book 6 (in particular with regard to the important variable R_0, pronounced 'are nought') and it is not discussed further in this book.

This discussion of conditions under which the pathogen population will increase or decrease is an example of wider ecological debate about the nature of stability of population dynamics and conditions for extinction and colonization. In the malaria case, we have a situation analogous to a ball balancing on a very fine point (Figure 3.6a).

It is mathematically possible for the ball to stay on the peak. But if there is even the slightest change in conditions (e.g. as represented in the malaria example above by alterations in daily bite rate), it will roll one way or the other. Thus, it is possible to have a population persisting with one infected host, but it requires all the variables to stay at the same value over a long period of time. This is highly unlikely! Much more likely is the situation in which the pathogen population increases or decreases. This then raises new questions. Will the decline in the pathogen be continued, ultimately resulting in its local extinction? Will the increase in the pathogen population continue until all susceptible hosts have been infected? It is likely that neither of these will occur. Instead, we may have either a high increase followed by (possibly dramatic) reductions in population size (Figure 3.6b) or reductions to a few infected hosts. Over longer periods of time, this may be seen as cycles of pathogen population abundance or at least fluctuations in pathogen population size. This is the subject of the next section.

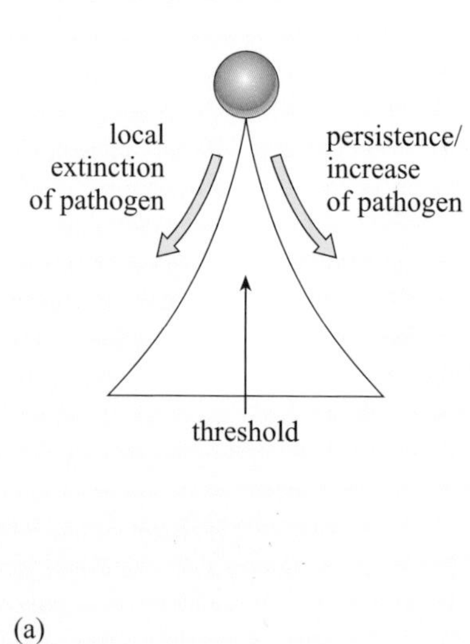

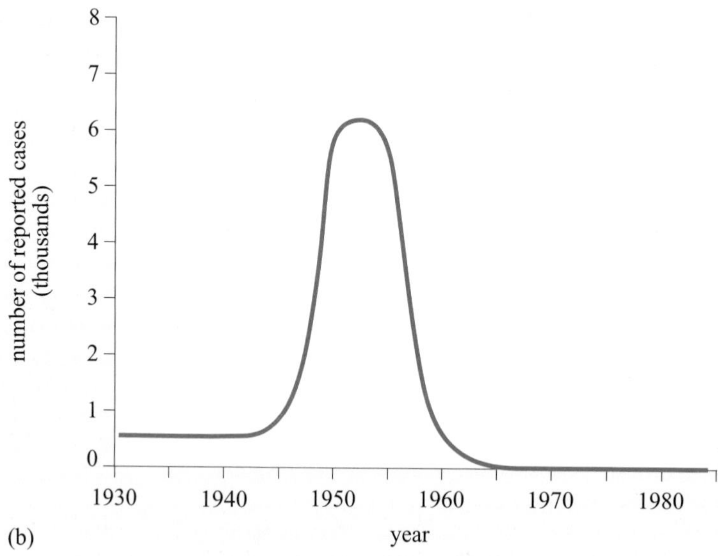

FIGURE 3.6 (a) Unstable dynamics and (b) example of an epidemic (polio, detailed in the *Polio* Case Study).

Summary of Section 3.2

1 A compartmental model is constructed to investigate the possible spread of malaria through a village. Four compartments of host and vector are recognized: susceptible, infected but latent, infectious and recovered.

2 The assumptions of the model include equal susceptibility of the hosts, a constant high vector population and the introduction of the pathogen by a single infected host.

3 Data on mosquito survival and longevity, daily bite rate and duration of the stages of the pathogen life cycle are sourced from the *Malaria* CD-ROM and other sources.

4 Changes in the numbers of hosts and vectors in the different compartments are calculated over a total of 34 days. In this example, comparison of the number of infected persons on day 34 with the number on day 1 (one person) show whether the pathogen will increase or decrease in the village.

5 Based on the assumptions of this model, a daily bite rate of 0.4 is required for persistence of the pathogen. This value is identified as a threshold for persistence.

3.3 Further examples of host–pathogen dynamics: cycles and fluctuations in abundance

Why might some diseases show cycles or predictable fluctuations in abundance? These fluctuations may be linked to seasons, e.g. the higher incidence of influenza in winter (Book 1, Figure 2.7, see further examples in Book 6, Section 5) or the onset of yellow fever with the rainy season, due to the hatching of eggs of previously infected mosquitoes. In these cases, there are clear reasons why the pathogen population should change in abundance – survival, fecundity and/or transmission of the pathogens can all be affected by the environmental conditions. Another more contentious example is the outbreaks of *Vibrio cholerae* infection which appear to be associated with climatic cycles and ocean plankton blooms (see the *Cholera* Case Study).

☐ With reference to Book 3, what else might be affected by the environmental conditions for a given pathogen species?

■ Defence of the host may be impaired (e.g. immunodeficiency, Book 3, p. 102).

These explanations of pathogen abundance driven by external environmental patterns, such as weather, are examples of factors **extrinsic** to the host–pathogen system. The same factors may have been responsible for shifts in the range of the pathogens over time.

In some cases, there appear to be no obvious extrinsic factors. In these examples, cycles or predictable fluctuations of outbreak years may occur over tens of years. A set of data on epidemics recorded in the United States from 1657 to 1918 by present-day genealogists is given in Figure 3.7.

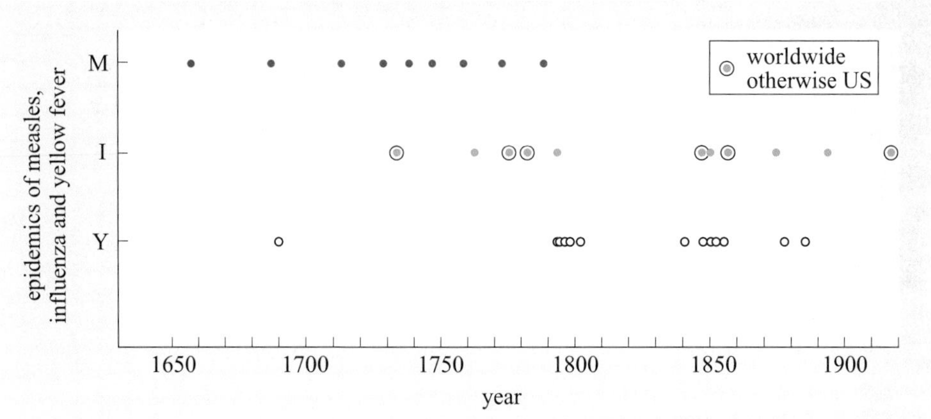

FIGURE 3.7
Epidemics of measles (M, red), influenza (I, green) and yellow fever (Y, black) from 1657 to 1918 recorded by genealogists.

- How reliable are these data? (*Hint*: think back to Book 4.)

- They depend on correct diagnosis at the time – this may be incorrect for influenza and possibly yellow fever (which may have been confused with hepatitis). They are also not a systematic sample – there is not a standard definition of an epidemic and they have not been taken from a fixed number of people in a standardized manner. (See Book 4 for discussion of notifiable diseases (p. 11) and Book 6 for examples of sampling epidemiological data.)

However, these data are indicative of the likely frequency of major outbreaks of given diseases. Note that they are not records of pathogen abundance but indications of disease prevalence. More reliable sets of data are provided in the returns of general practitioners and other health workers from the mid-twentieth century to the present day (see Book 6 for details).

- What conclusions can be reached about the frequency of occurrence of the epidemics of the three diseases listed in Figure 3.7?

- Some of the yellow fever epidemics are widely spaced, whilst others appear to be tightly clustered. There is no obvious pattern with the influenza epidemics. The measles epidemics may be increasing in frequency. Indeed, we can contrast this frequency of occurrence of these measles epidemics every ten years or more with those every two years in England and Wales from 1948 to 1982 (see Book 6, Figure 5.1).

As you will see in Book 6, the analysis of measles data has been particularly fruitful for its insights into cycles of pathogen abundance. For example, Grenfell and co-workers have used weekly statistics on measles data from 1944 to 1994 in England and Wales to illustrate waves of infection originating in large cities and then spreading to surrounding towns and villages. This gives the cycles of abundance a spatial dimension, i.e. the peaks of abundance are not restricted to one particular locality but are able to spread between localities. It may be that there are some correlations of the outbreaks with climate patterns, but this is not always the case.

Where there are no apparent extrinsic events driving the dynamics, we need to consider what **intrinsic** processes might be driving the dynamics of the pathogen and host, i.e. processes derived from the interaction between host and pathogen. We will consider a little later some details of these intrinsic processes. The search

FIGURE 3.8
Lynx chasing a snowshoe hare.

for intrinsic mechanisms that generate cycles in abundance is an issue that has fascinated ecologists for many years. It is a phenomenon that stretches far beyond host-pathogen interactions. Cycles of abundance can be found in organisms as diverse as lynx, herbivorous insects and grouse (Figures 3.8 and 3.9).

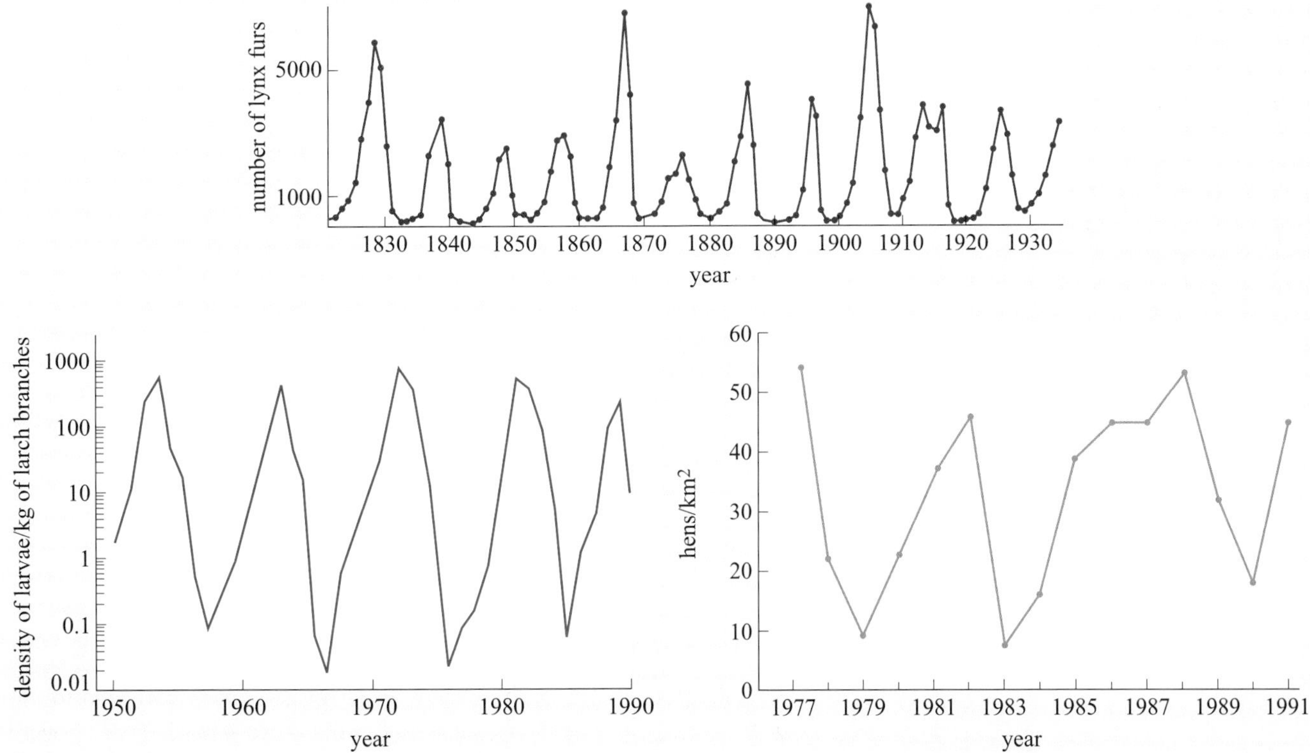

FIGURE 3.9 Cycles of abundance in (a) lynx (based on trap returns), (b) larch bud moth and (c) grouse (mature females).

What do the ecological systems in Figure 3.9 have in common with the host–pathogen system? First, they all involve (+/–) interactions as described in Chapter 1. But that is not unusual; many species are involved in such interactions. A second important property is that all the predators/pathogens/herbivores (i.e. those species that gain from the interaction) *specialize* on a small number of host or prey species. Indeed, they usually specialize on just one species. For example, lynx (where they show cycles in abundance) feed predominantly on snowshoe hare (Figure 3.8), and the larch bud moth (*Zeiraphera diniana*) feeds only on larch (*Larix decidua*). Grouse specialize on heather (*Calluna*) species, but in their case it is probably a parasitic nematode that specializes on them which is important. You encountered this parasite in Chapter 1 (Table 1.2). In the early 1990s, Dobson and Hudson used a combination of experiments and mathematical models to show that cycles of abundance in grouse could be due to the grouse's interaction with a parasitic nematode.

A consequence of this specificity is that changes in the abundance of one species are expected to lead to changes in the abundance of the other. To illustrate this, let us imagine a system of one predator and one prey species (the lynx and the hare). In this simple scenario, lynx only eat hares and hares only eat grass. Assume that grass is abundant and unaffected by the numbers of hare.

☐ What do you predict would be the effect of an increase in the number of lynx?

■ They would eat more hares and the number of hares would fall.

☐ What would be the effect on the lynx of this reduction in the number of hares?

■ The lynx would have less to eat and therefore their survival and/or fecundity would decline.

☐ What would be the effect of reducing survival and/or fecundity of the lynx?

■ They would reduce in abundance.

☐ What would be the effect of reducing numbers of lynx?

■ Hares would increase in abundance!

You will see from this set of questions and responses that it is easy to generate an intuitive argument (the real situation is inevitably more complex than this!) to explain why lynx and hare would cycle in abundance. This is particularly true if there is a **delay** in response of one species to changes in abundance of the other. For example, whilst reduced numbers of hares this year may result in reduced fecundity of lynx in the same year, this is not manifested as change in the abundance of mature lynx until several years later.

Very similar arguments were applied by Dobson and Hudson to the grouse–parasite system. They showed that birds treated with chemicals to kill the parasites had higher adult survival and higher hatching success. Furthermore, they showed that there were significant *delays* in the parasite life cycle, caused by the ability of the larval parasites to arrest their development after infecting a host. The authors' detailed mathematical studies demonstrated that cycles of abundance with a period of 8 or 10 years could be produced by a particular combination of larval arrestment duration (typically 2–4 months) and host birth rate.

FIGURE 3.10 A cicada.

Delays in the pathogen life cycle are found widely, including in human pathogens. They occur due to the duration of development and reproduction of the pathogen in the host (i.e. the latent period) and due to dormant periods, e.g. between the stages of syphilis. Dormancy also appears to be an important feature of prion and virus life cycles. What might be the adaptive explanation for long periods of dormancy? Clues come from comparison with other ecological systems where dormancy is a feature. Two examples of such ecological dormancy come to mind. The first is amongst annual plants, the seeds of which may remain dormant in the soil for many years, i.e. for periods of time which far exceed the generation time of the organism. The second example is the dormancy of cicadas (Figure 3.10; a type of plant-feeding insect whose loud noise in late afternoon and early evening is well known to anyone who has travelled in tropical and subtropical regions). These two examples represent two different reasons for dormancy. In the first, the benefit of dormancy is that the seeds of many annual plants are only able to germinate under certain conditions such as following physical disturbance, flooding or intermittent rains. These events may be infrequent and unpredictable in occurrence, e.g. in desert environments. Hence there is a selective advantage to plants that can persist during unfavourable conditions in the dormant state (which usually acts to protect them against the adverse environmental conditions) and respond quickly to intermittent favourable conditions.

In the second example, selection has favoured cicadas that emerge infrequently and thereby avoid predation. This is further supported by the emergence times of cicadas, for example every 13 or 17 years in Indiana in the United States.

- ☐ Why is emergence every 13 or 17 years favourable to a potential prey species?

- ■ Because 13 and 17 are prime numbers and cover a protracted period of time, which means that predators can only specialize on these prey by emerging at exactly the same time and with the same period. Predators that emerge with any other time period (or show peaks, e.g. every five or ten years) would rarely coincide with the peaks of prey abundance and therefore be unable to specialize on the prey.

Do either of these explanations for dormancy in non-pathogen species help with interpretation of patterns of dormancy in pathogen species? It is possible that both are relevant. The first explanation may be appropriate to pathogens that have specialized requirements within the host, e.g. contact with a limited set of cell types, or require the host to be at a particular developmental state, but have a broad type of transmission or unspecialized movements within the host. Thus, the pathogen cannot guarantee when and where it enters the host and needs to enter a dormant state before it encounters a part of the host in a receptive or suitable condition. Dormancy in malaria may be related to its exit strategy from the host. Hypnozoites of *Plasmodium vivax* and *P. ovule* in the liver can be reactivated up to 18 months later; this may be seasonal and coincide with reappearance of the vector (*Malaria* CD).

The second explanation may also be correct. The pathogen is seeking to evade the host's defences and may be aided by long periods of dormancy during which it remains undetectable by the host's defence. This links back to the examples of pathogens transmitted by direct contact that may spend many years inside the host (Table 1.4).

Given the presence of these delays, can the population dynamics argument applied to grouse and their parasites be applied to humans and their pathogens? Certainly we know that humans have host-specific pathogens, that those pathogens can have an effect on survival and fecundity and that those pathogens can have periods of dormancy in the host. A major difference from the grouse system is that humans have a much longer generation time and effects on human fecundity are not going to respond numerically in the manner of the grouse. In other words, humans cannot show great variation in 'hatching' success! Another problem is that humans may be interacting with a much wider array of pathogens than the grouse, or perhaps more accurately, that there is no one pathogen for humans that is of such overwhelming importance as the parasitic nematode is to the grouse (99% of juvenile birds in a sample of 2723 were infected). If there were situations in which humans were mainly interacting with one pathogen whose impact on human populations was high in terms of survival and/or fecundity (TB in pre-industrial England may have been a candidate), then we might expect to see cycles of host abundance. But such dynamics might be played out over tens or hundreds of years and therefore possibly be undetectable on the time-scales of scientific studies. With humans, the most interesting host–pathogen population dynamics are probably happening at the cellular level within a single individual, where the immune system is interacting with an array of pathogens. It is the cellular level to which we now direct our attention.

Summary of Section 3.3

1. Fluctuations or cycles of abundance of pathogens could be due to extrinsic causes, e.g. seasonal weather patterns.
2. Evidence from historical and current data point to diseases with a variety of time periods of outbreaks or epidemics.
3. Intrinsic processes underlying cycles in abundance in ecological systems have been linked to host specialization and delays in response of one population to changes in the other. These processes are illustrated by the interaction between grouse and its major parasitic nematode.
4. Delays in host–pathogen systems appear to be widespread, with pathogens benefiting by, e.g. avoiding the host defence and timing completion of the life cycle in the host with vector activity.
5. Cycles in abundance of human pathogens may be rare due to the variety of human pathogens, the long generation time of humans and the lack of numerical responses in fecundity. If they do occur, such cycles might be undetectable over the normal time-scales of scientific study.

3.4 Population dynamics of pathogens in the host

At several points in this chapter and in other parts of the course, we have discussed the potentially high rates of population increase of different pathogens. In this section, we will quantify some of these rates and discuss their implications for survival of the pathogen in the host. Note that in this section we focus on population dynamics *within* the host – the parallel story of spread of disease between hosts, drawing on similar methods, is given in Book 6, Section 1.2.1.

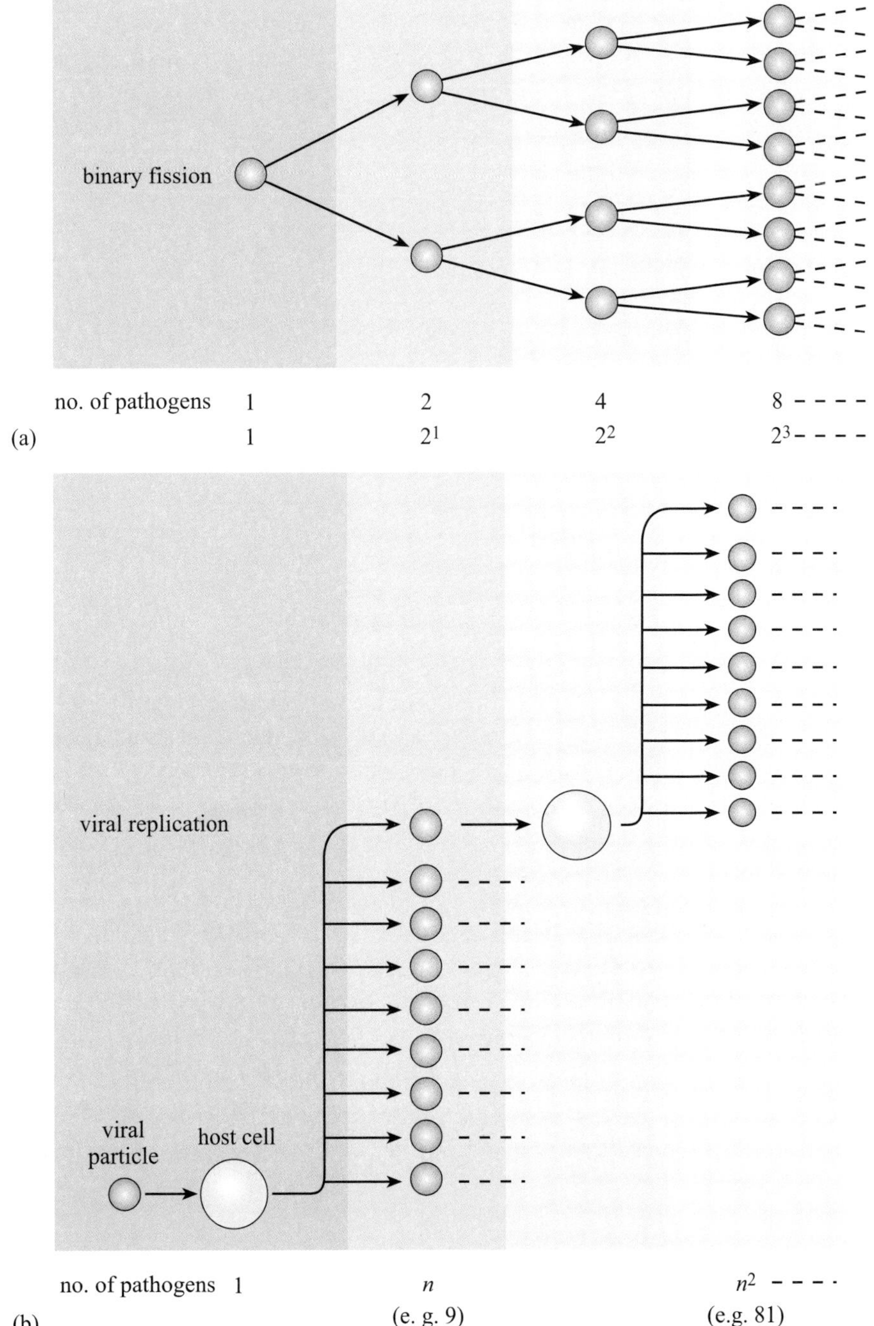

FIGURE 3.11
Increase in numbers of bacteria and viruses.

Consider first a bacterium that divides by binary fission. This means that each bacterium produces two new bacteria which then divide to produce four bacteria and so on (Figure 3.11). This doubling method of reproduction gives bacteria a characteristic population dynamic, at least in the early stages of increase when there is nothing to limit its increase.

In Book 2, p. 39, it was noted that *E. coli* may divide once every 20 minutes (referred to as the doubling time) although for other species it may be much longer. In contrast, on the same page of Book 2, the doubling time for lymphocytes, the host's cells mediating the adaptive immune response, is about six hours. What are the quantitative implications of this imbalance in doubling time?

- ▢ Assume a bacterium has a doubling time of 30 minutes and that we start with one individual. How many are present after six hours, i.e. the time taken for a lymphocyte to divide?
- ■ After 30 minutes there will be two individuals, after one hour there will be four, after 90 minutes there will be eight and so on. After six hours there will be a staggering 4096 bacteria (but only two lymphocytes).

There are two ways of calculating the number of bacteria after six hours. You can either keep doubling the numbers after every 30 minutes, i.e. repeat the calculation 12 times in total. This is rather time-consuming! Or, to speed the process up, you can note that after one 30-minute period there are 2^1 (2 to the power 1, i.e. 2) individuals, after two 30-minute periods there are 2^2 (2 to the power 2, i.e. 4) and so on. So, after twelve 30-minute periods (6 hours), there are 2^{12} bacteria, which is 4096.

Thus, any delay in detection of the bacteria by the host will result in a considerable numerical disadvantage to the host.

- ▢ Do you imagine that bacteria could maintain that rate of population increase?
- ■ No, otherwise the world would be covered with the species of bacterium with the shortest doubling time! Competition between individuals (and between species) will limit availability of resources and will result in the slowing of the population increase. Eventually, interactions with the host defence system (see Book 3) will also lead to a slowing down of the increase and even a reduction in numbers of the pathogen.

Let us consider a second example of pathogen increase in the host. In this case, we will go back to Chapter 2 of Book 1 and look at the influenza virus. Recall that antibody production against the virus begins 3 to 4 days after infection. Eventually, this may lead to elimination of the virus. But what numbers of the virus are present by the time that antibody production kicks in?

Viruses replicate by infecting a host cell and then producing multiple copies of themselves (Figure 3.11) that are released (usually) by lysing the host cell. Therefore, after each replication cycle, the number of viruses multiply by a certain number.

To estimate the number of virus particles after three days, we need to know three variables – the number of virions (V) at the start of infection (denoted by V_0, i.e. the number at time zero), the average number of virions produced per host cell (r) and the average time taken for replication (t). Before dealing with the specific values for influenza, let us generate a simple formula that could be used for any virus.

- ☐ What is the average number of viral replication cycles in 3 days?
- ■ $3/t$. But we need to be careful with the units! If the viral replication time is expressed in hours, then the total time under consideration also needs to be in hours. Thus, if viral replication time was 12 hours, the number of viral replications would be $36/12 = 3$.

In order to generalize, we will replace the number of hours over which replication is taking place (36 above) by T. Thus there are T/t replication cycles. If each viral replication produces r virions, then the equation for the number of virions after T hours (denoted by V_T) is:

no. of virions after T hours (V_T) = no. at start (V_0) × no. produced per replication cycle (r) to the power T/t, or

$$V_T = V_0 \times r^{T/t} \qquad \text{(Eqn 3.2)}$$

This uses the same logic as our bacterial example. In that case, the number of replication cycles was the number of doubling periods ($12 = 6/0.5$). The number of bacteria produced per replication cycle was 2, i.e. r was 2.

So Equation 3.2 is sufficiently general to be able to predict the number of bacteria after a fixed period of time (B_T), knowing the initial number (B_0) and the doubling time t. Equations of this type are used widely in ecology to describe the increase in the number of organisms over time, with the assumption that there is no limit to the rates of increase.

Summary of Section 3.4

1. The reproduction rates of bacteria and viruses are discussed in relation to the response times of the human host.
2. The number of bacteria and viruses produced after a given time can be described by a simple equation, given the initial number, duration of replication and number of offspring produced.

3.5 The role of other species in the ecology of human diseases

3.5.1 Host–pathogen communities

Earlier examples in this book have made it clear that many other species, in addition to human hosts and pathogens, are frequently involved in host–pathogen interactions. Indeed, in many cases it is not a simple host-pathogen interaction but a three-way or more interaction. This extends the area of study into **community ecology** that addresses the dynamics and other properties (such as relative abundance of species) arising from interactions of many species. An ecological community can be defined as a set of species, populations of which may interact with each other over a given area. We have already seen many ways in which hosts and pathogens may interact, not only with each other, but also with alternative or intermediate hosts and vectors. These interactions are summarized in Figure 3.12. We will adopt the shorthand of referring to these as **host–pathogen communities** (which may include intermediate or secondary hosts and vectors). The interactions within the host–pathogen community are generally played out over small areas, e.g. in the case of malaria it is limited by the flight of the female mosquito that in turn is linked to the availability of habitat for egg laying. This is not always the case, especially in human examples where infected milk or meat, or the hosts themselves, may travel hundreds of miles, thereby potentially spreading the range of the community. These host–pathogen communities, and ecological communities in general, may be described as more or less diverse, depending on the number of interacting species and their relative abundance in the community (Box 3.3).

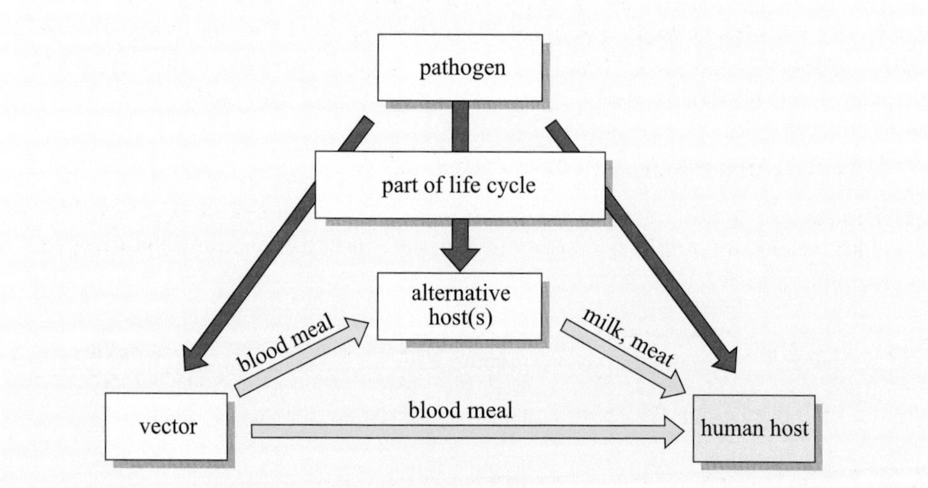

FIGURE 3.12
Generalized interactions within the host–pathogen communities.

In reviewing the role of other species, we should revisit the concept of zoonoses introduced in Book 1 and Chapter 1 of this book.

- Recall from Book 1, Box 1.2, the definition of zoonoses (singular: zoonosis).

- A disease caused by an infection that can be transmitted to humans from other vertebrates under naturally occurring conditions. This link is represented in Figure 3.12 by the arrow from alternative host(s) to human host.

BOX 3.3 Diversity of ecological communities

The term diversity is often used rather loosely to refer to the variety of species in an ecological community. In fact, ecologists recognize two components of diversity: richness and evenness. Richness is a measure of the number of different species in an assemblage. For example, this might be the number of hosts of the *Ixodes* tick larvae (see Figure 2.7 for details). Evenness, as the name implies, is a measure of the relative abundance of these different species. Again, with reference to the tick example, there may be four hosts (species richness is four), one of which is ten times more abundant than the other three combined. This would be a highly uneven community. Abundance can be measured as number of individuals (preferably as population density) or amount of biomass. You may come across ecological measures of diversity, i.e. indices that represent the degree of diversity in a community. These indices combine measures of richness and evenness. High richness and even abundance contribute to a high diversity value.

Here we will examine in more detail the various types of zoonosis. They can be classified into four groups depending in part on the manner of transmission: direct zoonoses, cyclozoonoses, metazoonoses and saprozoonoses.

Direct zoonoses involve transmission from the vertebrate host to a susceptible human by direct contact, fomite or by a mechanical vector. In this example, there is no developmental change or propagation of the organism during transmission. Examples of direct zoonoses include rabies and brucellosis. **Cyclozoonoses** require more than one vertebrate host but no invertebrate host and include human tapeworm infections (Book 2, Section 7.4). In **metazoonoses**, the agent multiplies and/or develops in an invertebrate host before transmission to a vertebrate host is possible. Examples include arboviruses, plague and schistosomiasis.

- ☐ Why is malaria not an example of metazoonosis?
- ■ Because, although the pathogen develops and multiplies in an invertebrate vector during transmission, it is usually transmitted between humans and not from a vertebrate host.

The final category of zoonoses are **saprozoonoses**. In this case, non-animal development sites or reservoirs are required, such as food plants, soil or other organic material. Examples in this category include some mycotic diseases.

3.5.2 Radiation of host–pathogen communities

Examples such as HIV show that pathogens are continually switching to new hosts. In so doing, they are creating new host–pathogen communities. One way of understanding the changing patterns of host–pathogen communities is to consider the different communities that have arisen amongst closely related pathogen species. In evolutionary terms, we can talk about the **radiation** of host–pathogen communities, in the same way that one might discuss the radiation of non-pathogen species, e.g. Darwin's finches in the Galapagos islands. The species of trypanosome provide an excellent example of the radiation of host–pathogen communities.

- ☐ Recall from Book 2 the characteristics and different types of trypanosome.
- ■ Trypanosomes are single-celled, animal-like cells with flagella. They include *Trypanosoma* species that cause a variety of diseases including trypanosomiasis (sleeping sickness). Another group of trypansomes are in the genus *Leishmania*, which cause a whole series of different types of disease.

The extraordinary diversity of host–pathogen communities associated with *Trypanosoma* and *Leishmania* are illustrated in Figure 3.13. For *Trypanosoma*, the interactions include a variety of vectors, especially flies (*Glossina* species – which includes tsetse flies – and horseflies or tabanids) and, in stark contrast, a reduvid bug which is the vector for Chagas' disease. The other vertebrates involved in these communities include semi-domesticated stock (horses, donkeys, cattle, camels) and wild animals (antelope and deer). Some of the communities do not include humans and the diseases that characterize them are diseases of the other vertebrates. In one case, there is no vector (dourine acute).

The communities associated with *Trypanosoma* show interesting geographical patterns. For example, the subspecies of *Trypanosoma brucei* in East Africa is transmitted by *Glossina morsitans* and causes acute sleeping sickness. In West Africa, another subspecies of *T. brucei* (*gambiense*) is transmitted by another *Glossina* species (*Glossina pallipides*, tsetse fly) and causes chronic sleeping sickness. Finally, a third subspecies of *T. brucei* (*brucei*) is widely distributed in Africa, transmitted by the tsetse fly, and causes a disease in domestic stock and wild animals (nagana acute). To complicate the story further, this same disease appears to be caused by two other *Trypanosoma* species (*vivax* and *congolense*), spread by *Glossina morsitans*. The relatively subtle shifts in trypanosome vector in Africa (e.g. between *Glossina* species) contrasts with the one New World example, where the vector is an entirely different order of insect.

The *Leishmania* communities in both the New and Old World all involve sandflies with at least five different pathogen species and three forms of the disease.

- ☐ What major difference in the composition of *Leishmania* and *Trypanosoma* associated communities is apparent from Figure 3.13?
- ■ *Leishmania* communities do not have an alternative vertebrate host, in contrast to all the *Trypanosoma* communities.

Interpretation of the evolutionary and ecological patterns of host–pathogen communities has been helped enormously by the analysis of phylogenetic trees (or phylogenies) derived from molecular data (RNA or DNA sequence data, e.g. from ribosomal RNA, rRNA). These trees show not only what is related to what but also the closeness of that relationship. The statistical analyses used to construct these trees are extremely complex and cannot be covered here. However, the cautionary tale is that there may be many, equally likely phylogenetic trees. Thus we should treat a phylogenetic tree as the latest in a series of hypotheses about the relationship between the species in question.

FIGURE 3.13 (Opposite) Global radiation of host–trypanosome communities.

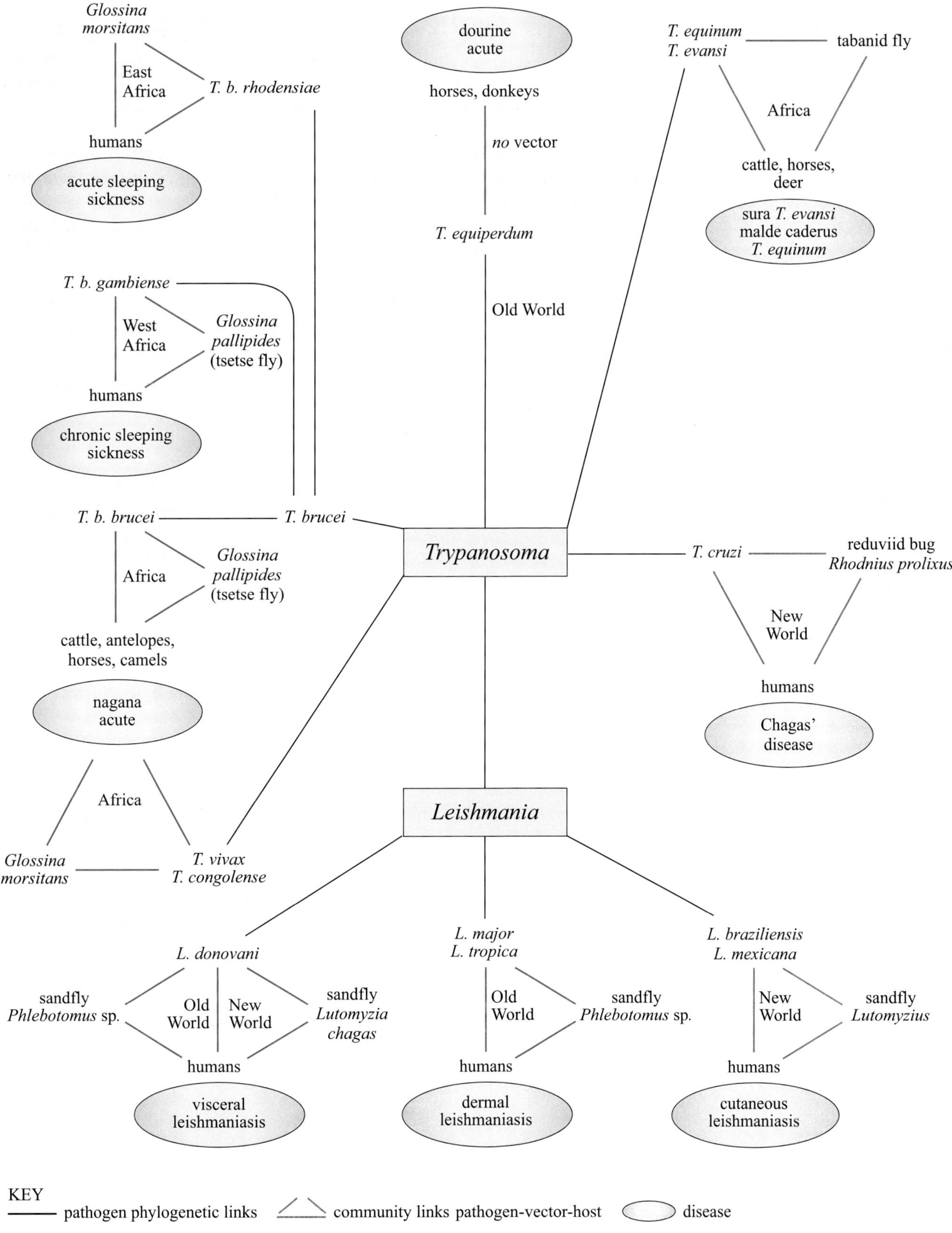
Glossina morsitans
East Africa
T. b. rhodensiae
humans
acute sleeping sickness
T. b. gambiense
West Africa
Glossina pallipides (tsetse fly)
humans
chronic sleeping sickness
T. b. brucei
T. brucei
Africa
Glossina pallipides (tsetse fly)
cattle, antelopes, horses, camels
nagana acute
Africa
Glossina morsitans
T. vivax
T. congolense
dourine acute
horses, donkeys
no vector
T. equiperdum
Old World
Trypanosoma
Leishmania
T. equinum
T. evansi
tabanid fly
Africa
cattle, horses, deer
sura T. evansi
malde caderus
T. equinum
T. cruzi
reduviid bug
Rhodnius prolixus
New World
humans
Chagas' disease
L. donovani
sandfly Phlebotomus sp.
Old World
New World
sandfly Lutomyzia chagas
humans
visceral leishmaniasis
L. major
L. tropica
Old World
sandfly Phlebotomus sp.
humans
dermal leishmaniasis
L. braziliensis
L. mexicana
New World
sandfly Lutomyzius
humans
cutaneous leishmaniasis
KEY
pathogen phylogenetic links
community links pathogen-vector-host
disease

The other important result that can be derived from the phylogenetic tree is the age of the relationships, i.e. given certain assumptions (such as the rate of mutation) the time before present at which species diverged can be estimated. Therefore, in theory we should be able to estimate how many million years ago *Leishmania* split from *Trypanosoma* (assuming they are both derived from a common ancestor).

The phylogenetic tree for trypanosomes (current in 1999) is shown in Figure 3.14. This showed that the trypanosomes were monophyletic, i.e. derived from a common ancestor. It also showed the ancient divergence of the so-called 'aquatic clade' from other groups. (A clade is a group of closely related species with a common ancestor.) The aquatic clade comprises species of trypanosome found in marine and freshwater fish and amphibia. These trypanosomes are spread by aquatic leeches. Indeed, one of the important findings of the phylogenetic analysis is to show the coevolution of the pathogens and their vectors – thus, closely related trypanosomes (comprising a single clade) tend to be transmitted by the same closely related set of vectors. But we also predict that the trypanosomes will coevolve with their vertebrate hosts. This has also been supported by the phylogenetic studies, for example, most of the *T. cruzi* clade are associated with South American mammals. The exceptions to this are an unnamed species that infects kangaroos and two species of European bat trypanosomes.

- ▢ Why would the kangaroo and European bat trypanosomes be related to the other *T. cruzi* affected species?

- ■ In the case of the kangaroo, this is because Australia was joined to South America via Antarctica much later than South America was joined to Africa. Thus, the *T. cruzi* clade may have evolved across South America, Antarctica and Australia. The European bats are mobile and may have been able to disperse over long distances (possibly linking South America and Africa).

The dating of the divergence of these clades suggests that trypanosomes have coevolved with their hosts over several hundred million years. For example, the *T. brucei* clade is predicted to have diverged from other clades during the Permian, when reptiles were the most advanced vertebrates and certainly when none of the current hosts were present. Therefore, as humans evolved in Africa, they were amongst trypanosomes whose evolution was already several hundred million years old and for which movement into a new (and increasingly abundant) primate host was simply a matter of time. In South America, as humans migrated into the continent 30 000–40 000 years ago, the *T. cruzi* trypanosomes also had a short host leap from their existing host range, which included primates.

Finally, consideration of the host–pathogen community is vital for understanding the reasons for changes in incidence of disease. For example, construction of the Aswan High Dam resulted in huge increases in the prevalence of *Schistosoma mansoni*, from 5% in 1968 to 77% in 1993. This was largely due to an increase in the snail intermediate hosts that benefited from the increased habitat associated with the dam and irrigation channels. Deforestation in Africa has also favoured *Anopheles gambiae*, by increasing its habitat. Understanding the host–pathogen community is also vital for understanding emerging infectious diseases.

- ▢ Recall from Book 2 the missing information on the host–pathogen community of the Ebola virus.

- ■ Ebola is a zoonosis, but the animal that carries it has not been found.

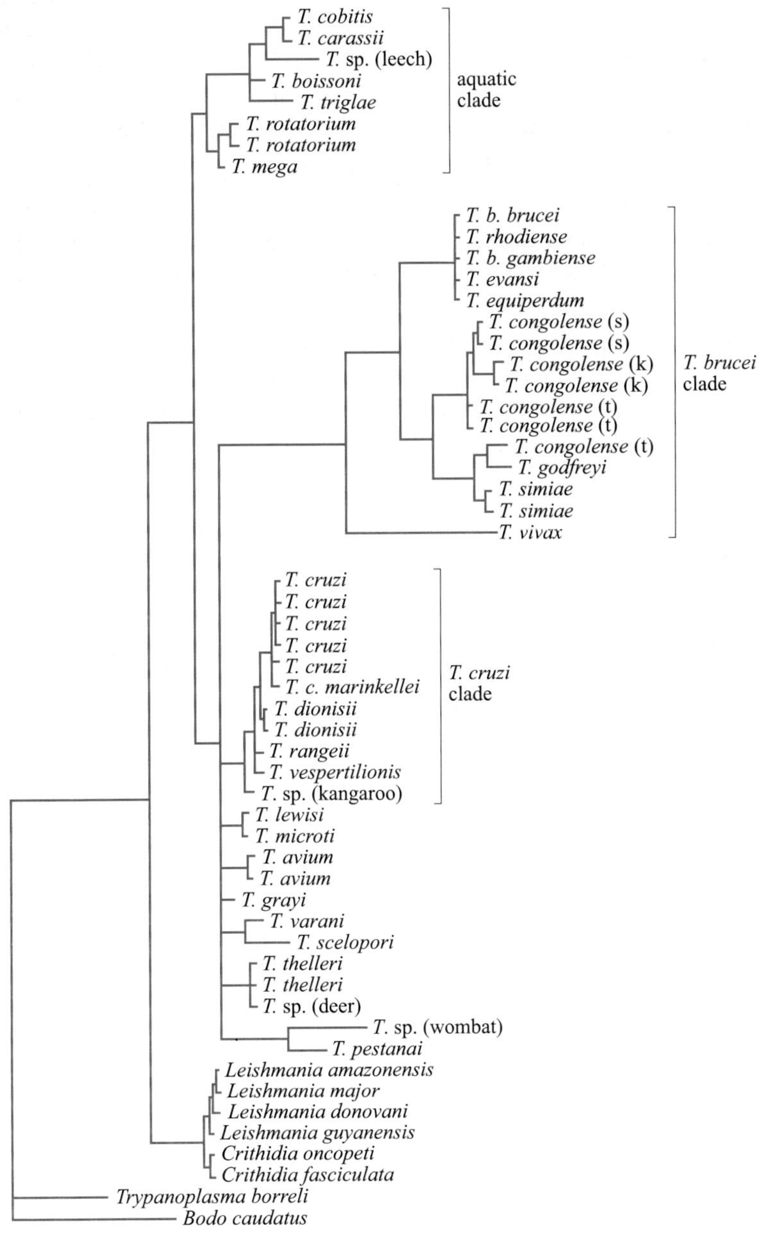

FIGURE 3.14
Phylogenetic tree of trypanosomes.

Summary of Section 3.5

1 Hosts and pathogens can be linked in various ways to comprise host–pathogen communities. These communities include zoonoses, classified into four groups depending in part on the manner of transmission: direct zoonoses, cyclozoonoses, metazoonoses and saprozoonoses.

2 The radiation of host–pathogen communities is illustrated by the global radiation of host–trypanosome communities. Understanding the patterns of radiation is aided by a detailed phylogenetic tree.

3 The incidence of disease in humans can often only be understood with reference to the whole host–pathogen community.

3.6 Ecological attributes of host–pathogen interactions

The compartmental model of malaria infection and the potential cycling in abundance of pathogen populations showed that the emergent dynamic properties of the host–pathogen system depend on details of the interactions between all the linked populations. In this final section, we will summarize aspects of the ecology (and biology) of the individuals and populations that characterize host–pathogen interactions and influence most heavily the abundance of the pathogen. In so doing, we will draw together material from Chapter 1 on life-history strategies, Chapter 2 on co-evolution and from earlier books in this course.

3.6.1 Body size

In all host–pathogen interactions, the host is very large compared to the pathogen. Where vectors are involved, the vector is of intermediate size. **Body size** is important for two reasons. The most apparent is one of physical constraints. A pathogen needs to survive and reproduce within or amongst the physiological apparatus of its host. In the most extreme examples – such as viruses – the pathogens need to access molecules such as enzymes, ATP and amino acids from within the cell of its host. This provides a clear constraint on pathogen size.

Secondly, body size is strongly correlated with the generation time of the organism. The smaller the body size, the more rapid the generation time. The pathogen needs to have a more rapid generation time than its host. Otherwise, it will fail to reproduce before the host dies.

In many host–pathogen interactions, the pathogen needs to have a much more rapid generation time than that of its host. This is because it needs to reproduce before the host's defence system has detected it. Ideally, it will have completed several replication cycles (Section 3.4) before the body has begun to respond – the rate of detection depending on the number of Tc cells in the body.

3.6.2 Active transmission

Many of the most effective pathogens use active forms of transmission from host to host. This includes employment of insect vectors and causing changes in the host's physiology and/or behaviour to elicit transmission.

- ▢ Can you give an example of changes in the human host's physiology and/or behaviour caused by the pathogen that favour its transmission?
- ■ Examples include sneezing (influenza), skin lesions (cowpox, smallpox) and diarrhoea (see Section 2.4 for more details).

These changes in host physiology and behaviour may also be linked to using waste products of hosts (urine, faeces) and causing a more rapid expulsion of these products as was illustrated for the *Vibrio cholerae* bacterium in Book 2 (p. 10). These changes may also be associated with a site-specificity on the host that maximizes transmission, e.g. around the genitalia – as noted in the *Syphilis* Case Study, humans find it hard to avoid reproducing (or at least attempting it). Transmission may also be increased by aggregation of the host, leading to a higher local density of hosts (see Section 3.1). Aggregation may be due to work (e.g.

malaria spreading through mining communities), poor and crowded housing (TB), lack of sanitation (cholera) or social behaviour (STIs, including HIV). Note that multiple sexual partners constitute a form of aggregation – not necessarily aggregation in one place at one time (!) but aggregation over a short time period.

The ecological parallel of transmission in populations that are not pathogenic is dispersal from one suitable habitat to another. Many of the most abundant species in the world are those that can successfully move from one habitat patch to another. This is especially true today with the increasing fragmentation of habitats. A patchy habitat is essentially what the pathogen experiences – a habitat comprised of a set of individual hosts separated in space. In this way, it is no different from a fly species that reproduces in patches of dung. It must first find the dung, lay eggs in it, complete its life cycle before the dung dries out and then move on to the next pile.

We have emphasized the active aspects of transmission. But what is passive transmission and are there any examples amongst pathogens? In passive transmission, pathogens will return to the environment and be picked up by passing hosts. This environment might include areas of soil, vegetation and water bodies. Ticks (and other ectoparasites, e.g. leeches) use this method of dispersal between hosts. They feed on a host, drop off into the vegetation or soil and then later get picked up by a passing host. In some cases, they may move a short distance to maximize their chances of a pick-up (they are part active). Whilst these ectoparasites are not infectious agents, they can be vectors of infectious agents, such as Lyme disease (Book 2 and Chapter 2 of this book).

3.6.3 Co-occurrence

Pathogens need to occur in the same areas and habitats as their hosts. We have already seen how some pathogens exist within a smaller fraction of the geographical range of their host (Section 3.1). One way that pathogens can increase their chances of interaction with their host is to exploit the resources required by the host, i.e. water and food. Alternatively, the pathogens exploit vectors or intermediate hosts associated with these resources.

☐ Can you give two examples of vectors or intermediate hosts associated with water bodies?

■ *Anopheles* mosquitoes (malaria vector) and aquatic snails (schistosomiasis or bilharzia intermediate host).

In both these examples, the vectors and pathogens are associated with water bodies close to human habitation or places of work (thereby increasing co-occurrence). In the case of schistosomiasis, the cercariae and their vectors are especially prevalent in irrigated fields where crops are grown or shallow rivers where people wash. Pathogens and vectors associated with water bodies are of enormous global importance in terms of the numbers of humans infected and the amounts of mortality or serious illness. Of particular note is the number of diseases associated with mosquito transmission (dengue, malaria, filariasis, yellow fever). When one extends this to other biting Diptera (flies), thereby including leishmaniasis (sandflies) and onchocerciasis (blackflies), the importance of water as breeding areas for flies as vectors of disease becomes overwhelming (Figures 3.15, 3.16). The reasons for the success of the pathogens that cause these diseases lies in their utilization of a vector that lives part of its life in water and part of its life aerially, feeding off humans. The pathogen therefore maintains an intimate relationship with both the individual host and one of his/her most essential dietary and domestic requirements: water. Moreover, these Diptera are able to utilize water bodies created by their hosts.

There are also examples of pathogens that are not exclusively associated with water and may be spread through contaminated food. Ascariasis, typhoid (*Salmonella typhi*) and cholera are all spread via food (contaminated hands, flies or utensils) and water contaminated with faeces and/or urine (in all cases, transmitted through the faecal–oral route, Book 2, p. 18). Thus, the resources of food and water are linked in these examples.

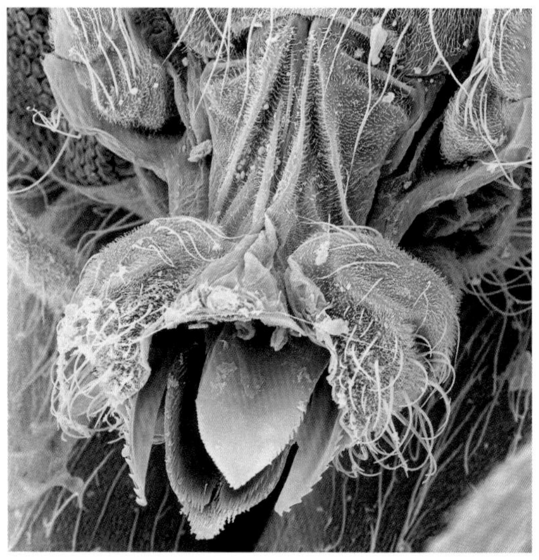

(a)

(b)

(c)

(d)

FIGURE 3.15
Co-occurence of human hosts with vectors or intermediate hosts associated with water:
(a) blackfly, showing mouthparts;
(b) sandfly;
(c) *Biomphalaria* snail; and
(d) workers in a rice paddy field.

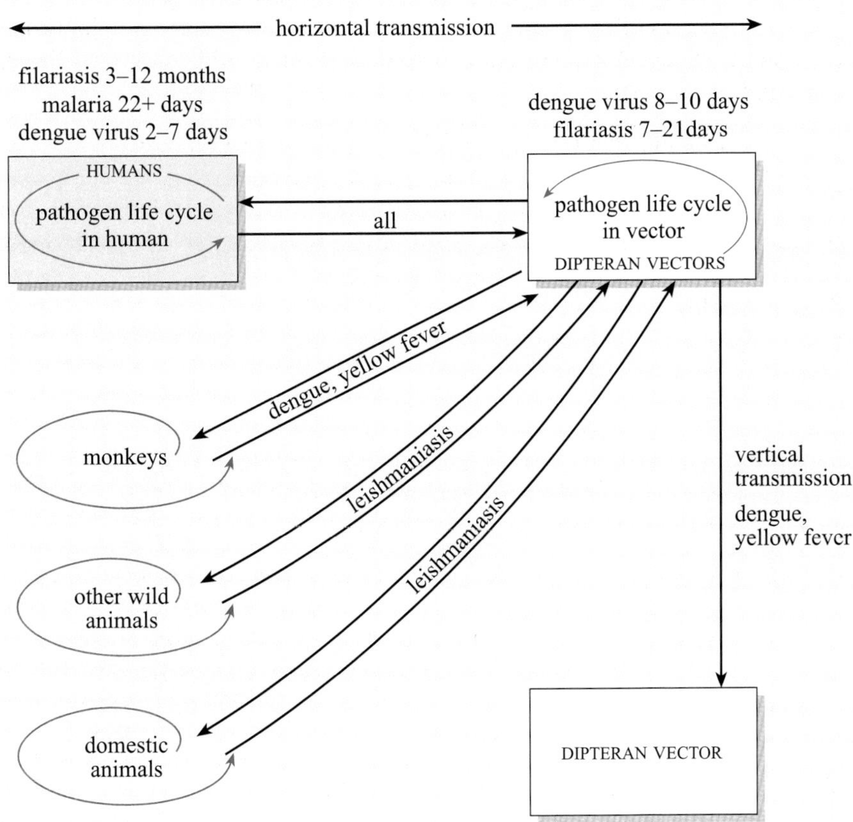

FIGURE 3.16 Summary of host–pathogen communities associated with dipteran vectors with aquatic stages.

3.6.4 Specialization

It is expected that pathogens will specialize on one or a few closely related hosts. This prediction results from a consideration of co-evolution (Chapter 2), with pathogens evolving ever more complex methods of living in hosts and overcoming their defences. The evolutionary responses of the hosts ensure that many pathogens become locked into an increasingly specialized relationship with one host or a few host species. Again, there are ecological parallels amongst non-pathogenic species. For example, herbivorous insects often specialize on plant species that are highly toxic to generalist predators. Through co-evolution, the plant feeders have overcome the defence systems of the plant (and the plant may have, in turn, evolved more toxic defence systems – which the herbivores have evolved to overcome, and so on). In some cases, the herbivores have used plant defence to their advantage, i.e. to defend themselves.

3.6.5 Overview and implications for emerging diseases

The four criteria listed in this section represent ecological and evolutionary constraints on the parasites and hosts. One can take the argument further and predict the most effective pathogens based on maximizing or minimizing these constraints. Thus, we would predict that the most abundant ('successful') pathogens would be those in which:

- body size is minimized (and replication rate is maximized);
- active transmission and co-occurrence are maximized;
- host (or part of host) specialization is maximized (especially with respect to defence against hosts or detection by hosts).

However, this is overly simplistic and we need to consider trade-offs. For example, smaller body size may be beneficial for faster replication but also carries costs if genome size is reduced. This is apparent in viruses: those with large genomes carry sophisticated host defence countermeasures, but replicate slowly. Viruses with small genomes rely on fast replication and have no spare genes for defence countermeasures.

- ☐ Are there any other criteria that we have discussed in this chapter that might also feature in this list?
- ■ Dormancy, discussed in Section 3.3.

Another way of looking at these criteria (implied above) is that they represent an evolutionary route for pathogens. Thus, we might predict that pathogens will evolve from large to small body size, from passive to active transmission, from high to low detection and generalist to specialist.

This concluding section of this book complements the discussion of Chapter 1, Section 1.3.4, where we attempted to identify the life-history strategies of pathogens according to their within-host and between-host attributes. We now have a complementary set of ecological attributes. Body size is important for within-host dynamics because it affects reproductive rate, survival and movement in the host. Active or passive transmission is clearly relevant to between-host variables. Co-occurrence is relevant to between-host variables, ensuring that all the members of the host–pathogen community coexist in the same place at the same time. Finally, specialization, through coevolution, underpins the host defence countermeasures of the pathogen.

Summary of Section 3.6

1. Four important ecological attributes of host–pathogen interactions are identified that impact on the dynamics of the pathogen and contribute to the incidence of the disease.
2. Pathogen body size affects both the ability to survive and reproduce in the host and the generation time of the pathogen.
3. Pathogens generally employ forms of active transmission (vectors, changes in host physiology and/or behaviour) to move between hosts.
4. Pathogens enhance their chances of transmission by occurring in the same habitat as their hosts and, where applicable, their vectors. Pathogens associated with water bodies are a globally important example of this phenomenon, especially those linked to dipteran vectors with aquatic and terrestrial life history stages.

5 Based on considerations of coevolution, many pathogens are expected to be (or become) highly specialized, utilizing one or a few closely related host species.

6 The implications of these ecological attributes for the evolution of host–pathogen interactions and emerging infectious disease are discussed.

Learning outcomes for Chapter 3

When you have studied this chapter, you should be able to:

3.1 Define and use, or recognize definitions and applications of, each of the terms printed in **bold** in the text. (*Question 3.1*)

3.2 Describe the geographical range of a host and its pathogen. (*Question 3.2*)

3.3 Interpret data on pathogen abundance patterns. (*Question 3.2*)

3.4 Interpret a simple compartmental model of host–pathogen dynamics. (*Question 3.2*)

3.5 Discuss the possible explanations for the fluctuations and cycling in abundance of some pathogen populations. (*Question 3.3*)

3.6 Distinguish between the different types of zoonosis. (*Question 3.1*)

3.7 Describe the composition, structure and evolutionary radiation of selected host–pathogen communities. (*Question 3.4*)

3.8 Describe and provide examples of the main ecological attributes of host–pathogen interactions. (*Question 3.5*)

Questions for Chapter 3

Question 3.1

Anthrax is commonly seen in cattle, sheep, horses, pigs and goats. These herbivorous animals are infected by ingestion of spores which are viable in soil for years. Humans are infected by handling contaminated carcasses, wool or hides and by ingestion or inhalation of the spores or bacteria (*Bacillis anthracis*). What category of zoonosis does anthrax fit best?

Question 3.2

Describe how the malaria compartmental model gives information on patterns of pathogen abundance and range.

Question 3.3

Why is the malaria compartmental model unlikely to lead to constant levels of pathogens over time?

Question 3.4

Based on trypanosome host–pathogen communities in the Old World, what predictions can be made about the future evolution of trypanosome communities in the New World?

Question 3.5

Why might co-occurrence with the host and host specialization not be important features in pathogens of emerging diseases?

REFERENCES

General reading

Anderson, R. M. and May, R. M. (1992) *Infectious Diseases of Humans*, Oxford University Press.

Ewald, P. W. (2000) *Plague Time*, The Free Press, New York.

Hudson, P. J., Rizzoli, A., Grenfell, B. T., Heesterbeek, H. and Dobson, A. P. (eds) (2002) *The Ecology of Wildlife Diseases*, Oxford University Press.

Karlen, A. (1995) *Plague's Progress. A Social History of Man and Disease*, Victor Gollancz, London.

Stearns, S. C. (1999) Introducing evolutionary thinking, in: *Evolution in Health and Disease,* S. C. Stearns (ed.) Oxford University Press, pp. 161–172.

Specific reading (chapter reference given in brackets)

Anderson, D. I. and Levin, B. R. (1999) The biological cost of antibiotic resistance, *Current Opinion in Microbiology*, **2**, pp. 489–493. *(Chapter 2)*

Austin, D. J., Kristinsson, K. G. and Anderson, R. M. (1999) The relationship between the volume of antimicrobial consumption in human communities and the frequency of resistance, *Proc. Natl. Acad. Sci. USA*, **96**, pp. 1152–1156. *(Chapter 2)*

Blount, J. D., Houston, D. C. and Møller, A. P. (2000) Why egg yolk is yellow, *Trends in Ecology and Evolution*, **15**, pp. 47–49. *(Chapter 1)*

Bull, J. J. (1994) Virulence, *Evolution*, **48**, pp. 1423–1437. *(Chapter 2)*

Bunyard, P. (2002) Breeding the superbug, *The Ecologist*, **32**, pp. 32–37. *(Chapter 2)*

Caren, L. D. (1991) Effects of exercise on the human immune system, *BioScience*, **41**, pp. 410–415. *(Chapter 1)*

Carey, C. (2000) Infectious disease and worldwide declines of amphibian populations, with comments on emerging diseases in coral reef organisms and in humans, *Environmental Health Perspectives*, **108** (Suppl. 1), pp. 143–150. *(Chapter 1)*

Chandler, M. and Claverys, J.-P. (2001) Genome diversity: sources and forces, *Current Opinion in Microbiology*, **4**, pp. 547–549. *(Chapter 2)*

Cleaveland, S., Laurenson, M. K. and Taylor, L. H. (2001) Diseases of humans and their domestic mammals: pathogen characteristics, host range and the risk of emergence, *Phil. Trans. Roy Soc. Lond. B*, **356**, pp. 991–999. *(Chapter 1)*

Colwell, R. R. (1996) Global climate change and infectious disease, *Science*, **274**, pp. 2025–2031. *(Chapter 3)*

Cowden, J. M. (2002) Winter vomiting, *British Medical Journal*, **324**, pp. 249–250. *(Chapter 1)*

Czárán, T. L., Hoekstra, R. F. and Pagie, L. (2002) Chemical warfare between microbes promotes biodiversity, *Proc. Natl. Acad. Sci. USA*, **99**, pp. 786–790. *(Chapter 1)*

Day, T. (2001) Parasite transmission modes and the evolution of virulence, *Evolution*, **55**, pp. 2389–2400. *(Chapters 1 and 2)*

Dobson, A. P. (1996) *Conservation and Biodiversity*, W. H. Freeman, New York. *(Chapter 1)*

Feil, E. J. and Spratt, B. G. (2001) Recombination and the population structures of bacterial pathogens, *Ann. Rev. Microbiol.*, **55**, pp. 561–590. *(Chapter 2)*

Fitzgerald, L. (1988) Exercise and the immune system, *Immunology Today,* **9**, pp. 337–339. *(Chapter 1)*

Fitzgerald, J. R. and Musser, J. M. (2001) Evolutionary genomics of pathogenic bacteria, *Trends in Microbiology*, **9**, pp. 547–553. *(Chapter 2)*

Gandon, S., van Baalen, M. and Jansen, V. A. A. (2002) The evolution of parasite virulence, superinfection, and host resistance, *Amer. Natur.*, **159**, pp. 658–669. *(Chapter 2)*

Gavazzi, G. and Krause, K.-H. (2002) Ageing and infection, *The Lancet Infectious Diseases*, **2**, pp. 659–666. *(Chapter 1)*

Gould, S. J. and Lewontin, R. C. (1979) The spandrels of San Marco and the Panglossian paradigm: a critique of the adaptationist program, *Proc. Roy. Soc. Lond. B*, **205**, pp. 581–598. *(Chapter 2)*

Gubler, D. J. (1998) Resurgent vector-borne diseases as a global health problem, *Emerging Infectious Diseases*, **4**. *(Chapters 2 and 3)*

Hawksworth, D. L. (1992) Microorganisms, in: *Global Biodiversity*, World Conservation Monitoring Centre, Chapman & Hall, London. *(Chapter 1)*

Hill, A. V. S. (2001) The genomics and genetics of human infectious disease susceptibility, *Ann. Rev. Genomics Human Genet.*, **2**, pp. 373–400. *(Chapter 2)*

Holmes, J. C. (1983) Evolutionary relationships between parasitic helminths and their hosts, in: Futuyma, D. J. and Slatkin, M. (eds) *Coevolution*, Sinauer, Sunderland, Mass., pp. 161–185. *(Chapter 2)*

Hughes, A. L. (2002) Evolution of the host defense system, in: *Immunology of Infectious Diseases.,* Kaufmann, S. H. E., Sher, A. and Ahmed, R. (eds), ASM Press, Washington DC, USA, pp. 67–75. *(Chapter 2)*

Hughes, K. A., Alipaz, J. A., Drnevich, J. M. and Reynolds, R. M. (2002) A test of evolutionary theories of aging, *Proc. Natl. Acad. Sci. USA*, **99**, pp. 14286–14291. *(Chapter 1)*

Jones, S. (1996) *In The Blood*, Harper Collins, London. *(Chapter 2)*

Kerr, C. (2002) Bloodsucking fly blamed for transmitting HIV, *The Lancet Infectious Diseases*, **2**, p. 265. *(Chapter 2)*

Levin, B. R. (1996) The evolution and maintenance of virulence in microparasites, *Emerging Infectious Diseases*, **2**. *(Chapter 2).*

Levy, S. B. (2001) Antibacterial household products: cause for concern, *J. Emerging Infectious Diseases*, **7**, pp. 512–515. *(Chapter 2)*

Lockhart, A. B., Thrall, P. H. and Antonovics, J. (1996) Sexually transmitted diseases in animals: ecological and evolutionary implications, *Biol. Rev.*, **71**, pp. 415–471. *(Chapters 2 and 3)*

Lycett, G. J. and Kafatos, F. C. (2002) Anti-malarial mosquitoes?, *Nature*, **417**, pp. 387–388. *(Chapters 2 and 3)*

May, R, M. and Anderson, R, M. (1978) Regulation and stability of host–parasite population interactions. II. Destabilising processes, *J. Anim. Ecol*, **47**, pp. 249–267. *(Chapters 1 and 3)*

Merrell, D. S., Butler, S. M., Qadri, F., Dolganov, N. A., Alam, A., Cohen, M. B., Calderwood, S. B., Schoolnik, G. K. and Camilli, A. (2002) Host-induced epidemic spread of the cholera bacterium, *Nature*, **417**, pp. 642–645. *(Chapters 2 and 3)*

Moore, S. L. and Wilson, K. (2002) Parasites as a viability cost of sexual selection in natural populations of mammals, *Science*, **297**, pp. 2015–2018. *(Chapter 1)*

Norris, K. and Evans, M. R. (2000) Ecological immunity: life history trade-offs and immune defense in birds, *Behav. Ecol*, **11**, pp. 19–26. *(Chapter 1)*

Ostfeld, R. S. and Keesing, F. (2000) Biodiversity and disease risk: the case of Lyme disease, *Conservation Biology*, **14**, pp. 722–728. *(Chapters 1 and 3)*

Pearce, F. (2002) Dung to death, *New Scientist*, 20 April, 15. *(Chapter 2)*

Penn, D. J., Damjanovich, K. and Potts, W. K. (2002) MHC heterozygosity confers a selective advantage against multiple-strain infections, *Proc. Natl. Acad. Sci. USA*, **99**, pp. 11260–11264. *(Chapter 2)*

Poulin, R. (2000) Manipulation of host behaviour by parasites: a weakening paradigm, *Proc. Roy. Soc. Lond. B*, **267**, p. 787. *(Chapter 2)*

Ridley, M. (1999) *Genome*, Fourth Estate, London. *(Chapter 2)*

Rigby, M. C., Hechinger, R. F. and Stevens, L. (2002) Why should parasite resistance be costly?, *Trends in Parasitology*, **18** (3), pp. 116–120. *(Chapter 1)*

Smith, D. L., Harris, A. D., Johnson, J. A., Silbergeld, E. K. and Morris, J. G. (2002) Animal antibiotic use has an early but important impact on the emergence of antibiotic resistance in human commensal bacteria, *Proc. Natl. Acad. Sci. USA*, **99**, pp. 6434–6439. *(Chapter 2)*

Steen, H., Taitt, M. and Krebs, C. J. (2002) Risk of parasite-induced predation: an experimental field study on Townsend's voles (*Microtus townsendii*), *Can. J. Zool.*, **80**, pp. 1286–1292. *(Chapters 1 and 3)*

Stevens, L., Giordano, R. and Fialho, R. F. (2001) Male-killing, nematode infections, bacteriophage infection, and virulence of cytoplasmic bacteria in the genus *Wolbachia*, *Ann. Rev. Ecol. Syst.*, **32**, pp. 519–545. *(Chapter 2)*

Taylor, L. H., Latham, S. M. and Woolhouse, M. E. J. (2001) Risk factors for human disease emergence, *Phil. Trans. Roy. Soc. Lond. B*, **356**, pp. 983–989. *(Chapter 1)*

ANSWERS TO QUESTIONS

QUESTION 1.1

Arguments for using the term pathogen. The course is concerned with infectious disease and as pathogen means causing harm (damage to host tissue) this is most appropriate, as opposed to parasite which includes any organism that lives in or on its host (irrespective of any damage it may cause). Pathogens are a sub-set of parasites. *Arguments against using the term pathogen.* The term parasite tends to be used in the ecological and evolutionary literature to include pathogens. This presents a problem for both you and the Course Team when searching the literature. However, as long as we are aware of that issue, using the term pathogen is most appropriate for a course on infectious disease.

QUESTION 1.2

Zoonoses are an obvious example. This may include pathogens that continue to be passed from animals to humans (e.g. vCJD) or pathogens that have previously crossed the host species barrier and are now routinely transmitted between human hosts (e.g. HIV). Ebola is an example of a zoonosis whose vertebrate host is unknown. Vector-borne diseases also warrant study of the pathogens not only in the vectors but also in alternative vertebrate hosts.

QUESTION 1.3

The normal life history of humans (in common with many vertebrates) is birth, growth, reproduction (possibly several times) and death. Pathogens also go through this sequence, but may reproduce only once (or many times). Reproduction may also vary in the number of offspring produced – possibly hundreds or thousands. The most important difference is that the life history of pathogens has to include transmission between hosts. Transmission events may occur at different points in the life history, e.g. during the juvenile (pre-reproductive stage). The whole life history may occur across several different hosts.

QUESTION 1.4

Cryptosporidium (Book 2, Figure 5.10) produces symptoms after 5 days, suggesting minimum duration in the host is short.

Trypanosoma brucei – trypanosomes have an outer protein coat (Book 2, p.101) and antigenic properties change. Minimum duration in the host is greater than 10 days. Transmission by insect vector.

Filarial roundworms have a minimum duration in human host of 3 months. Transmission by insect vector.

Herpes simplex. Direct host-to-host contact and long duration in host (>30 days). Remains undetected in nervous system.

Schistosomes. Long duration in host (>30 days and often for several years). Dispersal via water (can swim towards host).

TSEs. Long duration in host. Transmission is via consumption of infected meat (vertebrate or human host) so essentially host–host contact.

Given the above information, we can put the diseases into a new version of Table 1.4 (see Table A1.1):

TABLE A1.1 Pathogen life-history categories updated from Table 1.4 with the above diseases included **(bold)**.

		Within-host parameters		
	minimum duration in host	short (<10 days) (none)	medium (>10 days) (moderate)	long (>30 days) (complex)
Between-host (transmission) parameters	abiotic environment (air, soil, water)	influenza cholera ***Cryptosporidium***		**schistosomes**
	vector		malaria ***Trypanosoma brucei***	**filarial roundworms**
	host-to-host contact			syphilis, HIV, **herpes simplex, TSEs**

The inclusion of these six diseases fills in two more of the cells of the table but still suggests that this is a useful way of categorizing life-history strategies. In particular, it suggests that short duration in hosts and transmission by vector or host to host are not viable combinations for pathogens.

QUESTION 1.5

Reproductive status changes with age and it is expected that defence will be traded off against reproductive effort, especially under conditions of very low food availability.

QUESTION 2.1

The prudent pathogen model (and, ultimately, the incipient mutualism model). Virulence is defined as the ease of infection and the degree of damage. The prudent pathogen model predicts a reduction in damage to the host (and hence a reduction in virulence).

QUESTION 2.2

Sexual reproduction is identified (Section 2.2.1) as 'the major source' of genetic variation in large complex organisms such as humans (i.e. most hosts). Other sources of genetic variation are mutations and drift. Pathogens also show genetic variation due to mutation and drift but vary in terms of the amount of variation resulting from sexual reproduction. Some pathogens do not have sexual reproduction, although they may have other sources of genetic variation such as horizontal transfer.

QUESTION 2.3

In Section 2.4.1, three ways of looking at host manipulation are discussed. The third is possibly relevant to STIs: '... changes in the host caused by pathogen manipulation ... are adaptive for the pathogen, e.g. in aiding transmission.' This would indeed be the case if pathogens caused increased sexual activity. However, there is no evidence for this (Section 2.5.1). Therefore, it seems that these pathogens use sexual activity as a means of transmission but do not increase its likelihood. Having said that, by having little effect on host physiology during (at least) the early stages of infection, the pathogens do not reduce the likelihood of sexual activity.

QUESTION 2.4

The guidelines would cover the following areas: to ensure that the use of antibiotics is limited to all but the clearest cases of need and to ensure that as soon as resistance is detected the antibiotic is withdrawn.

QUESTION 2.5

Diptera (flies) contain most vectors of human disease (see Table 2.3). There are several reasons for this, including the evolution of piercing mouthparts and the aquatic and aerial stages of the life cycle. The aquatic component is important because it brings the flies into close proximity with their hosts (see Chapter 3). The aerial (adult) stage allows the fly to seek out its host.

QUESTION 3.1

Based on the information given in the question, anthrax falls into one of two categories: direct zoonosis or saprozoonosis. It could be said to be a combination of both as it is found in the soil (in keeping with saprozoonoses, although there is no development) and usually is transmitted by direct contact with the carcass of the other host. It does not require more than one host (therefore ruling out cyclozoonoses) and does not require an invertebrate host (therefore ruling out metazoonoses).

QUESTION 3.2

The model does not give information on the abundance of pathogens in any one host or vector. Instead, it gives information on the number of hosts or vectors containing pathogens and whether those hosts or vectors are infectious. The model describes changes in abundance through time in one place (a hypothetical village) so does not tell us anything about range. It would be possible to construct a compartmental model at many different locations and then include movement between locations – but this is potentially a huge task!

QUESTION 3.3

The construction of the model produces an output that changes around a given threshold, e.g. a certain value of daily bite rate. If the threshold is exceeded, the pathogen population will increase and if the threshold is not reached the pathogen population will reduce. The model only predicts a constant level of pathogens if all the variables, such as daily bite rate, stay at a certain constant value over time. This is ecologically impossible. More-sophisticated models can produce predictions of stable pathogen populations (or fluctuations within narrow limits).

QUESTION 3.4

Further radiation of host–trypanosome communities is expected in the New World. First, we might expect more interactions with semi-domesticated stock (there are many examples of this in the Old World). Secondly, we might expect other vectors of the *Trypanosoma cruzi* clade to evolve, possibly transferring other members of the clade into human hosts. The vectors might be relatives of the reduviid bugs or, more likely, they may be biting fly species.

QUESTION 3.5

Emerging diseases are usually caused by pathogen species with which we have not previously had contact. This may be because we have not coexisted with their normal hosts (e.g. in dense forest) or because they cannot be transmitted from their normal hosts. Pathogen species with high host specificity are less likely to transfer to new (human) hosts.

ACKNOWLEDGEMENTS

Grateful acknowledgement is made to the following sources for permission to reproduce material in this book:

Cover

Coloured scanning electron micrograph of *Clostridium botulinum* bacteria. Dr Gary Gaugler/Science Photo Library.

Figures

Figure 1.1: Daszak, P. *et al.* (2000) 'Emerging infectious diseases of wildlife-threats to biodiversity and human health', *Science*, **287**, 21 January 2000. Copyright © 2000 by the American Association for the Advancement of Science; *Figure 1.2*: Lee Berger and Alex Hyatt, CSIRO Australian Animal Health Laboratory; *Figure 1.3*: Roitt, I., Brostoff, J. and Male, D. (1996) *Immunology*, 4th edn, Mosby International Ltd.; *Figure 1.4*: © The World Health Organisation; *Figure 1.5*: Mims *et al.*, *Medical Microbiology*, 2nd edn. Copyright © 1998 Mosby International Ltd.; *Figure 2.2*: Liveley, C. M. (1992) 'Parthenogenisis in a freshwater snail: reproductive assurance versus parasitic release', *Evolution*, **46**, (4), Society for the Study of Evolution; *Figure 2.3*: Martyn F. Chillmaid/Science Photo Library; *Figure 2.4*: Wickler, W. (1968) *Mimicry in plants and animals*, Chapter 13, Orion Publishing Group Limited; *Figure 2.5*: Merijn Salverda; *Figure 2.6*: Welch, V. L. *et al.* (2001) *Ecological Entomology*, **26**, Blackwell Publishers Limited; *Figure 2.7*: Courtesy of American Lyme Disease Foundation; *Figure 3.1*: Jamoudi, A. and Sachs, J. D. (1999) 'The changing global distribution of malaria: a review', *CID Working Paper*, No. 2. Copyright Harvard University; *Figure 3.2*: Mims *et al.*, *Medical Microbiology*, 2nd edn. Copyright © 1998 Mosby International Limited; *Figure 3.3*: Peter Barker/Panos; *Figure 3.5*: WHO/TDR/Stammers; *Figures 3.8 and 3.9*: Anderson, R. M. and May, R. M. (1991) 'Microparasites', *Infectious Diseases of Humans*, from Registrar-General's weekly infectious disease return for England and Wales. Crown copyright material is reproduced under Class Licence Number Co1W0000065 with the permission of the Controller of HMSO and the Queen's Printer for Scotland; *Figure 3.8*: Alan Carey/Science Photo Library; *Figure 3.10*: Courtesy of Lacy Hyche, Associate Professor, Department of Entomology and Plant Pathology, Auburn University; *Figure 3.14:* Adapted from Stevens, J. R. *et al.* (1999) 'The ancient and divergent origins of the human pathogenic trypanosomes, *Trypanosoma brucei* and *T. cruzi*', *Parasitology*, **118**, pp.107–116; *Figure 3.15a*: Eye of Science/Science Photo Library; *Figure 3.15b*: Sinclair Stammers/Science Photo Library; *Figure 3.15c*: Courtesy of Rolf Mannesmann, Bielefeld University, Germany; *Figure 3.15d*: Sue Ford/Science Photo Library.

Every effort has been made to trace all the copyright owners, but if any has been inadvertently overlooked, the publishers will be pleased to make the necessary arrangements at the first opportunity.

INDEX

Note: Entries in **bold** are key terms. Page numbers referring to information that is given only in a figure or caption are printed in *italics*.